SIGNING *Naturally*

DAWNSIGNPRESS
San Diego, California

SIGNING *Naturally*

Signing Naturally Student Workbook, Units 7–12.

Published by DawnSignPress

ISBN: 978-1-58121-236-5

Printed in the United States of America

10 9 8

Table of Contents

Photo Credits and Permissions

Stream of Consciousness by Susan Dupor
Photo courtesy of Susan Dupor (page 1)

The Missing Jigsaw Pieces by David Call
Photo courtesy of David Call (page 71)

ASL Thrives by Nancy Rourke
Photo courtesy of Nancy Rourke (page 151)

Spirtuality of De'VIA by Ellen Mansfield
Photo courtesy of Ellen Mansfield (page 239)

untitled 1 by Tony Fowler
Photo courtesy of Tony Fowler (page 313)
Digital Painting

Deaf Profiles:

Arthur Kruger
Photo courtesy of Gallaudet University Archives (page 67)

Nathie Marbury
Photo courtesy of Gallaudet University Archives (page 138)

Eric Malzkuhn
Photo courtesy of Gallaudet University Archives (page 235)

Alice Terry
Photo courtesy of Gallaudet University Archives (page 303)

Chuck Baird
Photo courtesy of Gallaudet University Archives (page 384)

Introduction

The *Signing Naturally Units 7–12 Student Workbook* and videos are designed to compliment course work in American Sign Language (ASL) and build upon skills you learned previously in *Units 1–6*. These materials, along with class instruction, give you opportunities to:

- review and expand practice of the key grammar from *Units 1–6*
- practice other language functions and their key grammatical features
- expand vocabulary and range of topics
- increase narrative and conversational fluency
- compare aspects of ASL and English through translation exercises
- compare aspects of the Deaf culture, American culture and your own culture
- understand your role as an ASL student in the Deaf community.

Using the Student Workbook and Videos

The main goal of the *Signing Naturally* materials is to engage you in conversations utilizing appropriate cultural behaviors. Since the classroom experience may be limited to a few hours a week, the student materials are developed to supplement classroom learning and provide further practice. The video materials model the vocabulary, sentences, conversations, and narratives to be learned and the printed materials provide explanations, readings and resources. All with one goal in mind, to help you achieve meaningful interactions within the Deaf community.

WORKBOOK

Most homework is driven by the language presented on the video. The workbook provides instruction on how to work with the video materials to complete the homework activities. Homework activities have the following focuses:

Conversational homework activities focus on reviewing and practicing key vocabulary, phrases and grammar structures through conversations. Pay special attention to the section called **Learn the Dialogue** which highlights the key language phrases and structures introduced in class.

Skill building homework activities focus on practicing specific language elements such as numbers, fingerspelling, semantics, spatial and verb agreement, translating sentences, and negation.

Comprehension homework activities focus on strengthening and expanding the ability to understand what is signed by figuring out the meaning from context.

Production homework activities focus on developing signing fluency through narrating or storytelling. The section called **Learn the Narrative** highlights the key language phrases and structures to be incorporated in the presentation.

Culture homework activities focus on helping you develop a better understanding of appropriate cultural behaviors through reading, exercises and analysis.

Sections in the Workbook You Should Pay Attention To:

Assignment

At end of some homework, there is a section called **Assignment**, in which you are asked to develop or rehearse something for the next class. It is important you take the time to complete these assignments. These activities are designed to help you develop greater facility with the targeted language elements.

Vocabulary Review

At the end of the homework there is a **Vocabulary Review** that lists all the key vocabulary introduced in class. Printed video captures of the signs are numbered to correspond to the signs on video. The meaning of the signs are given by using pictures or written definitions.

New Vocabulary

In some minidialogues or narratives, under the heading **New Signs**, captures of new sign(s) from the video are shown along with their definitions. Learning these signs provides a good opportunity to expand your vocabulary.

Self-Assessment

At the end of each unit there is a **Self-Assessment**. Fill out the form thoughtfully as it will pinpoint areas where you need more practice. If you rate yourself with a 3 or below in any part of the assessment, you should formulate a plan of action to strengthen that particular skill. After a month, assess yourself again. Continue in this manner until you can honestly rate yourself with 4 or better in all areas.

Classroom Exercises

Included in the workbook are **Classroom Exercises**. Your teacher will tell you when to use them so be sure to bring your workbook to every class.

When you see this icon, it indicates the activity in the Workbook has a video component in the DVD. Be sure to read the information next to the icon before viewing the video.

Videos

There are two DVDs with the Workbook. One covers Units 7–9, and the other covers Units 10–12.

Introducing the Signers

The signers pictured below are the ASL models in the videos. In the workbook, they are identified by their first names, unless they use a different name for a story or dialogue.

Derrick Behm

Tonique Hunter

Iva Ikeda

Justin Jackerson

John Maucere

Melvin Patterson

Justin "JT" Reynolds

Lauren Ridloff

David Rivera

Terrylene Sacchetti

Ursula Smith

Suzanne Stecker

Amber Zion

Navigating the DVDs

The main menu on each DVD looks like this:

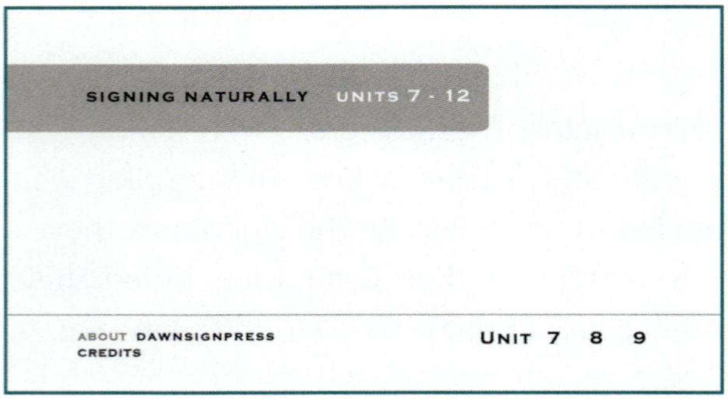

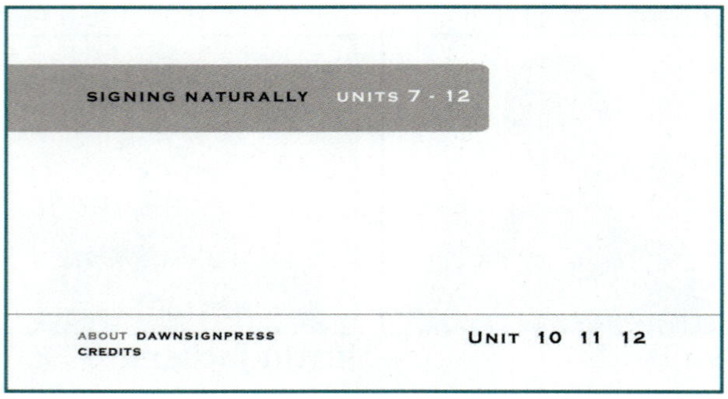

Click on the number for the unit you are working on to see its homework menu.

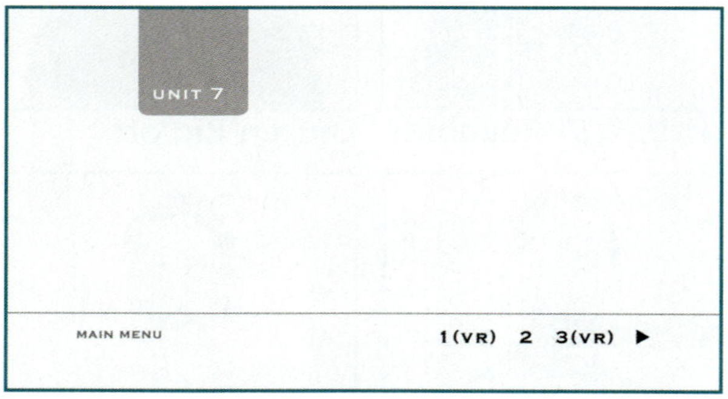

Then, click on the homework number. Read the information in the workbook before viewing the video. If you see (VR) to the right of the homework number, you will find the vocabulary review section at the end of the homework video clips.

As the video plays, the navigation bar indicates the unit and homework you are watching. For example, if the number shows 7:2, it means you are watching Homework 2 from Unit 7.

At the end of video clips that require you to write, draw, or answer, two symbols appear that allow you to play the section again, or move on to the next item. If the symbols do not appear and you need more time, pause the video yourself.

Remember when using the DVDs:

Read instructions in the workbook before starting the video activity. To skip forward in the DVD, use your remote control or DVD controls on your computer. The video must be playing to skip forward, you can't skip forward through the numbered sections of the DVD unless the video is playing.

Unit 12

Unit 12 is a storytelling unit. The goal of the homework activities is to introduce and rehearse different narrative elements needed to construct and present a coherent story. You may be assigned homework from this unit to accompany homework from other units.

THINGS TO REMEMBER AS YOU CONTINUE LEARNING ASL

Preparing for Class

Remember the more time you spend using ASL outside of class, the greater your ability to retain new vocabulary and language elements. Do your homework as soon as you can because in a single day a person can lose up to 40% of what they have learned.

Forming study groups with other classmates would be a helpful way to help you retain what you have learned. Remember that coming to class 10 minutes early and conversing in ASL with your classmates or your teacher would be a good reinforcement of your growing signing skills.

Maintaining Clear Sightlines

The classroom is most likely set up to help everybody maintain clear sight lines, such as chairs arranged in a semi-circle so you and other students can see each other. Take responsibility to situate yourself and ask others to do the same in order to maintain clear sightlines. Developing this habit will benefit you and others when interacting within the Deaf community.

Using English and Voice

All communication in your classroom will continue to be primarily in ASL. This approach, as you may know, is the best and fastest way to become comfortable with the language, to retain what you have learned, and to develop your comprehension and production skills. Your efforts to support this approach will benefit your progress in learning, enable your classmates with theirs, and in build good habits that show respect for Deaf people.

Also, remember that when one speaks (or thinks with) English words while signing, it may feel helpful, but in reality, it results in incorrect ASL syntax and semantic usage and good, clear and respectful communication goes out of the window.

A primary goal for you to achieve at this level in learning ASL is to start "thinking" in ASL. Reaching this threshold signals that you have successfully begun to negotiate meaning through the target language (ASL) rather than filtering the information through English.

To help with this, signs are reviewed or defined with pictures or by written definitions instead of giving single English word equivalents.

A BRIEF OVERVIEW: VIEWS ON DEAF PEOPLE

In taking this next level, you are continuing to learn more about American Sign Language and about the culture and history of Deaf people in the United States and Canada. But, the best thing about achieving this level is the opportunity to learn more about yourself and how you relate to both your own and other languages and cultures.

By now, you probably have used ASL with Deaf people. You may have seen ASL used in theatre, on television, or on the internet—people signing a song, or attempting to; little toddlers signing to their parents; Deaf people debating contemporary issues affecting society, their community and ASL. You probably have read articles or online posts concerning ASL and, or Deaf people ranging from "miraculous cures" for hearing loss, to computer applications that can translate ASL into English and vice versa, to stories about successful Deaf individuals.

While there are plenty of interesting things in the media, the information presented is often contradictory. Some of the inconsistencies in the media are rooted in how Deaf people are viewed. Examining the following views will hopefully broaden your understanding of what is behind society's depictions of Deaf people, and help clarify what informs your view.

The medical view focuses on the Deaf individual's inability to hear and speak, and seeks medical interventions. This view emphasizes the "loss" and sees Deaf people as individuals who live isolated lives, separated from humanity. This view concludes that the best way for Deaf people to escape this life of isolation, and live a more "normal" life, is to overcome what they see as their hearing and speech impairments. The idea of living or associating with other Deaf people and using Sign Language is not considered by the medical view as a desirable way to live.

At this time, most Deaf people are born into hearing families, so the medical view has a big impact on the Deaf community. From the very beginning, with mandatory newborn hearing screening in a hospital, many Deaf children's lives are shaped by this view. Taking the advice of the medical world, parents consent to medical procedures and start down the road of extensive sound and speech recognition training for the child. People working with the child, including the parents, are discouraged from using Sign Language. Meeting other Deaf people is warned against, believing it will distract the child from his or her auditory and speech development. As a result, ironically, many children struggle with their fluency in English, and ASL as well.

These medical procedures, including surgeries, are serious and invasive and are not without risk to the child. These procedures, can leave the child vulnerable to infections, meningitis, headaches, neurological damage and even death. They often do not provide the child with the range of hearing needed to master the spoken language and its cultural nuances in order to participate in society on an equal footing.

Additionally, the psychological, social and emotional toll of the medical view can leave the Deaf child and their families with an enduring sense of failure. There are numerous personal stories circulating in the community confirming that, even when the Deaf person manages to hear and speak adequately, denying one's identity is painful and too costly.

The biggest failure of the medical view is its complete lack of regard for Deaf people and their community.

The social view focuses on gaining access into the general society and inclusion for individuals with disabilities, including Deaf people. This view emphasizes "... that societies should be built and managed with all their members in mind, taking responsibility to ensure equal access and full citizenship for all." (Ladd, 2003)

While the social view provides advantages for Deaf people on certain levels such as giving access to sounds and spoken language through flashing light doorbells, special telephones, FM systems, captions on TV's, interpreters, and video relay services, it does not address the central issues related to sign language and Deaf culture. Utilizing the social view has unintentionally created linguistic and cultural barriers.

The social view's ultimate goal of mainstreaming disabled individuals into society, unwittingly isolates the Deaf person from their own people and language. For example, authorities with this view believe it is more socially responsible to mainstream Deaf senior citizens in facilities that provide "reasonable accommodations" like hiring interpreters as needed, rather than placing them in a facility with other Deaf seniors where everybody signs. For Deaf people, such attempts at inclusion often result in loneliness and isolation.

Another example is in education. The social view believes it's more appropriate to place the Deaf child in their local school with accommodations such as hearing aids, FM systems and interpreters. This practice is fraught with problems, starting with the teacher and administrator who usually know very little about American Sign Language and Deaf Culture. There are no quality assurances of interpreters hired and the assumption is that everything is fully accessed whenever accommodations are provided. Even if an interpreter is highly qualified and fluent in ASL, the child's access to information and even social activities continues to be funneled through (and filtered by) one person all day, everyday.

The social view does not take into account the unique situation Deaf children are in. Over 90% of the children have hearing parents who usually know nothing or very little about the Deaf community, its language, history or culture.

Traditionally Deaf children learn about themselves and ASL from others while attending Deaf residential schools. But with the onset of mainstreaming Deaf children, this traditional avenue has been interrupted. As a result, most mainstreamed students suffer gaps in their cultural literacy and fluency in

ASL. For many, this gap has affected their acquisition of English as well. and hampered their social skills. Public schools, generally, do not have qualified Deaf teachers and trained administrators to oversee the curriculum and the education of the whole child. Until Deaf children are recognized as members of a linguistic and cultural minority, mainstreaming will continue to isolate Deaf children, and create barriers to an education that provides a positive self image, healthy relationships and a sense of community.

The cultural-linguistic view focuses on recognizing Deaf people as minority cultural groups with their own natural Sign Languages. This view promotes the right of Deaf people to have a collective space within society to develop and pass on their languages, traditions and customs.

Few members from the general public are aware of the vibrant and complex Deaf community. Like other cultures, Deaf communities have their own histories, traditions, values and social norms, which are passed down the generations. There are Deaf theater companies, film festivals, and poetry jams. There are Deaf owned businesses such as restaurants, consulting firms, charter schools, publishing companies, etc. There are Deaf social workers, directors, doctors, financial consultants, lawyers, carpenters, pastors, professors etc. There are international, national and local Deaf political, professional, social and sports organizations.

Deaf people in the U.S., as members of a minority culture, are surrounded by the majority culture and language, American Culture and English, and have daily experiences, both positive and negative, with people from the majority culture whose actions affect Deaf people on many levels. Three examples of significant actions in Deaf history are the founding of Gallaudet University, the 1880 International Congress on the Education of the Deaf (ICED), and the influence of Alexander Graham Bell on educating Deaf children.

Gallaudet University was signed into existence in 1864 by U.S. President Abraham Lincoln and its land donated by Amos Kendall, a former Postmaster General. This paved way to higher education and college degrees for Deaf students, who become teachers and other professionals in the Deaf community. This university continues to use Sign Language as the language of instruction and continues to be a beacon of inspiration for Deaf people all over the world.

The 1880 ICED that occurred in Milan, Italy, was an event where a small group of self selected hearing "professionals" in the field of Deaf education convened and voted nearly unanimously to ban Sign Language from Deaf children's education, and declared speech (Oralism) as the preferred method. As a result, Deaf teachers and administrators were laid off in large numbers. In most places around the world the number went down to zero, because the Oralist, argued Deaf teachers were unable to teach or evaluate speech.

Around that time of the Milan conference, Alexander Graham Bell, the holder of the telephone patent, was rising in prominence and power. Before the telephone, Bell was dedicatedly working on mechanisms and ways to teach Deaf people speech and lipreading. Even though he could sign, he believed that Deaf people should accommodate the "majority" who did not sign by learning how to speak and lipread. With the advent of the telephone and the rise of scientism (the belief that science holds the most valuable view, to the exclusion of all other views), Bell's point of view shaped the society's view, Oralism dominated Deaf children's education, and Sign Language and Deaf culture became either invisible to or regarded negatively by the public.

The pendulum began to swing in the favor of the Deaf community in the 1960's when research emerged that showed Oralism was a dismal failure, and when linguists published research showing Sign Language to be a "bona fide" language. The Deaf community began to experience a cultural and linguistic resurgence. Schools began to reintroduce signing in the classroom as the language used to teach Deaf children. Colleges and universities began to offer American Sign Language classes for credit, and Deaf people felt renewed pride in their language and heritage.

However, despite the recognition given to ASL in the linguistics field and related academic communities, Deaf people still struggle to be recognized as a cultural group, especially in the political and educational arenas because the medical and social views continue to be prevalent in these areas.

In most cases, the general public is not aware of issues the Deaf Community faces and thus pay no or very minimal attention. The Deaf community is exploring strategies to reduce this lack of awareness by increasing the language's prestige, the community's legitimate power in the eyes of the dominant community, and creating a strong presence in the education system. As Ladd (2003) mentioned, "...This will take some planning, and the social and cultural implications and agendas must be as clear as those being constructed by other linguistic minorities like Welsh, Catalan and Basque people."

Like other minority cultures, the Deaf community's desire is to have a place to come together, opportunities to further explore our heritage, and a system to share our traditions with future generations. Central to this is complete access to Sign Language for Deaf people from birth to adulthood; a way to ensure Deaf children have the opportunity to develop positive identities and a sense of accountability to both the majority and minority cultures; and ways to promote bilingualism for all people.

Summary

We live in a time where social acceptance of diversity is on the upswing and yet we live at a time where our ability to eliminate differences has made alarming advances, as we see in the rise of genetic engineering. These opposing trends force us to think about how we feel about protecting diversity, how we feel about medical interventions when there is no real medical necessity, and the acceptability of the potential elimination of a "people." As a continuing student of Deaf culture and

American Sign Language, it is hoped that you will help raise awareness about the issues facing the Deaf Community. Embrace the idea that membership in a Deaf community is a positive life experience, that Deaf people have the right to continue to exist and that every Deaf child has the right to access and learn Sign Language—their natural language—and their Deaf cultural heritage.

Stream of Consciousness
Susan Dupor

oil on canvas
40" x 30"
2003

UNIT 7

Describing People and Things

Homework 7:1

CONVERSATION 1

Iva (A) and Melvin (B) demonstrate this dialogue in which Terrylene is identified and a message is relayed.

Signer A: Identify a person in the room, using
- body position
- appearance
- clothing

Signer B: Add another description to confirm

A: Confirm, ask B to relay a message to that person

B: Relay the message

Key Grammar

IDENTIFYING A PERSON

When identifying a person, describe one or two things that helps the listener spot the person quickly and easily. Consider things that also distinguish the person from others. The description(s) should include:

- body position: arms or legs (see pages 8–9 for examples)
- appearance: height, body type, head and face, or hair (see pages 9–12)
- clothing: color and pattern (see page 12–13).

View. See how Iva identifies Terrylene by the shirt she wears, and Melvin describes her body position to confirm.

Notice the sign, pictured on the next page, is used to both ask and to confirm the person. The key difference is in the facial expression. Melvin raises his eyebrows when asking Iva if that's the right person, and Iva nods and continues to nod when confirming.

asking to confirm person

confirming person

Describing Size

When describing the relative size of someone's height, body type or clothing patterns, add the following facial expressions, especially for the mouth, to indicate what is being described is smaller or thinner, or larger or thicker than normal or expected:

smaller or thinner

larger or thicker

If the size of what you are describing is standard or ordinary, then use the following facial expression:

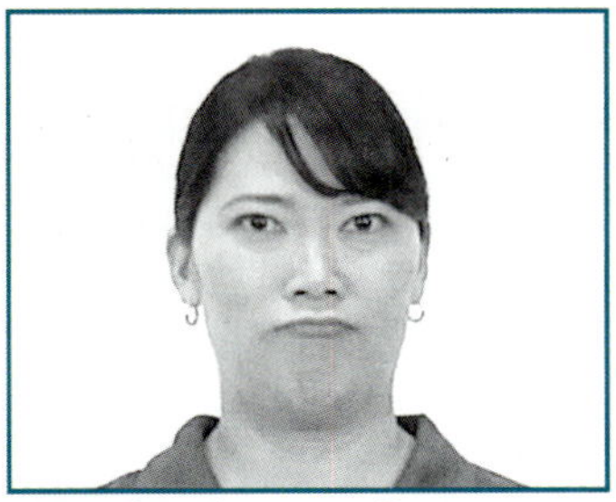

standard or ordinary

RELAYING A MESSAGE

When relaying a message, your personal pronoun and possessive adjective must agree with the location of the person sending the message and the location of the person receiving the message.

View. See how Melvin shows agreement when relaying Iva's message. The personal pronoun ("she") is oriented in the direction of Iva's location and the possessive adjective ("your") is oriented toward Terrylene to indicate "that she (Iva) likes your (Terrylene's) blouse."

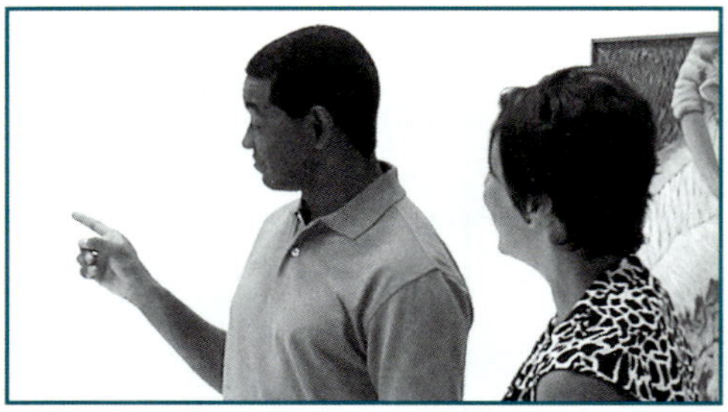

refers to Iva (personal pronoun)

refers to Terrylene's blouse (possessive adjective)

A SIGN OF CAUTION: It can cause confusion or misunderstandings if you mix up the handshapes for personal pronouns (made with the "index" hand) and possessive adjectives (made with the "open B" hand). Often these signs are mistakenly interchanged in sentences like "I like ***her***," (in which case, you would use the personal pronoun) or "I like ***her*** house," (in which case, you would use the possessive adjective).

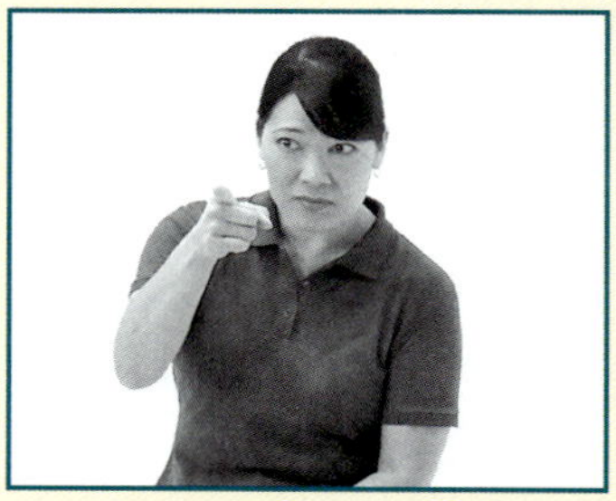

personal pronoun "you, him, her, it"

possessive adjective "your, his, hers, its"

MINIDIALOGUES

Watch the minidialogues and answer the questions below. Observe the signers respond by either confirming, or negating and correcting information.

Minidialogue 1

1. How does David identify his uncle?

2. What additional information do Iva and David give to confirm they are talking about the same person?

3. What explanation does David give for his uncle's appearance?

4. How does Iva identify the second man?

5. What does Iva think of him?

Minidialogue 2

1. What comment does Tonique make about Ursula's brother?

2. Why did the brother change his appearance?

3. What does he also do?

New Signs

to move in water by moving limbs; to swim

to race; to compete

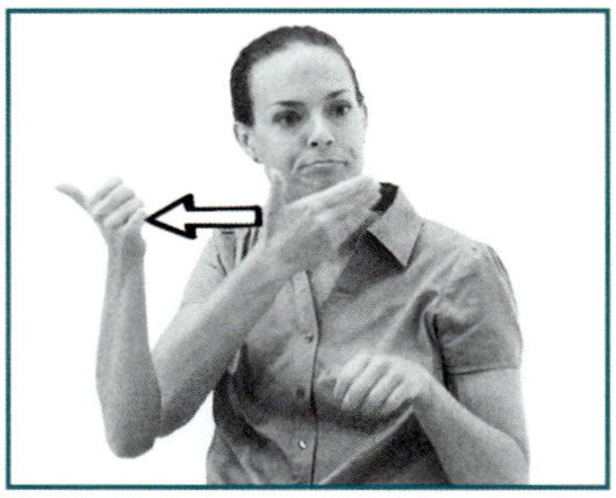

more appropriate; better

Answers given in class.

VOCABULARY REVIEW

Review the vocabulary on the video.

Body Position: Legs

1.

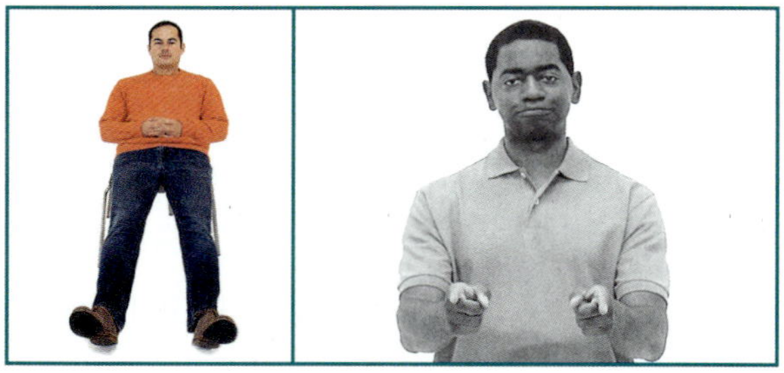

2.

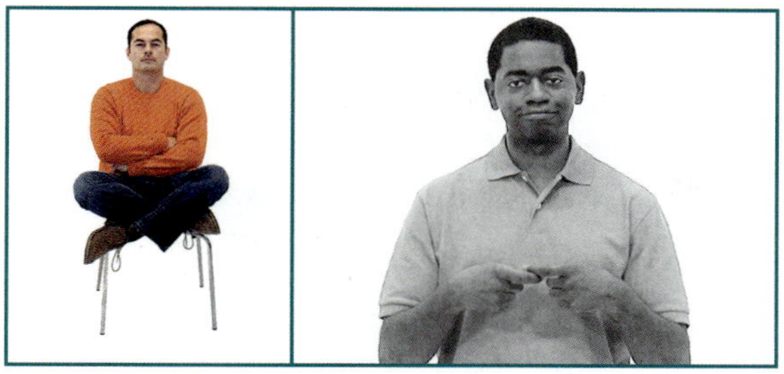

3.

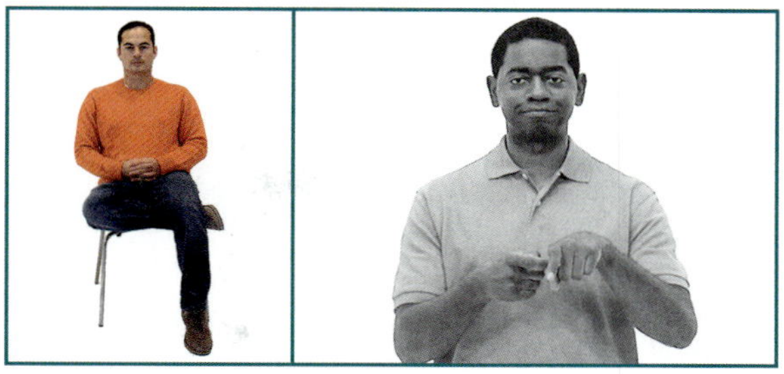

4.

5.

6.

Appearance: Height ____________________

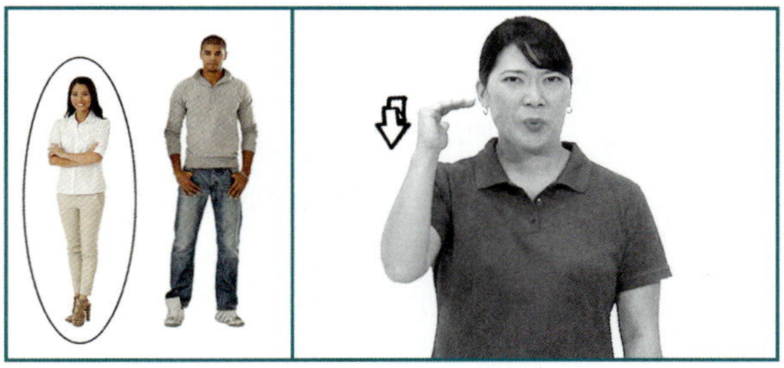

7.

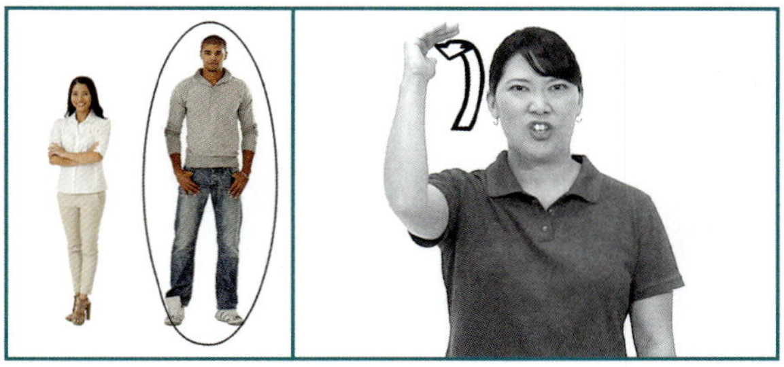

8.

Appearance: Body Type ____________________

9.

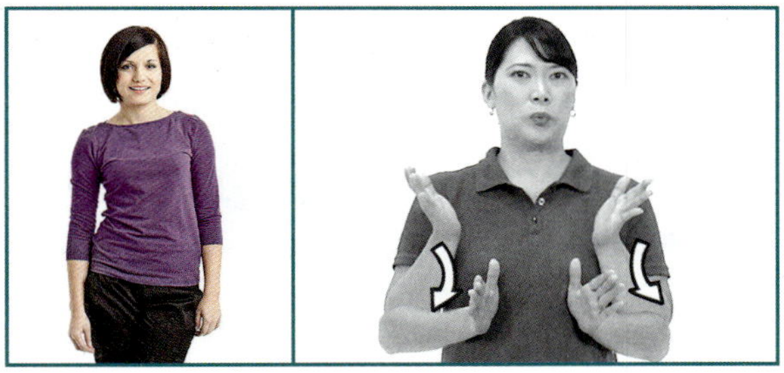

10.

11.

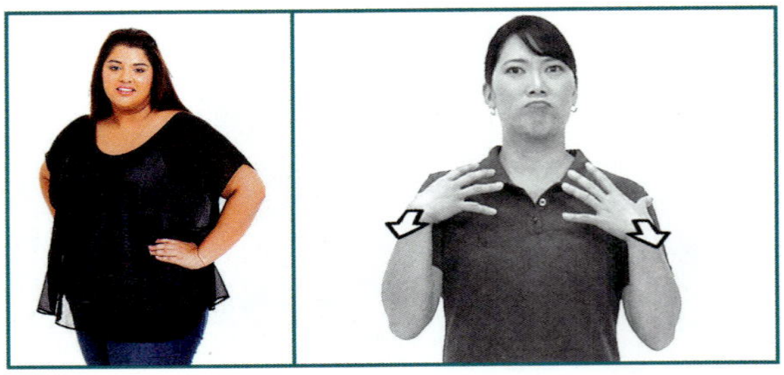

12.

Appearance: Head and Face

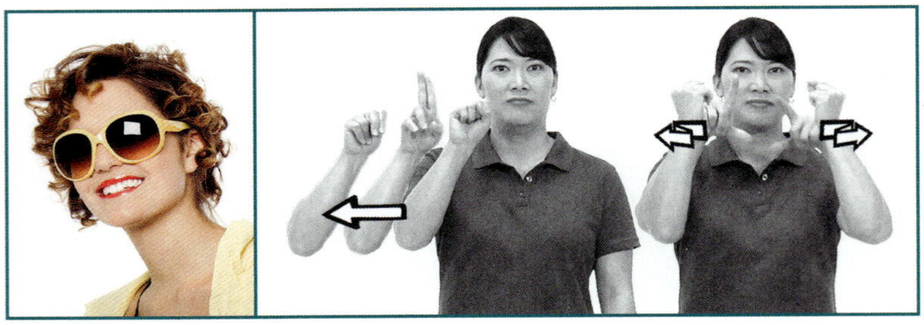

13.

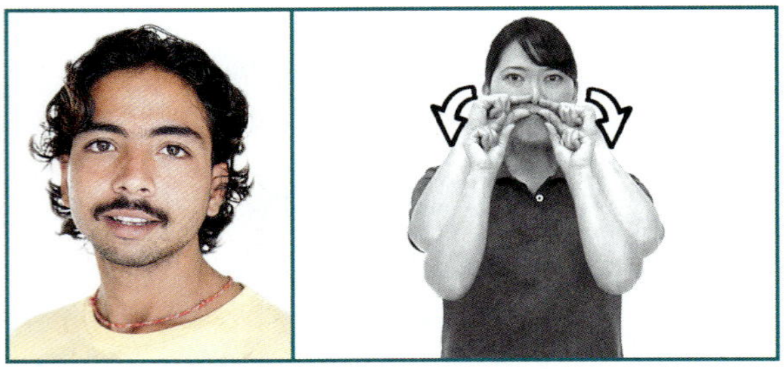

14.

15.

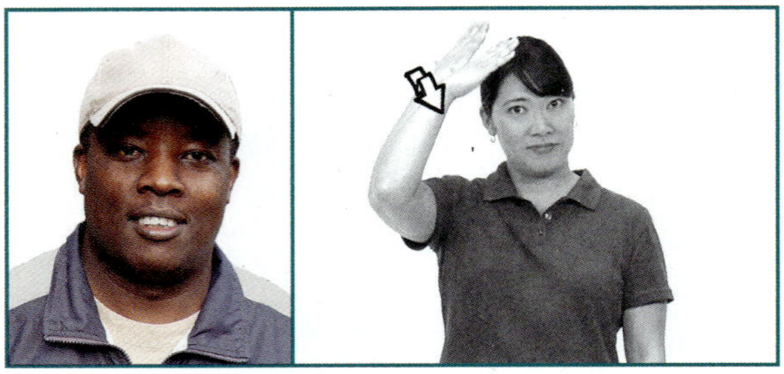

16.

17.

Appearance: Hair

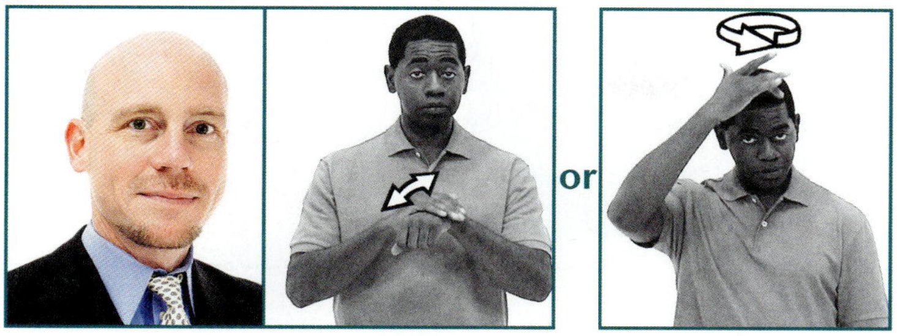

18.

19.

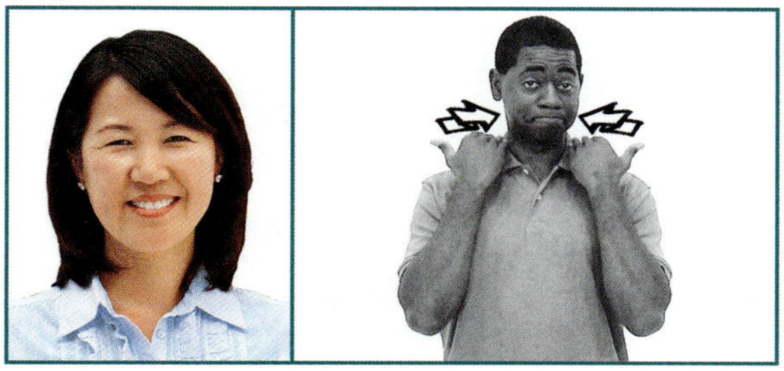

20.

21.

22.

23.

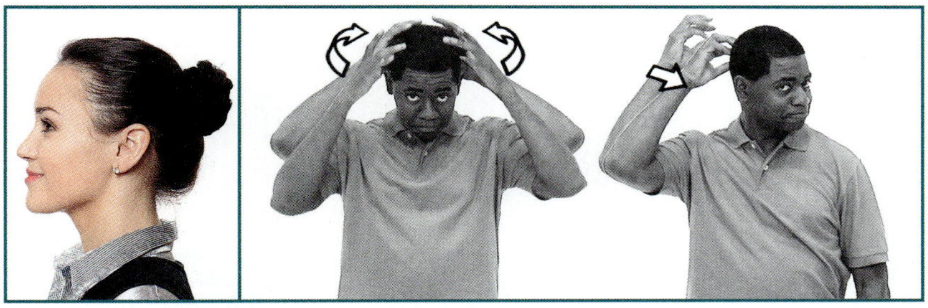

24.

25.

26.

27.

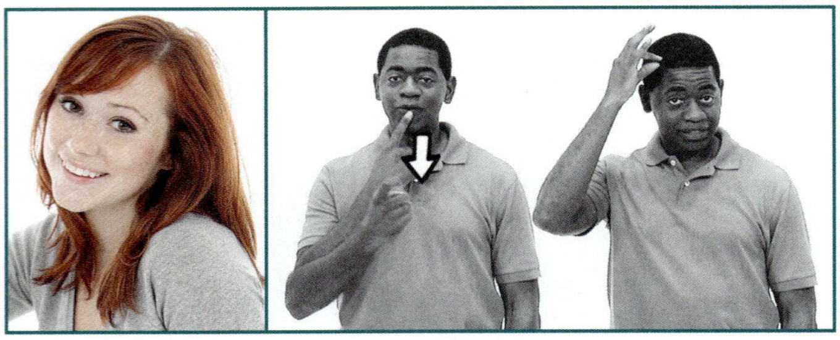

28.

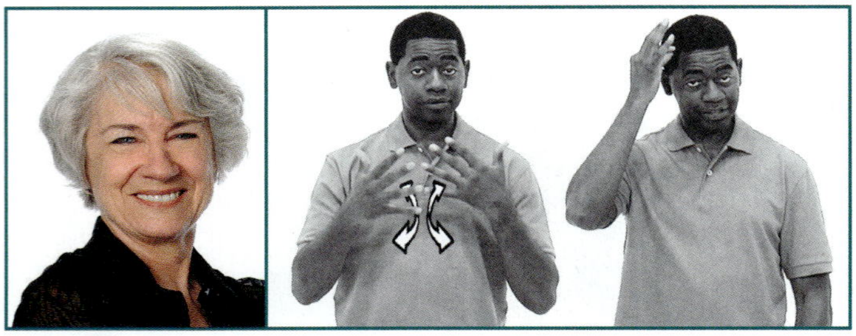

29.

Clothing: Patterns

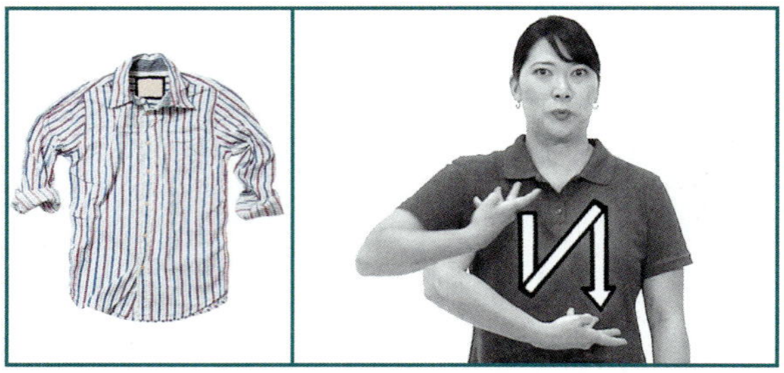

30.

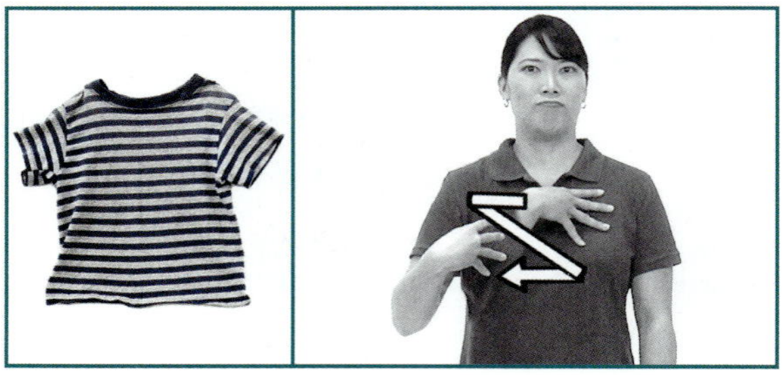

31.

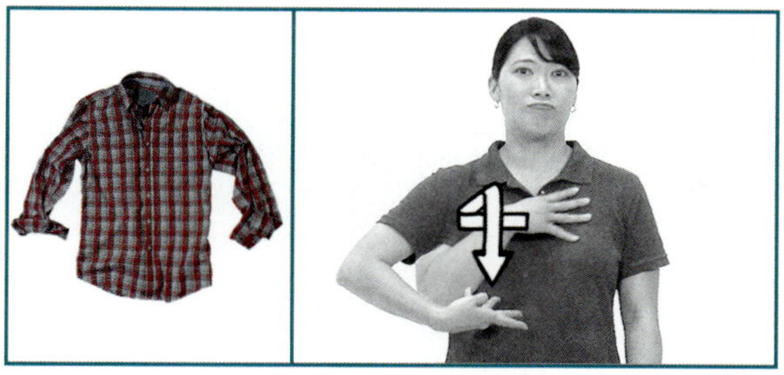

32.

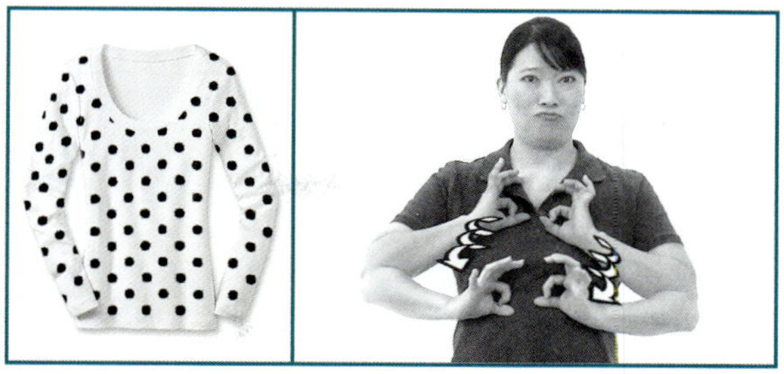

33.

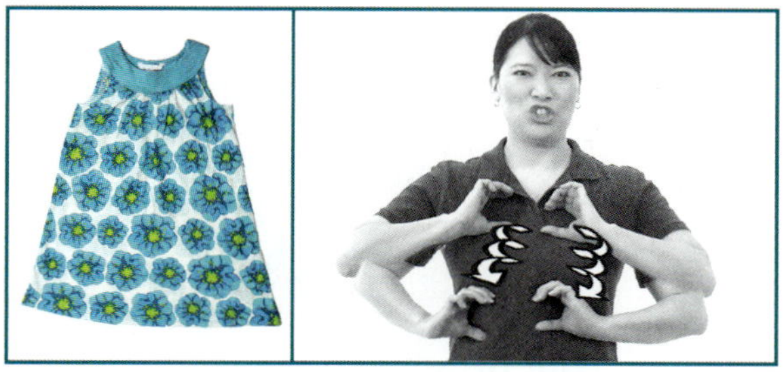

34.

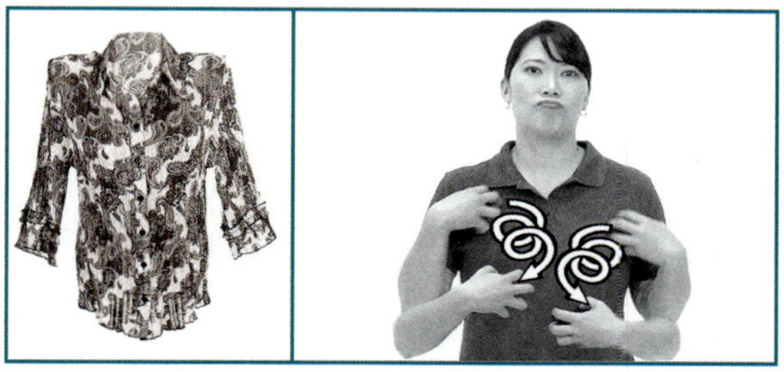

35.

36.

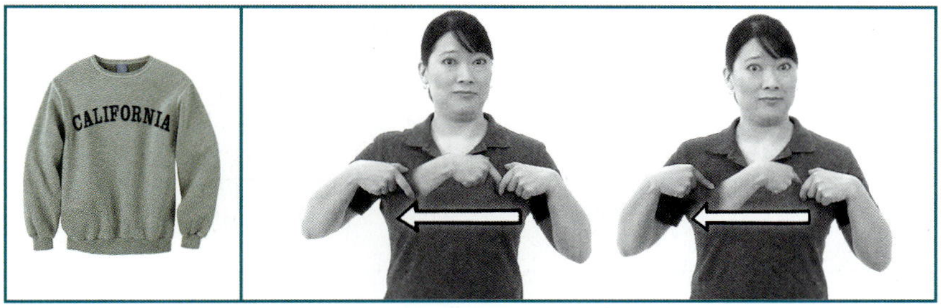

37.

Homework 7:2

CLOTHING-RELATED WORDS

Write the Word

David, Iva and Tonique give sentences with a fingerspelled word from this list. Write only the fingerspelled word.

plastic	suede	size	boots
nylon	fleece	style	sunglasses
silk	gold	cell phone	vest
cotton	silver	suit	bag
fur	copper	tuxedo	
wool	polyester	wallet	

1. ____________ 12. ____________

2. ____________ 13. ____________

3. ____________ 14. ____________

4. ____________ 15. ____________

5. ____________ 16. ____________

6. ____________ 17. ____________

7. ____________ 18. ____________

8. ____________ 19. ____________

9. ____________ 20. ____________

10. ____________ 21. ____________

11. ____________ 22. ____________

Answers on page 504.

Word List

John demonstrates how to fingerspell the following words. Notice the hand positions and movements used to spell each word.

1. plastic

The "p" begins with palm oriented downward and tilted sideways, then twists to front to spell "l"; the "i" is formed while holding "t"

2. nylon

The "y" has palm oriented downward

3. silk

The "i" is formed while holding "s," also the "l" is formed while holding "i"

4. cotton

Bouncing is used with double letter "t"

5. fur

The "u" begins with palm tilted slightly sideways and twists to front to spell "r"

6. wool

Hand slides sideways with double letter "o"

7. suede

The "u" and "d" move up slightly

8. fleece

Hand slides sideways with double letter "e"

9. gold

The "g" has palm oriented inward

10. silver

The "i" is formed while holding "s," the thumb and the ring finger maintain contact while spelling "ver"

11. copper

Bouncing is used with double letter "p"

12. polyester

The "p" begins with palm tilted sideways, then twists to front to spell "ol"; the "y" has palm oriented slightly downward

13. size

The "e" is positioned where the "z" ends

14. style

The "y" has palm oriented downward

15. cell (phone)

Bouncing is used with double letter "l"

16. suit

Smooth transition between letters

17. tux

The hand twists sideways and forward to spell the "x"

18. wallet

Bouncing is used with double letter "l"

19. sun (glasses)

The "u" moves up slightly

20. boots

Hand slides sideways with double letter "o"

21. vest

Smooth transition between letters

22. bag

The "g" has palm facing sideways

Challenge Yourself

In a day or two, get a separate piece of paper, replay the **Word List** segment and write down the words John fingerspells. Replay this segment until you can recognize the word without hesitation.

Homework 7:3

GUESS MY NUMBER

Watch how signers use cardinal numbers 1–100 to play this game.

Guess My Number 1

John and Iva play the game in which John tries to guess the number Iva has in mind. Write down John's guesses by recording the number and circle the type of question asked (above, below, or between).

1. ______________ above below between
   number(s)
2. ______________ above below between
   number(s)
3. ______________ above below between
   number(s)
4. ______________ above below between
   number(s)

Guess My Number 2

This time, Lauren guesses what number Melvin has in mind.

1. ______________ above below between
2. ______________ above below between
3. ______________ above below between
4. ______________ above below between
5. ______________ above below between
6. ______________ above below between
7. ______________ above below between
8. ______________ above below between

New Sign

a limit on what is allowed or permitted; restricted; limited to

Guess My Number 3

Justin guesses what number JT has in mind.

1. ____________	above	below	between
2. ____________	above	below	between
3. ____________	above	below	between
4. ____________	above	below	between
5. ____________	above	below	between

New Sign

one more; another

Answers on page 504.

VOCABULARY REVIEW

 Review the vocabulary on the video.

1. to have something in mind, in this case, a number

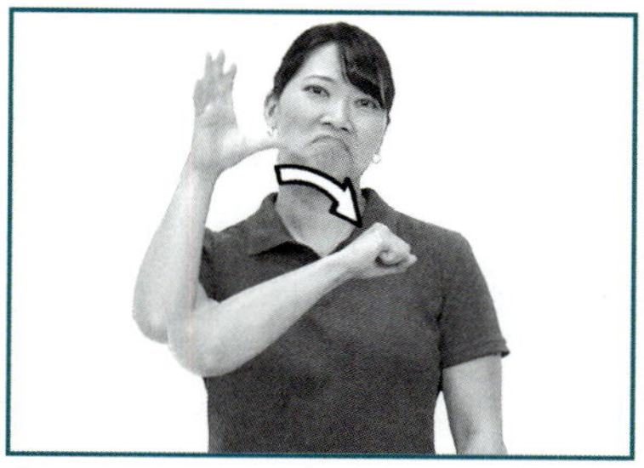

2. to guess or come up with (a number)

3. above (a certain number)

4. below (a certain number)

5. between two numbers

Homework 7:4

CONVERSATION 2

Lauren (A) and Amber (B) demonstrate this dialogue where they discuss an item Lauren bought.

Signer A: tell how you got the item
situation 1—bought for event
Signer B: respond, ask to describe what it looks like
A: describe
(use the correct sequence for the item)
B: ask what the item is made of
A: tell kind of material
B: comment on item

Key Grammar

DESCRIBING PERSONAL ITEMS

In **Lesson 7:1**, you learned to identify a person in the room by describing one or two things about the person that quickly distinguishes him or her from those around them.

In this lesson, you learn to describe items that are not present. The challenge is to give a clear detailed description of the item. Your description should move from the general to the specific, for example, begin with size, shape, cut and end with details like zipper, pockets, etc. These video segments demonstrate the sequences to follow to describe a top, a coat, a bag and a pair of eyeglasses pictured on the next pages.

DESCRIBING TOPS OR COATS

To describe a top or a coat, describe it as if you were wearing it, using your body as the reference point. Use this sequence as a guideline:

1. name item (give color if only one)
2. describe neckline, and sleeve length
3. describe pattern (name base color, then other colors)
4. describe other details (pockets, snaps, sheer, beads, hood, zipper, fur trim, puffy)

Describing Tops

Observe how Lauren follows the sequence to describe this top. Notice the fourth part of the sequence does not apply since the blouse doesn't have any other details.

Describing Coats

Observe how Amber follows the sequence to describe this coat. Notice the third part of the sequence does not apply since the coat has no pattern.

BAGS

To describe a purse or bag, describe it in neutral space in front of you. Use this sequence as a guideline:

1. name item (give color if only one)
2. describe size, shape and its handle
3. describe details (pattern, fastener, zipper, pockets, or flaps)
4. tell how it is handled or carried

Describing Bags

Observe how Lauren follows the sequence to describe this bag.

EYEGLASSES

To describe a pair of eyeglasses, describe them as if you were wearing them on your face. Show the size and shape on your face. Use this sequence as a guideline:

1. name item (give color if only one)
2. describe size and shape of lenses
3. describe details (tortoise shell, logo, rhinestones, or transparent plastic)

Describing Eyeglasses

Observe how Amber follows the sequence to describe this pair of eyeglasses.

Learn the Dialogue

Practice the key phrases for this dialogue.

Signer A: tell how you got the item[1]
- situation 1—inherited item
- situation 2—received as a gift (for birthday or holiday)
- situation 3—bought for an event or on a trip
- situation 4—person didn't want item so it was given to me
- situation 5—found it at garage sale/second hand store
- situation 6—took it from someone

Signer B: respond, ask what the item looks like[2]
- A: describe (use the correct sequence for the item)[3]
- B: ask what is the item is made of[4]
- A: tell kind of material; ask if B wants to see item
- B: say yes
- A: show item (picture on card)
- B: comment on item

1. **tell how you got the item**
   (see pages 33–34 **Tell How Got Item** to select a phrase)

2. **respond, ask what the item looks like**

3. **describe (use the correct sequence for the item)**
   See pages 21–22 for the correct sequence for items.

4. **ask what the item is made of**

MINIDIALOGUES

Watch the minidialogues and answer the questions below.

Minidialogue 1

1. How did Ursula get the item?

2. Draw and describe the item.

3. What is it made of?

4. What did Ursula think of it?

Minidialogue 2

1. How did Terrylene get the item?

2. Draw and describe the item.

3. What is it made of?

4. What did Terrylene think of it?

Minidialogue 3

1. How did Melvin get the item?

2. Draw and describe the item.

3. What is it made of?

Minidialogue 4

1. How did Justin get the item?

New Sign

exactly right; precisely

2. Draw and describe the item.

3. What is it made of?

4. Describe the costume.

Minidialogue 5

1. How did Lauren get the item?

2. Draw and describe the item.

3. What is it made of?

4. When Suzanne asked Lauren if she liked the sunglasses, why do you think Lauren didn't reply to the question directly?

Answers given in class.

Assignment

BRING TO CLASS

Bring the following items to class:

- a shirt or jacket (with pattern or detail)
- a bag, like a backpack or purse
- a pair of sunglasses (with pattern or logo)

VOCABULARY REVIEW

Review the vocabulary on the video.

Materials

1. leather

2. rubber

or

3. glass

4. translucent; semitransparent; something that can be seen through but not quite; sheer

5. something padded, puffy

6. fake, not real

7. authentic, real

8. fabric, cloth

9. something made of metal

Tops and Coats

10.

11.

12.

13.

14.

Fingerspell VEST

15.

Necklines

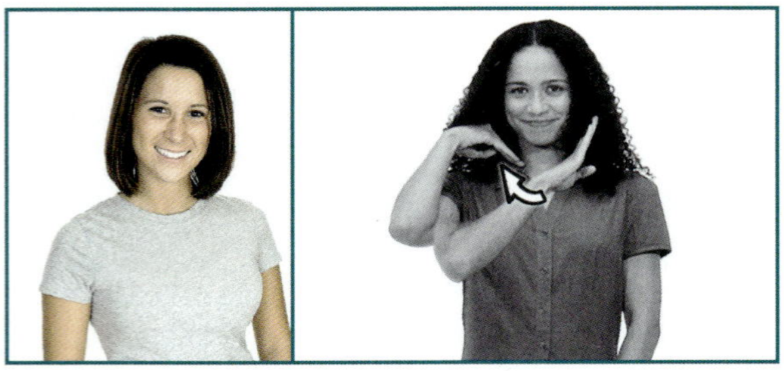

16.

17.

18.

19.

20.

21.

Sleeve Lengths

22.

23.

24.

25.

Other Details

26.

27.

28.

29.

30.

31.

Bags

32.

or

33.

Size and Shape of Lenses

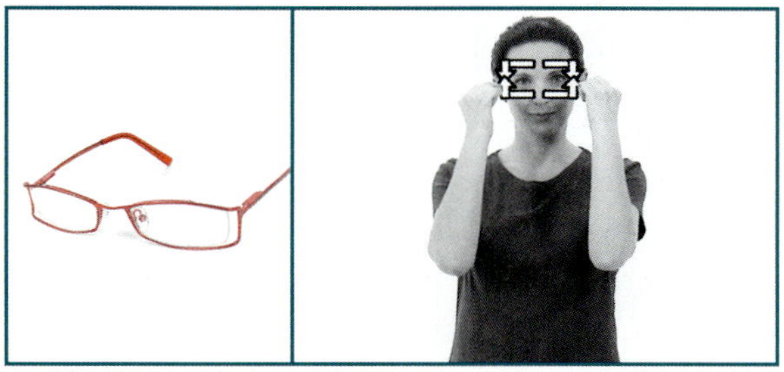

34.

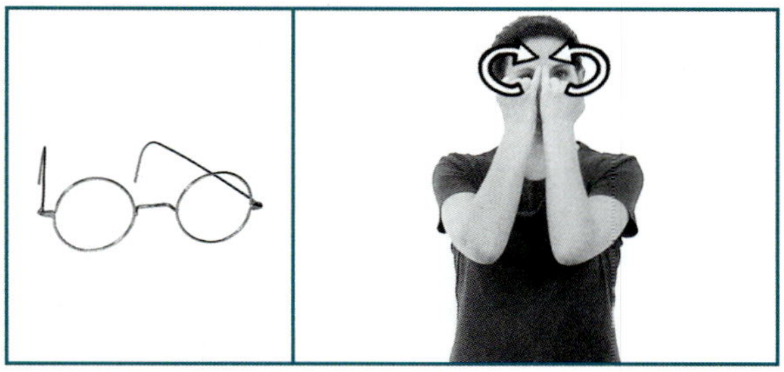

35.

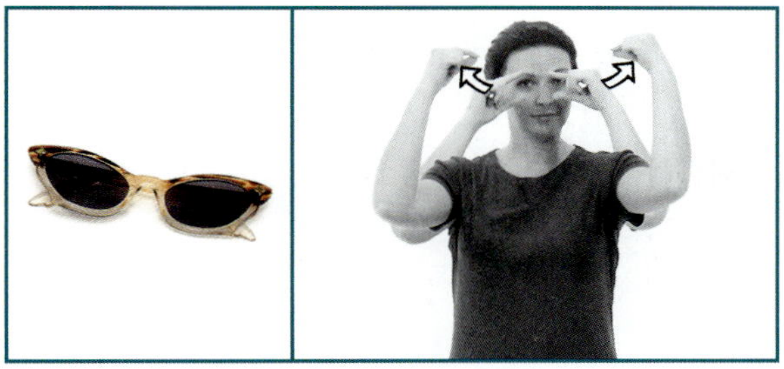

36.

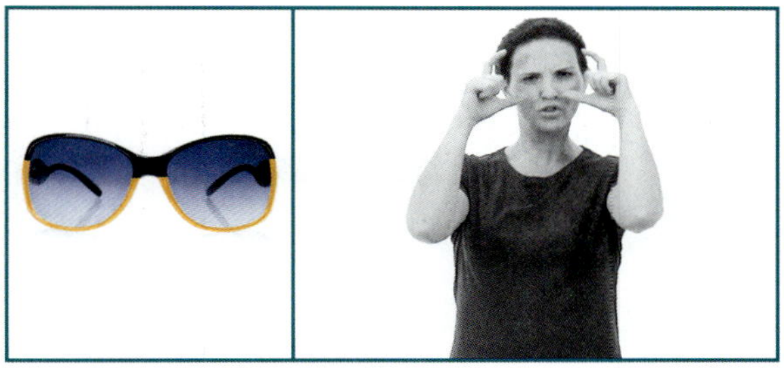

37.

38.

Comments

39. pretty, beautiful

40. unusual, odd

Fingerspell COOL

41. nifty, hip, chic

42. very good; swell

43. something never seen (before)

44. not like the others; different

45. no longer in style; not modern; old-fashioned

46. not pretty; unattractive; ugly

47. strong, bold color

Tell How Got Item

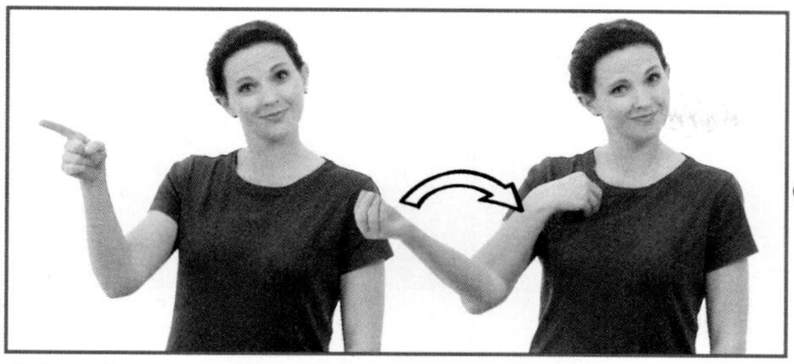

or

48. phrase telling item was inherited or given to

49. phrase telling item was a gift for Valentine's Day

50. phrase telling the item was bought on a vacation trip

51. phrase explaining the other person didn't want the item and gave it to me

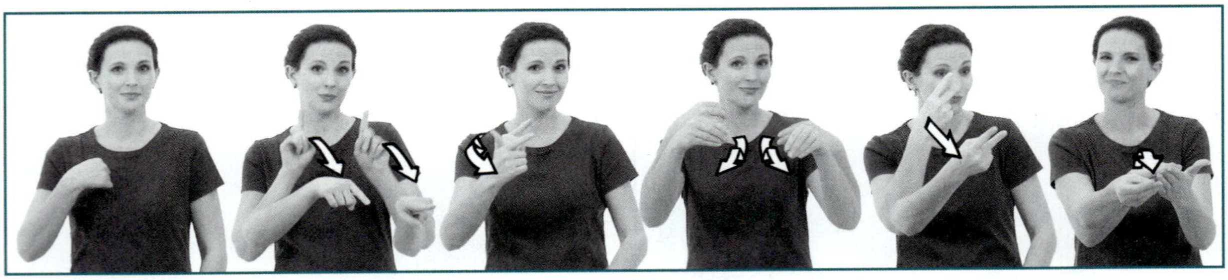

52. phrase telling the item was found at a second hand store

53. phrase explaining the item was taken from someone

Ask for More Information

54. phrase asking what item is made from

or

55. phrase asking what item looks like

56. asking to describe item

Homework 7:5

TRANSLATING SENTENCES WITH "HAVE" 1

The English word "have" has several meanings. To translate a sentence with "have," first figure the meaning it has within the sentence, then determine which sign best conveys the meaning in ASL.

Here are five example English sentences to translate:

The hotel has a pool.
The "has" in this sentence means to exist or to be present. In other instances, it can mean to be in possession of, to own, as in this sentence "He has a cat." The sign equivalent for these definitions would be:

Translation A

Watch how David translates "The hotel has a pool."

I have to go to work.
The "have to" in this sentence means to be obligated to, or to be required to. The sign equivalent for this definition would be:

Translation B

Watch how David translates "I have to go to work."

He has written two books.
The "has written" in this sentence means to have completed or to have accomplished. The sign equivalent for this definition would be:

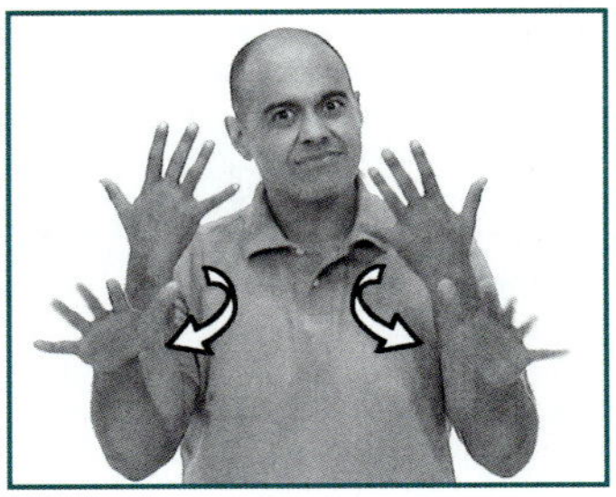

Translation C

Watch how David translates "He has written two books."

I don't have a jacket.
The "don't have" in this sentence means to not possess. It can also mean item is not present, or doesn't exist. The sign equivalent for these definitions would be:

Translation D

Watch how David translates "I don't have a jacket." The negation sign is accompanied by a side-to-side headshake.

I haven't received a letter.
The "haven't" in this sentence means the action (receiving a letter) is not yet completed or accomplished. The sign equivalent for this definition would be:

Translation E

Watch how David translates "I haven't received a letter." The negation sign is accompanied by a side-to-side headshake and a slight protrusion of the tongue.

ACTIVITY

Read each sentence and determine which of the signs (A, B, C, D or E) you would use to translate the sentence. Write the letter in the blanks.

___ **1.** I have no money.

___ **2.** I have a car.

___ **3.** I already had cake.

___ **4.** I haven't told Jose.

___ **5.** I have to tell Jose.

___ **6.** I have told Jose.

___ **7.** I have a HDTV.

___ **8.** I have to buy a jacket.

___ **9.** I have done my homework.

___ **10.** I have to call my mother.

___ **11.** I don't have any ice cream.

___ **12.** I didn't have any ice cream.

Answers given in class.

Practice. Now, practice your translations. Focus on both the word order and the facial expressions.

VOCABULARY REVIEW

Review the vocabulary on the video.

1. to exist or to be present; to be in possession of, to own

2. to be obligated to, to be required to

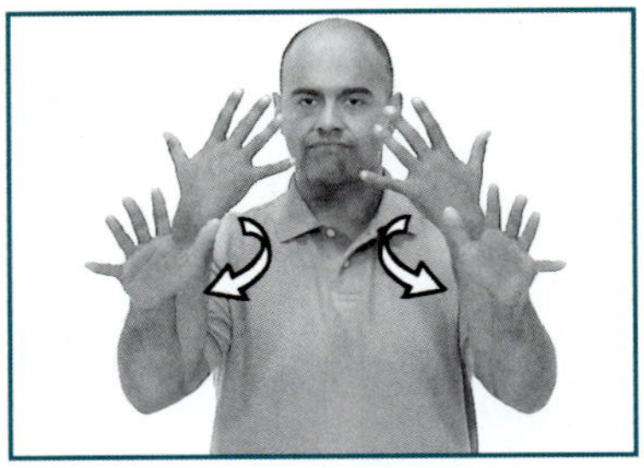

3. to have completed or accomplished

4. to not possess; is not present, or doesn't exist

5. not yet completed or accomplished

Homework 7:6

TRANSLATING SENTENCES WITH "TO DRIVE," "TO TAKE," AND "TO PICK UP" 1

Speakers of the English language learning ASL as a second language may experience interference from their native language when they sign in ASL. Here, we address some of the common errors students make with the verbs "drive to," "take (someone) to," and "pick (someone) up."

"...DRIVE TO..."

In English, this verb phrase can be used without a direct object, "I drove to work," or with a direct object (her), "I drove her to work." However, the ASL sign for "drive to" does not take a direct object, so to translate the sentence "I drove her to work," we need to add another verb sign meaning "take someone" (see below) to accommodate the direct object.

Sentence 1

Suzanne demonstrates a translation for "I drove to work." Notice Suzanne begins the movement of the sign for "drive to" close to her body, and ends it out in front to indicate the location for "work."

Sentence 2

Suzanne demonstrates a translation for "I drove her to work." Notice Suzanne establishes the woman on her right and uses the verb sign for "take someone" beginning in the woman's location and ends in her own location (since Suzanne is the one driving). Then, she begins the movement for the verb sign "drive to" from her own location and ends where "work" is located.

Sentences 3 and 4

Suzanne demonstrates two other ways to translate the sentence "I drove her to work." In both sentences, the locations of the woman and "work" remain the same.

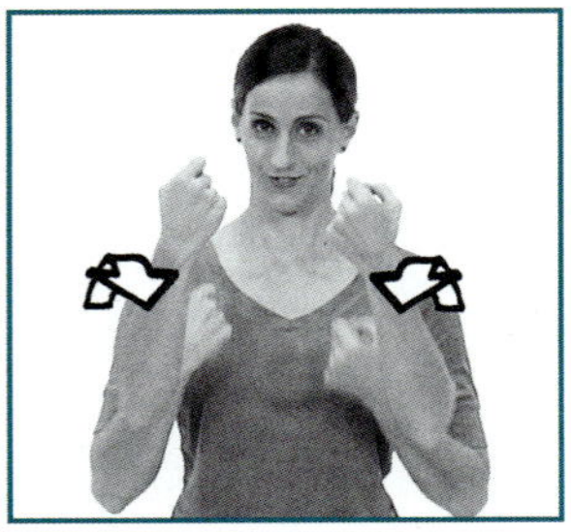
Sentence 1

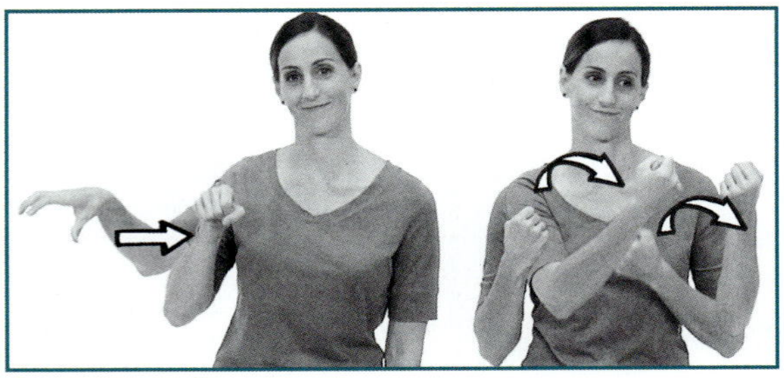
Sentence 2

Sentence 3

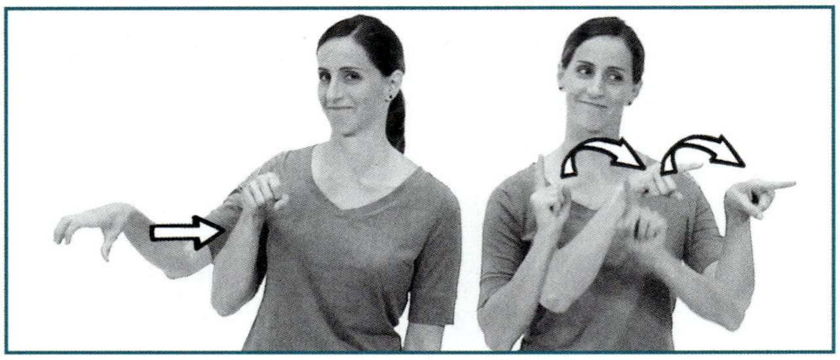
Sentence 4

"...TAKE (SOMEONE) TO..."

In this English sentence, "I took her to school," the verb means both to get and to transport a person. However, in ASL, the sign equivalent for "take" means only the action of getting a person. To add the idea of transporting someone in ASL, we would use another verb. See examples below:

Sentences 5–7

Suzanne translates this sentence "She took me to school" using two verb signs, one to indicate the woman getting Suzanne, and the other to indicate the woman transporting Suzanne to school. Notice that Suzanne begins the sign for "take someone" in her own location and ends in the woman's location (which was previously established). Then, she begins the second sign from the woman's location (since the woman is doing the driving), and ends it in the school's location.

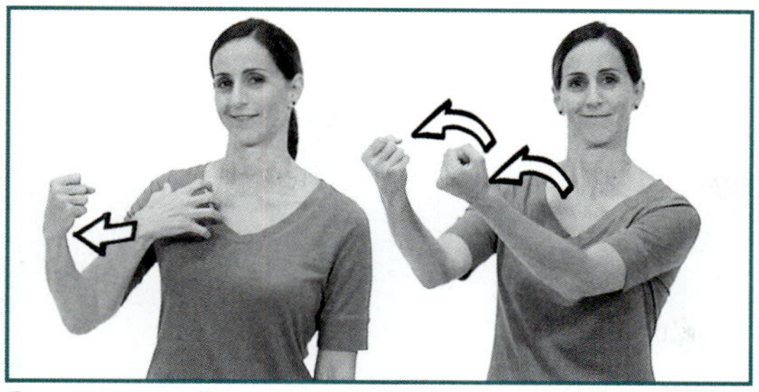

Sentence 5

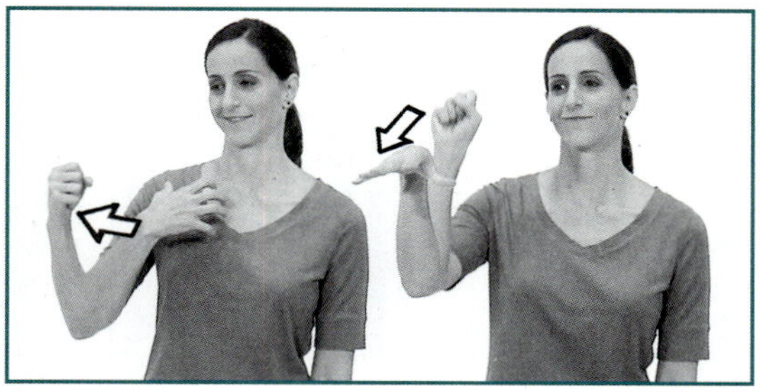

Sentence 6

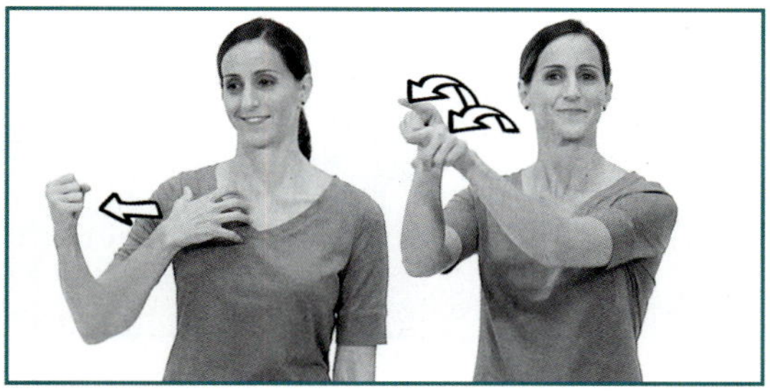

Sentence 7

"...PICK UP (SOMEONE)..."

In this English sentence, "I picked her up at school," the verb means to go to a location and get someone. However, in ASL, the sign equivalent for "pick up" means only "to get the person," so another verb would be needed to express the idea of "go to a location." See examples below:

Sentences 8–10

Suzanne translates this sentence "I picked my nephew up from his house and took him to school." She precedes the sign for "pick up" with the sign for "to go."

Observe how the movements for all three verbs in each sentence agree with the locations for herself, the nephew and the school.

Sentence 8

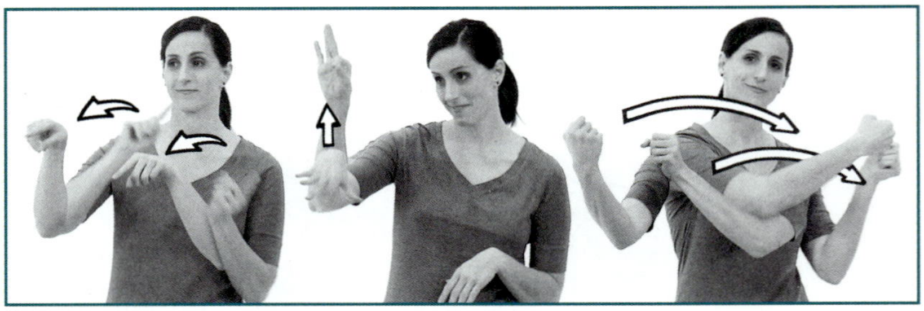

Sentence 9

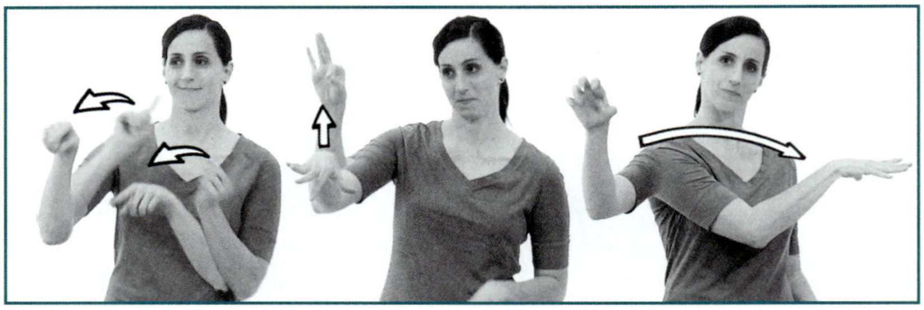

Sentence 10

INSIGHT

BEST WAY TO LEARN A NEW LANGUAGE

Typically, students learning American Sign Language assume that for every word in their first language, like English, there is a single translation equivalent in ASL. They assume that word-for-word translation equivalence is the best way to learn a language. So it is not surprising to see students in the ASL classroom asking their teacher to give English word equivalents for signs or vice versa—ASL signs for English words. This is not a very productive approach and can be misleading or incorrect. This approach creates grammatical errors and miscommunication when students use English equivalents and structures to construct ASL sentences.

To attain mastery of ASL involves moving beyond English equivalence to immersing yourself in the language—understanding ASL by using ASL.

WRITE THE TRANSLATION 1–5

For each sentence, indicate the locations by labeling each location L1, L2, and L3. Then, write an English translation for that sentence.

Example:

Write the translation *My sister will bring my son home from camp.*

1.

Write the translation ____________________

2.

Write the translation ____________________

3.

Write the translation ______________________________

4.

Write the translation ______________________________

5.

Write the translation ______________________________

Answers on page 505–506.

Homework 7:7

ASKING HOW MANY

How Many

For each dialogue, write the topic of the question, and the amount given. Then circle the number that corresponds to the reaction to the amount given.

1 ordinary, common, expected
2 less than expected
3 more than expected
4 unbelievable, ridiculous, outrageous

	Topic	*Number Given*	*Reaction Used*
1.	______	______	1 2 3 4
2.	______	______	1 2 3 4
3.	______	______	1 2 3 4
4.	______	______	1 2 3 4
5.	______	______	1 2 3 4
6.	______	______	1 2 3 4
7.	______	______	1 2 3 4
8.	______	______	1 2 3 4
9.	______	______	1 2 3 4
10.	______	______	1 2 3 4
11.	______	______	1 2 3 4
12.	______	______	1 2 3 4
13.	______	______	1 2 3 4
14.	______	______	1 2 3 4
15.	______	______	1 2 3 4

Answers on page 507.

New Sign

VOCABULARY REVIEW

Review the vocabulary on the video.

Reactions

1. react to information that is ordinary, common, expected

2. react to a given number that is less than expected

3. react to a given number that is more than expected

4. react to information that is beyond expectation; express astonishment

5. react to information that is unbelievable; ridiculous; outrageous

Homework 7:8

CONVERSATION 3

JT (A) and Suzanne (B) demonstrate this dialogue about a cap JT lost.

Part 1 *(A approaches B)*
- A: tell what is lost, ask if B has seen it
- B: say no, ask A to describe it
- A: describe
- B: tell A you will check

Part 2 *(B returns without the item)*
- B: add another description to confirm
- A: confirm or correct
- B: explain you will go get the item.

Part 3 *(B returns with the item)*
- B: ask if it is the correct item
- A: confirm, express gratitude
- B: respond

Key Grammar

DESCRIBING PERSONAL ITEMS

In this lesson, you continue to learn how to describe items that are not present. Remember, your description should move from the general to the specific, for example, begin with size and shape of the item and ending with details like pattern, logo, or fringes. These video segments demonstrate the sequence to follow to describe a hat and a scarf pictured below.

HATS

To describe a hat, describe as if you were wearing it on your head. Use this sequence as a guideline:

1. name item (give color if only one)
2. describe basic size and shape
3. describe details, like trim, colors, pattern, or logo.

Describing Hats

Observe how JT describes this hat following the sequence on the previous page.

SCARVES

To describe a scarf, describe it in neutral space in front of you. Use this sequence as a guideline:

1. name item (give color if only one)
2. describe basic size and shape
3. describe pattern or details, like fringes, or how the scarf is put on

Describing Scarves

Observe how Suzanne describes this scarf following the sequence above.

FILL IN THE BLANK

On the video, signers will describe items in random order. Number the items in the order they are described (1–12) and write the information given.

For 1–6 ______________________________

For 7–12

Answers given in class.

VOCABULARY REVIEW

Review the vocabulary on the video.

Nouns

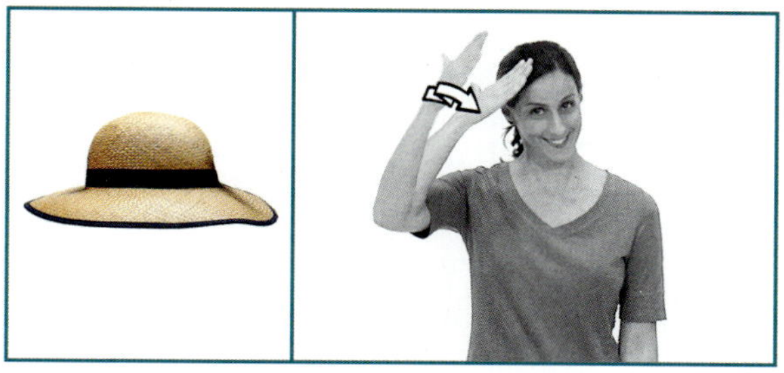

1.

2.

Sizes and shapes of hats

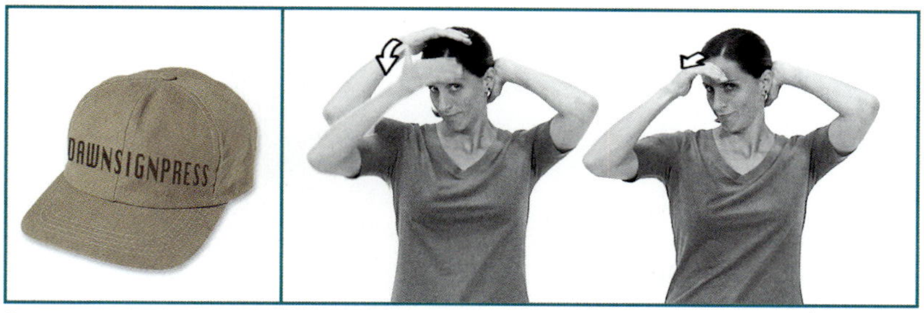

3.

4.

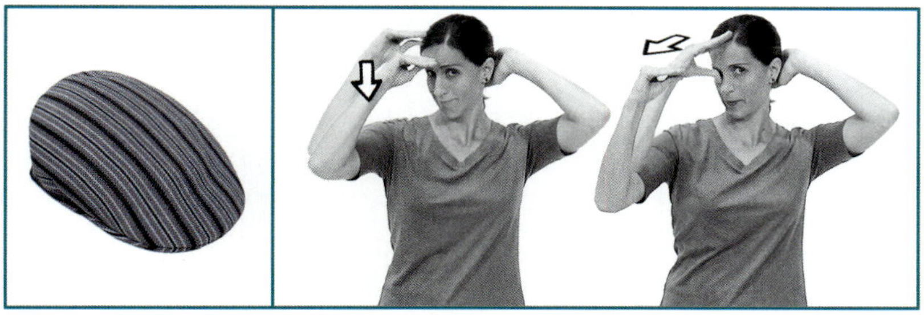

5.

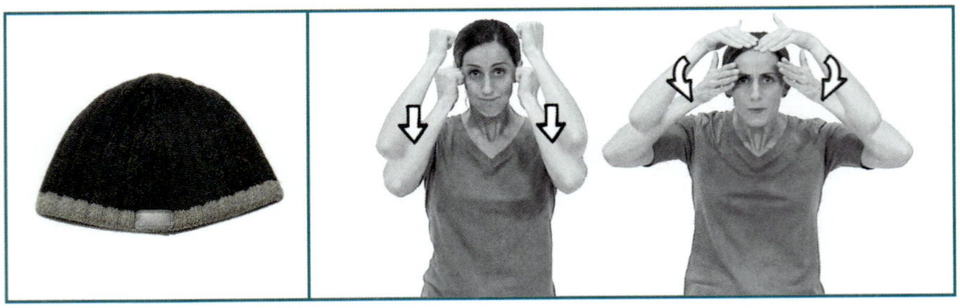

6.

7.

Homework 7:9

TELLING THE YEAR

Watch Iva demonstrate how to tell years.

Basic Year Numbers

To sign the year, divide the 4 digits into two sets of numbers. For instance, to give the year 1984, sign 19, then move your hand slightly to your dominant side before signing 84.

Iva demonstrates numbers for years 1984, 1992 and 1775. Practice signing the numbers. Make sure to move your hand out slightly between the two sets of numbers.

Years with 11–15

For years beginning or ending with numbers 11 through 15, the movement for these numbers is not repeated. For numbers 13, 14 and 15, the fingers move outward instead of inward.

Iva demonstrate numbers for years 1911, 1492, 1913, and 1712. Practice signing the numbers. Make sure you don't repeat the movement for 11 through 15. Likewise, the movement for 10 is not repeated.

Years beginning with 20

For years with beginning with 20 and ending with numbers 10 or higher, sign the number 20 first, followed by your hand's slight move to your dominant side before signing the last two numbers. The tapping movement for the number 20 is not repeated.

Iva demonstrate numbers for years 2010, 2011, 2018, 2030 and 2045. Practice signing the numbers. Make sure you do not repeat the movement for 20.

Years ending with 01–09

For years ending with numbers 01 through 09, the final two digits are signed as individual numbers. For instance, to give the year 1907, sign 19, then move your hand slightly out from your body on your dominant side to sign 0, then move your hand slightly forward for the 7.

Iva demonstrate numbers for years 1907, 1801, and 1603. Practice signing the numbers. Make sure the palm faces out for numbers 1–5.

Years with 00 in the middle

For years with two zero numbers like 2000–2009, after first giving the number 2, slide your hand out from your body on your dominant side before stopping to give the final number. Make sure the palm faces out for numbers 1–5.

Iva demonstrate numbers for years 2000 through 2009. Practice signing the numbers. Make sure to slide your hand out toward your dominant side when signing 00.

Bonus

In 2069 Iva will be 100 years old, how old is she now? ________

WRITE THE YEAR

Write down the year each event took place. Events will be given in random order.

topic	*year*
The sinking of the Titanic	________
Start of World War I	________
Wright brothers' first flight (with engine)	________
Young women's hair style of that period	________
First crossword puzzle	________
First car Ford sold	________
Barack Obama is elected President of the U.S.	________
Hippie clothing style of that period	________
San Francisco earthquake and fire	________
London, England hosting the Summer Olympics	________

Answers on page 507.

VOCABULARY REVIEW

Review the vocabulary on the video.

Past Years

or

1. Last year or one year ago

or

2. Two years ago

or

3. Three years ago

or

4. Four years ago

or

5. Five years ago

Future Years

6. Next year or one year from now

7. Two years from now

8. Three years from now

9. Four years from now

10. Five years from now

Homework 7:10

TRANSLATING SENTENCES WITH "HAVE" 2

Sentences 1–8

Write translations for the sentences Melvin signs. Make sure your translations contain the word "have."

1. ______________________________

2. ______________________________

3. ______________________________

4. ______________________________

5. ______________________________

6. ______________________________

7. ______________________________

8. ______________________________

Answers on page 508.

Homework 7:11

CULTURAL

GREETINGS AND LEAVE-TAKINGS

To be part of the close-knit Deaf community, where relationships with each other are valued, it is important to learn to function as a member of the group. Greeting and saying goodbye to each other are simple, yet important ways to develop and maintain your ties with the group.

Saying Hello. In a situation where you see people regularly, such as the classroom, it would be expected that you greet people when you enter the room and say goodbye when you leave.

If someone says "hello" or "hi" to you, you are expected to return the greeting. It is considered very rude if you do not return someone's greeting.

If you know the person and have not seen them for a while, then a "hello" is often accompanied by a hug or a handshake and a follow-up question like "how are you?" or "how's it going?"

After class or later in the day if you happen to run into an ASL student or an ASL teacher, it is customary to acknowledge the person with a "hello," a quick comment or a simple nod. Passing by the person without acknowledging him or her in some way is not considered polite or friendly.

GREETINGS

There are three common ways to greet a person.

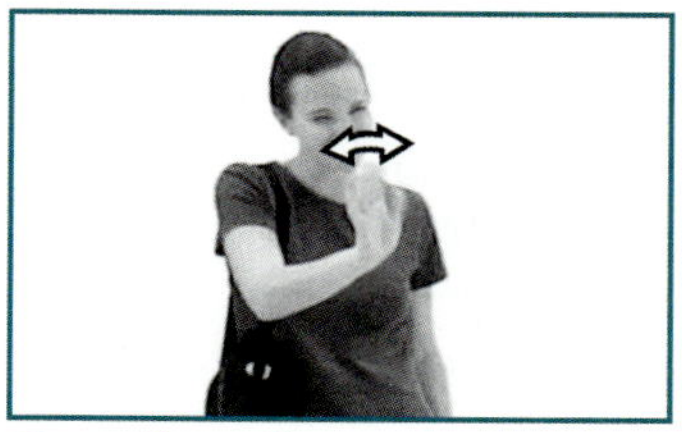
Greeting 1

Greeting 2

Greeting 3

Greetings 1–3

Amber, Suzanne and JT demonstrate three ways to greet classmates as they enter the classroom. Notice they scan the room and greet those that make eye contact with them. Also notice how the teacher greets the whole class.

Follow-up after Greeting 1–6

Suzanne demonstrates different follow-up phrases to use after greeting someone.

Follow-up 1: ask how someone is

NOTE: Responding with just "I'm fine, thanks" is acceptable, but if you include how you are really doing, it is not viewed as awkward.

Follow-up 2: ask for an update

NOTE: This sign usually follows a greeting as a way to invite a more involved conversation. To answer simply "nothing" with no elaboration on how ordinary the days have been would give the impression you are not interested in talking to that particular person. So some sort of elaboration is in order.

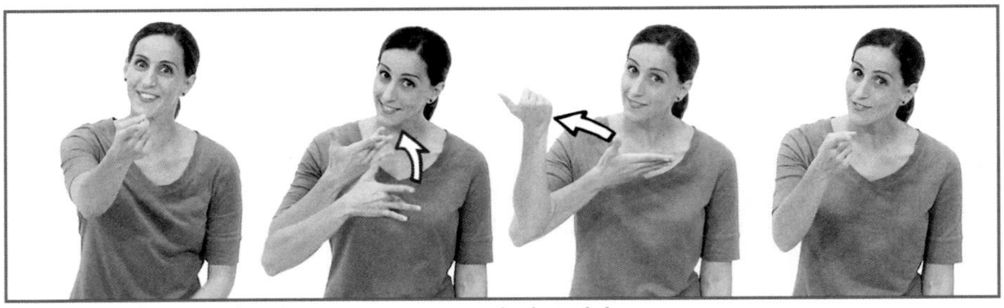

Follow-up 3: ask about someone's health

Follow-up 4: commenting on absence to person you don't know well

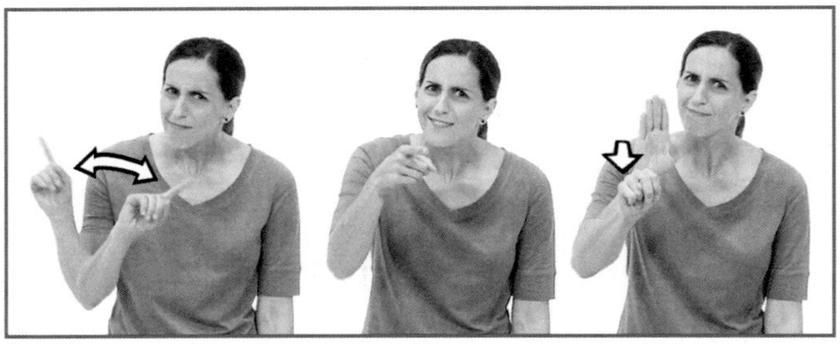

Follow-up 5: commenting on absence to person you know well

Follow-up 6: another way to comment on absence to person you know well

Reply 1–3

Justin demonstrates replies to Follow-ups 1–3.

Reply 1 (to Follow-up 1): tell you are all right

Reply 2 (to Follow-up 2): tell everything is the same, that there is nothing new

Reply 3 (to Follow-up 3): tell you are definitely better

SIGNING GOODBYE

When you leave a group setting like the classroom, making an effort to say goodbye to others is considered polite. Make it a habit to scan the room as you leave to say goodbye to those who make eye contact with you.

Leave-takings 1–5

These are five common ways to sign goodbye to someone.

Leave-taking 1

Leave-taking 2

Leave-taking 3

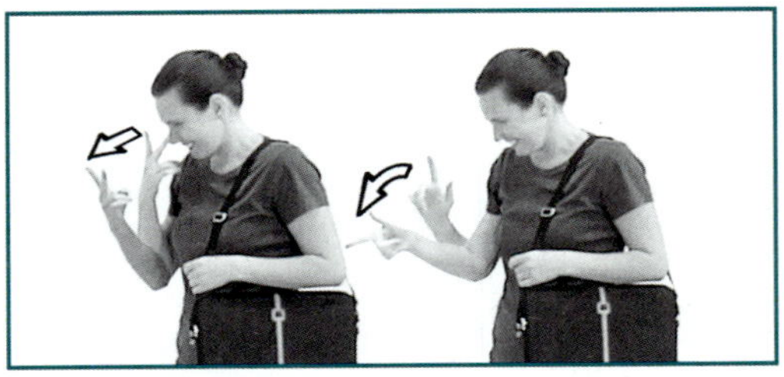

Leave-taking 4

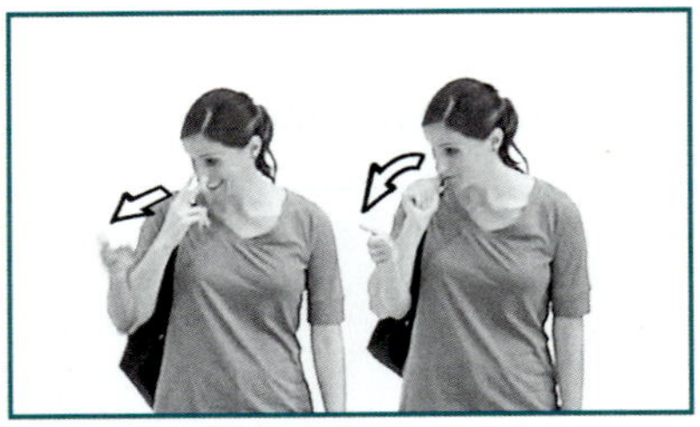

Leave-taking 5

Leave-Taking 1–5

Several classmates say goodbye to their peers as they get up and leave the classroom. Notice them making eye contact with each other when they sign their goodbyes.

Assignment

OBSERVATIONS: GREETINGS AND LEAVE-TAKING

Attend an organized activity where Deaf and hearing people gather, for example, Deaf Coffee Night, Pizza Night, Deaf/ASL Theatre, Signing Weekend, or Deaf Expo.

Observe how Deaf people greet each other and what questions or comments they use after the greeting. Then observe how they end the conversation and say their goodbyes. See if there are any differences in usage and behaviors between females and males, young and old, and strangers and friends.

On a separate paper, type your observations covering these:

- name of event
- date, including the time you arrived and departed the event
- how many people attended, including the estimated number of Deaf people
- general description of the event
- summarize your observations. For each observation, identify
  - the gender and age of the participants
  - kind of relationship (strangers or friends)
  - what greetings were used
  - what follow-up questions or comments were made
  - what leave-taking phrase(s) were used
- compare these behaviors with those from your own culture.

Homework 7:12

TRANSLATING SENTENCES WITH "TO DRIVE," "TO TAKE," AND "TO PICK UP" 2

Translate the sentences below. When translating the sentences, make sure the movement of the verbs agree with the locations of the person(s) and place(s). **Homework 7:6** has notes to review on spatial agreement as well as the lexical and grammatical differences.

1. My friend will take me home after school.
2. I drove four of my friends to see the show.
3. I brought my mother home from the party.
4. Yesterday I took my niece to soccer practice.
5. When will you drive your family to San Francisco?
6. We need to take the baby to the hospital.
7. My friend took me to the ballgame.
8. My daughter wanted to come home, so I went and got her.

Assignment

PRACTICE THE SENTENCES

Be prepared to sign these sentences next class.

Homework 7:13

STORY: A MEMORABLE COSTUME

View the story **A Memorable Costume** then answer the questions below.

1. How old were Amber and her brother?

2. What traditionally happens at school for Halloween?

3. One Halloween, what did Amber and her brother want to be?

4. Explain what they did to make the costume.
– the head

– the body

5. What did they win?

Answers given in class.

NEW SIGNS

Use these definitions to help your understanding of the story.

1. a residential school for the Deaf

2. on every occasion; without fail; always

3.

4. personal pronoun for "a group of us"

5. a set of clothes worn for Halloween; costumes

6. expression meaning "how cute" or "how adorable"

7. to achieve a prize, trophy, or victory; or to achieve the first place in a competition; to win

8.

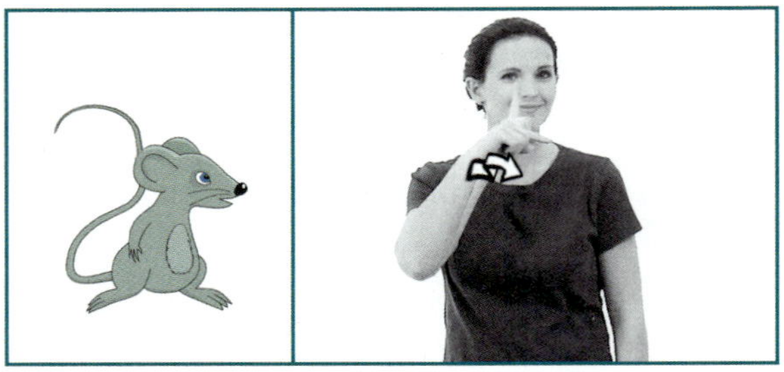

9.

10.

11. to become solid, firm or be hardened

12. to take pleasure in; to enjoy

DEAF PROFILE

ARTHUR KRUGER (1911–1992)

Arthur "Art" Kruger was passionate about sports all his life, and turned that passion into a lasting legacy as the "father" of the American Athletic Association of the Deaf (AAAD), now the US Deaf Sports Federation (USDSF), and as a tireless trailblazer who championed US Deaf sports at the international level.

Arthur Kruger was born in 1911 in Philadelphia. He graduated from the Pennsylvania School for the Deaf in 1927, and from Gallaudet College in 1933. All through his school years Art was an avid sports fan, writing for his school newspapers.

Art's work was not only on the front lines, but touched every aspect of supporting Deaf athletes. He raised approximately $2 million to support the AAAD over the years.

He continued his sports journalism. Art had a 50-year custom of choosing the Schools for the Deaf Basketball All-American selections (1936-1986). He wrote for the *Silent Broadcaster* starting in 1944, and served as the sports editor of the *Silent Worker* beginning in 1949.

In 1945 Art organized the first National Deaf Basketball tournament in Akron, Ohio. The night before the tournament. leaders of various Deaf sports clubs agreed to establish the American Athletic Union of the Deaf, soon to be renamed the AAAD, and elected Art as the first president. By 1954 Art was the first person inducted into the AAAD Hall of Fame for leadership and sports writing.

With a thriving US Deaf sports organization established, Art next turned his attention to the international sports scene. The Deaf World Games (later known as the Deaflympics) had been held, with a 10-year hiatus in the 1930s, since 1924. By 1953, in the history of the Deaf World Games, only three US athletes had ever participated. With Art's assistance, fourteen athletes participated in the 1953 games. While Art served as Team Director between 1957 to 1983, he helped send 12 teams and hundreds of athletes and coaches to the World Deaf Games. In 1975 he was also the President of the Pan-American Games for the Deaf Foundation, extending his help to Central and South American athletes.

Art's work was not only on the front lines, but touched every aspect of supporting Deaf athletes. He raised approximately $2 million to support the AAAD over the years. In addition to the accolades already mentioned, he received countless awards and recognition for his work with Deaf athletes worldwide, including the Edward Miner Gallaudet Award in 1980, and an honorary doctorate degree from Hofstra University in New York in 1982.

At its height the USDSF had over 200 clubs and 25,000 members. Gallaudet named Art Kruger a visionary leader in October 2013 as part of the school's 150th anniversary celebrations, a fitting tribute to a leader who created lasting organizations that touched the lives of Deaf people.

Did You Realize...Once There Were Five Iron Men?

Left to right: Don Padden, Earl Roberts, Paul Baldridge, Roy Holcomb, Harold Weingold

Seeded last in Mason-Dixon Conference Basketball Championship tournament of March 1943, the Gallaudet University* men's team overcame huge odds to win the championship and were dubbed "The Five Iron Men." In the first game, the men faced second-ranked Randolph Macon College, a team they lost to twice in the regular season, yet managed to upset them by the score of 48–39. The Gallaudet men, being the last-seeded team had to change their clothes in the hallway since there were no dressing rooms left. But this didn't dampen their enthusiasm for playing the game. The Gallaudet team went on to win the next two games against American University, and the University of Delaware to capture the championship. What was remarkable was that the same five players played the entire three games without substitution. Even more remarkable was that all five men were named to the all-star team.

* Gallaudet University, located in Washington, D.C., was established in 1864 by an act of Congress. It is the world's only liberal arts university whose mission is to serve Deaf students.

Unit 7 Review: Self-Assessment

Write the number of: classes you missed: _____
homework assignments not completed for class: ____
hours you practiced/used signs outside of the classroom per week: _____

Now that you are done with this unit, rate yourself using the list below: **5** indicates feeling the most comfortable and confident about your skill in that area and **1** indicates feeling the least confident.

NOTE: If you marked 3 or lower, you should review that portion of the workbook and write down steps you plan to take to improve your skills in that area.

1.	I can describe one or two things to successfully point out a person.	5	4	3	2	1
2.	I can use the correct sequence to describe items that are not present.	5	4	3	2	1
3.	I can ask for confirmation about or confirm a person being identified.	5	4	3	2	1
4.	I can translate English sentences with the word "have" correctly into ASL.	5	4	3	2	1
5.	I can correctly fingerspell clothing-related words.	5	4	3	2	1
6.	I understand how to use the signs for "drive to," "take to" and "pick up" to correspond to the assigned locations in the narratives.	5	4	3	2	1
7.	I can give year numbers using the correct number patterns.	5	4	3	2	1
8.	I understand how to do "greetings" and "leave-takings" with consideration of the person, time and place.	5	4	3	2	1
9.	When viewing the story "A Memorable Costume," I'm able to figure out the meaning even though I don't know every sign used.	5	4	3	2	1

Steps I will take: ______________________________

NOTES:

The Missing Jigsaw Pieces
David Call
12" x 18"
Linocut
2012
www.eyehandstudio.com

UNIT 8

Making Requests and Asking for Advice

Homework 8:1

CONVERSATION 1

Tonique (A) and David (B) demonstrate this dialogue in which a request has been made.

Signer A: explain situation, make request
Signer B: decline, give reason

New Signs

to deliver; or bring here

to be enthusiastic or and eager

give instructions

suggestion phrase "Why don't you..."

use a videophone

yourself; on your own

expression meaning "Let's try" or "Let's see how it works"

to make an effort to do something; to try

Key Grammar

EXPLAINING A SITUATION

Because you are asking a favor of someone, which involves their time and resources, you need to explain the situation to justify your request.

View. Watch Tonique give a detailed explanation of her situation.

1. she gets David to recall she bought the shelves
2. she was thrilled when the shelves arrived yesterday
3. when she opened the box, she realized she had to assemble the shelves herself
4. after reading the instruction manual, she realized she needed some help

MAKING A REQUEST

After you explain the situation, use this sign to signal you are making a request. Also, use a pleading expression while you sign the request.

View. Observe Tonique making the request.

MINIDIALOGUES

Watch the minidialogues and answer the questions below.

Minidialogue 1

Signer A

explain situation: ______________________________

request made: ______________________________

Signer B

reason for declining: ______________________________

New Signs

to volunteer

to give food to animals; to feed

animals

past the agreed-on time; to be late

(business) not open; to be closed

Minidialogue 2

Signer A

explain situation: ______________________________

request made: ______________________________

Signer B

reason for declining: ______________________________

New Signs

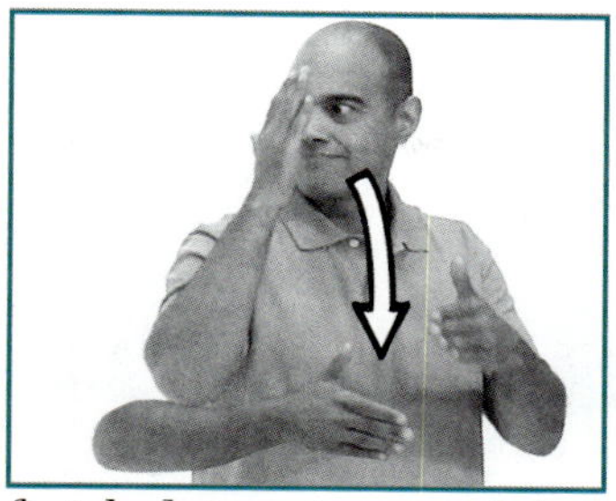

finish doing; to complete (something)

story; narrative

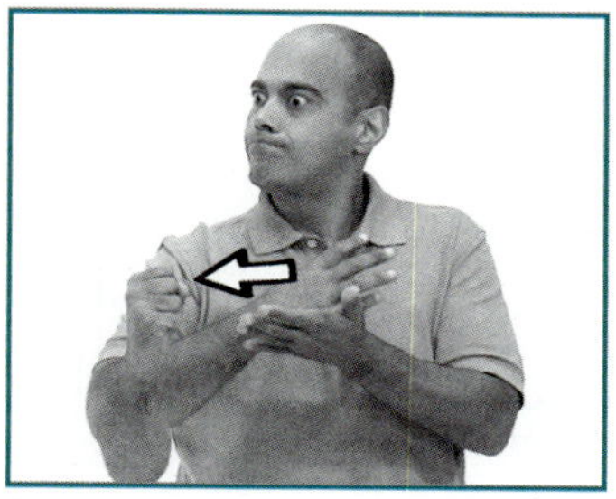

to use up; to run out of

to put coins in the meter

Minidialogue 3

Signer A

explain situation: ______________________________

request made: ______________________________

Signer B

reason for declining: ______________________________

suggested solution: ______________________________

New Signs

along with; accompanied by

to reach or arrive at a location

put together; set up

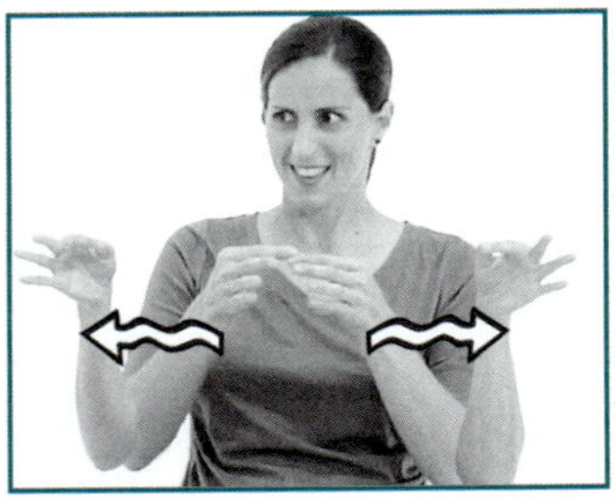
language

a character-based writing system like Chinese

Minidialogue 4

Signer A

explain situation: ______________________________

request made: ______________________________

Signer B

reason for declining: ______________________________

New Signs

to request something be supplied; to order

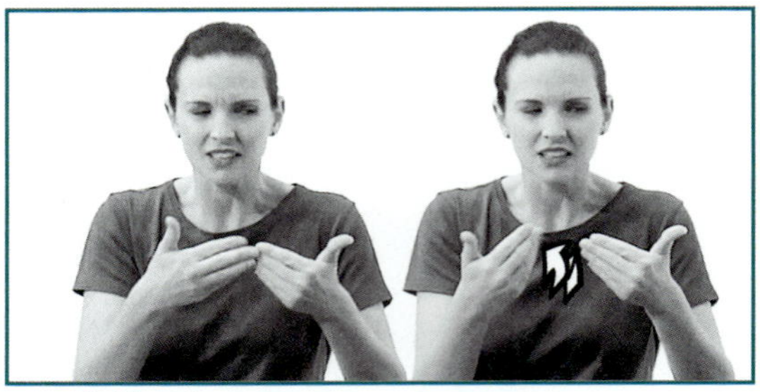
not difficult; easy

Minidialogue 5

Signer A

explain situation: ______________________________

request made: ______________________________

Signer B

reason for declining: ______________________________

suggested solution: ______________________________

New Signs

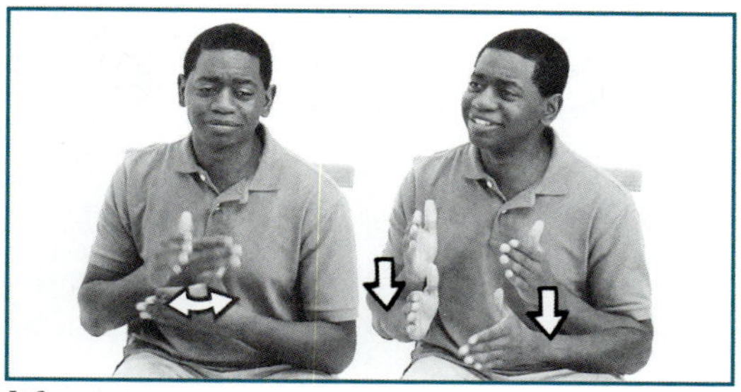

life partner

taking a very short time; quickly

Minidialogue 6

Signer A

explain situation: ____________________

request made: ____________________

Signer B

reason for declining: ____________________

suggested solution: ____________________

New Signs

to write using the keyboard; to type

to do swiftly; speedily

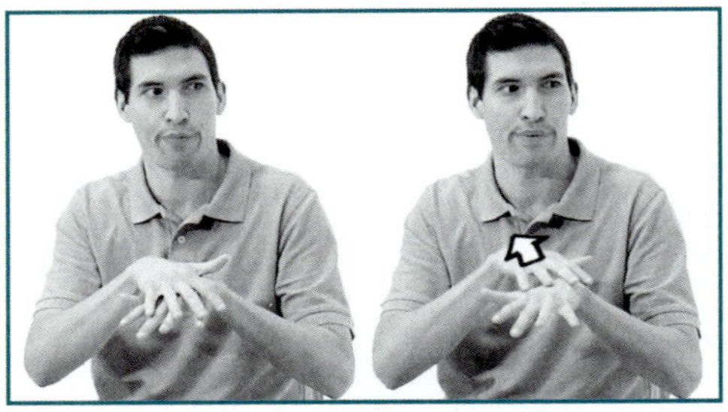

to move at a slow speed; to be slow

Answers given in class.

Learn the Requests

REQUESTS 1–6

Memorize these requests introduced in class. When rehearsing them, be sure the movement of the verbs agrees with the established locations of the people or places in each situation. Be prepared to sign the requests in class.

Request 1

Request 2

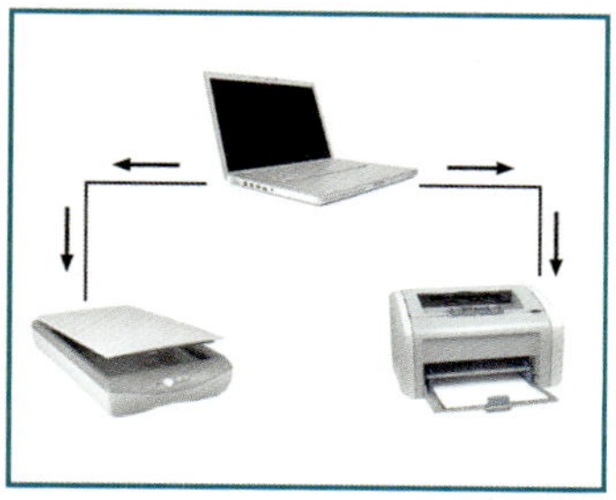

Request 3

Request 4

Request 5

Request 6

Assignment

MAKE YOUR OWN REQUESTS

Create three requests of your own to use in class. Each request should include the following:

- explanation of the situation (with three to five details and at least one new sign learned)
- the request itself.

Memorize all three before going to class.

VOCABULARY REVIEW

Review the vocabulary on the video.

Requesting

1. phrase used to make a request

Declining

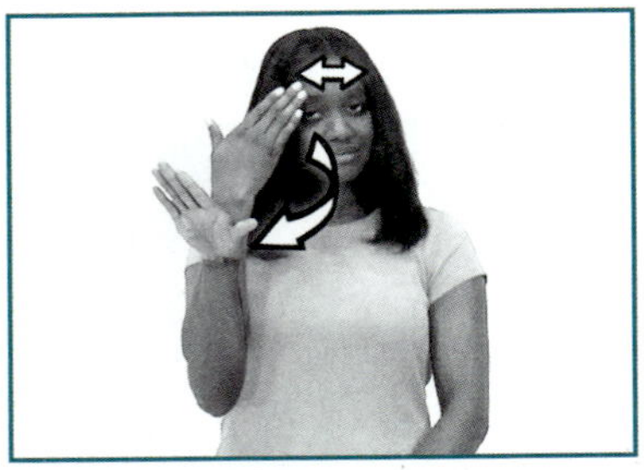

2. not knowing how (to do or fix something)

Verbs

or

or

3. to use

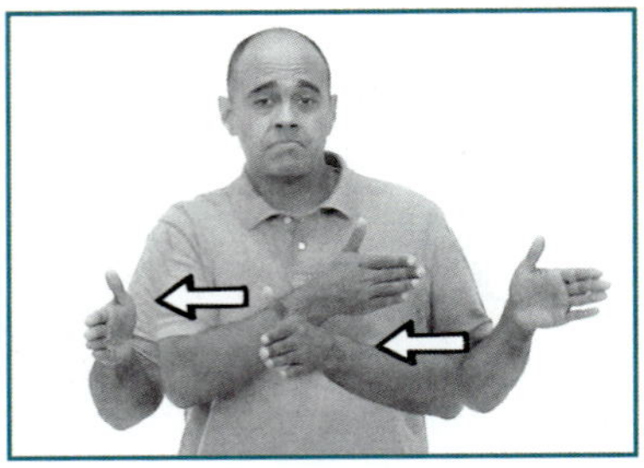

4. to plan to do (something)

5. to put off, postpone

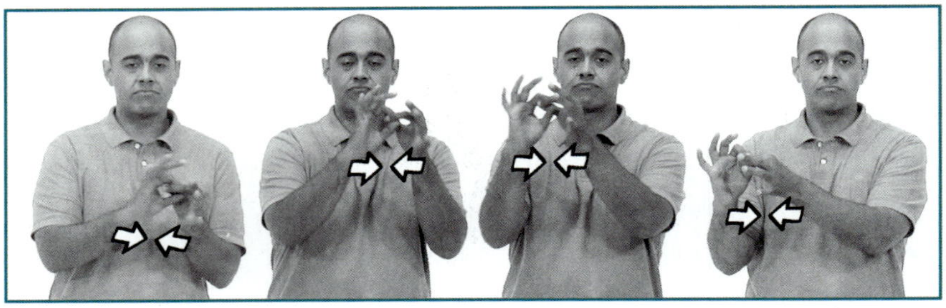

6. to assemble; to put components or parts of a unit together

7. to lose or misplace something

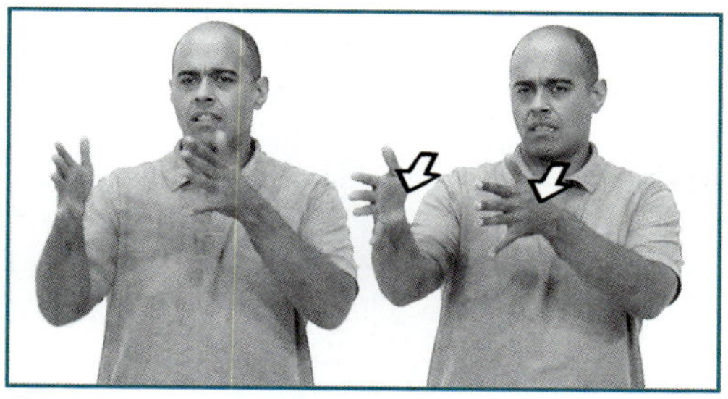

8. to leave behind

9. (plane) taking off or departing

10. to wait for a good while

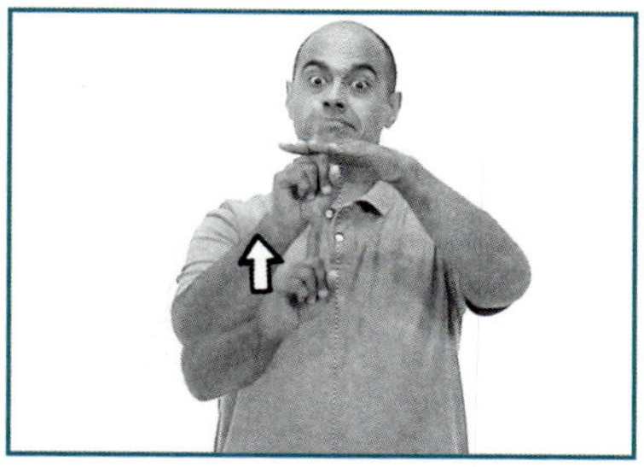

11. to show up; to appear

12. to be curious to know something

13. to fall behind

14. to finish what has not been done; to catch up on work

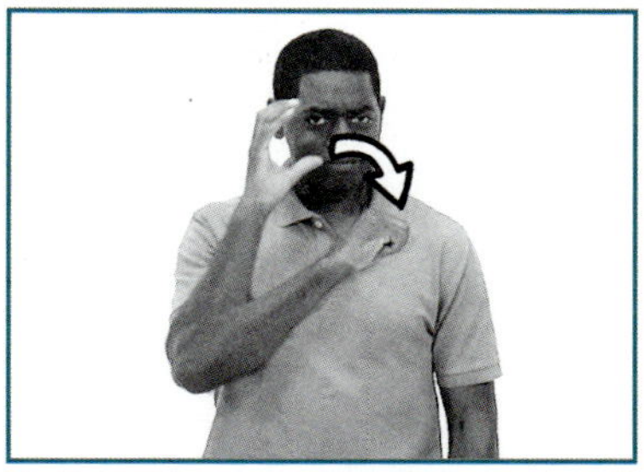

15. to be absent from class

Technology-related

16. a device that prints

17. a device that scans

18. the internet

State of Being

19. to be ignorant about something

Time-related

20. not long ago; recently

Pronoun

21. myself

Nouns

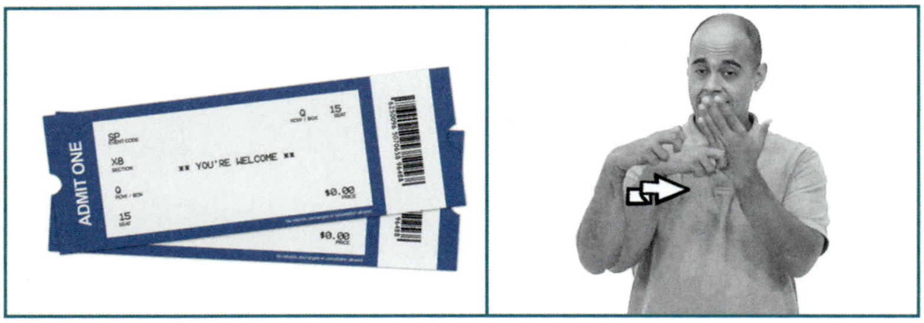

22.

23. address of a location

24. a play; theatre

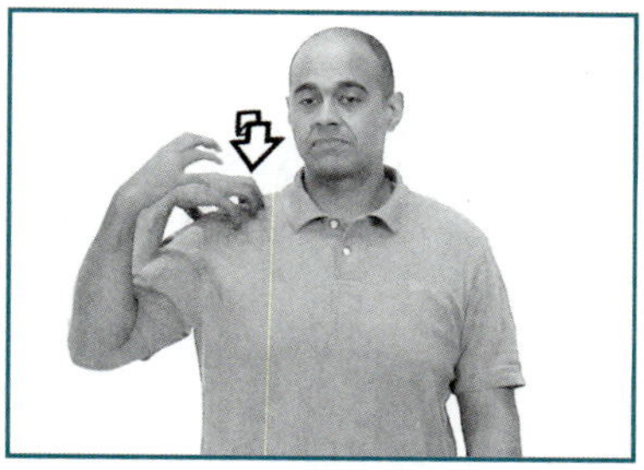

25. a higher authority at a workplace; boss

26. New York

27.

28. a program or procession honoring someone who died; a funeral

Other Signs

Fingerspell
OT

29. time in addition; overtime

30. by way of or by means of; through

31. perhaps; maybe

32. contains everything

SIGNING NATURALLY

Homework 8:2

TALKING ABOUT MONTHS

John demonstrates how to sign the months using fingerspelling. Notice how certain letters are positioned, or combined to spell each word.

January (fingerspell JAN)

"A" begins with the palm facing sideways

February (fingerspell FEB)

"E" pulls back slightly, then moves forward to form "B"

March (fully spelled out)

"C" twists wrist (like turning a doorknob) to form "H"

April (fully spelled out)

"A" begins facing sideways, then transitions to "P" and "R" in one continuous circular movement

May (fully spelled out)

The hand moves downward to form "Y"

June (fully spelled out)

"U" is formed with palm facing inward and held as the hand rotates forward

July (fully spelled out)

"U" is formed with palm facing inwards and as the hand rotates forward, it becomes "L"

August (fingerspell AUG)

Palm of the hand faces sideways for "G"

September (fingerspell SEPT)

"T" pulls back slightly

October (fingerspell OCT)

"C" moves slightly upward

November (fingerspell NOV)

"O" pulls back slightly before moving forward for "V"

December (fingerspell DEC)

"E" pulls back slightly, before moving forward for "C"

WRITE THE MONTH

Signers will sign sentences with months. Write the month and what it refers to.

	month(s)	*what the month(s) refer to*
1.	________________	__________________________

New Signs

usually; have a tendency to

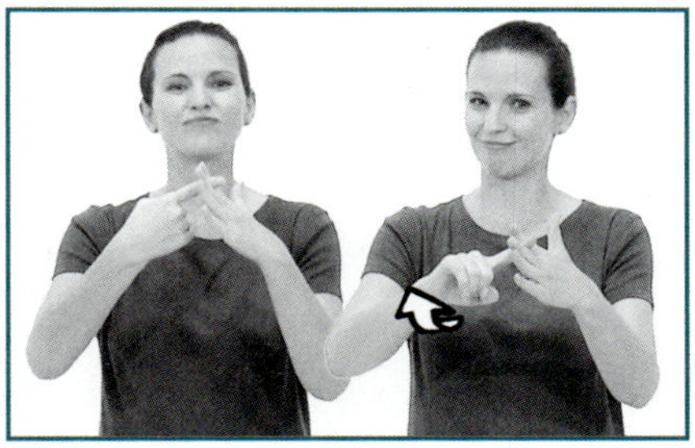

to begin: to start

2.	________________	__________________________
3.	________________	__________________________

month(s) | *what the month(s) refer to*

4. ______________ ______________________

New Signs

great amount of time

short amount of time

5. ______________ ______________________

New Signs

a rock or stone

6. ______________ ______________________

7. ______________ ______________________

New Signs

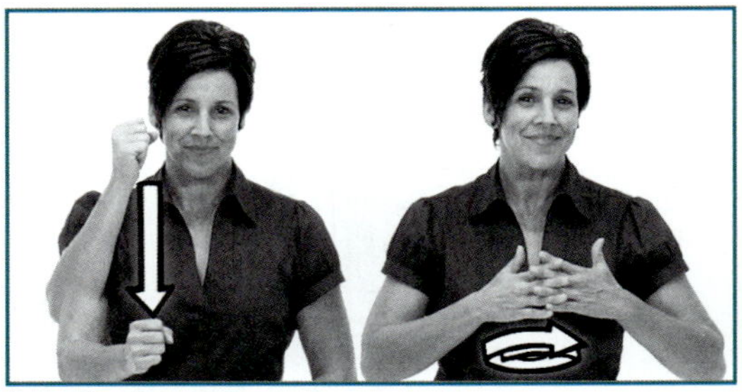
South America

having a high temperature; hot

8. ____________________ ________________________________

New Signs

Valentine

Answers on page 509.

TELLING HOW MANY MONTHS

To tell how many months, numbers 1–9 are incorporated in the sign for month. Form the numbers with the palm facing inward.

3 months
number is incorporated

7 months
number is incorporated

For 10 months or more, the number is not incorporated in the sign for month. Give the number, then the sign for month.

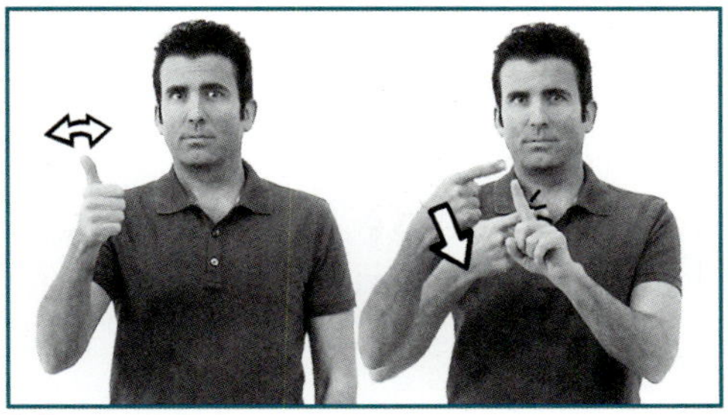

10 months
number is *not* incorporated

To specify when in the future or in the past something will or did occur, sign the following.

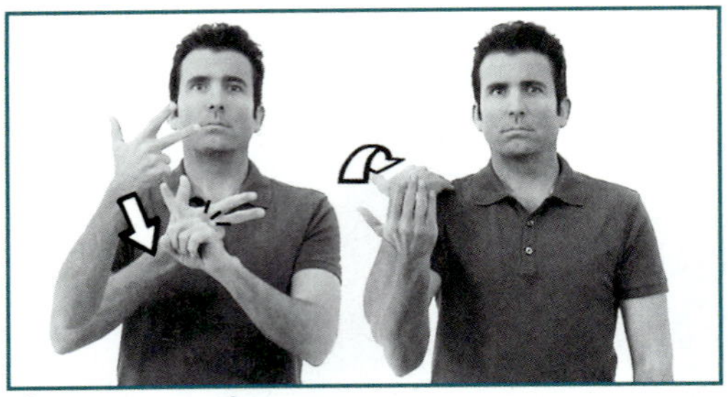
three months ago

seven months from now

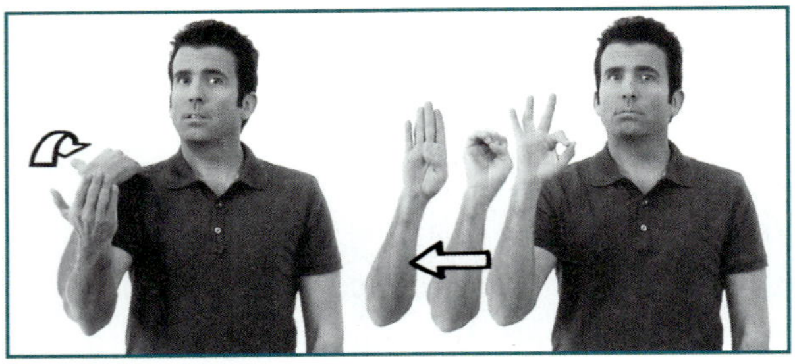
last February

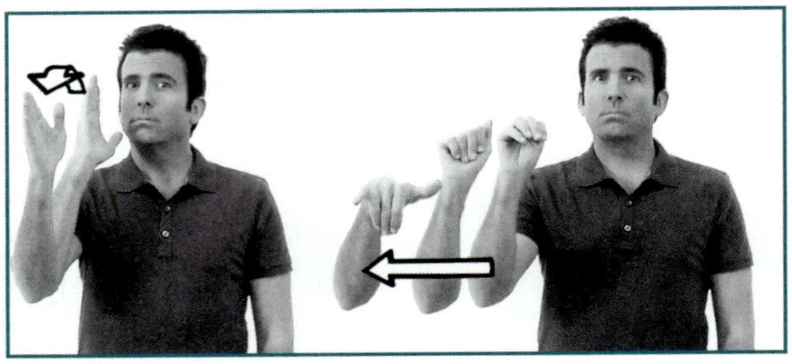
next May

When an event occurs repeatedly, like every year or every two years, repeat the sign. When you want to specify when during the year, the event occurs, give the month.

every year

every two years

Assignment

FIVE QUESTIONS

Develop five questions that require your partner to name a month.

VOCABULARY REVIEW

Review the vocabulary on the video.

Calendar Time Signs

1. every year: annually

2. every other year: biannually

Seasons

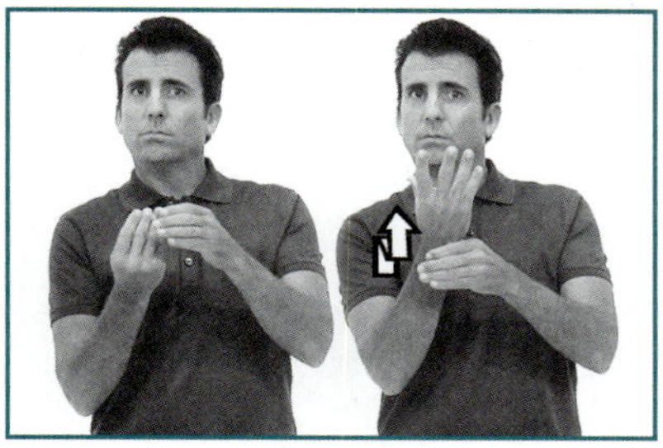

3. the season including March, April and May

4. the season including June, July and August

5. the season including September, October and November

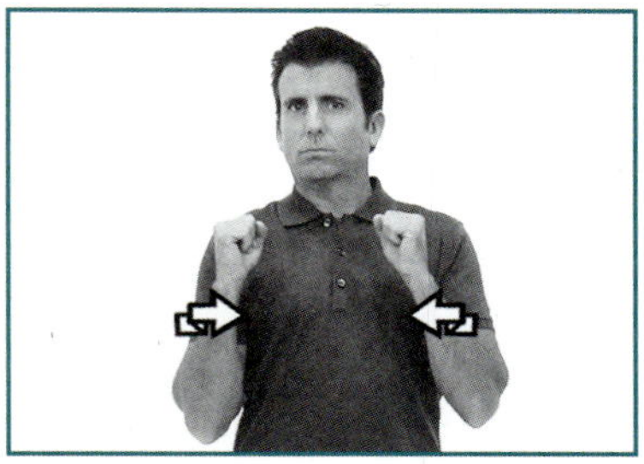

6. the season including December, January and February

SIGNING NATURALLY

Homework 8:3

AGREEMENT VERBS 1

Agreement verb signs can be modified to show the subject and the object of the sentence. The agreement verb usually begins in the location of the subject and moves in the direction of the object.

View. For each verb sign below three different movements are shown on video, each one indicating different subject-object relationships.

- "from me to you"
- "from you to me,"
- "from someone to another."

Here is the list of verbs to practice.

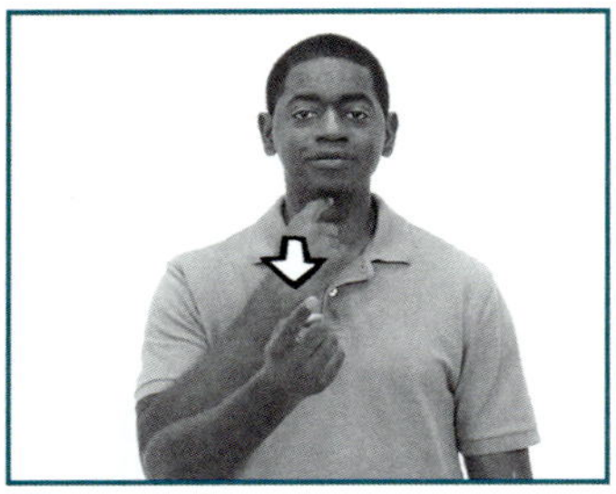

1. to tell or to communicate something

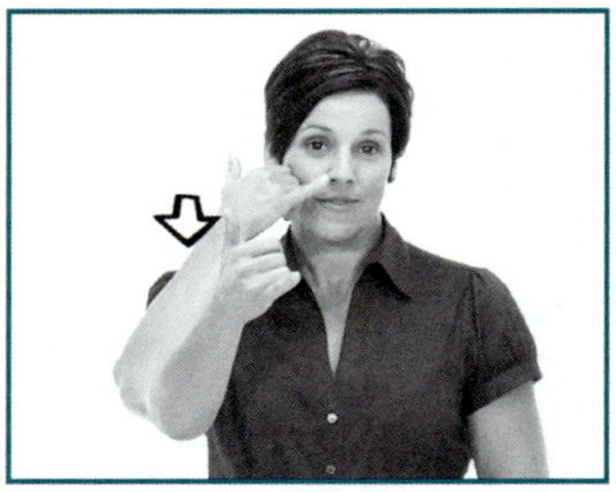

2. to call someone by phone

3. to send or mail something

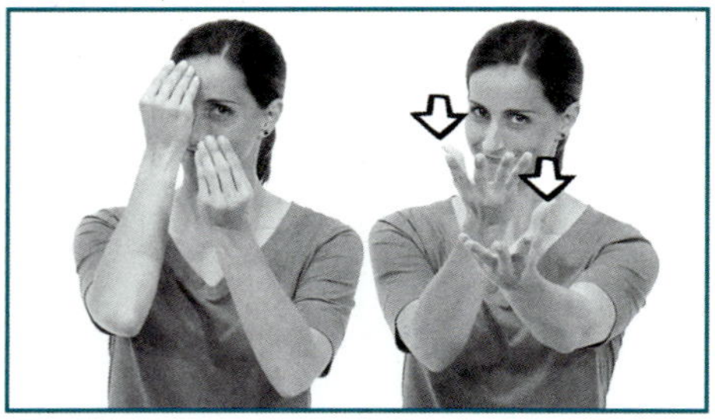

4. to give news, announcements, or warnings

5. to give money for services rendered; to pay

SENTENCES

You will see two signed sentences (A and B). Put a check in the box for the one that best matches the meaning of the English sentence.

Sentence 1

"I told Renee to send you the flowers but instead she sent them to me."

A ❑ or **B** ❑

Write the English translation for the other signed sentence.

____

Sentence 2

"Lee called to tell me you have not paid him."

A ❑ or **B** ❑

Write the English translation for the other signed sentence.

____

Sentence 3

"Renee informed me that Lee has already paid her, so I will now send Lee the package."

A ❑ or **B** ❑

Write the English translation for the other signed sentence.

____

Answers on page 510.

NARRATIVES

After viewing each narrative, answer the questions below.

Narrative 1

What did the dentist call JT about? ______________________

____

What was JT's response? ______________________

____

Narrative 2

What did Suzanne buy and when will it be delivered? ______________________

____

What happened when she got ready to pay? ______________________

____

Answers on page 510.

VOCABULARY REVIEW

Review the vocabulary on the video.

For each definition below, three different movements are shown, each one indicating these subject-object relationships:

- "from me to you"
- "from you to me,"
- "from someone to another."

1. to tell or to communicate something

2. to call someone by phone

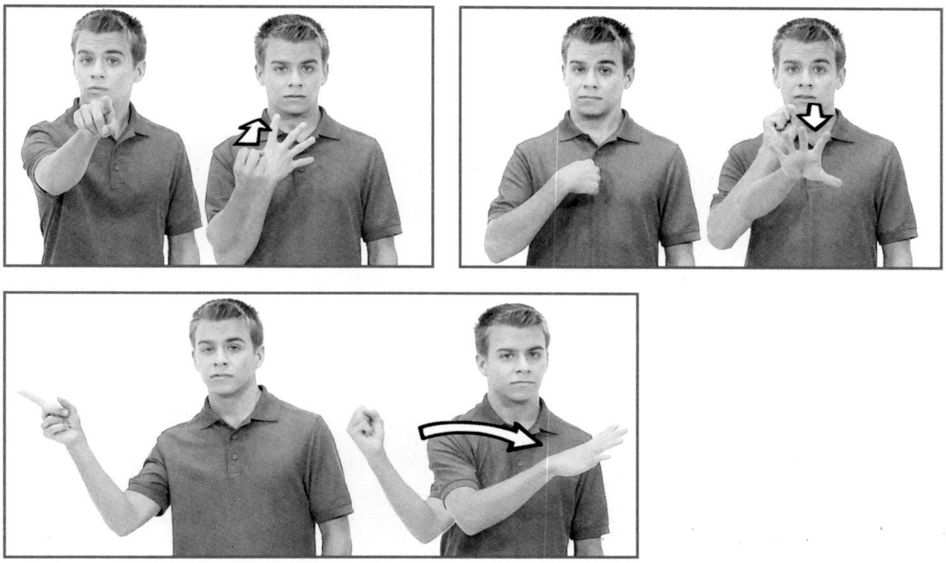

3. to send or mail something

4. to give news, announcements, or warnings

5. to give money for services rendered; to pay

Homework 8:4

CONVERSATION 2

Derrick (A), Melvin (B) and Terrylene (C) demonstrate these dialogues in which Melvin and Terrylene agree to Derrick's request with conditions.

Signer A: explain situation, ask what he should do
Signer B: make suggestion
A: reply, make request
B: agree with condition (what must happen first)
A: reply
B: respond

(Signer A goes to see Signer C)
A: explain situation, make request
C: agree with condition
(what is expected in return)
A: agree

New Signs

to park (a vehicle)

a place designated for parking

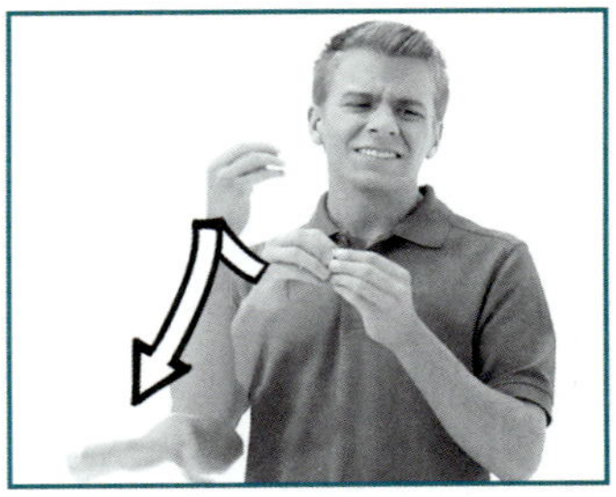

too costly or expensive

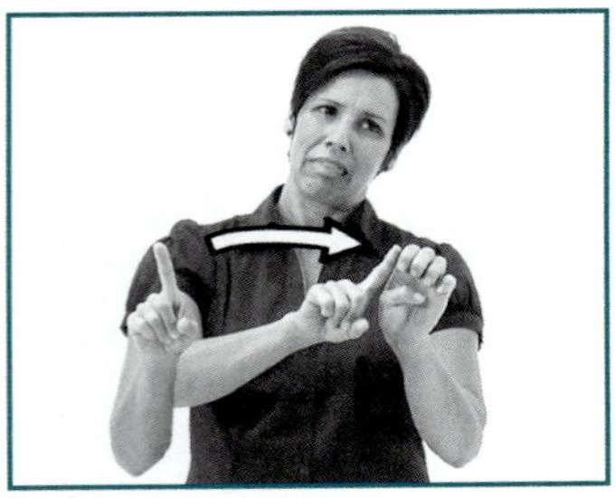

fuel gauge needle on empty

Key Grammar

AGREEING WITH CONDITION

There are two ways to agree with a condition to a request:

- **by telling what must happen first**
  1. express willingness (nod)
  2. give condition (raise head and brows, shift to side)
  3. tell what you will do (when clause, nod)
  4. check if person agrees (raise brows, lean head forward, hold sign)
- **by telling what is expected in return**
  1. express willingness (nod)
  2. give condition (raise head and brows)
  3. tell what is expected
  4. check if person agrees (raise brows, lean head forward, hold sign)

Agree with Condition 1

Observe Melvin stating what must happen first when agreeing to Derrick's request, beginning with this sign.

Agree with Condition 2

Observe Terrylene explaining what is expected in return as a condition to agreeing to Derrick's request, beginning with this sign.

Identify the Situation 1–6

Each signer demonstrates how to agree to a request with a condition. Identify the situation each response refers to, then write the number in the box.

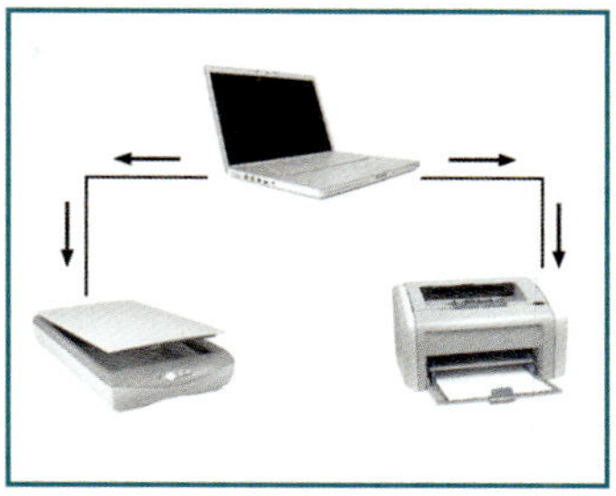

New Signs

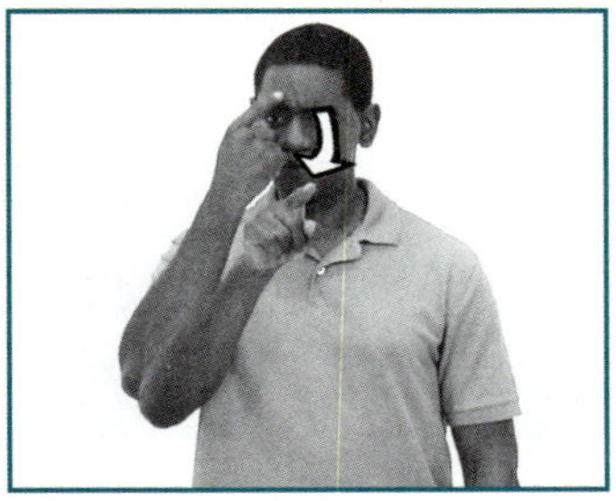

phrase meaning "for you"

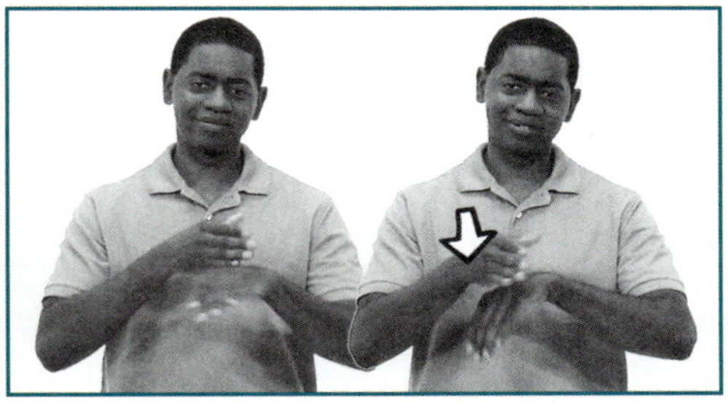

time following (an event); after

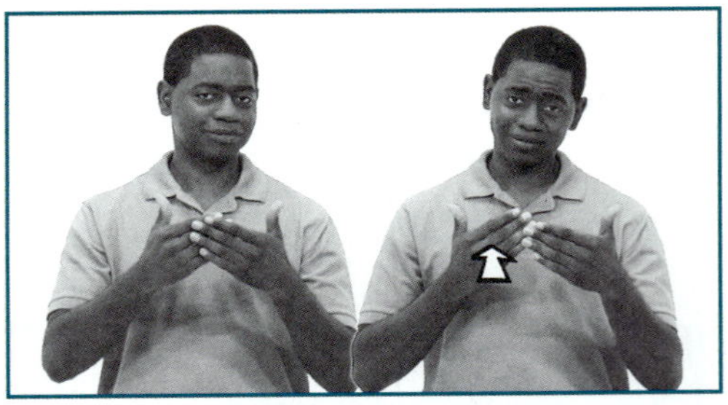

time preceding an event or a time; before

to search; to look for

to fill with gasoline

Answers on page 511.

Assignment

AGREE WITH CONDITION

Requests 1–4

Prepare a response to each request (signed on video) using one of the two ways to agree with a condition. Rehearse your responses for class.

New Signs

portable computer; laptop

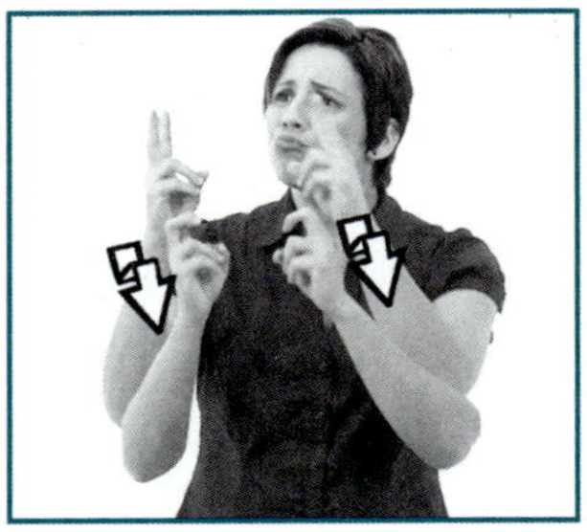

to transfer data; to download

VOCABULARY REVIEW

Review the vocabulary on the video.

Conditions

1. what must happen first

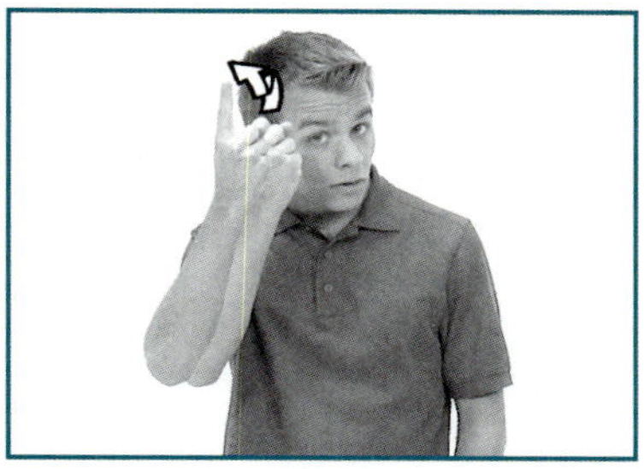

2. provided that; with the stipulation that; with the understanding that

Agreeing

3. "it's fine with me;" "no problem"

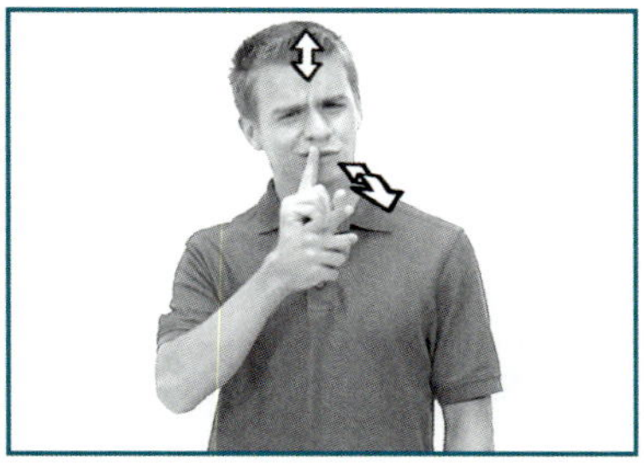

4. "sure thing"

5. "be glad to"

Other Signs

6. to duplicate a document or make a copy; to xerox

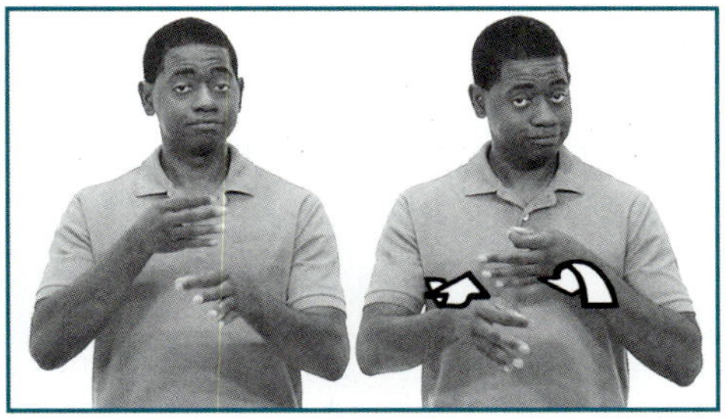

7. in return; in exchange

8. conjunction meaning "but" or "however"

Homework 8:5

NEGATIONS 1

To translate negative English sentences, follow this structure:

- establish time if specified (raise brows)
- establish location if specified (raise brows)
- name the topic (raise brows)
- end with a negation (shake head)

Be aware that there will be exceptions, however this strategy will help you most of the time.

View. Observe JT translating the sentences using the negation signs pictured below the sentences. Notice how he raises his brows with the topic, and shakes his head with the negation sign.

1. I don't have your phone number.

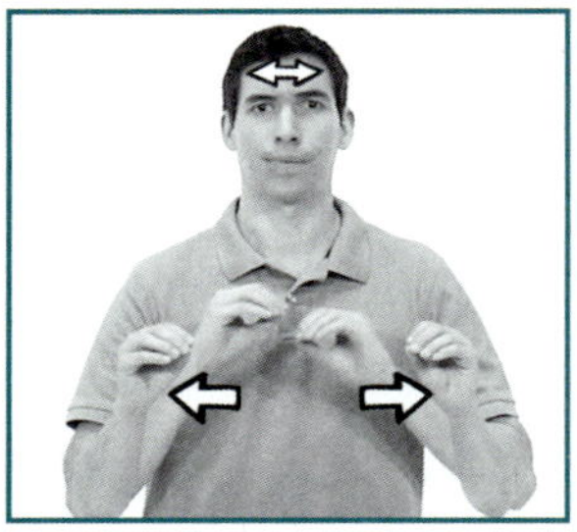

or

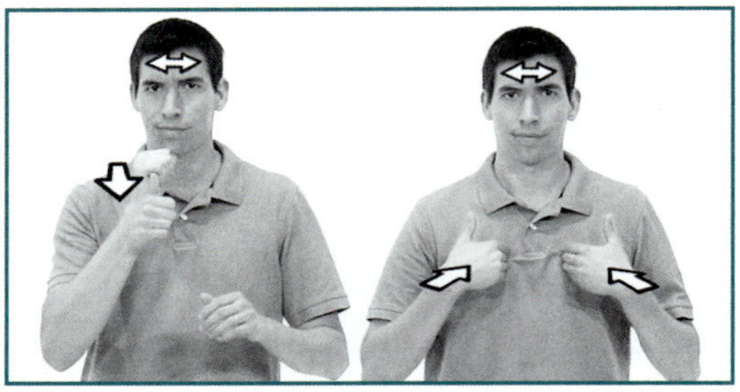

2. My nephew won't eat peas.

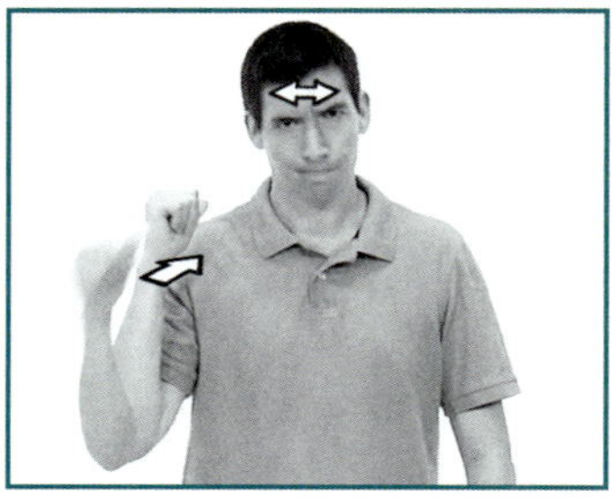

3. There is no class Thursday.

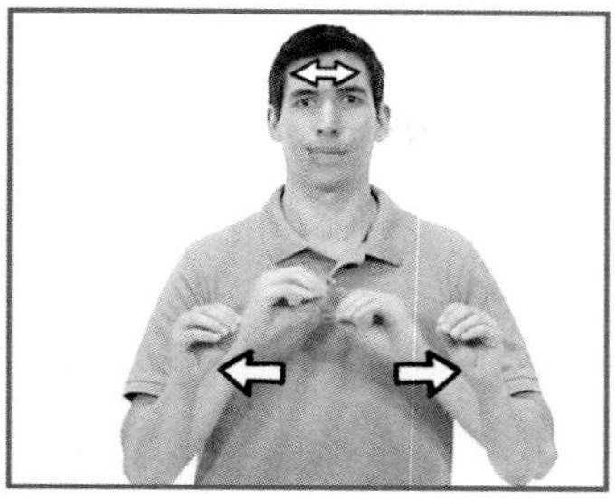

4. Don't chew your nails.

5. You can't smoke in restaurants.

or

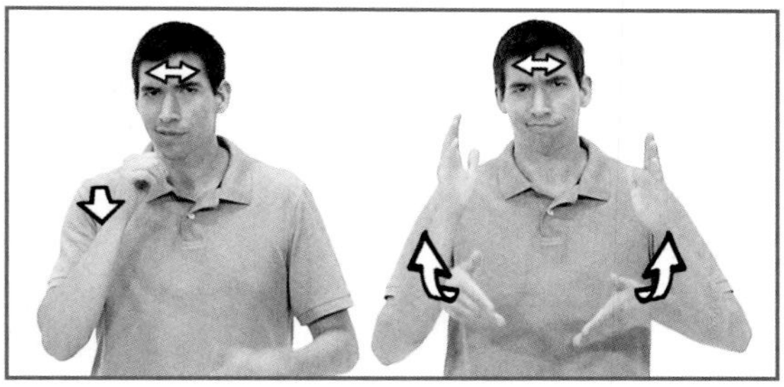

6. I haven't met your mother.

7. Please don't forget to bring your book.

8. I don't want Jack to come.

9. I didn't finish my homework.

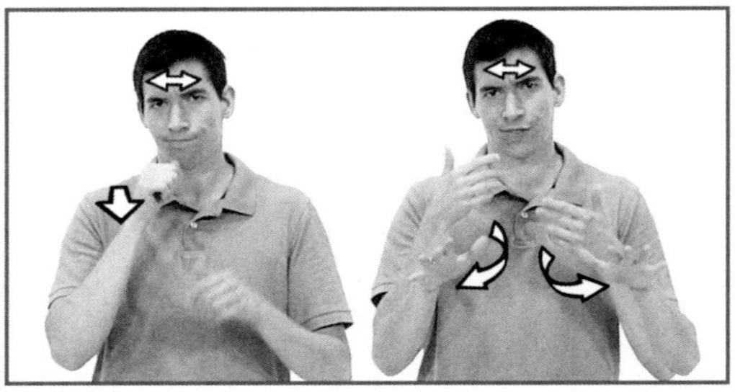

10. These cookies are sugar free.

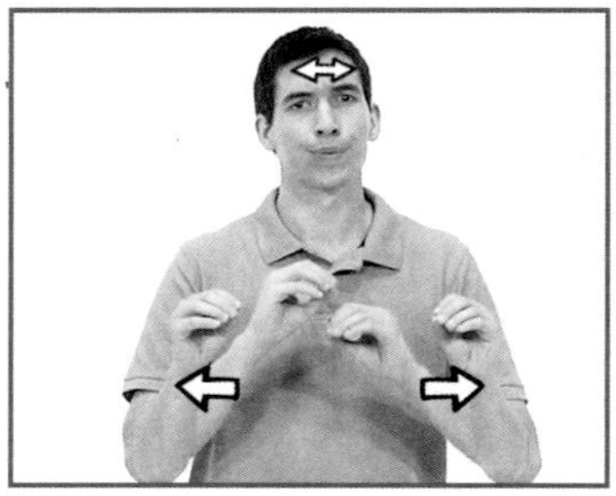

11. You don't have to pay me back.

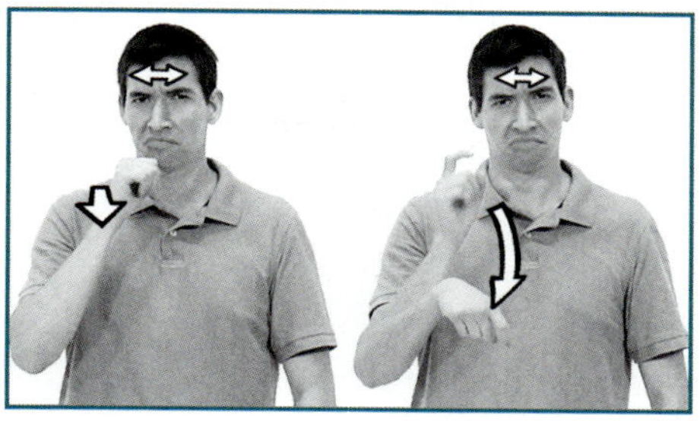

12. You should not read her mail.

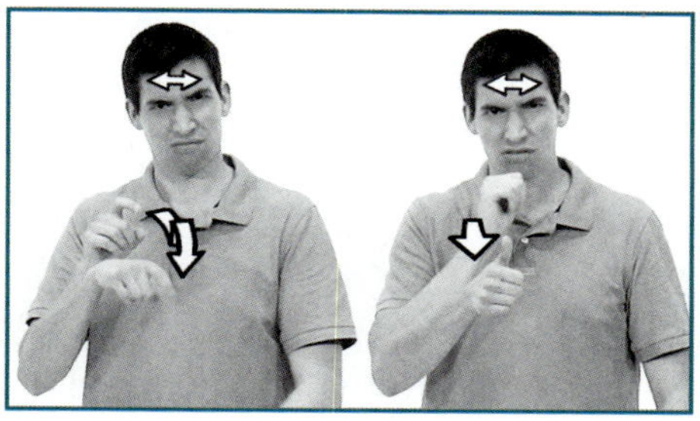

Practice. Now practice the sentences. Be mindful of the phrasing of the signs and the facial expressions. Be prepared to sign them in class.

VOCABULARY REVIEW

Review the vocabulary on the video.

Negation Signs

1. used to express negation, denial or refusal

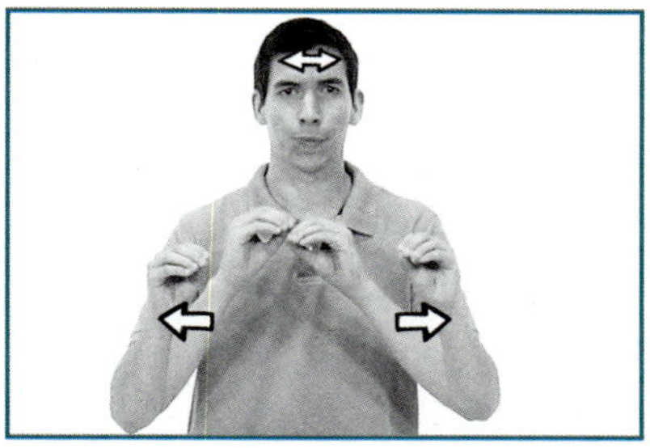

2. not in possession of, doesn't have something, doesn't exist, there is none

3. (gesture) to warn or advise against doing something

4. to refuse; not willing to

5. to prohibit; to forbid; to not allow

6. to not allow or permit

7. not yet (completed or accomplished)

8. to have no desire to; to have no interest in doing something

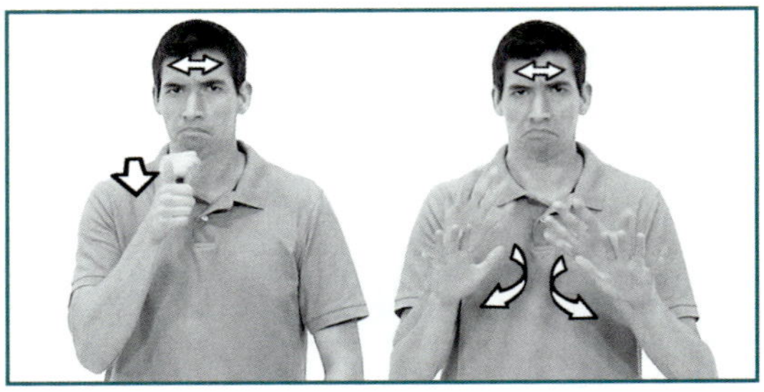

9. not done; incomplete

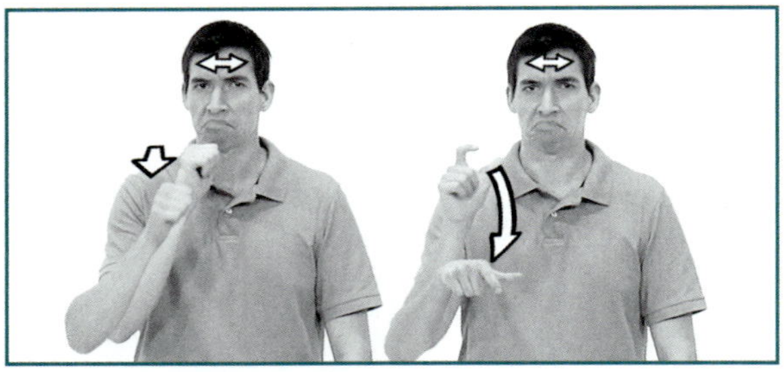

10. don't have to do; no need to; not obligated to

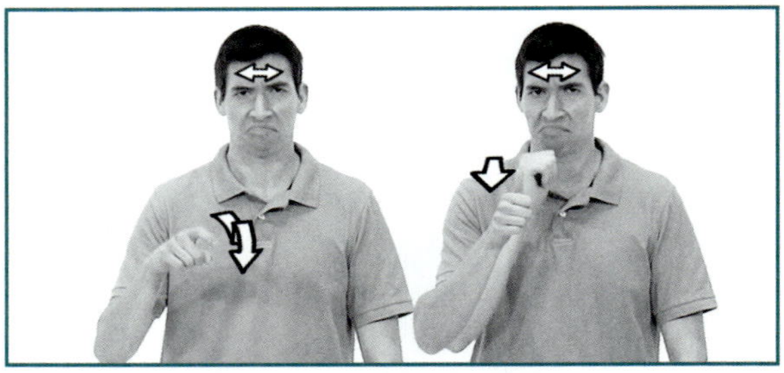

11. should not; inappropriate

Homework 8:6

GIVING PHONE NUMBERS

The number patterns used for giving zip codes, social security numbers, house numbers, and phone numbers are called *identification numbers.* Here we focus on phone numbers.

When giving an identification number the palm faces outward for the numbers 1–5, as opposed to cardinal numbers where the palm faces inward.

Phone Numbers

Iva discusses how to sign the phone number **707-235-3104.**

For area code 707: split the digits into a 1-2 pattern, 7-07.

For the next three digits, 235: the same principle applies. Split the digits into a 1-2 pattern, 2-35. If the first two digits are the same, 223, then either use the 1-2 pattern, 2-23, or treat each digit as a single number, 2-2-3. It is not correct to sign 22-3. This rule for grouping numbers also applies to numbers used to give area codes.

For the final four digits, 3104: split into a 2-2 pattern, 31-04. If the middle digits are the same, 6119, then either use the 2-2 pattern, 61-19, or treat each digit as a single number, 6-1-1-9. The latter is more common. It is not correct to sign 6-11-9.

Now, write the phone number Iva gives for her school.

(   )   - ____________________

Notice how Iva pauses and moves her hand slightly to the right (her dominant side) as she gives each set of numbers.

WRITE THE PHONE NUMBER

Different signers will sign a phone number. Write the number.

1. ______________________ (For the White House switchboard)
2. ______________________ (For the New York U.S. Senator's office)
3. ______________________ (For the National Association of the Deaf office)
4. ______________________ (For the DawnSignPress, Inc.'s office)

Replay the segment and observe how each signer pauses and moves their hand slightly to their right as they give each set of numbers.

Answers on page 511.

Useful Numbers

Different signers will explain what each three-digit number refers to. Fill in the blanks below.

411 ____

____

New Signs

to ask what something is for

sign that begins a hypothetical situation

abbreviation for "company" (commercial business)

511 ____

____

New Signs

something that needs a solution; problem

restoration of a place; renovation

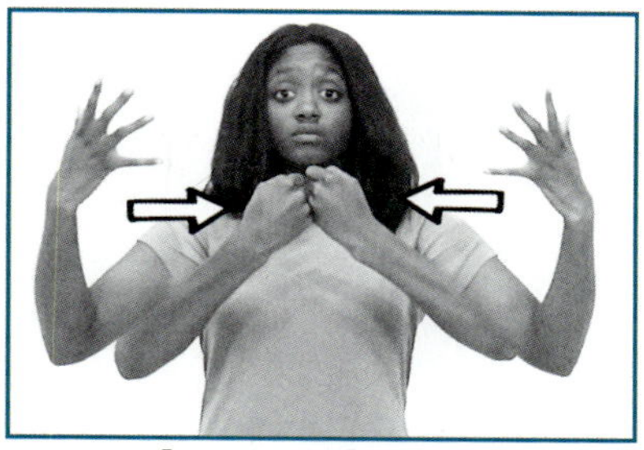

an incident in which damage occurs to vehicles; an accident

611 ____

____

New Signs

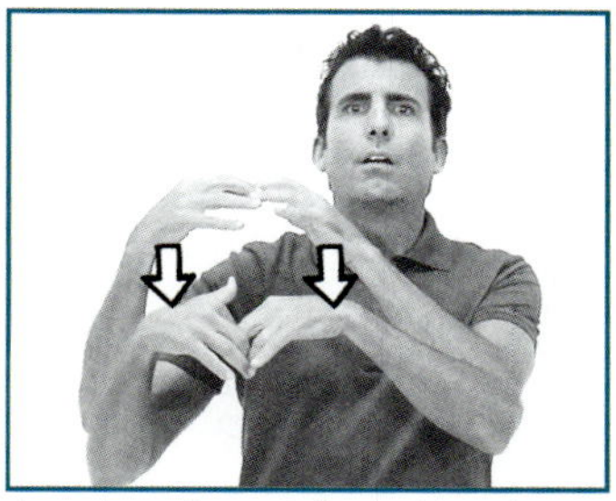

(system) not functioning

911 ____

____

New Signs

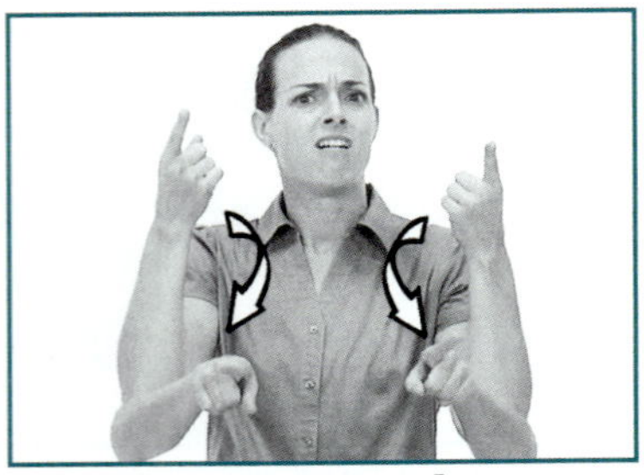

something occurred, something happened

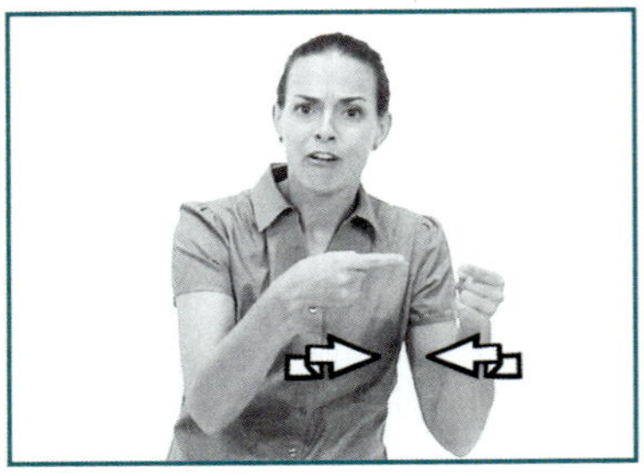

to be in pain; to be hurting

to pass away; to die

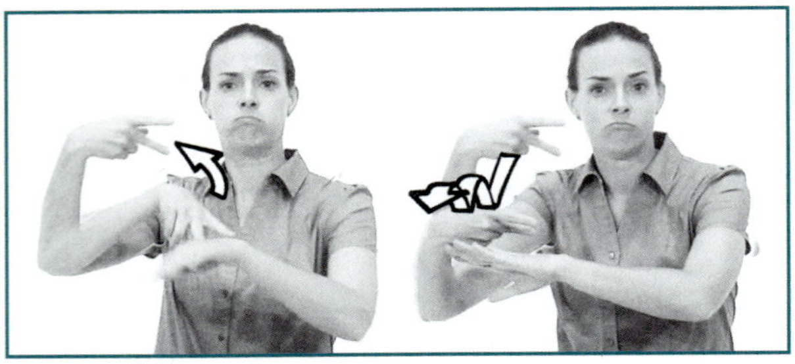

person falling down

to have difficulty breathing

to move or act with haste; to hurry

Answers on page 511.

Practice. Review the vocabulary and explanation for each number listed above. Practice until you can explain the purpose of each number for next class.

INSIGHT

Deaf people often experience discrimination when applying for a job or training especially when others perceive being able to hear essential to the job. In this case, Jessica, who is Deaf, applied to the nursing program and received this feedback from the program director:

"To pass the skills test to be certified as a Nurse's Aide, you are asked to take a person's blood pressure, and that means listening through a stethoscope. I'm afraid people's lives could be put at risk because you are Deaf. Therefore we are denying your request to enter the Associate Degree Nursing program."

Luckily, Jessica was persistent and eventually was admitted into the nursing program. Jessica was able to demonstrate that she could get consistently accurate blood pressure readings by palpating the patient. She completed the program, received her certificate and graduated highest in her class.

What to take away? What Jessica experienced is not uncommon among Deaf people. The public's opinions are informed by what they hear in school, from friends and in the media. The message, somehow, always focuses on what Deaf people don't have (hearing) rather than what they do have (intelligence, skills and experience in adapting situations to their needs). As you learn more about Deaf people and understand they are your peers, your actions and attitudes will help contribute to changing society's perception of Deaf people.

Homework 8:7

CONVERSATION 3

Tonique (A) and Iva (B) demonstrate this dialogue in which Tonique explains she forgot to give the house key to her guest before she left for school.

Signer A: explain problem, ask for advice
- **tell when**
- **explain situation**
- **tell what you forgot to do (use conjunction)**
- **ask for advice**

Signer B: give advice

A: respond

New Signs

asking what is the matter

be prevented from

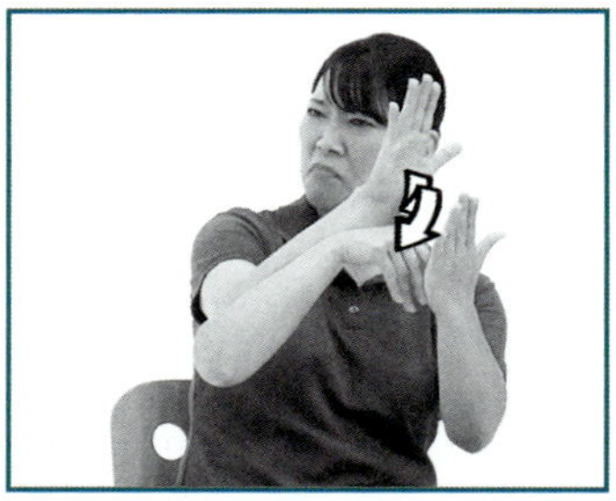
to apply paint to a surface

Key Grammar

CONJUNCTION—WHAT YOU FORGOT TO DO

Use this sign to tell when you realized you forgot something. To use the conjunction first tell what you were doing, like walking, driving, watching T.V., then use the conjunction to transition into telling what you forgot to do.

View. See how Tonique first tells what she was doing at the time (on her way to school) then uses the conjunction to tell what she forgot (her car key).

ASKING FOR OR GIVING ADVICE

Use these signs:

ask for advice

give advice

Helpful Tip

For "explain situation," most students tend not to give enough of an explanation, so in order to receive helpful advice, you must ensure the listener has a good understanding of the problem. This requires you to describe the situation thoroughly.

MINIDIALOGUES

Watch the three video minidialogues and fill in the information below.

Minidialogue 1

1. situation:

2. what was forgotten:

3. advice given:

New Signs

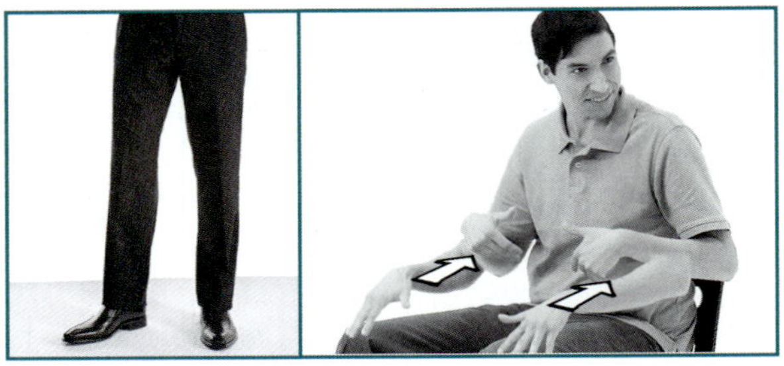

to turn under the edge of pants or dress by hemming

Minidialogue 2

1. situation:

2. what was forgotten:

3. advice given:

New Signs

to enter (facial expression signifies entering without permission or lacking respect for one's property)

to take something that is not yours; to steal

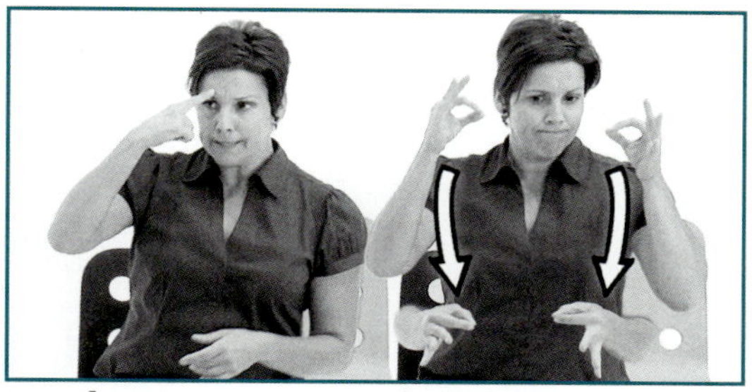

to select as a course of action; to decide

to install; to put in

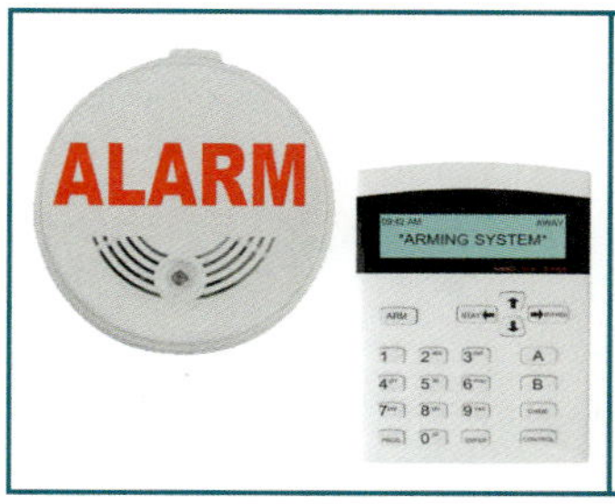

to set up (alarm)

occasionally; sometimes

Minidialogue 3

1. situation:

2. what was forgotten:

3. advice given:

New Signs

to video or film oneself

to move or transfer contents to the USB in the person's hand

Answers given in class.

VOCABULARY REVIEW

Review the vocabulary on the video.

Conjunction

1. the idea or thought came to me

Suggestion Phrase

or

2. "Why don't you…"

Respond to Suggestion

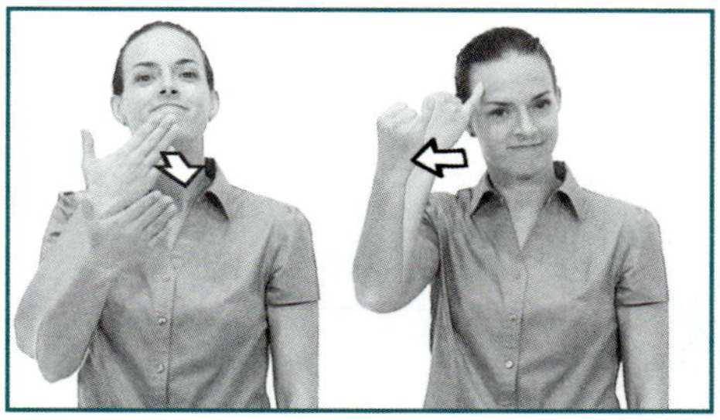

3. "Good idea"

Verbs

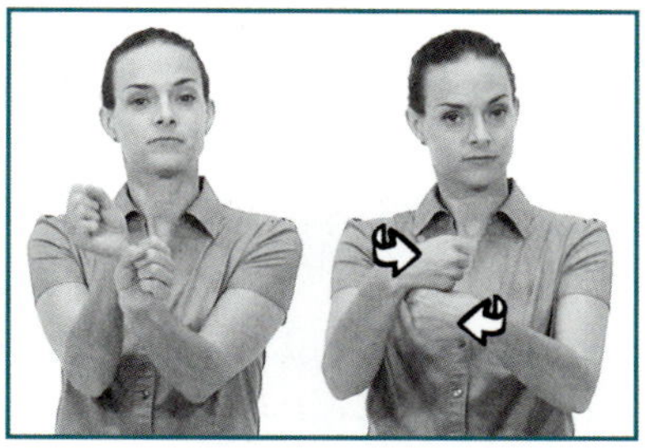

4. to make; to produce; to create

5. to lock (a door)

Nouns

6.

7. someone living next to you; neighbor

Homework 8:8

ASKING FOR A SIGN

When you do not know or have forgotten a sign, use one of these strategies to ask for the sign.

1. list things in the category
2. use opposites
3. describe or act out
4. give definition

Often when ASL students want to know the sign for something, they will fingerspell the word. This is not the best strategy. "Why?" you may ask. When you fingerspell a word to ask for the sign, what you get may not be correct for what you had in mind.

For example, suppose you want to sign "your nose is *running*" but you don't know the sign for "running" and you fingerspelled the word, the signer most likely will assume you mean "a person running" and give you this sign:

Then if you used that sign to say "your nose is running," it would literally mean "your nose is running down a road." Wouldn't that be a sight to see! However, had you used one of the strategies above, which requires you to give more context, you would get this more accurate sign for "a runny nose":

Using context plays an important role in getting the right sign. So becoming adept in using these strategies will go a long way toward getting the sign you're looking for.

FIGURE THE MEANING

On video, the signers will use one of the strategies listed on the previous page to ask for a sign. Write the concept you think the signer is trying to get across and identify the strategy used.

	concept	*strategy*
1.		
2.		
3.		
4.		
5.		
6.		
7.		
8.		
9.		
10.		

Answers discussed in class.

Practice. Watch the video again and practice the strategies the signer uses to describe the concepts. Be prepared to use these strategies in class to get the sign for the concepts from your teacher.

SIGNING NATURALLY

Homework 8:9

AGREEMENT VERBS 2

Remember that with agreement verbs the direction in which the verb moves indicates the subject and the object of the sentence. The verb usually begins in the location of the subject and moves in the direction of the object.

View. For each verb sign below, three different movements are shown, each one indicating a different subject and object. The first movement shows the verb action

- "from me to you"
- "from you to me,"
- "from someone to another."

Here is the list of verbs to practice.

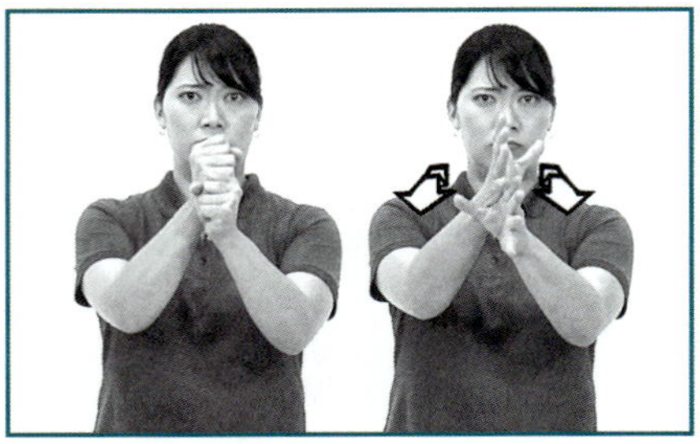

1. to reprimand; to bawl out

2. to irritate (someone); to bother

3. to tease (someone)

4. to borrow from (someone)*

5. to ignore (someone)

* For this verb, the movement begins in location of the object instead of the subject to indicate "from" instead of "to."

NARRATIVES

View the narrative, then write a translation of the narrative.

Narrative 1 ______________________________

____

____

Narrative 2 ______________________________

____

____

Narrative 3 ______________________________

____

____

Narrative 4 ______________________________

____

____

Narrative 5 ______________________________

____

____

Answers on page 512.

Assignment

CREATE NARRATIVES

Create two narratives that involve you and two other people. Use at least two agreement verbs from the previous page in each narrative. Be prepared to sign your narratives in class.

VOCABULARY REVIEW

Review the vocabulary on the video.

For each definition below, three different movements are shown, each one indicating these subject-object relationships:

- "from me to you"
- "from you to me,"
- "from someone to another."

Agreement Verbs

1. to bawl out or reprimand (someone)

2. to irritate or bother (someone)

3. to tease (someone)

4. to borrow from (someone)

5. to ignore (someone)

Others

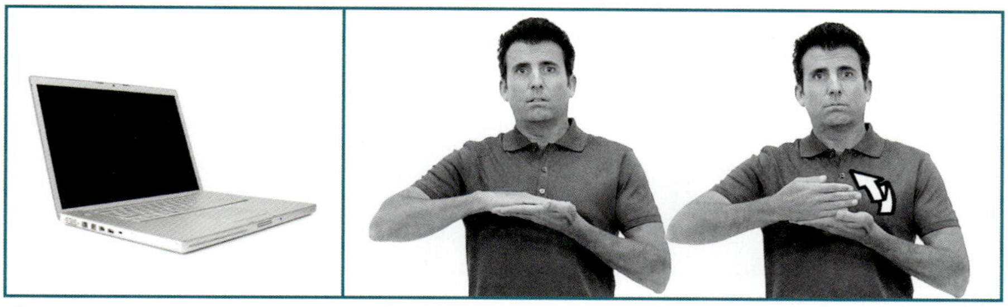

6.

Homework 8:10

CONVERSATION 4

View. Iva (A) and Tonique (B) demonstrate this dialogue in which Iva asks for Tonique's advice about a boy not telling his mother he broke a window.

Signer A: explain problem, ask for advice
- tell when
- explain situation
- tell what unexpectedly happened (use conjunction)
- ask for advice

Signer B: give advice

A: respond

New Signs

time sign indicating "some time in the future"; after awhile; later

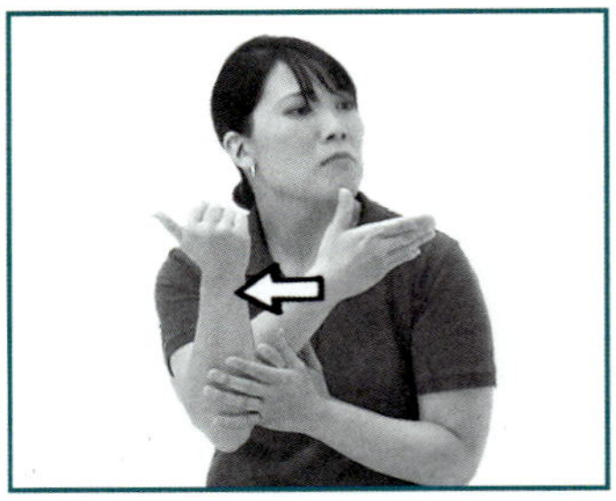

more appropriate; better

Key Grammar

CONJUNCTION—WHAT UNEXPECTEDLY HAPPENED

This sign is used as a conjunction to signal something unexpected happened. To use the conjunction first tell what the person was doing at the time, then use the conjunction to transition into telling what unexpectedly happened.

View. See how Iva first established what the boy was doing (playing) before she used the conjunction to tell what happened next was unexpected (breaking the window).

EXPLAINING SITUATION

In this lesson, you learned to describe three types of situations when asking for advice.

1. incidents involving liquids
2. awkward conversations
3. something one's not supposed to do

Spills

When describing incidents involving liquids, such as spills, follow this sequence:

1. tell what the person or animal was doing
2. [name liquid,] describe movement of liquid (element classifier)
3. tell where, describe how the liquid lands (element classifier)

Element classifiers (ECLs) describe the flow or movement of liquids. Specific handshapes are used to represent the physical aspect of a liquid, and the movement depicts the direction and flow of the liquid. For example:

mustard drips from sandwich landing on pants

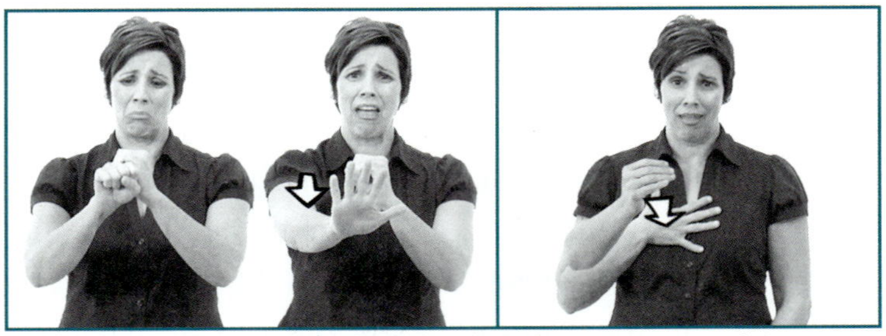

ketchup expels from bottle, landing on my shirt

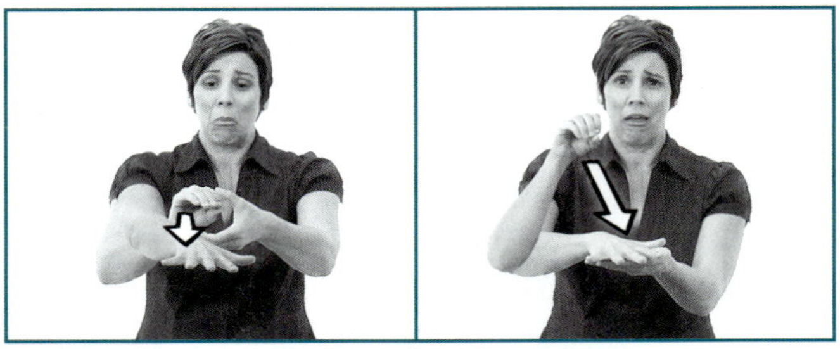

soda spills out of glass, landing on the rug

Be sure to name the liquid (mustard, ketchup, soda) before describing its movement, then tell where (pants, shirt, rug) before describing how it lands.

View. Observe Ursula describing an incident involving a cat and her laptop. Notice Ursula matches the cat's vomit with the location of the laptop. Also, notice how Ursula uses the conjunction to signal what follows is unexpected.

Awkward Conversations

Role shifting is an essential tool to use to describe conversations. To describe incidents involving an awkward conversation, follow this sequence:

1. describe what you and another person were doing at the time
2. role shift the other person asking or saying something uncomfortable or awkward
3. tell how you responded or reacted
4. tell the other person's reaction

View. Observe Amber describing an awkward conversation between her daughter and herself. Notice Amber ends the conversation with her daughter's reaction (step 4 in the sequence above). Also, notice how Amber uses the conjunction to signal what follows is unexpected.

Something One's Not Supposed to Do

Role shifting is also an essential tool to use to describe a person's actions. To describe this type of incident, follow this sequence:

1. describe what went on before the incident
2. role shift to describe something one's not supposed to do

View. Observe Justin describing an incident involving his brother's phone. Justin uses role shifting to show himself playing games on the phone and to show his reaction to the mishap. Notice how Justin uses the conjunction to signal what follows is unexpected.

MINIDIALOGUES

Watch the three video minidialogues and answer the questions below. Observe the signer using the conjunction before stating what unexpectedly happened.

Minidialogue 1

1. situation:

2. what happened:

3. advice given:

New Signs

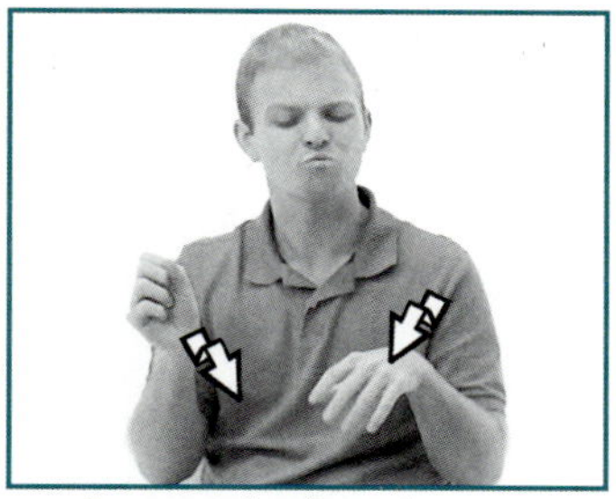

to throw clothes (in a washing machine)

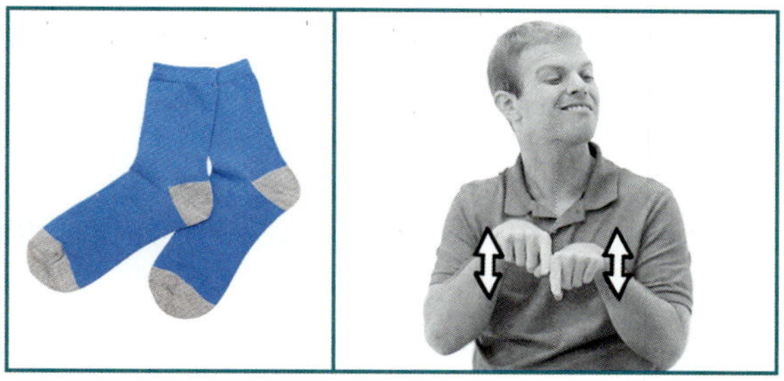

to dissolve, to fade

to lessen, to reduce

Minidialogue 2

1. situation:

2. what happened:

3. advice given:

New Signs

phrase meaning to "feel bad"

Minidialogue 3

1. situation:

2. what happened:

3. advice given:

Answers given in class.

Assignment

Develop three "ask for advice" situations:

- one describing a spill
- one describing an awkward conversation
- one describing a person doing something she or he was not supposed to do.

For each situation, be sure to explain the problem and ask for advice using this sequence:

- tell when
- explain the situation
- tell what unexpectedly happened (use conjunction)
- ask for advice.

Review the **Key Grammar** (pages 127–129) to help you develop the situations. Finally, rehearse your situations until you can sign them without hesitation.

VOCABULARY REVIEW

Review the vocabulary on the video.

Conjunction

1. conjunction meaning unexpectedly; suddenly

Time-Related

2. time sign indicating "recently" or "just now"

Food-Related

3.

4.

5.

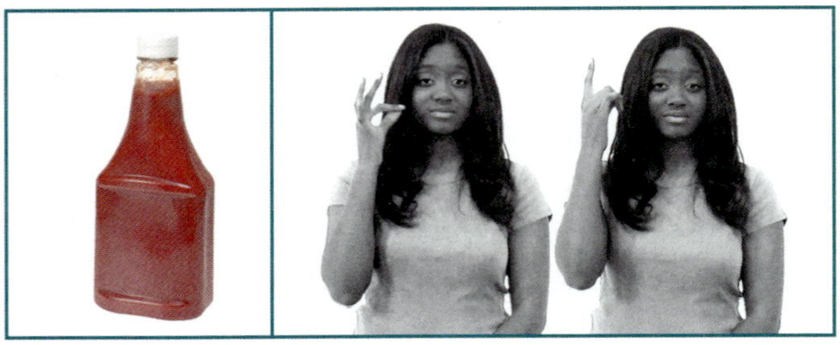

6.

Fingerspell
MUSTARD

7.

8.

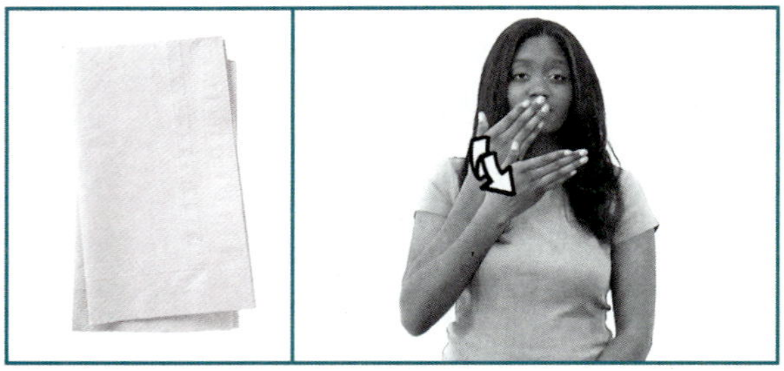

9.

10.

11.

12.

Verbs

13. to break (something)

14. to throw up; to vomit

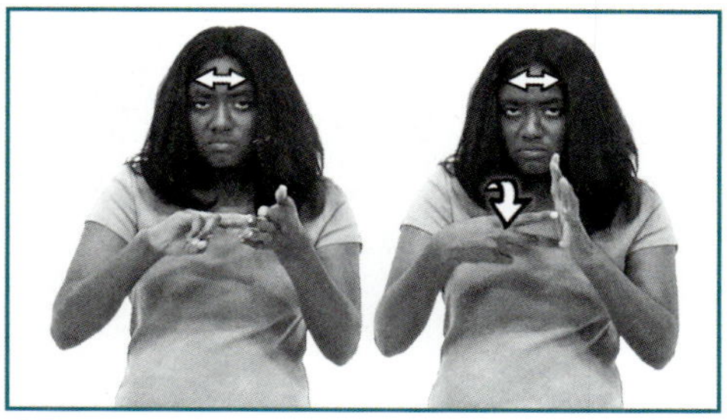

15. to ask what something means

Nouns

or

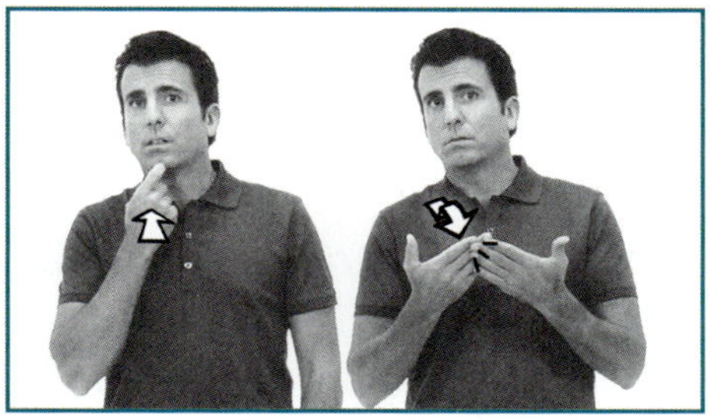

16. material made of glass

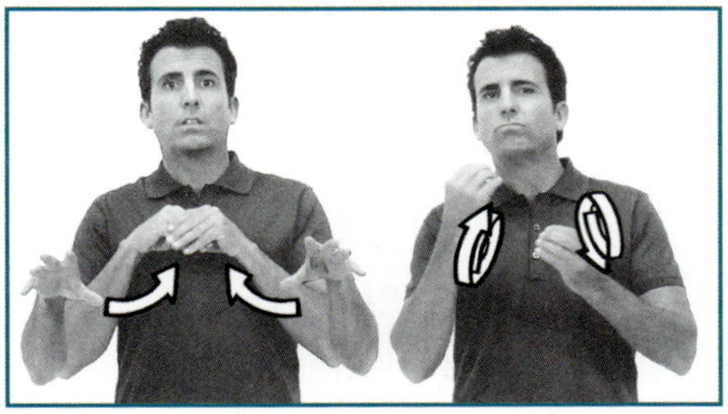

17. wedding reception

18. calendar; timetable; schedule

Other Signs

19. to indicate you are quoting an expression

20. something that is cracked and damaged

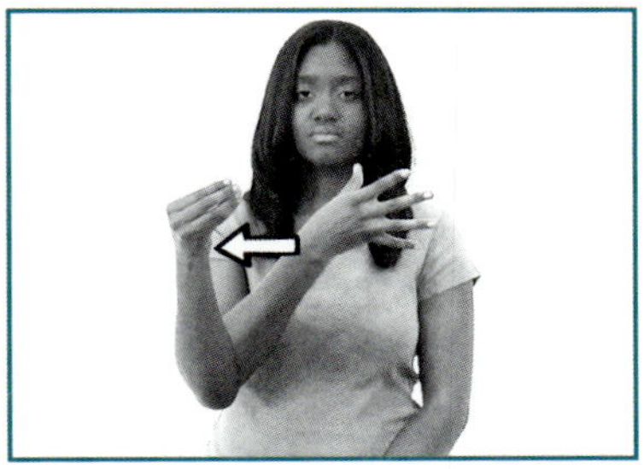

21. conjunction meaning "and"

Homework 8:11

NEGATIONS 2

To translate sentences with tag questions, follow this structure.

- establish location, if specified (raise brows and head)
- name the topic (raise brows and head)
- end with a negation sign (shake head and furrow brows)
- add a tag question (raise brows and lean head forward)

Be sure to integrate facial grammar with each part of the sentence.

Negations 1–12

Observe JT integrating facial grammar with each part of the translated sentences.

1. I have no money. Do you?
2. I don't eat meat. Do you?
3. I didn't bring my USB. Did you?
4. I don't want to see the movie. Do you?
5. I don't know how to make coffee. Do you ?
6. My parents don't allow smoking in the house. Is it the same with your parents?
7. I have not been to Hawaii yet. Have you?
8. The teacher told me I don't have to take the test again. Do you have to?
9. I have not received last semester grades. Have you?
10. No one informed me that class was canceled. Were you informed?
11. My name is not on the list. Is yours?
12. The sign says "No eating or drinking." Did you know that?

Practice. Now practice the sentences. Be mindful of the phrasing of the signs and the facial expressions. Be prepared to sign the sentences in class.

VOCABULARY REVIEW

Review the vocabulary on the video.

1.

2.

3.

4. have been to (a place)

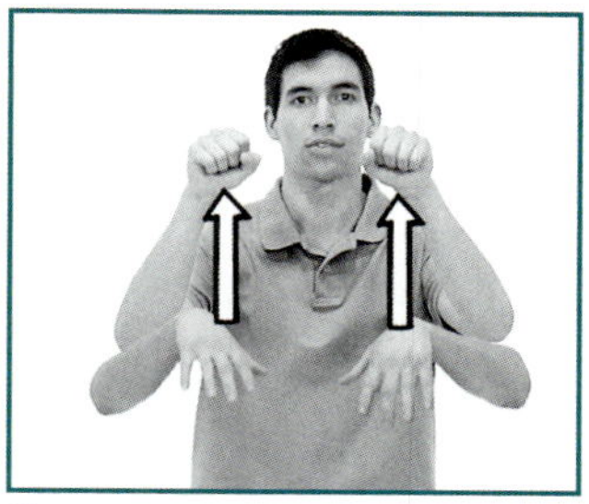

5. to undertake (something), e.g. a test

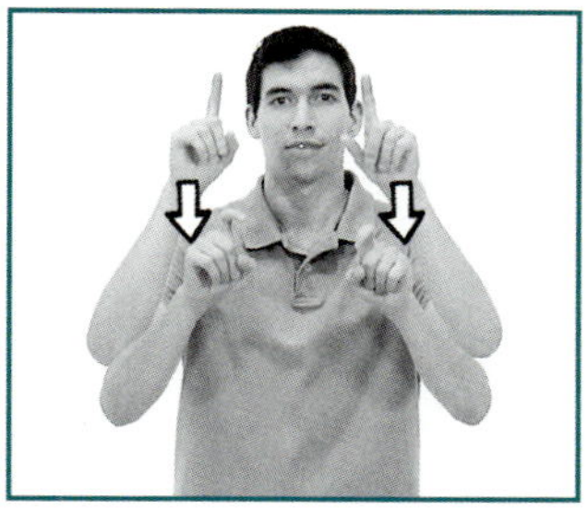

6. test, exam

7. 15–18 weeks in an academic year; a semester

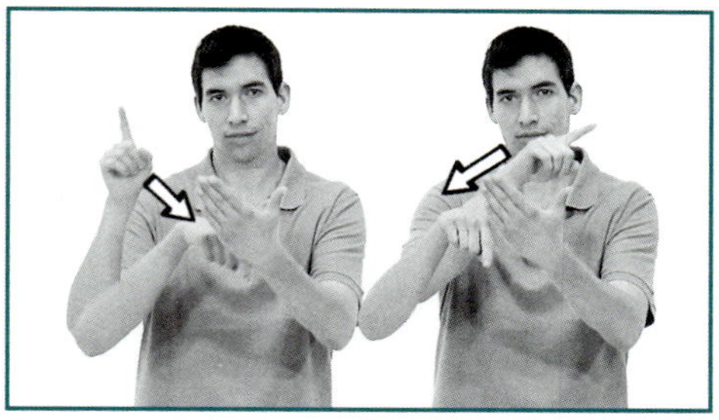

8. to decide an event will not take place: to cancel

9. someone; something

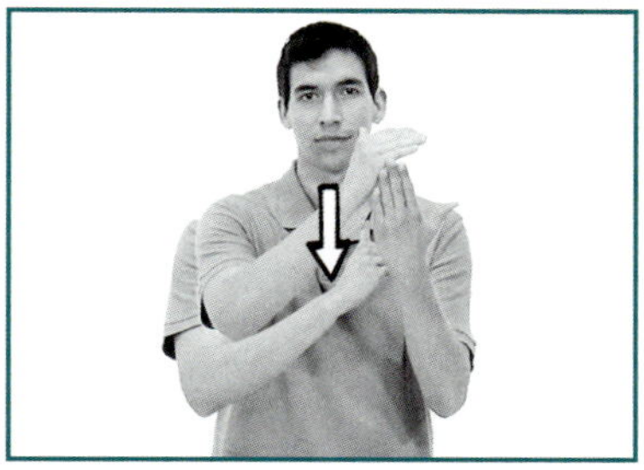

10. a number of names or items written consecutively; a list

11. phrase used to ask "did you know that...?"

Homework 8:12

STORY: THE MOTEL STORY

View. Watch **The Motel Story**, then write a summary of the story and tell why it is funny.

Answer discussed in class.

Practice. Learn the story well enough to re-tell it in class.

NEW VOCABULARY

Use these definitions to help your understanding of the story.

1. vacation

2. going on a trip; traveling

3. the whole day; all day

4. getting dark

5. to stop at; to pause

6. to make a request

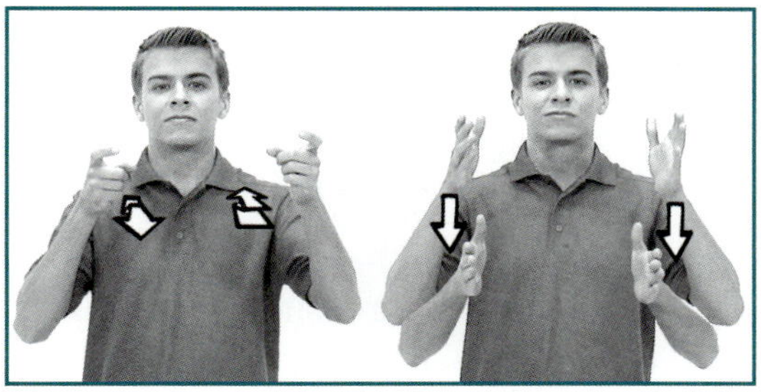

7. one who manages or operates a business; manager

8. the last one

9. room

10. to feel relieved

11. use a car horn to honk

DEAF PROFILE

NATHIE MARBURY (1944-2013)

"I love teaching... it's my first love..."

Nathie Marbury was a well-known storyteller and poet, beloved educator, and an inspirational role model for the Black Deaf community.

Nathie was born in Grenada, Mississippi in 1944 and grew up in Pennsylvania where she graduated from the Western Pennsylvania School for the Deaf (WPSD) in 1962. She asserted that WPSD saved her life by caring for her and providing her with a good education. As a result, she was the only member of her family to attend college. She earned her Bachelor's degree in Home Economics from Gallaudet University in 1975. In the following year she received two Master's degrees from California State University at Northridge (CSUN), one in Special Education and one in Administration and Supervision. She was the first Black Deaf woman to complete a Doctorate in Deaf Studies/Deaf Education at Lamar University in 2007.

There were several more firsts for Nathie as a Black Deaf woman, notably the first Black Deaf person entering the National Leadership Training Program for the Deaf at CSUN, becoming the first Black Deaf teacher at Kendall Demonstration Elementary School for the Deaf, and being the first Black Deaf woman to serve on the National Association of the Deaf (NAD) board as a Member-at-Large.

Nathie's African-American heritage became increasingly important to her later in life. In her dissertation, she described a pivotal moment in her mid 40's. A Black ASL student told her he wanted to practice his new language skills and wanted to know where could he find the Deaf Black community. Nathie wrote "I was flabbergasted at this question because back then I never considered that there might be two communities." After this encounter, the student became Nathie's personal Black Studies/Culture mentor. The relationship was an extraordinarily long and unwavering friendship. So inspired by what she learned and her journey, she helped form the organization Deaf Ujima, whose goal was to have Black Deaf students learn about, honor and celebrate their Black culture as well as their Deaf culture.

In her 35-year career of teaching, whether with children or adults, Deaf or hearing, one thing remained constant—her passion for teaching. In a video interview, she remarked "I love teaching...it's my first love," before flashing one of her famous brilliant smiles. The last 14 years of her career, she taught at Austin Community College (ACC) in Austin, Texas. Toward the end of her life, she donated her entire collection of books and videos to The Nathie Marbury ASL/ Deaf Studies Collection housed in ACC's library. On March 2, 2013, colleagues, friends and students gathered for a dedication ceremony, to praise and thank Nathie for her invaluable contributions to the field of ASL teaching. The ceremony ended with the announcement of the creation of the annual Dr. Nathie L. Marbury Masters in Sign Language Education Academic Achievement Award to be given to an outstanding Gallaudet University graduate student. This plaque is written in both ASL and English.

In August of 2013, Nathie posthumously received the Lifetime Achievement Award from the National Black Deaf Advocates (NBDA). In their announcement of the award, the organization recognized, "her distinguished career and outstanding service to the Black Deaf community, the American Deaf Community, and the Professional Interpreting Community." The announcement further stated, "We celebrate her many accomplishments, and recognize that we have lost a legend."

SIGNING NATURALLY

Homework 8:13

CULTURAL

MINIMIZING INTERRUPTIONS

Keeping each other informed is essential in Deaf culture. In this homework we will discuss how to keep your teacher informed while minimizing the interruption to his or her presentation when you arrive late or must leave the class.

Arriving Late

What do you do if you are late and class has begun? There are several things you need to take into consideration.

- ***The right time to interrupt***
  Wait at the door or just outside the semicircle until an appropriate break in the teacher's presentation before moving forward and getting the teacher's attention.
- ***How to briefly apologize and get permission to take your seat***
  When the teacher notices you, you should briefly apologize and explain your tardiness, using the phrase below. After getting the teacher's permission, you may take your seat.

View. Amber apologizes for being late to class. Notice she moves quickly and as inconspicuously as possible to her seat to show her respect for the teacher and the class.

Leaving During Class

If you need to leave during class, how do you interrupt the teacher without disrupting the class? It is not considered polite to just walk out quietly. Instead you need to consider the following.

- ***The right time to interrupt***
  Wait for an appropriate break in the teacher's presentation before getting up or getting the teacher's attention. If urgent, go ahead get up and as you move toward the door, look at the teacher.
- ***How to apologize and get permission to leave***
  After getting the teacher's attention, briefly excuse yourself and explain why you need to leave, using the sign below. After getting the teacher's permission, you may leave the room.

View. Suzanne minimizes the interruption by waiting for a pause in the teacher's signing before getting up and telling the teacher in one sign why she has to leave class.

NOTE: ***What to do if you are unable to get your teacher's attention?***

In the event you arrive late and are unable to get the teacher's attention, because she or he is either talking with another student or working with a group, you should go ahead and take a seat. Likewise, if you need to leave and cannot get the teachers' attention, you should leave an explanation with a fellow classmate to deliver to the teacher when she or he is free.

Assignment

COMPARING NORMS

Describe the "norm" for handling arriving late and leaving early in spoken English classes and then contrast this with how to conduct oneself in the ASL classroom.

Homework 8:14

CULTURAL

NAME SIGNS

A name sign is used when referring to a person or when pointing out a person. It's not used to address the person directly. Name signs are given in a number of ways. The most obvious is from parent to child. However, since most Deaf children have hearing parents that don't sign, the naming responsibility usually falls to Deaf adults, and sometimes children's peers in the school and community.

There are two types of name signs: *descriptive* and *arbitrary*.

Descriptive Name Signs

In many Deaf communities throughout the world, descriptive name signs are the norm. Such name signs are derived from a physical or behavioral characteristic of a person—such as "dimples," "frizzy hair," "big eyes," or "laughs a lot." Sometimes, descriptive name signs are derived from what the person's written name refers to. For example, a person whose last name is Fish might get a name sign implying "fish."

Examples of descriptive name signs for a person who:

has a dimple

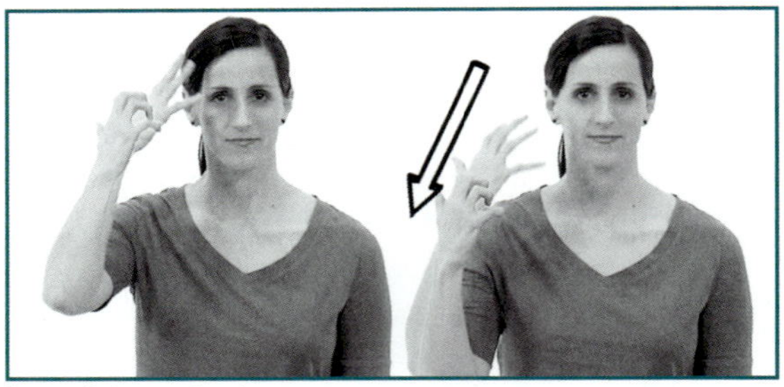
has frizzy hair

has big eyes

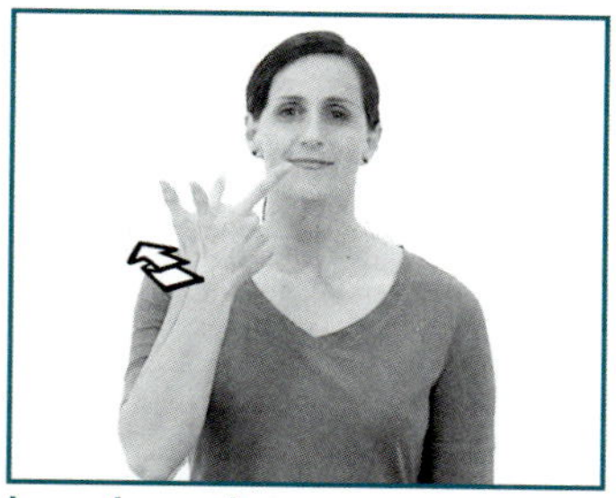
laughs a lot

In the US, descriptive name signs are mostly used among children and young adults to identify others—teachers or houseparents in the school—but are usually shed in adulthood for the more traditional arbitrary name signs.

Arbitrary Name Signs

In American Deaf communities, arbitrary name signs have long been the norm, although there is a growing trend among Deaf parents to give descriptive name signs to their children.

Arbitrary name signs have no intrinsic meaning connected to the person's identity other than the initial(s) of their written name. Sometimes, a family may aim to maintain a similar pattern for the name signs of all members such as different name signs on the same location of the body, or the same handshape in different locations. You may recall this from **Sam's Name Sign** shown in class.

An arbitrary name sign uses the initial of a person's first or sometimes their last name. The handshape of the initial, along with its contact point, location and movement are rule-governed to create possible and acceptable name signs.

Following are some examples of possible name signs for a person whose first or last name's initial is "L." Note the locations, movements and the contact points of the handshape.

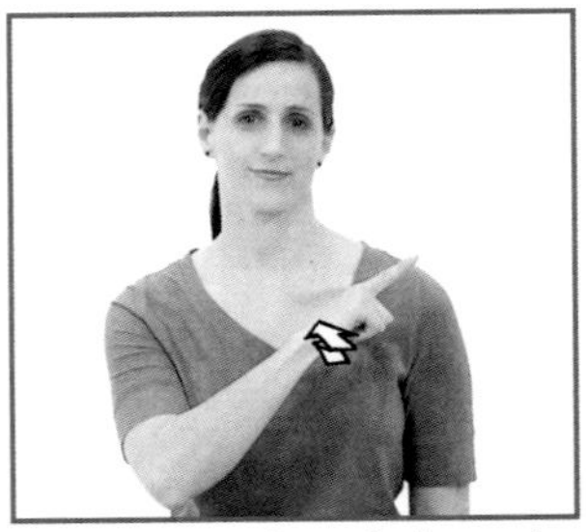

contact: *tip of thumb*
location: *single*
movement: *tap twice*

contact: *palm side of hand*
location: *dual*
movement: *tap once at each location*

contact: *palm side of hand*
location: *single*
movement: *tap twice*

contact: *tip of thumb*
location: *dual*
movement: *tap once at each location*

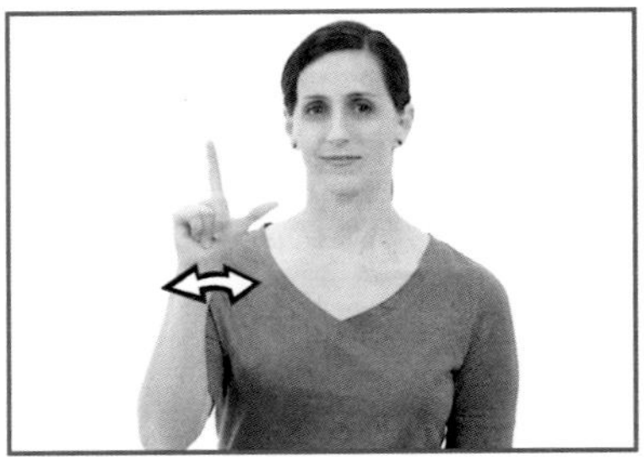

contact: *none*
location: *neutral space*
movement: *shake*

Supalla (1992) suggests that the arbitrary naming system was probably made by the educators of the Deaf in the early nineteenth century, one of whom was Laurent Clerc, a Deaf Frenchman. In that period in France, signs incorporating the initial fingerspelled letter of a corresponding spoken word were used in Deaf schools, and we can surmise this influence transferred to the US schools for the Deaf, where the teachers probably encouraged the use of initialized name signs among the pupils.

Changing Name Signs

A person's name sign may change throughout his or her life if the situation prompts it. In a case where two people in the same community have the same name sign, the name sign of one or both persons is modified to distinguish one from the other, such as adding a second handshape to refer to the last name, or a sign to refer to a difference between the two people, like their heights.

Usually, the name sign is modified for the person who is younger or a newcomer, like a person who has moved from another community, a new hearing employee in the community or an ASL student.

Another example of changing one's name sign is when individuals enter professional careers where it's considered more proper to spell their last names or to use the initial of their last name rather than their first name.

In the next video you will see a story about one man's name sign saga.

Eugene's Changing Name Signs

See David explain how Eugene's name sign (both arbitrary and descriptive) has changed over the years.

1. What name sign did Eugene's parents give him?

2. In grade school his name sign changed. Why and how?

3. At Gallaudet University, how did students refer to each other?

4. At Eugene's first job, what name sign did the children give him? Why?

5. At Eugene's second job, what name sign did the children give him? Why?

6. At Eugene's third job, what name sign did the children give him? Why?

7. What name sign did Eugene end up with and why?

Answers on page 513.

New Signs

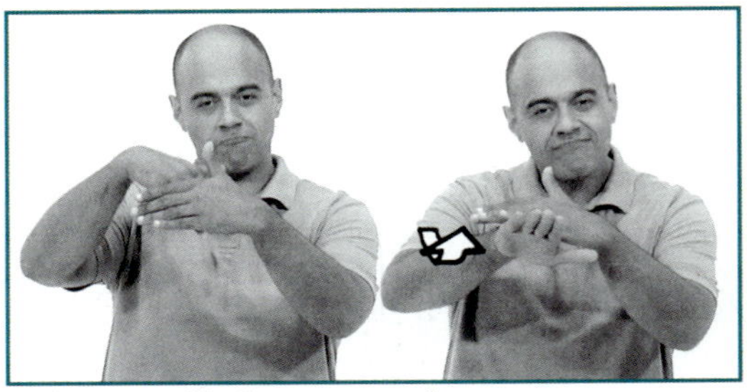

to be enrolled; to attend

residential school for the Deaf

Gallaudet University

usually; have a tendency to

to fingerspell a name or word

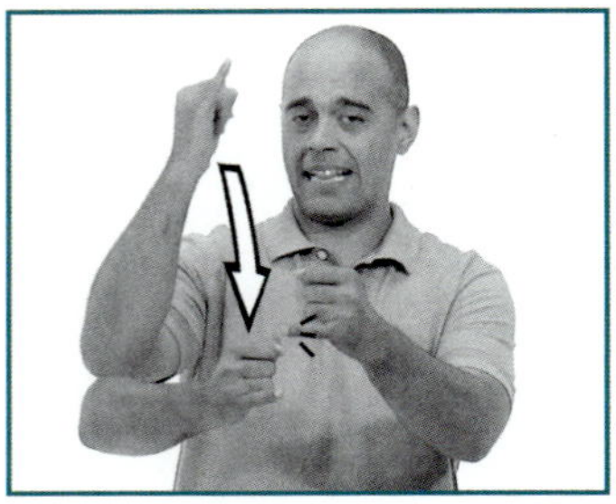

last (as in "last" name)

A SIGN OF CAUTION: Over the years a non-traditional type of name sign has surfaced in the community. These name signs, usually combining the initial from the person's name with some descriptive feature or interest of the person, as shown below.

Kathy who loves playing music

These non-traditional name signs may be the result of increasing number of students taking ASL classes and asking their teachers or Deaf friends to give them a name sign or taking it upon themselves to come up with their own. Name signs are properly given after the person has been involved in the community on an on-going basis, either through work or social relationships, and based on need and familiarity. You will know the time is right when Deaf people give you the name sign without you having to ask for it. It is not appropriate to go ahead and assign yourself a name sign.

Reference: *"The Book of Name Signs: Naming in American Sign Language"* by Samuel D. Supalla.

Assignment

YOUR NAME

For next class, be prepared to tell how you got your name and the different names you go by, if any.

Unit 8 Review: Self-Assessment

Write the number of: classes you missed: _____
homework assignments not completed for class: ____
hours you practiced/used signs outside of the classroom per week: _____

Now that you are done with this unit, rate yourself using the list below: **5** indicates feeling the most comfortable and confident about your skill in that area and **1** indicates feeling the least confident.

NOTE: If you marked **3** or lower, you should review that portion of the workbook and write down steps you plan to take to improve your skills in that area.

1. I know how to thoroughly explain the situation before requesting a favor.	5	4	3	2	1
2. I know how to politely decline a request or agree to it with conditions.	5	4	3	2	1
3. I can ask for advice by explaining a situation, and using the conjunction that tells what I forgot to do.	5	4	3	2	1
4. I can ask for advice by explaining situations involving spills, awkward conversations or something one should not do, and using the conjunction that tells what unexpectedly happened.	5	4	3	2	1
5. I can correctly name the months; use numbers to tell in how many months something will occur; and modify number signs to tell an event occurs repeatedly.	5	4	3	2	1
6. I can modify an agreement verb to show the subject and object of the sentence.	5	4	3	2	1
7. I know the structure to follow when translating negative English sentences.	5	4	3	2	1
8. I know the structure to follow when translating negative English sentences that end with a tag question.	5	4	3	2	1
9. I can give phone numbers using identification number patterns.	5	4	3	2	1
10. I can use all four strategies to ask for a sign.	5	4	3	2	1

11. I know how to minimize interruptions and when to share why I am arriving late or leaving early with the teacher.	5	4	3	2	1
12. I know the differences between arbitrary and descriptive names signs, how they are formed, given and used.	5	4	3	2	1
13. When viewing **The Motel Story**, I'm able to figure out the meaning of what is signed even though I don't know every sign used.	5	4	3	2	1

Steps I will take: ____

____

____

NOTES:

ASL Thrives

Nancy Rourke

oil on canvas
30" x 40"
©2011

UNIT 9

Describing Places

SIGNING NATURALLY

Homework 9:1

DESCRIBING A NEIGHBORHOOD 1

David's Neighborhood

Watch how David uses this narrative outline to discuss his neighborhood.

1. **tell where you live**
   - **kind of residence, what city or district**
   - **for how long and with who**
2. **tell what your neighborhood is like**
   - **type of neighborhood or area**
   - **what is nearby and convenient**
   - **who lives in the neighborhood**
3. **tell what is next to your residence**
4. **tell what you like and don't like about the area**
5. **tell about future plans**

Amber's Neighborhood

Watch Amber discuss her neighborhood then fill in the blanks below.

1. where Amber lives
   - kind of residence, what city or district ______________________
   - for how long and with who ________________________

     ____ .
2. tell what Amber's neighborhood is like
   - type of neighborhood or area __________________________

     ____ .

- what is nearby and convenient ______________________

  ____.

- who lives in her neighborhood ______________________

  ____.

3. tell what is next to her residence ______________________

   ____.

4. tell what she likes and doesn't like about the area ______________

   ____.

5. tell about her future plans ______________________

   ____.

mixture of (types and styles of residences)

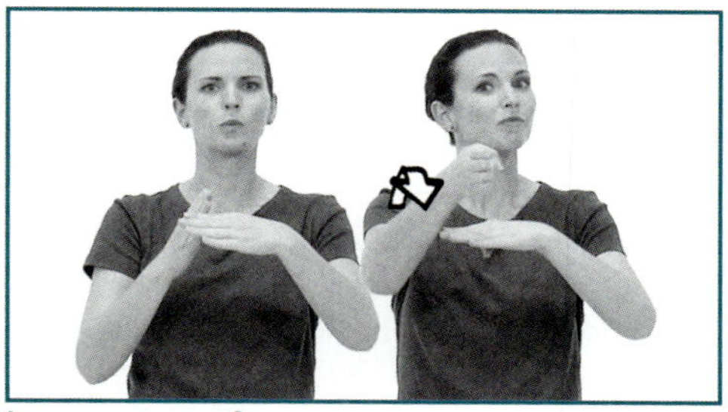

in excess of; over

Answers given in class.

Did You Realize... Everyone Signed on Martha's Vineyard?

For several centuries up until the 1950's, on an island off Cape Cod in Massachusetts called Martha's Vineyard, especially in the towns of Chilmark and West Tisbury, practically every family had Deaf members, so everybody in the town "spoke sign language." Islanders viewed Deaf people not as "handicapped" but "just Deaf" and often remembered their being Deaf as secondary to their occupations or memorable activities. Deaf people owned businesses, held public office, served as church elders—there was no office or position they could not hold or didn't hold at one time or another. Deaf people were an integral part of the community.

Although the signing community on Martha's Vineyard no longer exists, there are other signing communities around the world that have developed naturally and have existed for generations. They have been found in Mexico, Bali, Ghana, and the most recent discovery, in a Bedouin village in Israel.

It is the hope of many here in America, that with more and more people learning ASL and respecting Deaf people as a cultural-linguistic group, creating another "Martha's Vineyard" becomes possible once again.

NOTE: Historical records have shown that the Sign Language used on Martha's Vineyard can be traced to the now extinct Old Kentish Sign Language, which was used in the county of Kent in the southern part of England in the 16th and 17th centuries. It was during this time when many families emigrated to Massachusetts. Jonathan Lambert, himself a Deaf carpenter and farmer, and his hearing wife, settled in Martha's Vineyard and bore two children who were Deaf. This was the first recorded case of hereditary deafness on the island.

VOCABULARY REVIEW

Review the vocabulary on the video.

Areas

1.

2.

3.

4.

5.

6.

Fingerspell
HILLS

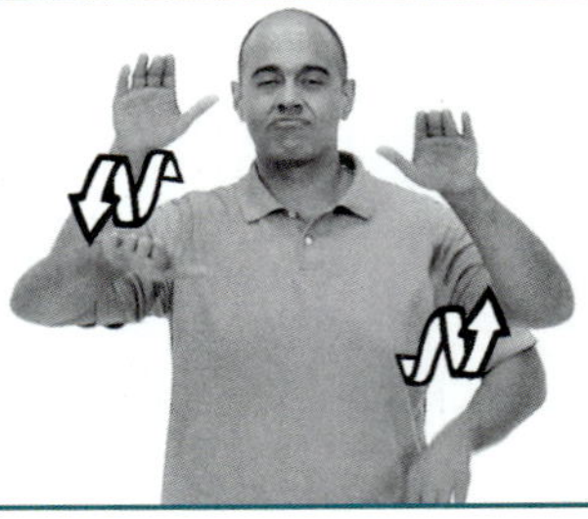

7.

Fingerspell
APT

8.

Fingerspell
LOFT

9.

Fingerspell
CONDO

10.

Neighborhoods *(continued)*

11.

12.

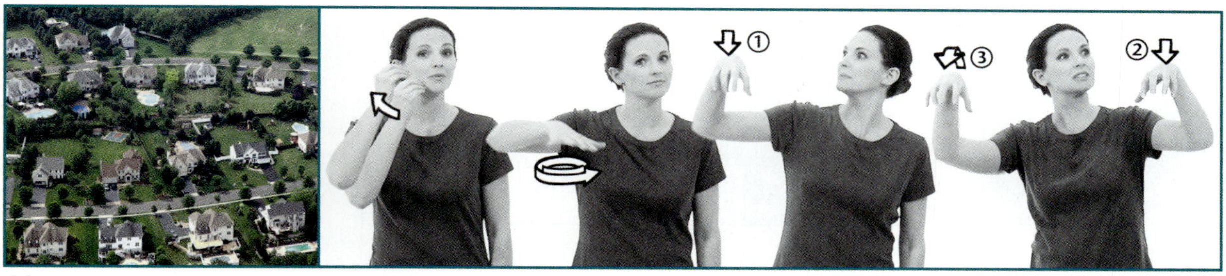

13.

Places Nearby

14. close by; near

or

15.

Fingerspell
POOL

16.

Fingerspell
STUDIO

17.

Fingerspell
TRAIL

18.

Fingerspell
MARKET

19.

Fingerspell
FERRY

20.

People in the Neighborhood

21.

22.

23.

24.

People in the Neighborhood *(continued)*

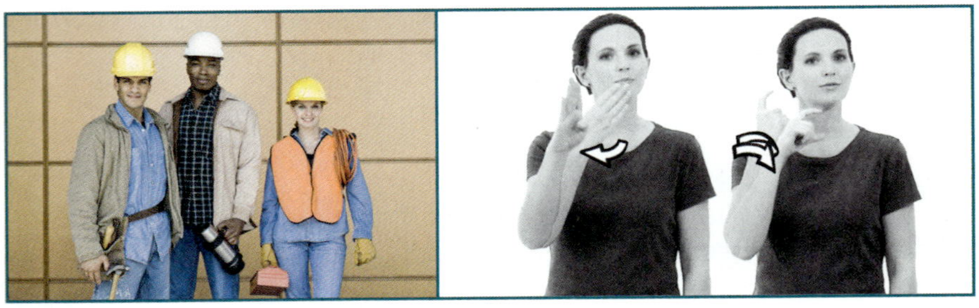

25.

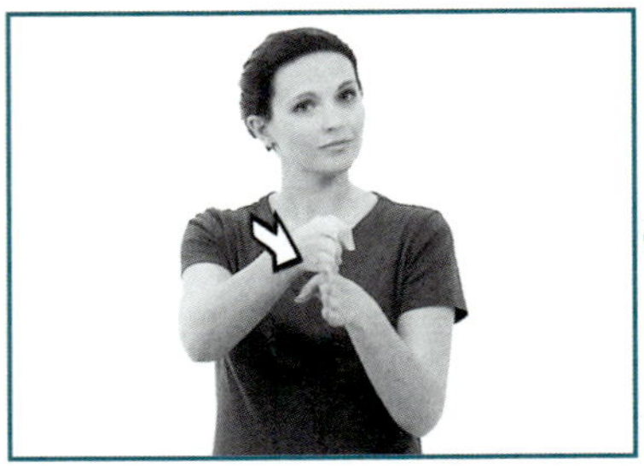

or

26. professional working people

27. retired

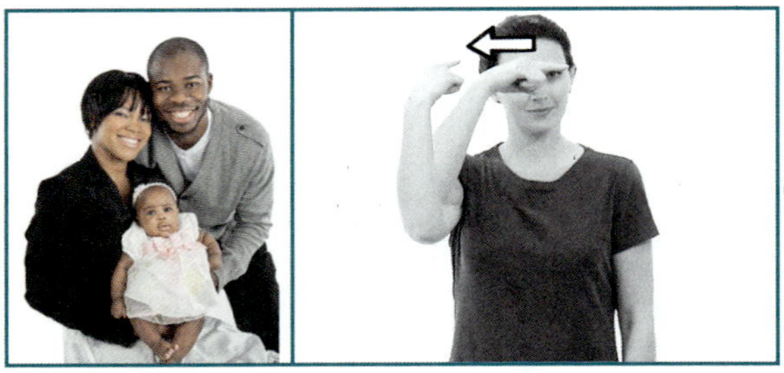

or

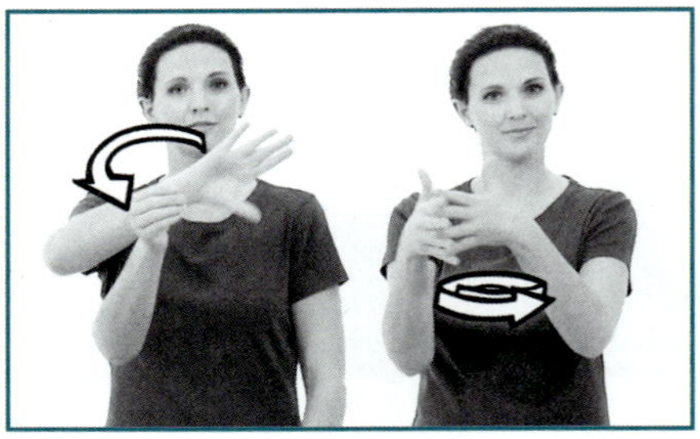

28.

or

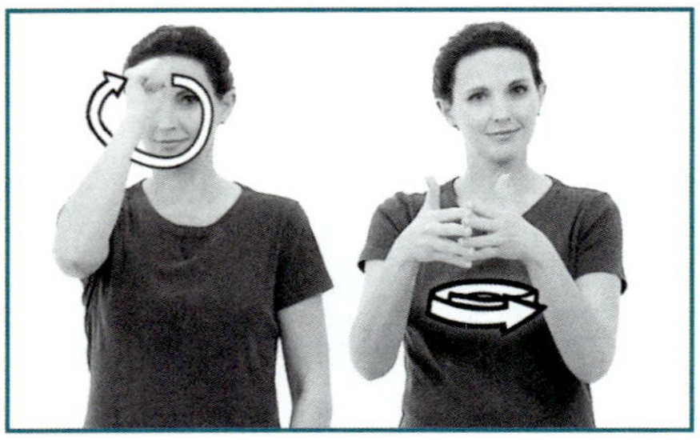

or

29.

30.

31.

32.

Surroundings

33. across the street from (here)

34. in the rear; behind my house

35. on the right side

36. on the left side

Comments about Neighbors

37. cheerful; friendly

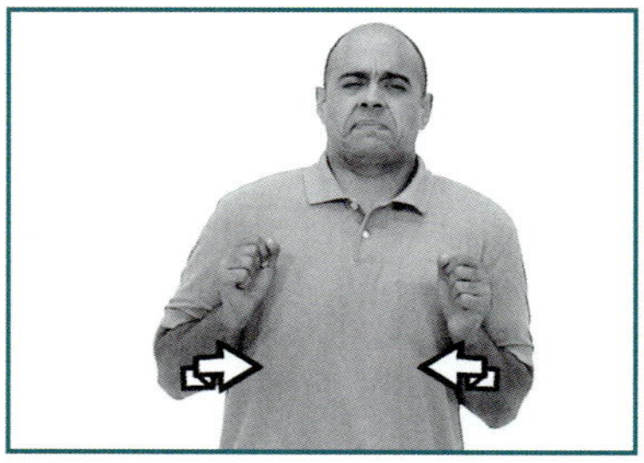

38. not friendly; cold

39. crabby; grouchy

40. snoopy; nosy

What People Like and Don't Like About the Area

Noise Level

41. tranquil, quiet

42. not quiet; noisy

Safety Level

Fingerspell SAFE

43.

44. unsafe; dangerous

Traffic Level

45. no one on the street, empty street

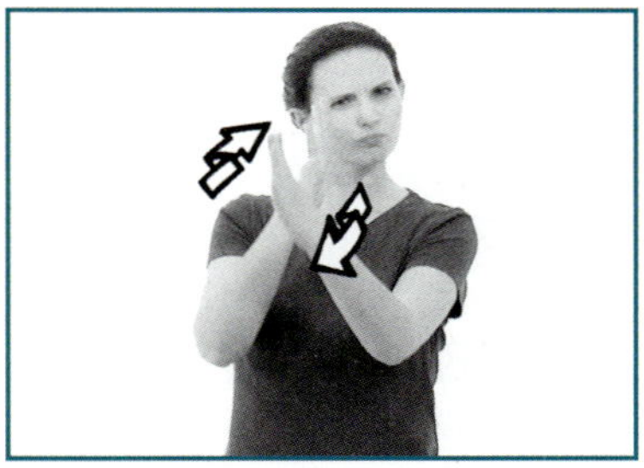

46. a lot of foot traffic or car traffic

Level of Cleanliness

47. neat, clean

48. filthy, dirty

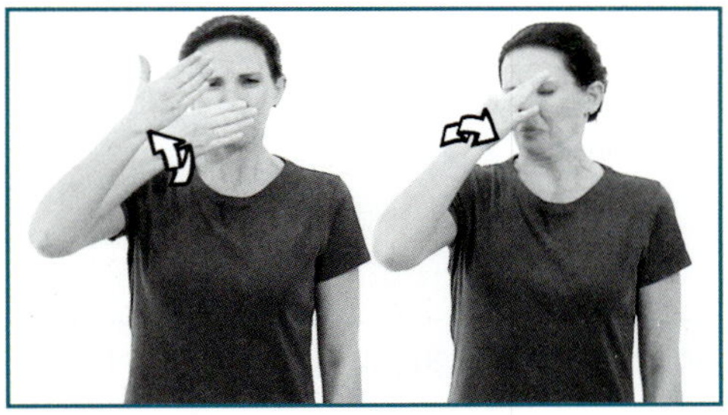

49. stinky; smelly

Activity Level

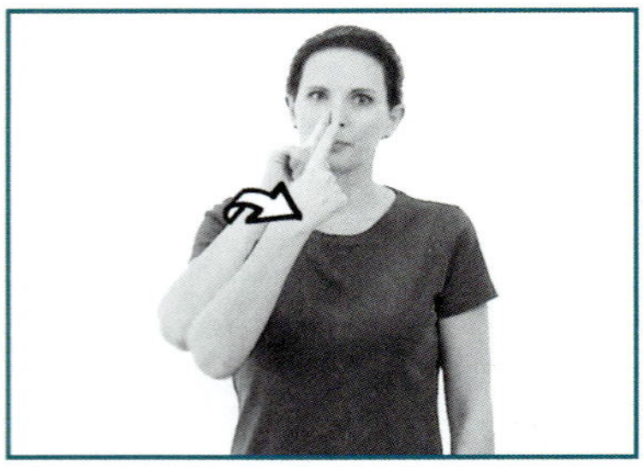

50. boring, unexciting, dull

51. bustling; high level of activity

Cost of Living

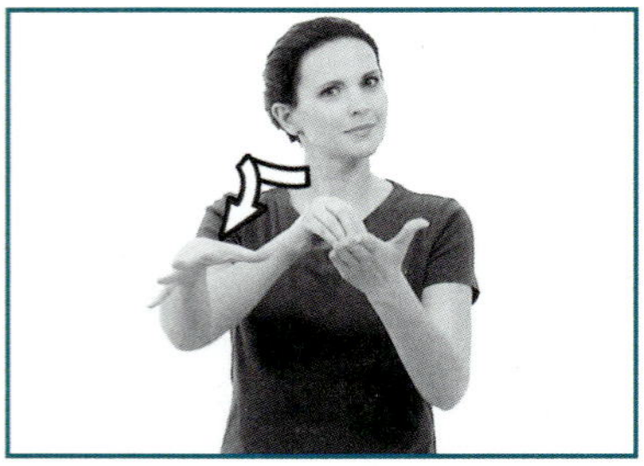

52. costing a lot of money; expensive

53. low in price; inexpensive; cheap

Other Signs

54. referring to a span of time beginning in the past and continuing to the present

55. many years ago; long time ago

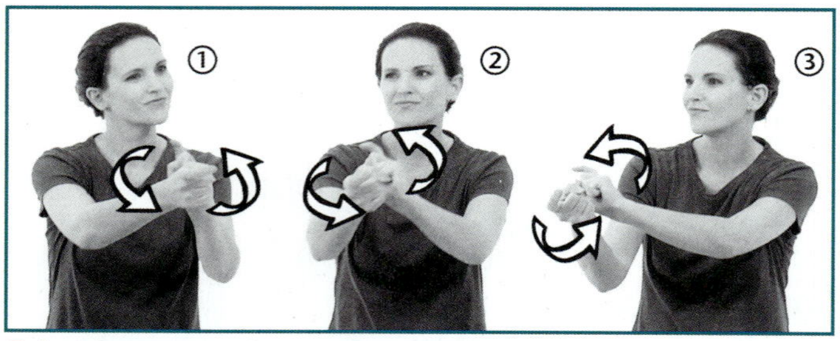

56. changes taking place over time

57. pretty; beautiful

58. nothing in common; all different

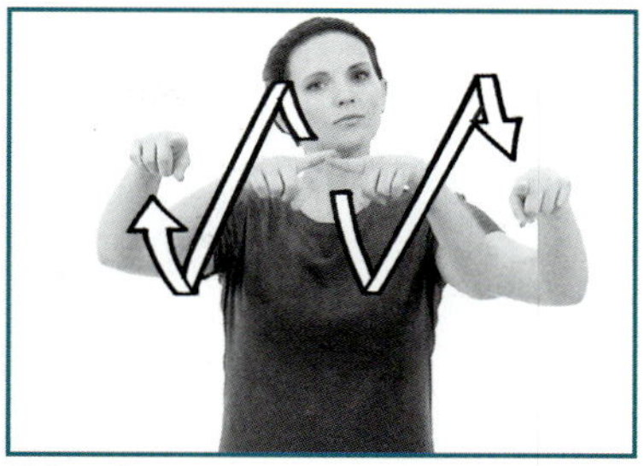

59. diverse; variety

60. 61. 62.

all ———————————————— none

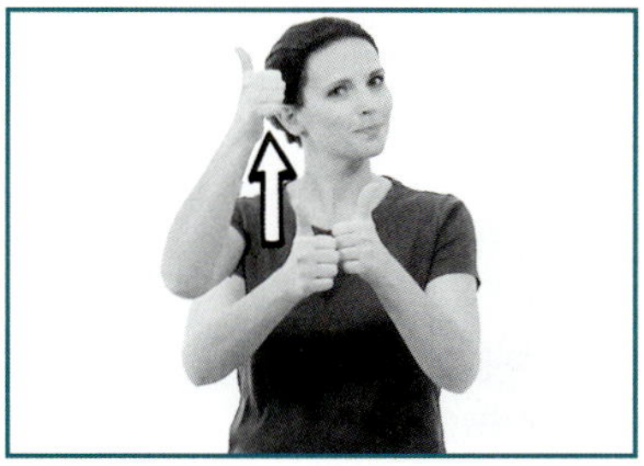

60.

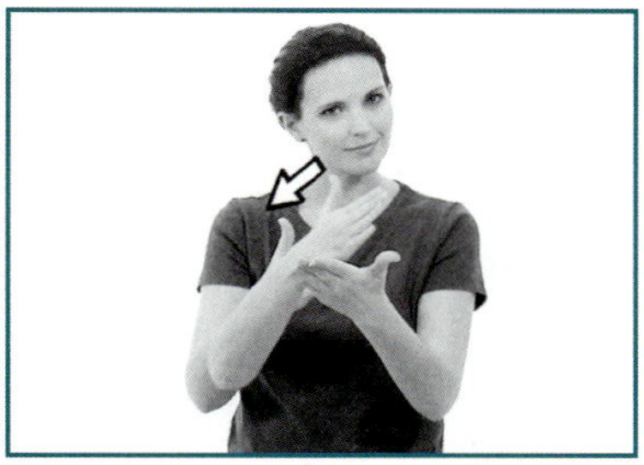

61.

62.

SIGNING NATURALLY

Homework 9:2

PLACES IN THE NEIGHBORHOOD

VOCABULARY REVIEW

Review the vocabulary on the video.

Names and Types of Businesses

Fingerspell
HYATT

1. type: hotel

Fingerspell
REMAX

Fingerspell
RE

2. type: real estate business

3. type: coffee house

Curves

Fingerspell
CURVES

4. type: exercise facility

5. type: fast food

IKEA

Fingerspell
IKEA

6. type: home furnishings (furniture)

AAA

Fingerspell
AAA

7. type: auto insurance business

macy's

Fingerspell
MACY'S

Fingerspell
DEPT

8. type: department store

Names and Types of Businesses (continued)

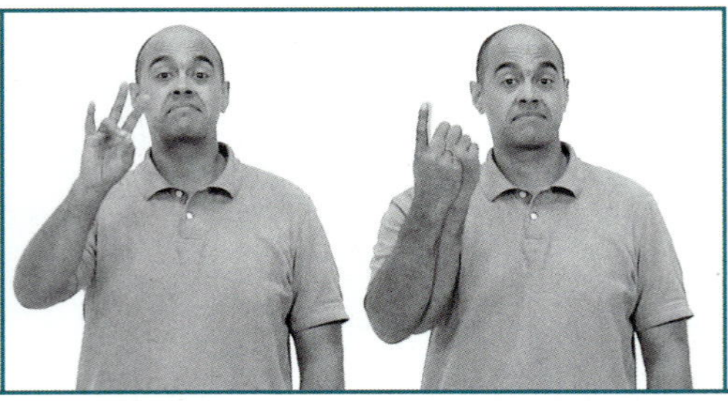

9. type: late-night convenience store

Fingerspell ABC

10. type: liquor sales

Fingerspell ACE

Fingerspell HARDWARE

11. type: hardware store

Fingerspell SAM'S DELI

or

12. type: sandwich shop

Fingerspell
ATT

13. type: phone store

14. type: discount store

Fingerspell
ADAMS

15. type: funeral home

Government Services and Facilities

Fingerspell
CITY HALL

16.

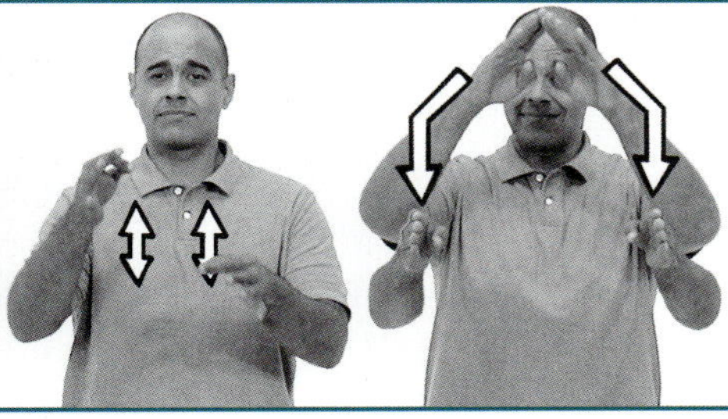

17.

Government Services and Facilities *(continued)*

18.

or

19.

20.

Did You Realize...There Were Stamps Featuring ASL?

It is an involved process to get a particular theme selected to be on stamps by the U.S. Postal Service and to get a Deaf or American Sign Language theme on stamps is even more challenging. At first, the U.S. Postal Service wasn't receptive to the idea of creating the stamps, but the America Postal Workers Union, which represented nearly 2,500 Deaf workers at the time, lobbied for the stamps and won the approval of the postmaster general to create the stamps. In 1993 the U.S. Postal Service released two stamps celebrating American Sign Language; one featuring the "I Love You" handshape (combination of the letters "I," "L" and "Y"); and the other one showing a mother cradling a baby in one arm and sharing the ILY sign with the child. Many Deaf Americans, thrilled with the public recognition, bought sheets of stamps as a keepsake to commemorate the event.

Homework 9:3

GIVING THE TIME 1

Hour Numbers

When giving the time on the hour for 1:00 to 9:00, the number is formed by:

- tapping the index finger on the wrist
- moving the hand outward and shaking the hand
- having the palm face out.

When giving the time on the hour for 10:00 to 12:00, form the numbers by:

- using either a repeated or a single movement
- tapping the index finger on the wrist.

View. Iva demonstrates the form for hour numbers 1:00 to 12:00.

Practice signing the numbers.

Hour and Minute Numbers

When giving a time that includes minutes, the numbers are formed by:

For hours:

- tapping the index finger on the wrist before giving the hour number
- not shaking the hand for hours 1–9 and not repeating the movement for the hours 10–12

For minutes:

- before giving minute number, the hand moves slightly to the side
- the palm faces out for minutes :01–:09
- for minutes :10–:15 and :20, it is best to use an emphatic, singular movement, but repeated movement is acceptable
- for :30, :40 and :50 these numbers use an emphatic, singular movement only.

View. Iva demonstrates these hour and minute combinations:

1:05	4:20	7:35	10:50
2:10	5:25	8:40	11:55
3:15	6:30	9:45	12:30

Practice signing the numbers.

WRITE THE TIME

Iva gives the time. Write in the blanks below.

1. ________	6. ________	11. ________	16. ________
2. ________	7. ________	12. ________	17. ________
3. ________	8. ________	13. ________	18. ________
4. ________	9. ________	14. ________	19. ________
5. ________	10. ________	15. ________	20. ________

Answers on page 514.

FILL IN THE TIME

John and Tonique give the activities and the times. Fill in the blanks below.

	Activity and Places	*Time 1*	*Time 2*
1.	________________	________	________
2.	________________	________	________
3.	________________	________	________
4.	________________	________	________
5.	________________	________	________
6.	________________	________	________

Answers given in class.

VOCABULARY REVIEW

Review the vocabulary on the video.

Verbs

or
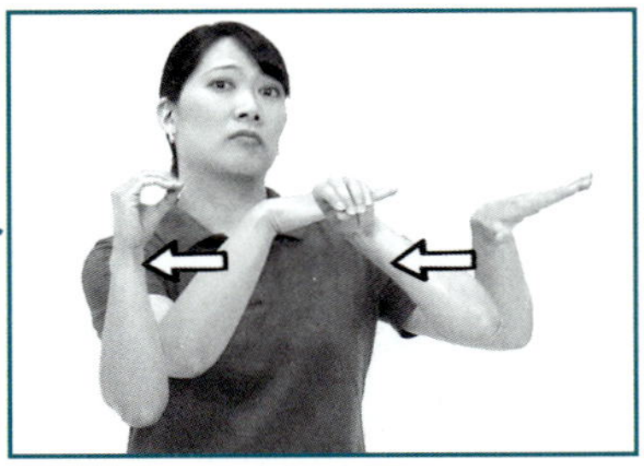

1. to leave or depart from

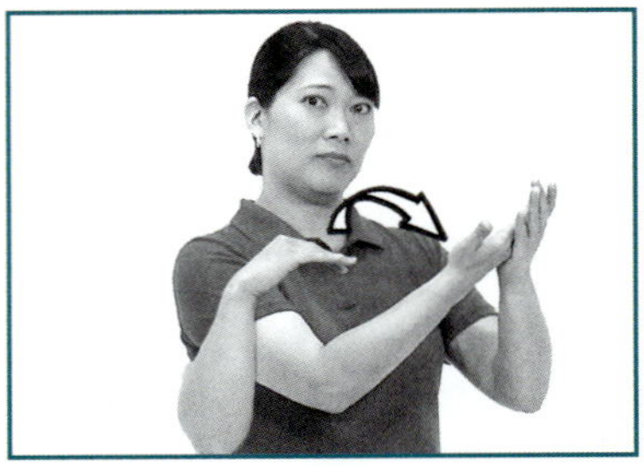

2. to arrive or reach at

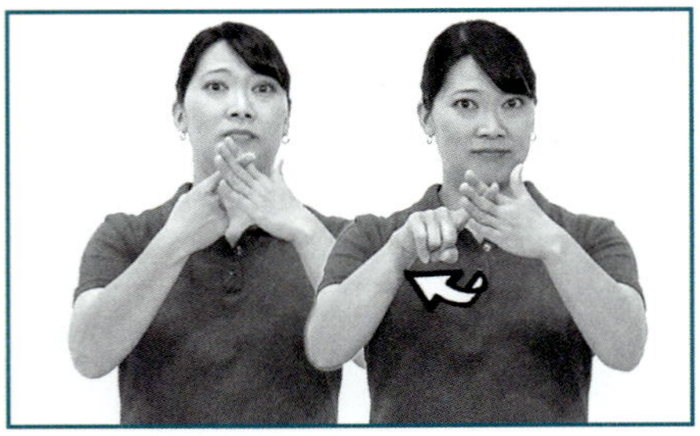

3. to begin; to start

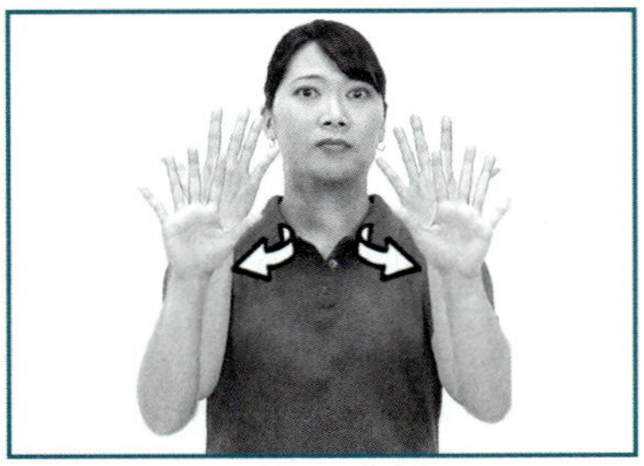

4. to finish; to end; to complete

5. to arise from bed; to get up

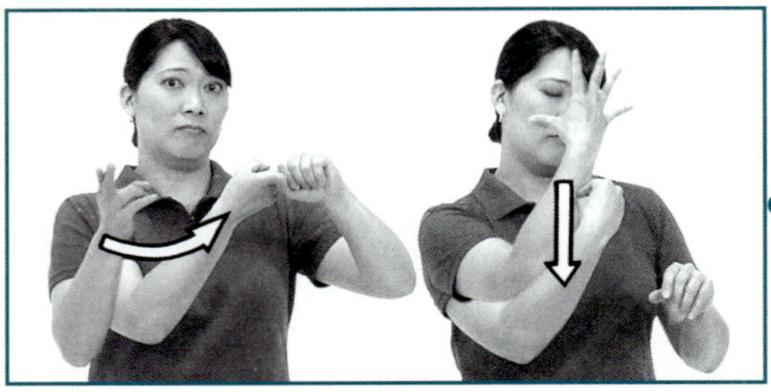
or
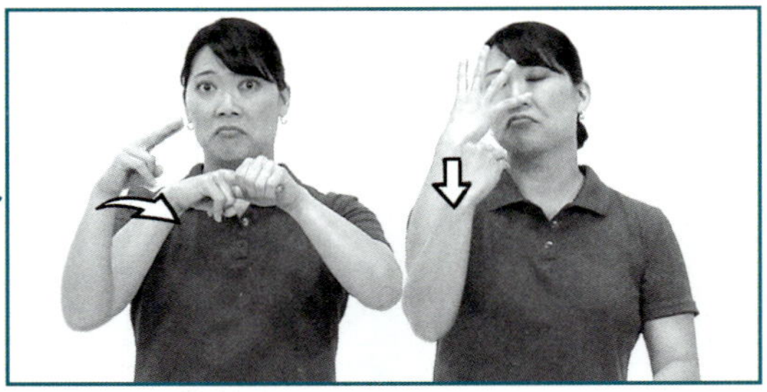

6. to go to bed

Wh-word Question

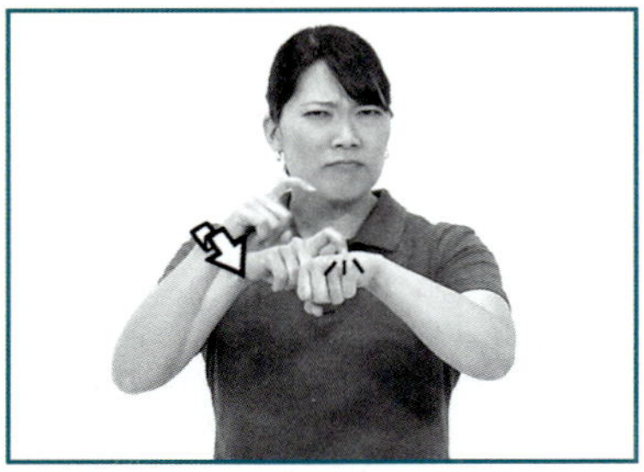

7. asking what time

Homework 9:4

DESCRIBING A NEIGHBORHOOD 2

Lauren's Neighborhood

Lauren uses the narrative outline to describe her neighborhood.

Narrative Outline

1. tell where you live
   - kind of residence, and what city or district
   - for how long and with who
2. tell what your neighborhood is like
   - type of neighborhood or area
   - what is nearby and convenient
   - who lives in the neighborhood
3. tell what is next to your residence
4. tell what you like and don't like about the area
5. tell about your future plans

New Signs

a panoramic view

Key Grammar

USING RHETORICAL QUESTIONS

One of the ways a narrator engages his audience is by using rhetorical questions to draw attention to the topic he will discuss next. A rhetorical question is followed by the answer. For example the narrator could use a rhetorical question to ask, "What is my neighborhood like?" Then give the answer "It's a mixed area with apartment buildings, lofts and warehouses." A rhetorical question is similar to a wh-word question in structure, but instead of furrowing the brows, the signer raises his brows. A good signer purposefully intersperses his narrative with rhetorical questions to make his telling more engaging to the audience.

Rhetorical Questions 1–3

Watch Lauren demonstrate how to sign rhetorical questions to transition to the next segment of the narrative. Notice Lauren raising her brows, tilting her head slightly and shaking her head when signing the rhetorical question.

1. For "tell what your neighborhood is like"

2. For "tell what you like about the area"

3. For "tell what you do not like about the area"

Learn the Narrative

Practice the key elements of the narrative outline.

Narrative Outline

1. tell where you live
   - kind of residence, and what city or district
   - for how long and with who
2. tell what your neighborhood is like
   - type of neighborhood or area
   - what is nearby and convenient
   - who lives in the neighborhood
3. tell what is next to your residence
4. tell what you like and don't like about the area
5. tell about your future plans

For "• *how long*"

For "• *type of neighborhood or area*"

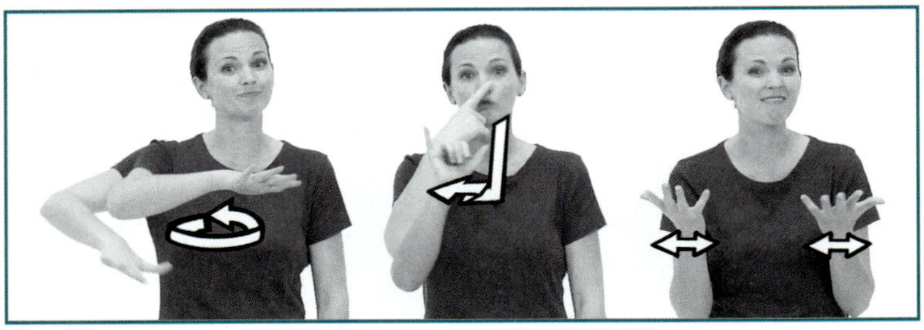

Remember to use a rhetorical question.

For "• *what is nearby and convenient*"

nearby (over there)

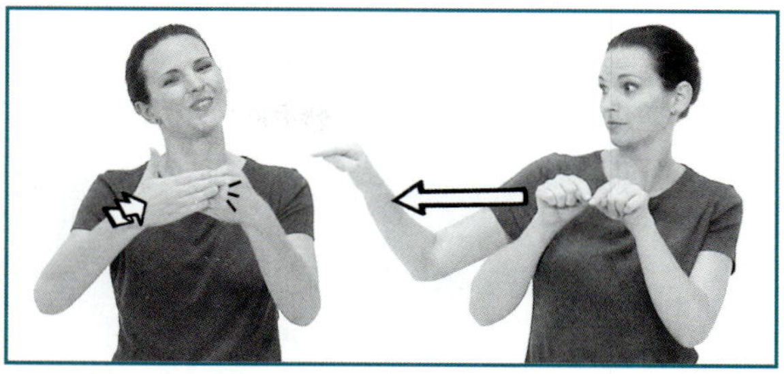

nearby in that direction

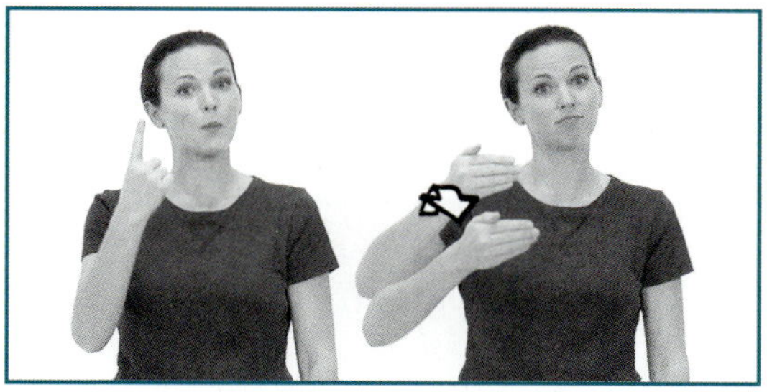

one block away

For "• *who lives in the neighborhood*"

tell about composition of population

tell about diversity

For *"3. tell what is next to your residence"*

across the street from here

on the right side

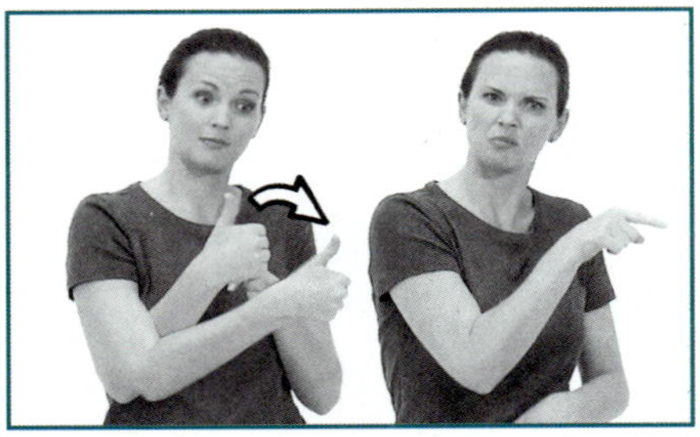
on the left side

behind my house

Remember to add information about the facility, building, or neighborhood.

For "*4. tell what you like and don't like about the area*"

(describe what you like about the area)

(describe what you don't like about the area)

Remember to use a rhetorical question.

For "*5. tell about your future plans*"

(event)

Assignment

YOUR NEIGHBORHOOD

Develop a narrative about your neighborhood.

Follow the narrative structure on page 177. Incorporate phrases from **Learn the Narrative**, pages 180–183, and vocabulary from **Homework 9:1**, pages 156–167.

Review **David's Neighborhood**, **Amber's Neighborhood**, and **Lauren's Neighborhood** as examples. Practice your narrative until you can recall the information without notes. Be prepared to present your narrative in class.

Homework 9:5

GIVING DIRECTIONS: NEXT TO, ACROSS FROM

To give directions to a place, use the horizontal map orientation to describe the area "with a street view" as opposed to "reading a map." To properly understand and follow the directions you need to use the signer's perspective. It's as if you become the signer and and see the location from the signer's eyes.

Iva describes locations of four businesses pictured on the map below, using the corners as a reference point.

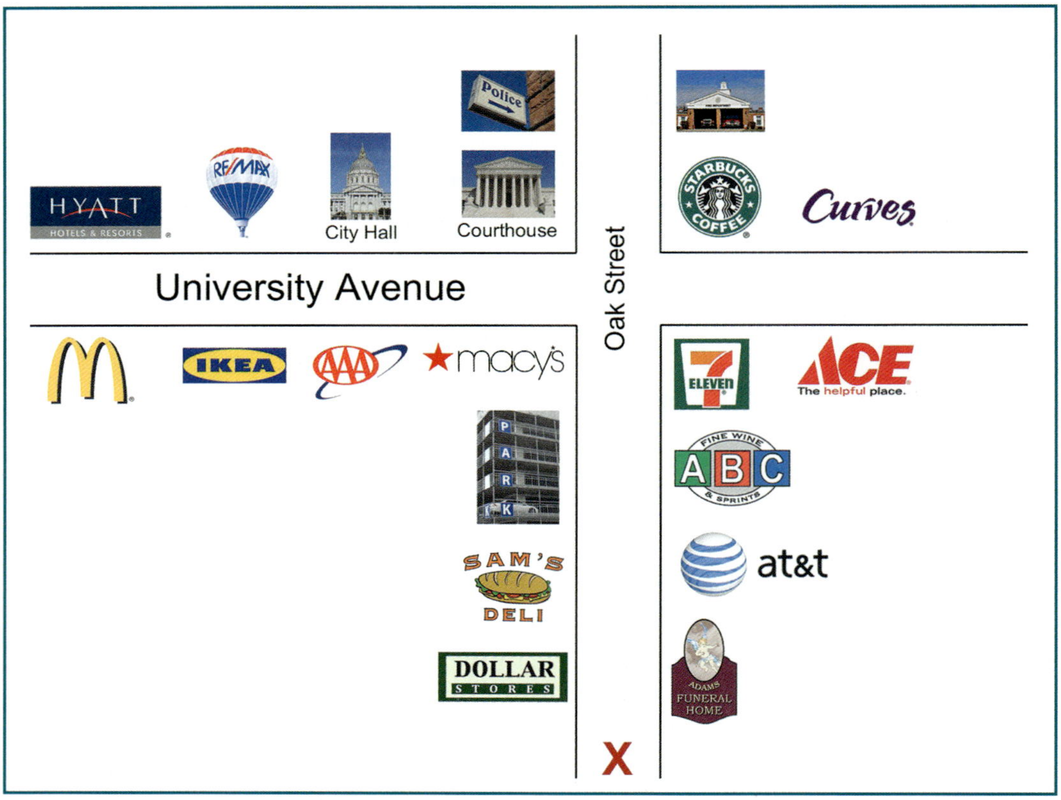

From a Corner 1

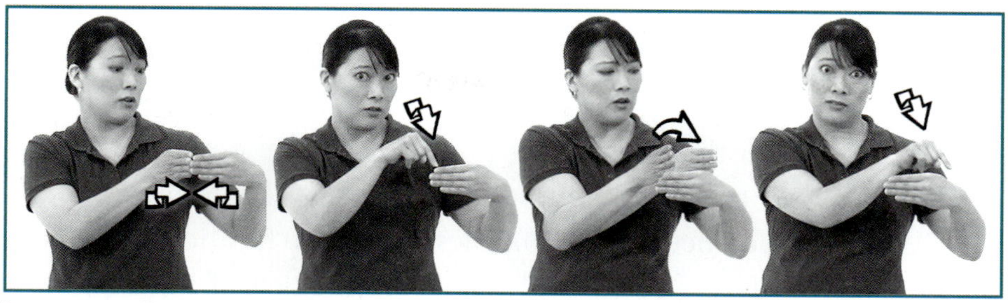

location of AAA

From a Corner 2

location of ABC Liquor

From a Corner 3

location of Police Station

From a Corner 4

location of Curves

Observe how Iva uses:

- the horizontal map orientation (from the "x" marked red on the map)
- facial expressions to indicate whether the corner is closer or further away
- her non-dominant hand to maintain the location of the corner (reference point) while describing the location of the business,
- nods and points at the end to make clear the location.

Sign Tip

If taking the signer's perspective is difficult for you, try standing next to your monitor so you and Iva are looking in the same direction, and have the same perspective.

For the following examples Iva describes locations of four businesses pictured on the map using other businesses as a reference point.

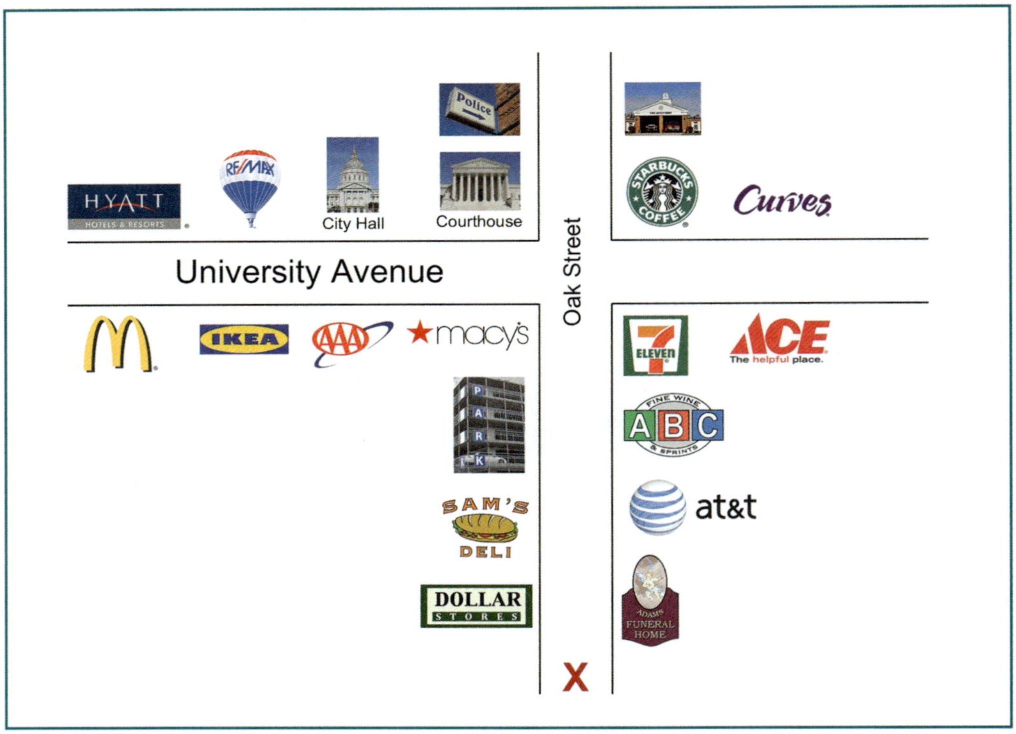

Across from a Place 1

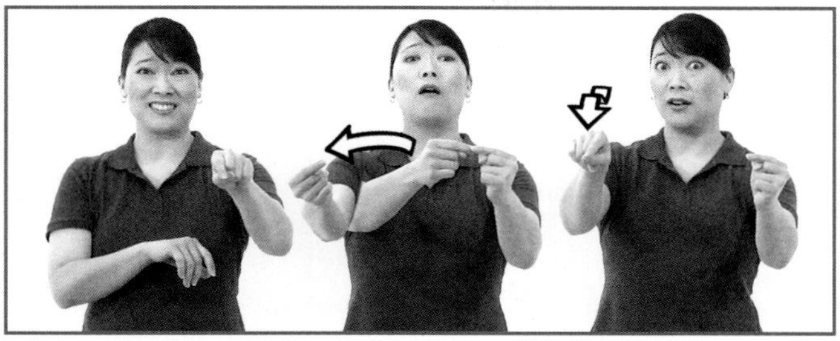

location of firehouse (across from the Police Station)

Across from a Place 2

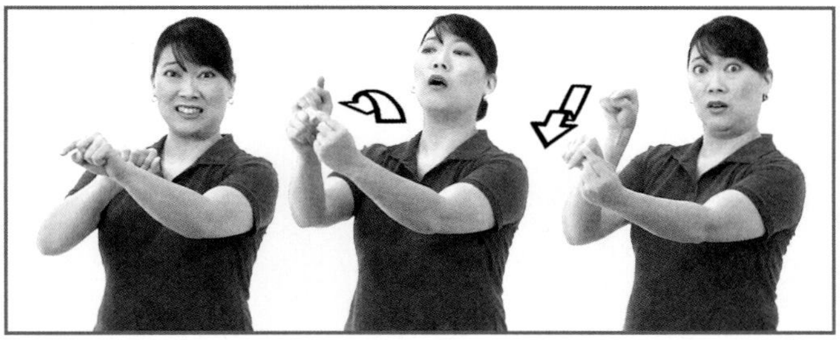

location of ACE hardware (across from Curves)

Across from a Place 3

location of Sam's Deli (across from AT&T)

Across from a Place 4

location of the Hyatt Hotel (across from McDonald's)

Observe how Iva uses:

- horizontal map orientation (street view)
- her non-dominant hand to maintain the location of the business (reference point) while telling the location of the intended business
- nods and points at the end to make clear the location.

FILL IN THE SPACE

Iva tells where businesses are located. Write the name of the business in the correct location on the map.

(**NOTE:** The locations of businesses on the map have been changed.)

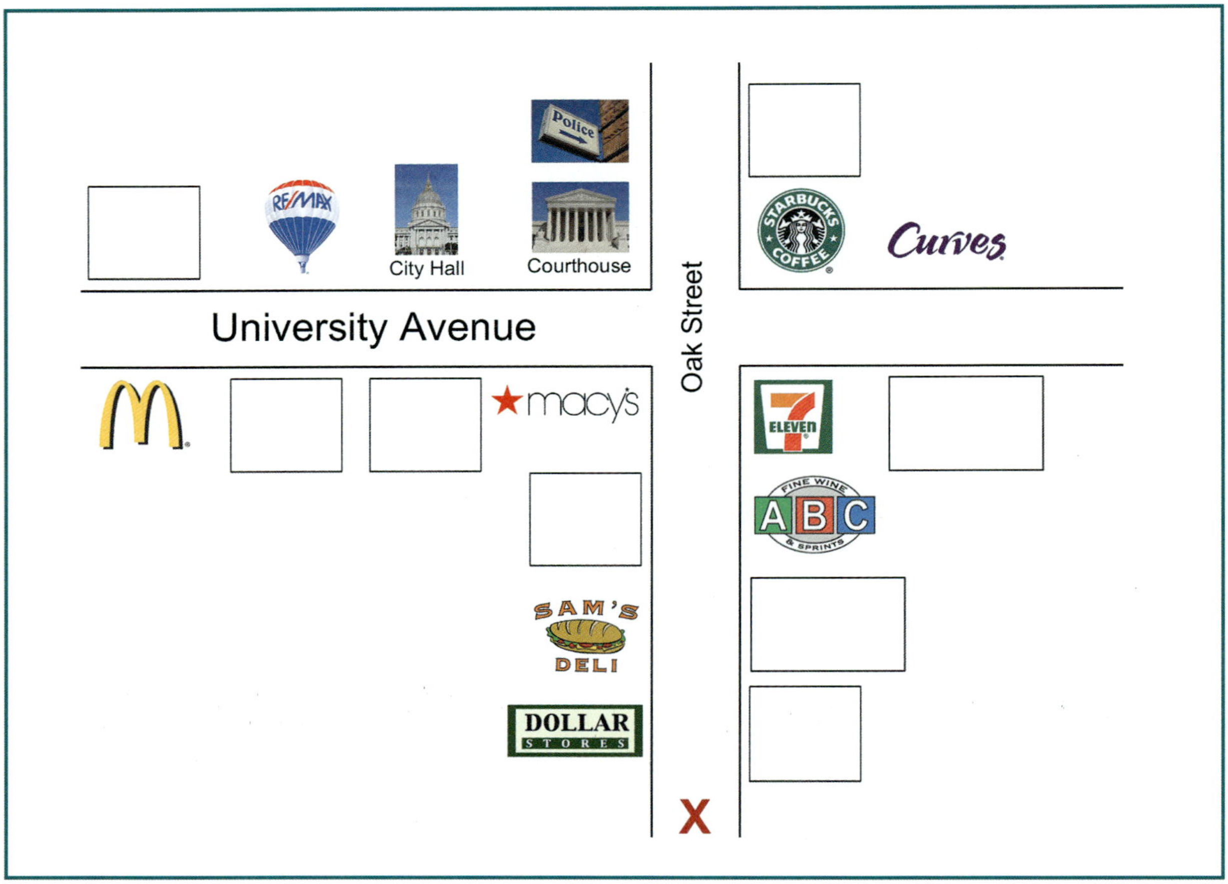

Answers on page 514.

Homework 9:6

YES–NO QUESTIONS 1

Identify the topic of each question by underlining the topic.

1. Do you like coffee?
2. Do you know how to fix a car?
3. Do you like to iron clothes?
4. Have you tried Thai food?
5. Do you read a newspaper daily?
6. Do you have more than 100 books?
7. Have you been to Paris?
8. Do you know how to download music off the Internet?
9. Are you afraid of spiders, bugs or frogs?
10. Do you like to get up early?

To translate yes-no questions, follow this word order:

- establish time if specified (raise brows)
- establish location if specified (raise brows)
- name the topic (raise brows)
- end with a question (raise brows, head tilt forward, hold last sign)

Example

1. Do you like coffee?

Name the topic, end with a question.

Sign Tip

For sentence 2 and 8, when translating the phrase "know how" it is better to fingerspell "how." The signs following should not be used.

sign used in common phrases borrowed from English such as "How are you?" or "How do you know?"

sign used in wh-word questions to ask how something is done, such as, "How did you come to class?" or "How do you make coffee?"

View. Tonique signing translations of the questions above. Practice signing the questions. Focus on word order, facial grammar and phrasing. Be prepared to sign the sentences in class.

VOCABULARY REVIEW

Review the vocabulary on the video.

Fingerspell HOW

1. phrase used to ask if a person knows how to do something

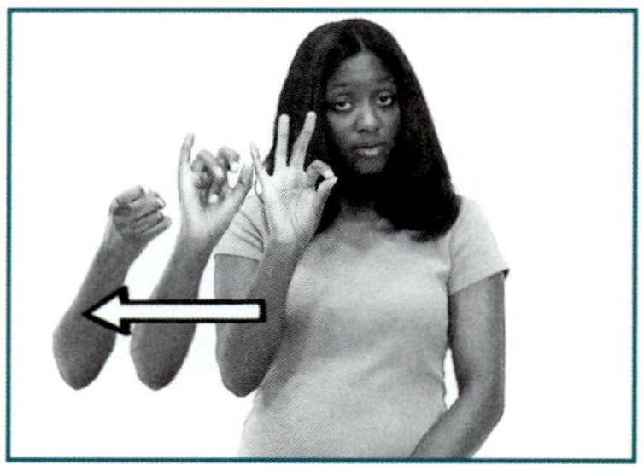

2. to fix; to repair

3.

4. everyday, daily

5. above or more than a certain number

6. to have experienced or have been to a place—like a country, a city, a park, a beach, etc.

7. the city of Paris, France

8. computer network providing email and information; the internet

9. to get data; to download

10.

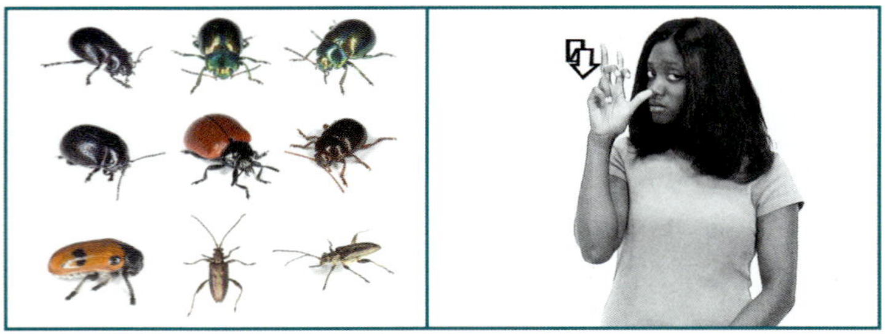

11.

12.

13. to be afraid of

or

Fingerspell EARLY

14. early

Homework 9:7

CONVERSATION 1

JT (B) describes a certain restaurant to Justin (A) and tells what food is served there.

A: ask if B has been to a certain restaurant
B: say yes
A: ask what it looks like
B: describe, include:
- **table or counter and seating arrangement**
- **wall decorations**
- **lightings**

A: ask what kind of food is served
B: tell what is served (use listing)
A: ask if food is good, and if it's expensive
B: give opinion
A and B: closing

New Signs

to look forward to

Key Grammar

DESCRIPTIVE, LOCATIVE AND ELEMENT CLASSIFIERS

To describe the environment of a restaurant, include all or some of the following:

- table or counter and seating arrangement
- wall decorations
- lighting

Then describe the restaurant's unique features such as unusual facade, a table, menu, and view to help your listener understand why this particular restaurant stands out from the rest.

ASL classifiers are essential language tools needed to provide an effective description of an environment. Classifiers are specific handshapes used to represent nouns according to:

1. their *shape*, flat, cylindrical, bulky
2. their *location*, on the wall, on the floor, on the table
3. their *movement*, flashing, flowing, splatter, dripping, and
4. their *arrangement*, in a row, in a U-shape, randomly placed

The following classifiers are emphasized in this lesson.

Descriptive classifiers (DCLs) describe the size and shape of counters and tables, the shapes, patterns and textures of the walls.

Locative classifiers (LCLs) indicate the arrangement of tables in the area and objects on the walls.

Element classifiers (ECLs) describe the intensity, movement and direction of things that are not solid, such as rays of light, mist of water, fire in a forest and wind (air).

View. JT describes the restaurant **The Mercer** from the front facade to the menu on the iPad. Notice his eye gaze when he uses classifiers to refer to the locations of objects.

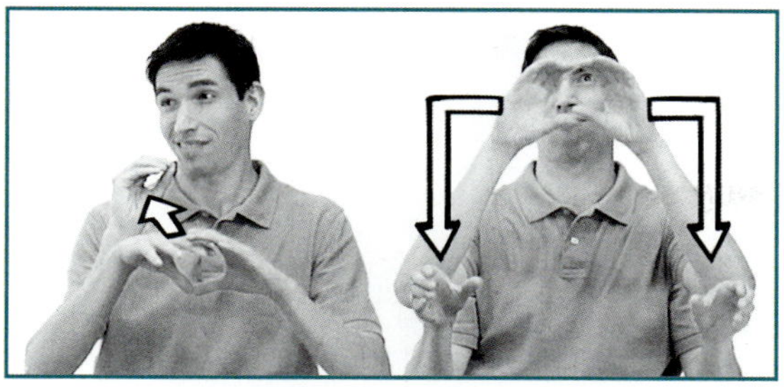

- **the front facade** – describing the shape of the front facade using DCL

- **the front door** – describing the glass surface of the front door using DCL

- **the bar counter** – describing the shape and the location of the bar counter using DCL

- **the bar stools** – telling the location of the bar stools using LCL

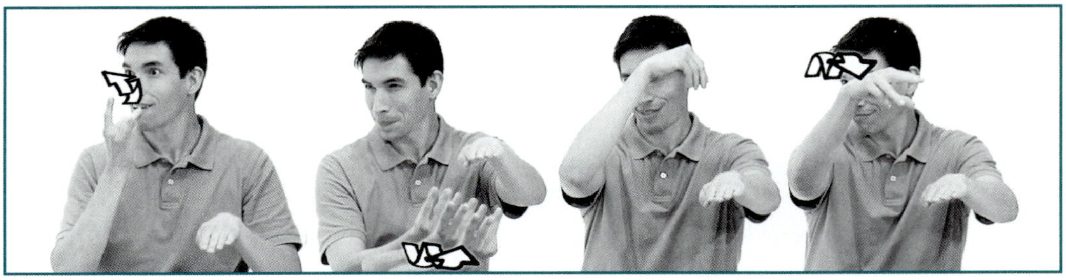

- **the lighting** – describing lighting below and above the counter using ECL

- **the stone wall** – describing the stone wall (from floor to ceiling) using DCL

- **the tables** – telling the tables are randomly arranged around the room using LCL

- **the iPad** – telling the location of the iPad, which contains the menu, using LCL

LISTING

When you list several items in a given category, for example, food served at a restaurant, nod when naming each item to separate one from the other.

View. Observe JT naming types of dishes (Italian), then nodding each time he names a food item. Items can be signed in different locations to emphasize and make clear the items the signer is listing.

DESCRIBING RESTAURANTS

Restaurant 1

Derrick describes a restaurant. Watch the narrative and fill in the blanks below.

1. name of restaurant ______________________________

2. dining area location ______________________________

3. draw the tables and their arrangement (or write the description)

4. draw the arrangement of the boats and the fish sculptures (or write the description)

5. draw the arrangement of the surfboards (or write the description)

6. type of food served at the restaurant ____________________

Restaurant 2

Terrylene describes another restaurant. Watch the narrative and fill in the blanks below.

1. name of restaurant ______________________________

2. what is seen before reaching the restaurant ______________

   ____

3. what the restaurant used to be ____________________

   ____

4. fill in the room with details

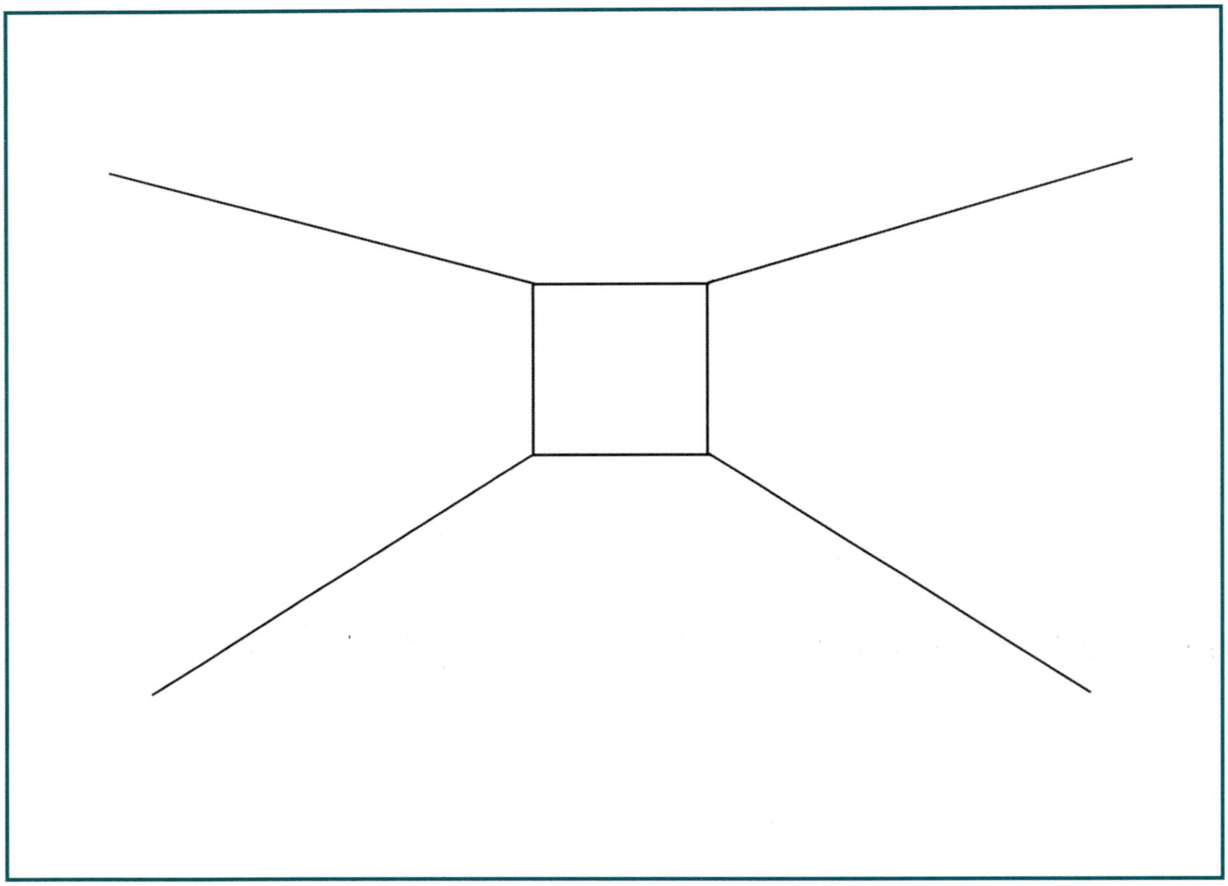

5. type of food served at the restaurant ______________

Answers on page 515–516.

VOCABULARY REVIEW

Review the vocabulary on the video.

Wh-word Question

1. ask what kind

Places to Eat

2.

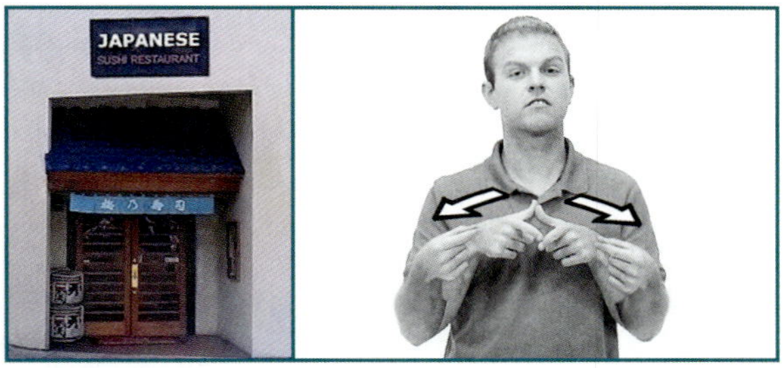

3.

4.

5.

or

6.

Places to Eat *(continued)*

7.

8.

9.

10.

11.

or

Fingerspell BAR

12.

Opinions: Prices

13.	14.	15.	16.
$$$$	$$$	$$	$

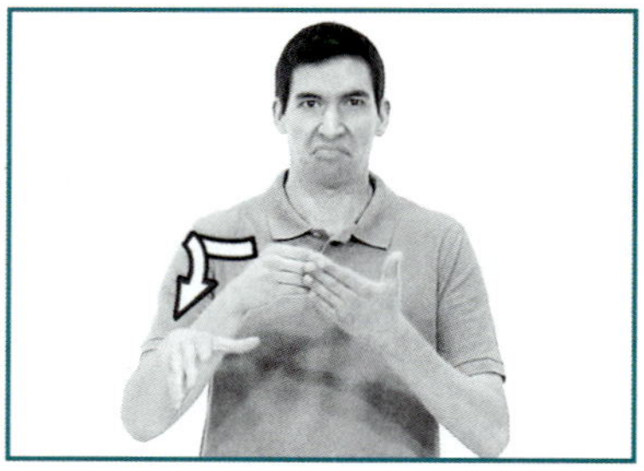

13.

14.

15.

16.

Opinions: Food

17.–18.	19.	20.–22.	23.–26.
★★★★	★★★	★★	★

or

17.

18.

19.

20.

21.

22.

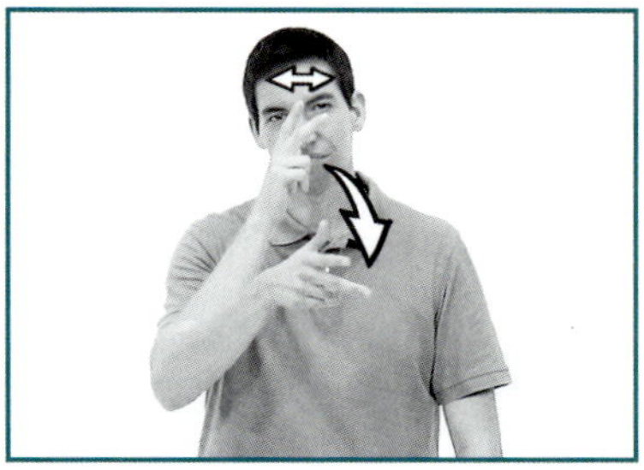

23.

24.

Opinions: Food (continued)

25.

26.

Describing Counters

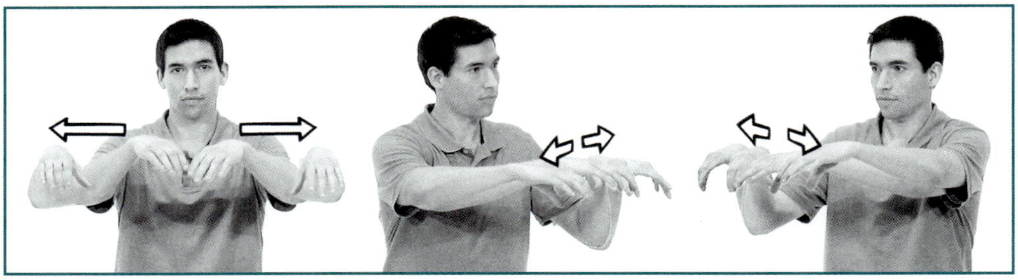

27. descriptive classifier sign indicating counters in various locations

Describing Tables

28. locative classifier sign showing arrangement and shape of long tables

29. locative classifier sign showing random arrangement of round tables

30. locative classifier sign showing rows of tables

31. descriptive classifier sign showing an island table with a stove in the middle

Describing Seatings

32. locative classifier sign showing rows of chairs facing each other

33. locative classifier sign showing chairs around several round tables in the room

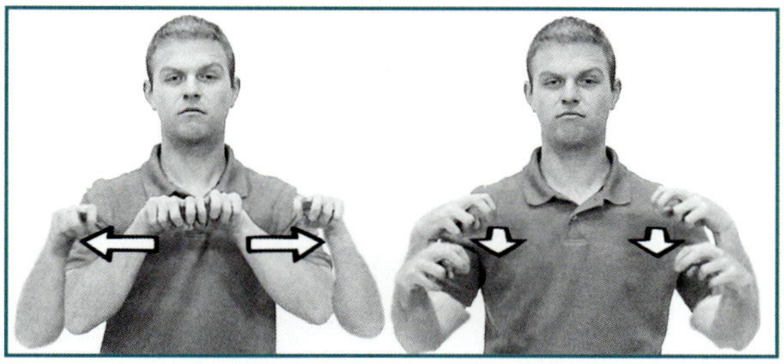

34. locative classifier sign showing chairs around the three sides of a table

Food and Drinks

Fingerspell PIZZA

35.

36. (see 2 other variations on page 170 with Sam's Deli)

37.

38.

39.

Fingerspell BBQ

40.

41.

42.

43.

44.

45.

Food and Drinks *(continued)*

Fingerspell
RICE

46.

47.

48.

49.

50.

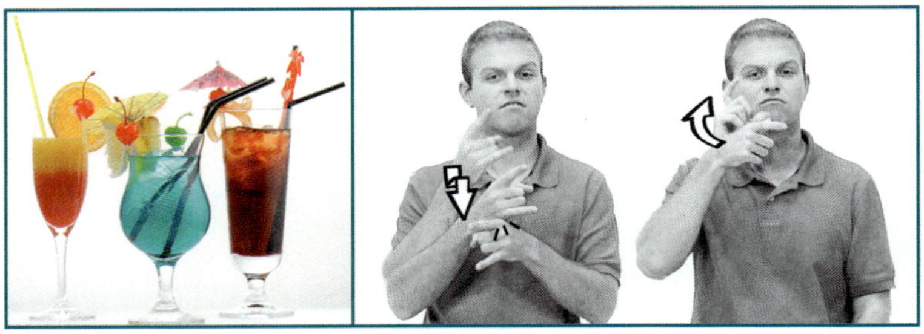

51.

52. home-made, made by hand

53. variety of, et cetera, so forth

Describing Walls

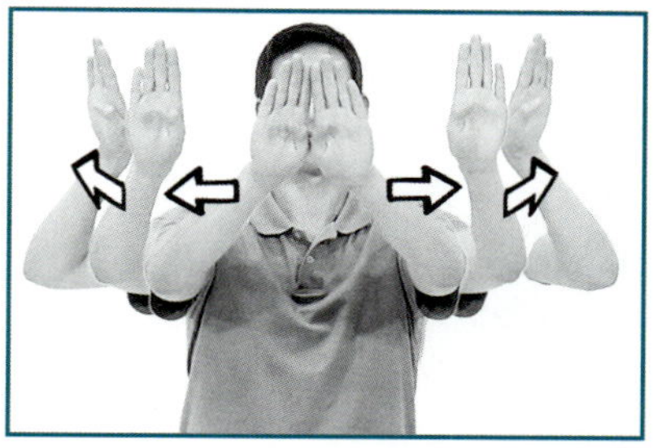

54. locative classifier sign indicating all three walls in a room

55. locative classifier sign indicating the left wall

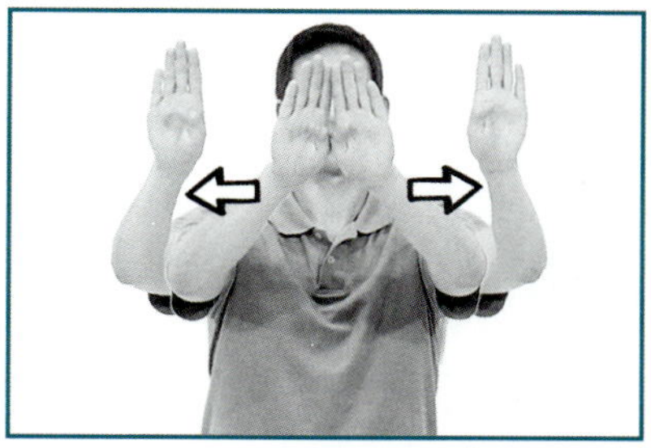

56. locative classifier sign indicating the center wall

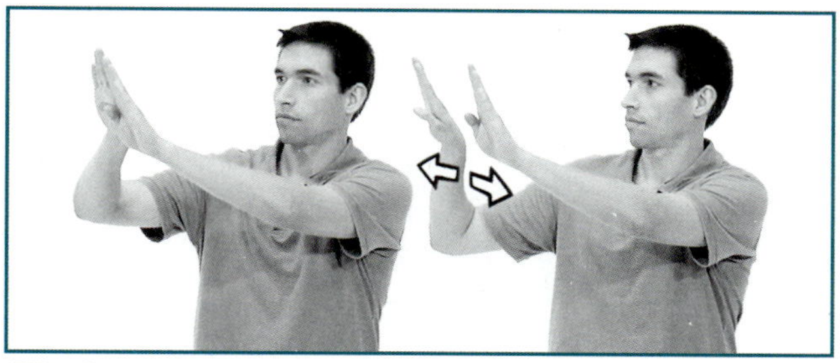

57. locative classifier sign indicating the right wall

Describing Things on a Wall

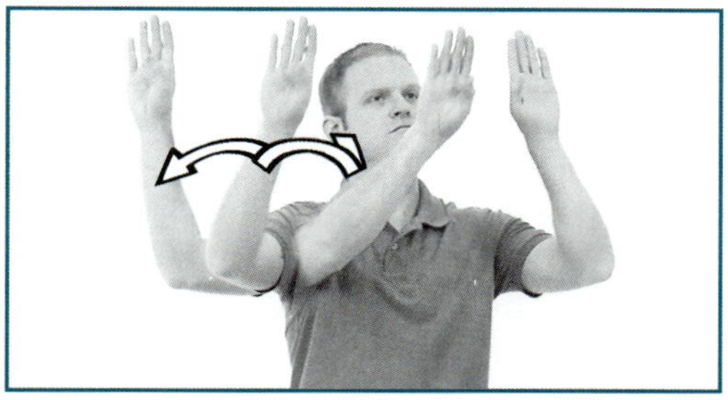

58. locative classifier sign indicating flat and square or rectangular objects arranged on wall

59. locative classifier sign indicating round-shaped objects arranged on wall

Describing Things on a Wall (continued)

60. locative classifier sign indicating long narrow objects arranged on wall

Describing Lights

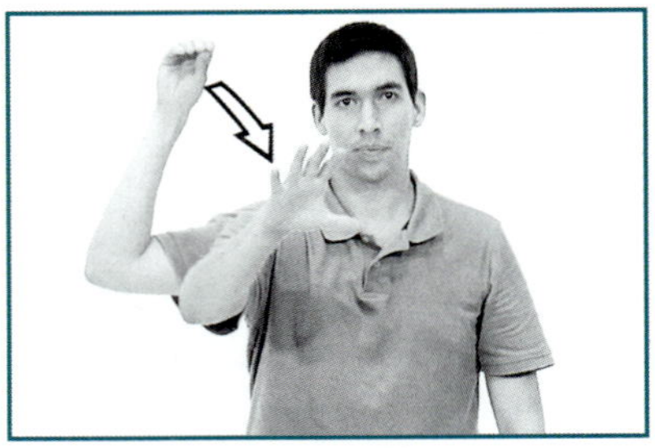

61. element classifier sign showing the light shining down on wall or stage

62. element classifier sign showing the light being dimmed

63. element classifier sign showing circle of lights blinking

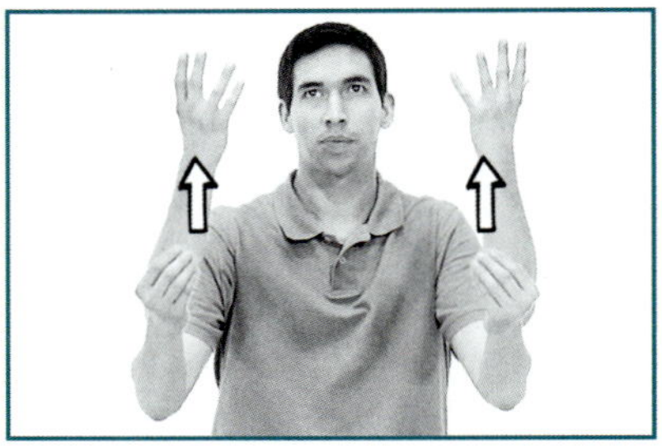

64. element classifier sign showing uplighting

Materials

65.

or

66.

67.

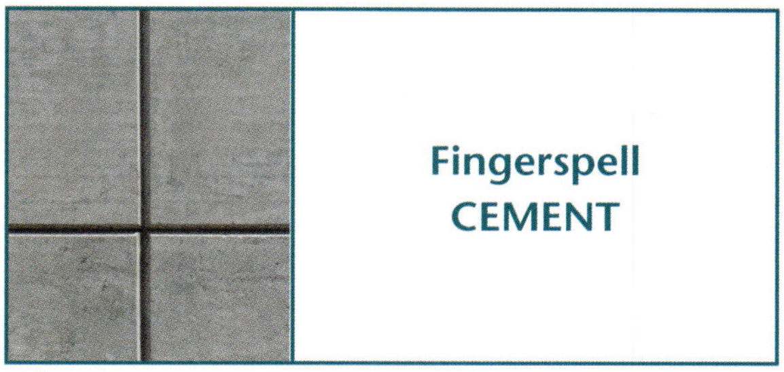

68.

69.

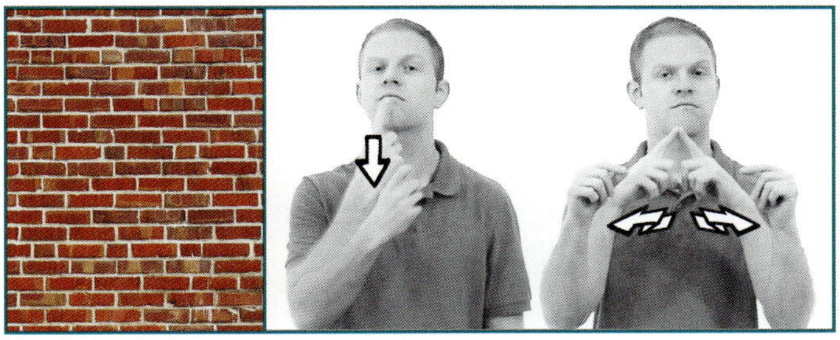

70.

71.

Opinions: Environment

72. something that is interesting

Homework 9:8

GIVING DIRECTIONS: WHERE TO TURN

There are three ways to tell where to turn within city blocks when giving directions:

1. tell how far (distance), number of blocks, all the way down
2. refer to a landmark, such as a corner with a business on it, stop light, school
3. refer to the intersection, naming the cross street

Then, tell which direction to turn (left or right).

Using the map on page 211 as a reference, observe Iva demonstrating the sequence above to tell where to turn.

Where to Turn 1

Notice Iva:

- nods her head for each block as she indicates three blocks down
- uses a "when" clause when naming the corner to make the turn
- uses her right hand to sign "right turn."

Where to Turn 2

Notice Iva:

- uses single movement when signing "all the way down"
- uses a "when" clause when naming the school (landmark) and the intersection before telling where to turn
- uses her left hand to sign "left turn."

TURNS 1–8

Iva and David will tell you where to turn. For each turn draw arrows on the map (page 211) to indicate where to turn and write in the number for the turn. Don't forget to take the signer's perspective to determine whether the turn is to the left or right.

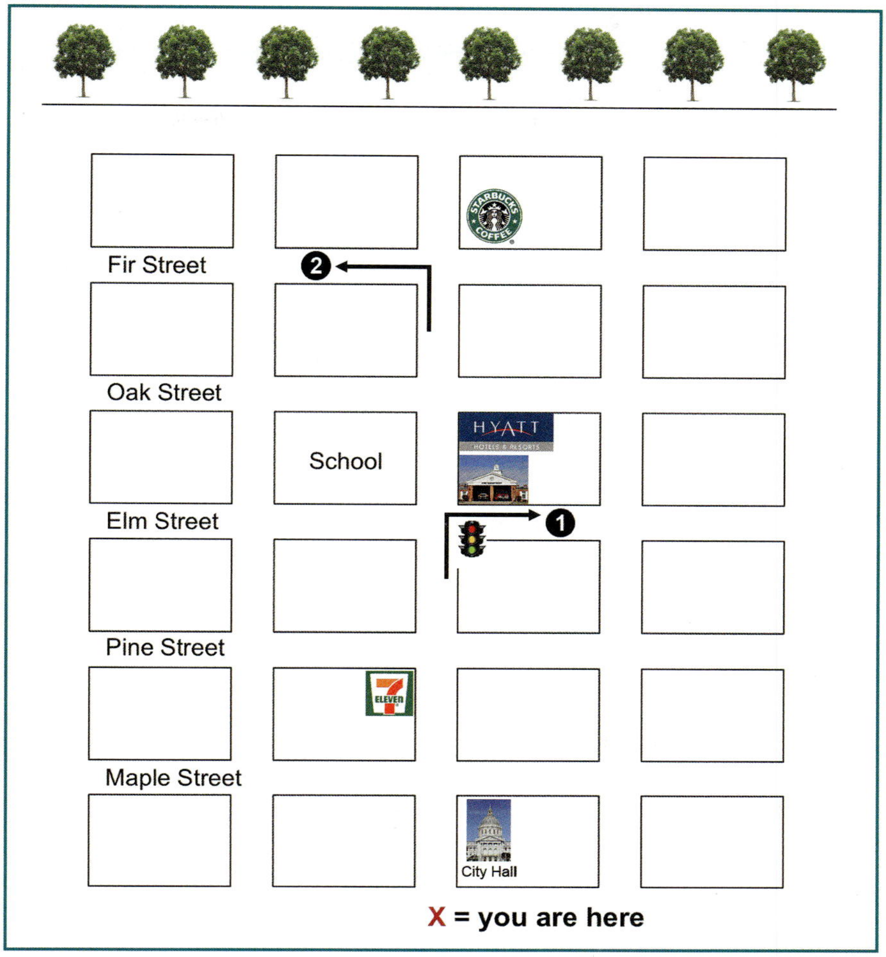

Answers on page 517.

VOCABULARY REVIEW

Review the vocabulary on the video.

Distance

1. to go straight ahead; to go all the way down the street

2. the end of the street

3. blocks ahead

Landmark

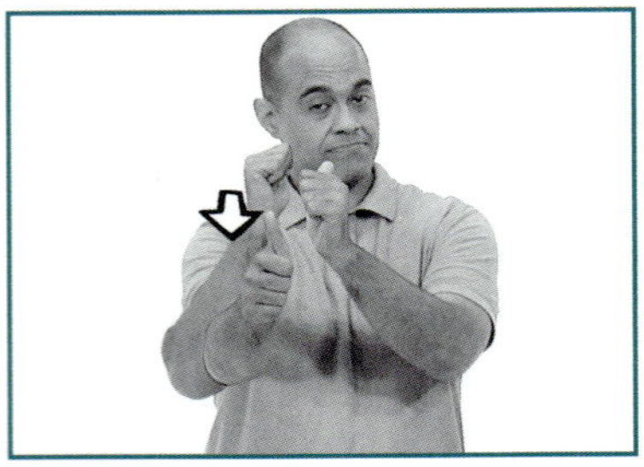

4. to go past

5. traffic stop light

Intersection

6. intersection, then the cross street

Where to Turn

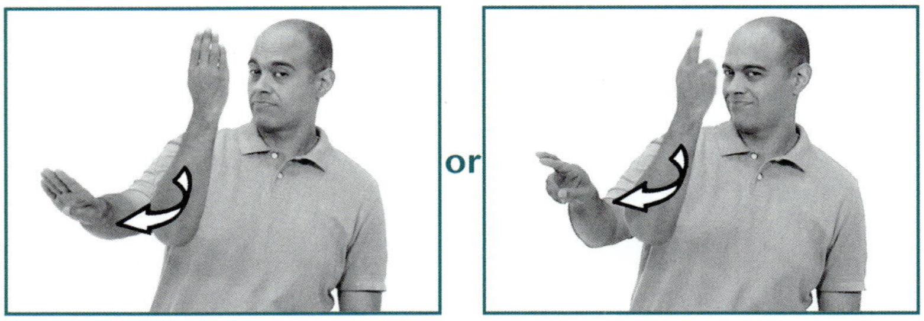

7. to turn right

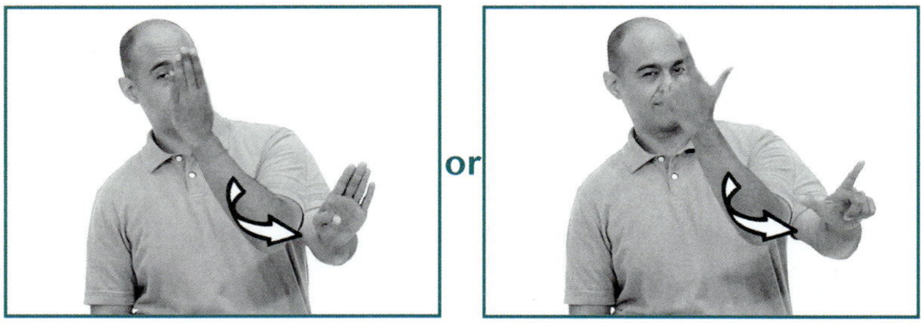

8. to turn left

Homework 9:9

GIVING THE TIME 2

What Happens When

Signer tells what happens at a certain time of the day.
You write in the information given.

	Time	*Who*	*What Happens*
1.	________	________	________________
2.	________	________	________________
3.	________	________	________________
4.	________	________	________________
5.	________	________	________________
6.	________	________	________________
7.	________	________	________________
8.	________	________	________________
9.	________	________	________________
10.	________	________	________________

Answers on page 517.

NUMBER TUNE UP

Review the four different number types you have learned so far:

cardinal (counting)

age

year

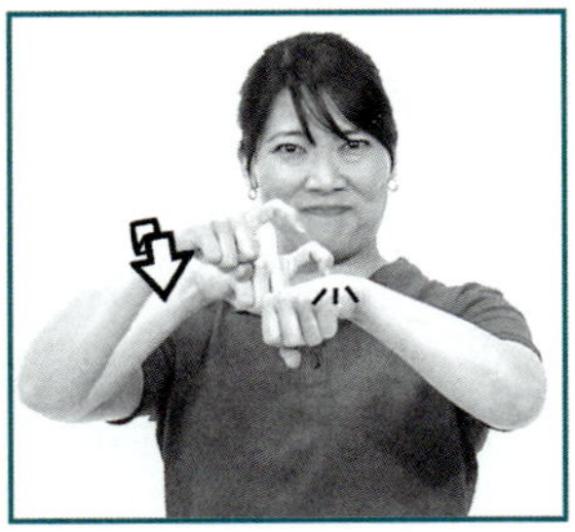
clock

View. Iva reviews the differences among the four number types for the numbers 11, 13, 15, 20 and 30.

The Number 11

cardinal: 11
age: 11 years old
year: 2011 (20 and 11 are not repeated)
clock: 7:11 (sideways movement)

The Number 13

cardinal: 13
age: 13 years old
year: 2013 (20 and 13 are not repeated)
clock: 8:13 (sideways movement)

The Number 15

cardinal: 15
year: 2015 (20 and 15 are not repeated)
clock: 6:15 (sideways movement)
age: 15 years old

The Number 20

cardinal: 20
age: 20 years old
year: 2020 (20 is not repeated)
clock: 9:20 (sideways movement)

The Number 30

cardinal: 30
age: 30 years old
year: 1930 (30 is not repeated)
clock: 1:30 (sideways movement)

Rehearse the number form and movement associated with each type of number, particularly clock numbers. Be prepared to demonstrate them in class.

Assignment

FIVE QUESTIONS

Come up with five questions that ask what time. Rehearse signing the questions. Pay attention to the structure of the question. Remember to name the activity, then ask what time at the end. Don't forget to furrow your brows and lean your head forward with the question.

VOCABULARY REVIEW

Review the vocabulary on the video.

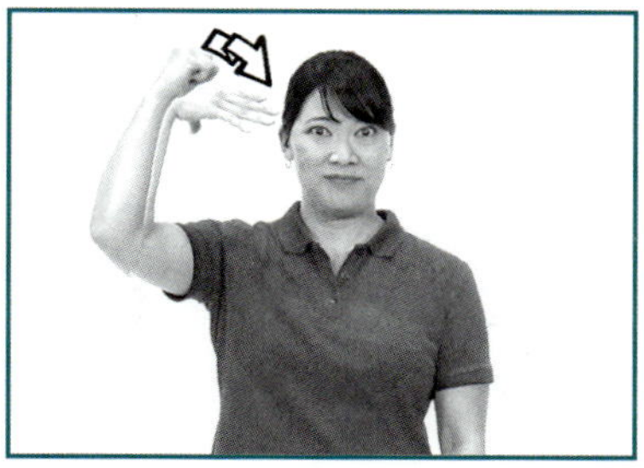

1. to take a shower

2. to brush teeth

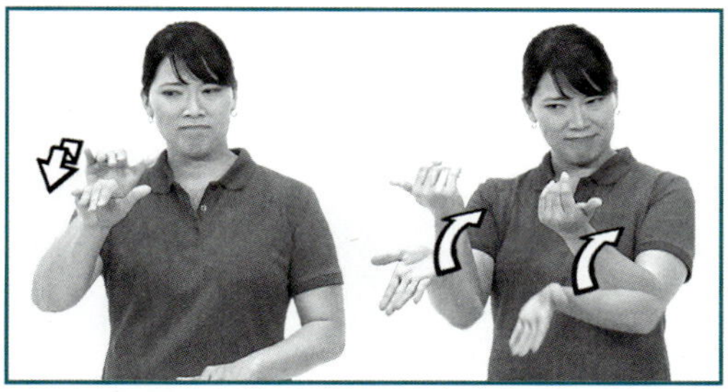

3. to awaken someone

4. to get dressed

5. to take a bath

Homework 9:10

SUGGESTING A PLACE TO EAT

Watch the three video conversations and answer the questions below.

Minidialogue 1

1. Who does Suzanne want to take out to eat?

2. Describe each restaurant.

Amber's recommendation

Restaurant's name ______________________________

Information given:

Drawback:

Lauren's recommendation

Restaurant's name ______________________________

Information given:

Drawback:

3. Why does Lauren think Amber's recommendation is not ideal?

4. Which restaurant does Suzanne decide on? Why?

5. Why does Amber disagree with Suzanne's choice of restaurant?

New Signs

overnight; all night long

hot dog

worth it; worth your time

crowded or popular; constantly packed

to feel full

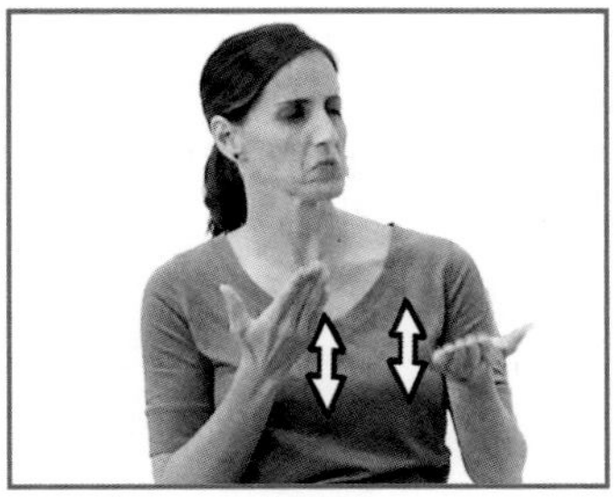
maybe; probably

sign used to disagree with the choice made

same old thing; too common

Minidialogue 2

1. Who does Justin want to take out and why?

2. Describe each restaurant.

   Amber's recommendation

   Restaurant's name ________________________________

   Information given:

   Drawback:

   Suzanne's recommendation

   Restaurant's name ________________________________

   Information given:

   Drawback:

3. Which restaurant does Justin really want? Why? Why does he end up picking the other restaurant?

4. What problem does Suzanne have with Amber's restaurant suggestion?

5. How does Justin defend his decision?

New Signs

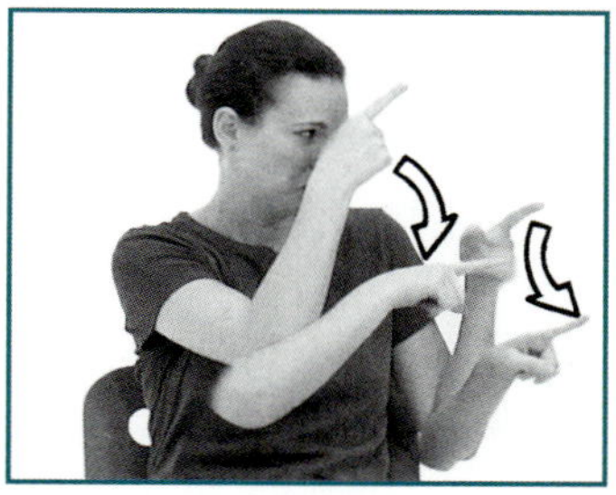
to agree with; to concur with

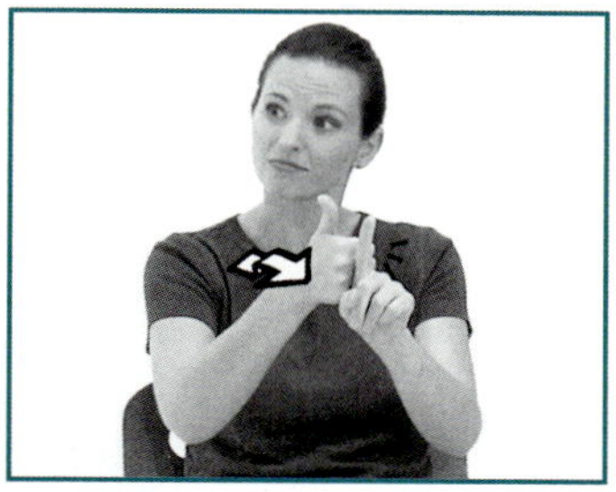
itself

duck

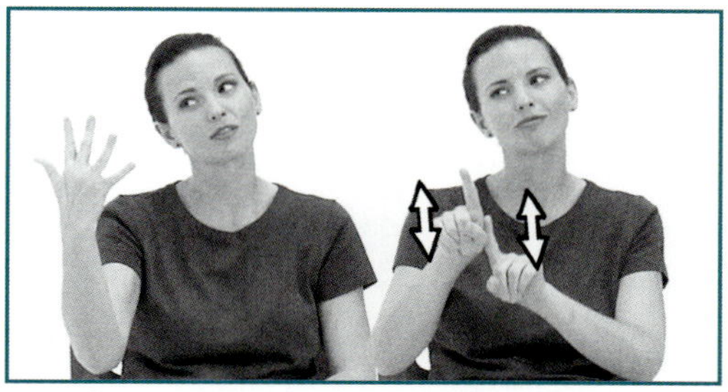
rated 5 stars

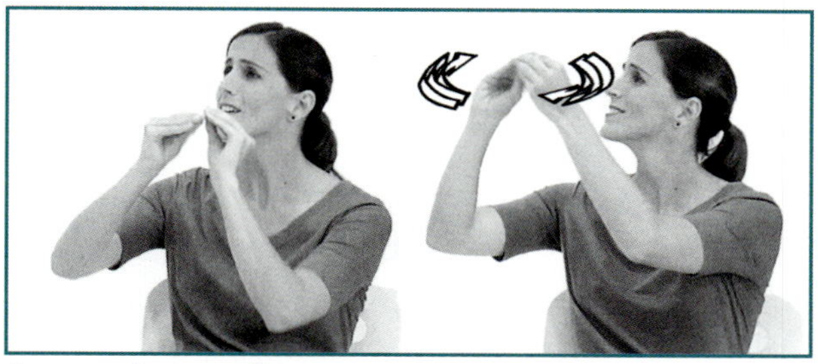
decorations; adornments; trimmings

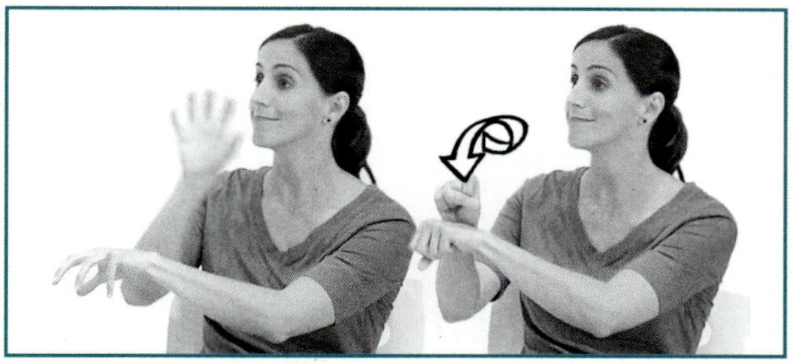
to make a reservation

famous, well-known, prominent

gaze in each other's eyes

Minidialogue 3

1. Who does Melvin want to take out and why?

2. Describe each restaurant.

   Justin's recommendation
   Restaurant's name ______________________________
   Information given:

   Drawback:

   JT's recommendation
   Restaurant's name ______________________________
   Information given:

   Drawback:

3. Which restaurant does Melvin decide on? Why?

4. How does Melvin respond to Justin's concern about missing the sunset?

Answers given in class.

New Signs

to think over;
to mull over

prior to

comfortable; cozy

fireplace; hearth

not of this country;
foreign

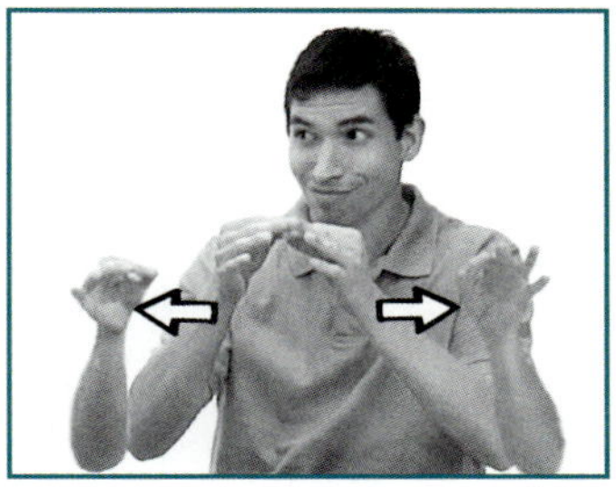

captions, subtitles

to miss out on something
or on an opportunity

VOCABULARY REVIEW

Review the vocabulary on the video.

Recommending

1. to suggest or
recommend (a place)

Explaining a Drawback

2. phrase used to caution about a possible
downside or drawback; to warn

Homework 9:11

GIVING DIRECTIONS: PERSPECTIVE SHIFT

Directions to Fire Station

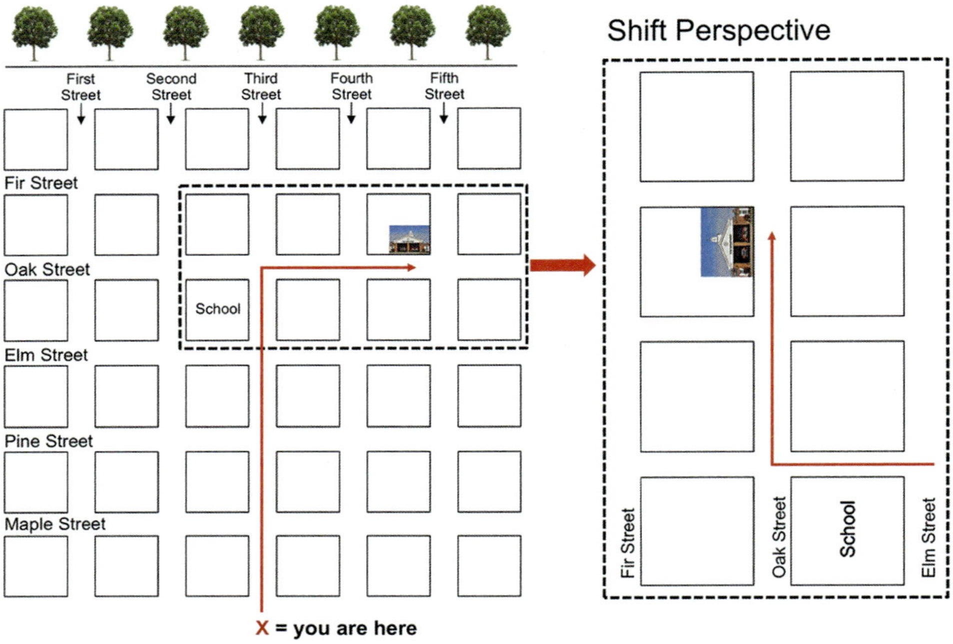

looking down 3rd Street

looking down Oak Street

Give directions from the point of view of looking down a street as if it were in front of you. When you describe a turn, you must shift your perspective and continue the directions as if that street is directly in front of you.

For directions to the fire station indicated on the map above, begin the directions by looking down Third Street, and at Oak Street "shift" your view with the turn and look down Oak Street to complete the directions.

Perspective Shift 1

David tells where ABC Liquor is located. After indicating where to turn, he shifts perspective to complete the directions.

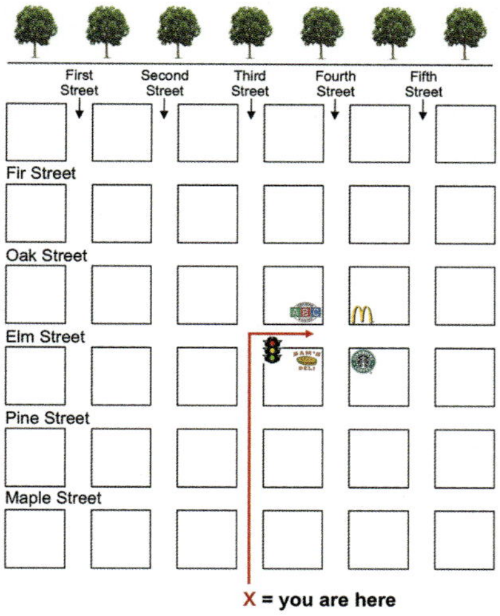

Notice David uses a "when" clause (raised brows) when telling to turn at the traffic light.

Perspective Shift 2

David tells where the police station is located. After indicating where to turn, he shifts perspective to complete the directions.

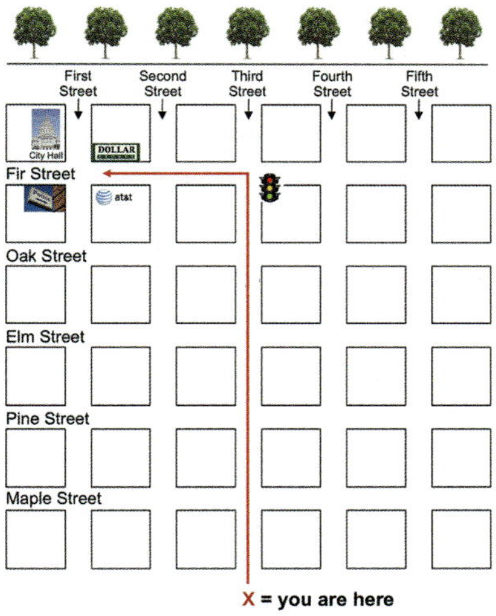

Notice David uses a "when" clause (raised brows) when telling to turn at the traffic light and also when naming the cross street (Fir).

Locations 1–10

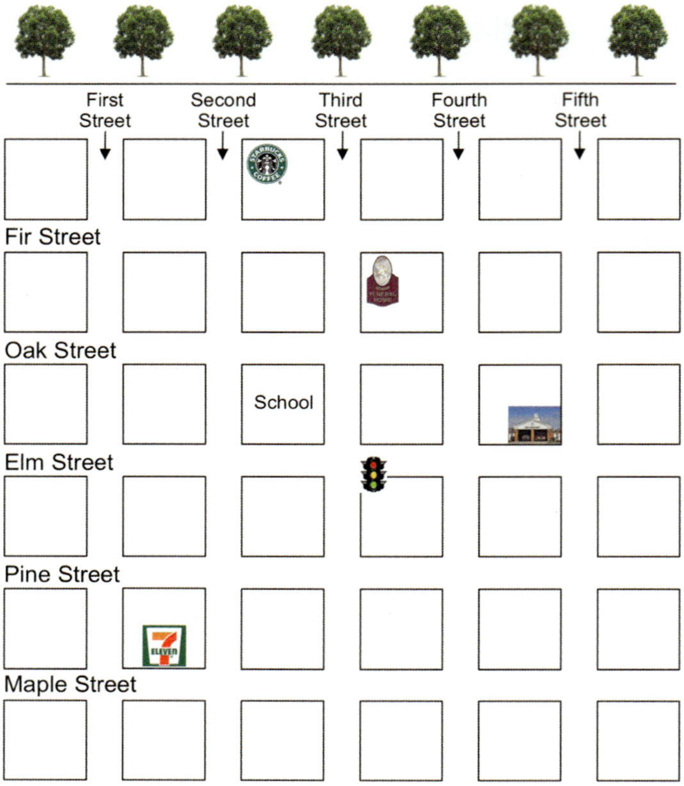

X = you are here

Signers will tell you where to go to find a store or place. For each business named, write the number in the location on the map above. Then, in the corresponding blanks below, write in the name of the business and the reason for going there.

name of business *reason for going*

Location 1. ____________________ ______________________________

New Signs

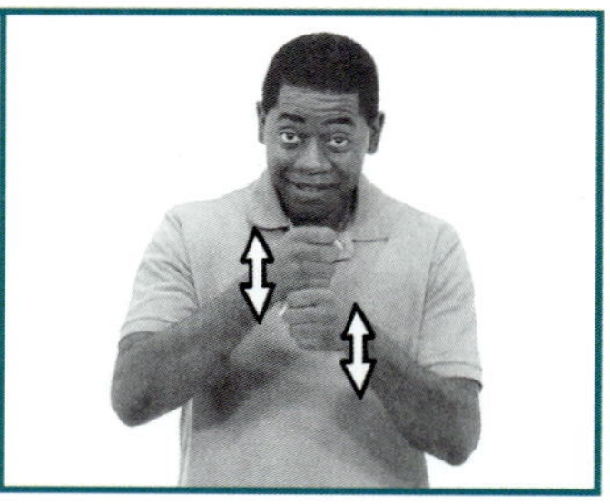

Location 2. ____________________ ______________________________

Location 3. ____________________ ______________________________

Location 4. ____________________ ______________________________

Location 5. ____________________ ______________________________

New Signs

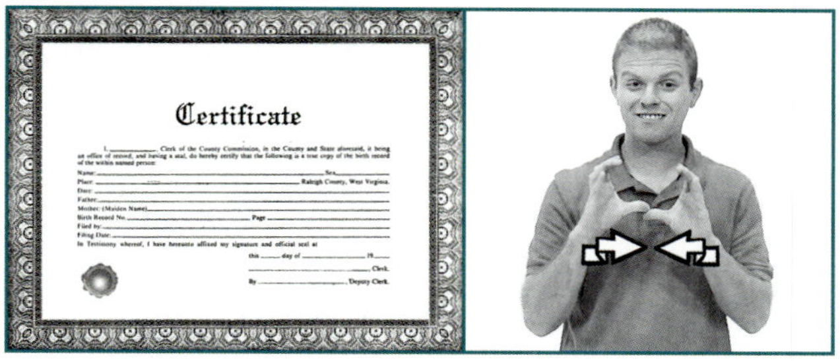

Location 6. ____________________ ______________________________

New Sign

supply of electric current to a building for lighting or heating

Location 7. ____________________ ______________________________

Location 8. ____________________ ______________________________

New Signs

driving at a speed above the legal limit; speeding

Location 9. ________________ ________________________

New Sign

having no space left; to be full

Location 10. ________________ ________________________

New Sign

far; a long way from here

Answers on page 518.

Homework 9:12

YES–NO QUESTIONS 2

Underline the topic of each question.

1. Do you like meeting new people?
2. Do you like foreign films?
3. Have you ever tried eating raw fish?
4. Have you ever experienced raising a rabbit?
5. Do you write poetry?
6. Do you know how to scan pictures into the computer?
7. Can you cross your eyes?
8. Have you ever tried snowboarding?
9. Can you name three famous painters (artists)?

View. Watch Suzanne follow the sequence below to sign translations of the questions above.

- establish time if specified (raise brows)
- establish location if specified (raise brows)
- name the topic (raise brows)
- end with a question (raise brows, tilt head forward, hold last sign)

Practice the questions, focusing on both the structure and the facial grammar.

Assignment

FIVE NEW QUESTIONS

Now, pick five questions from above and change the topic to make new questions. For example, for Question 1:

> ***original:*** Do you like meeting new people?
> ***new:*** Do you like tasting different foods?

Rehearse signing your new questions. Be prepared to sign them in class.

VOCABULARY REVIEW

Review the vocabulary on the video.

1. mingling with many people

2. new

3. people; human beings

4. from another country; foreign

5. to take care of; tend to

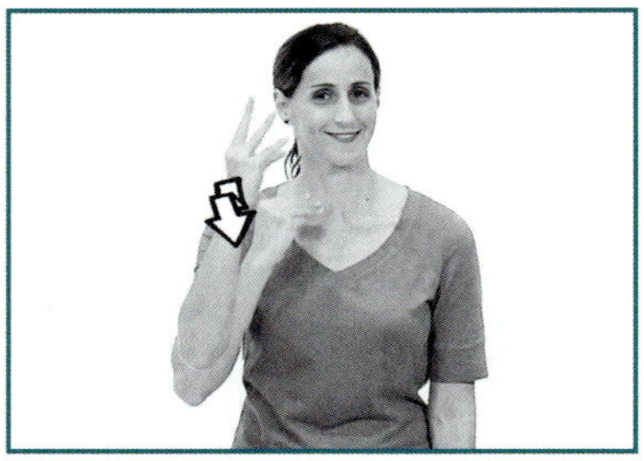

6. to experience

7.

or

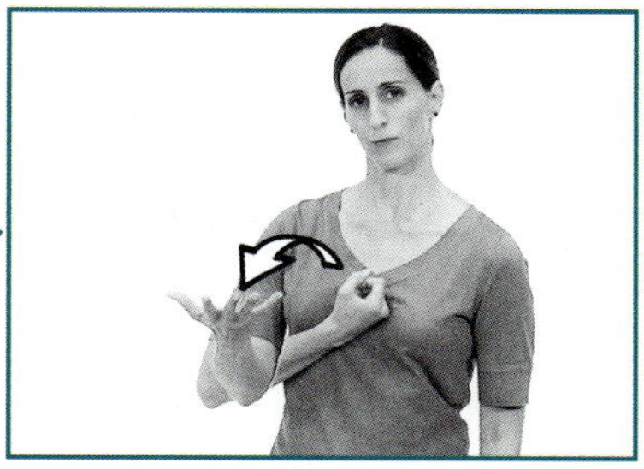

8. written or spoken poetry; signed poetry

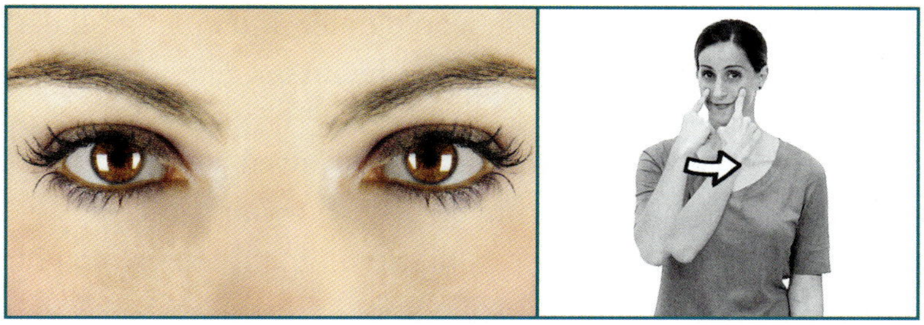

9.

10.

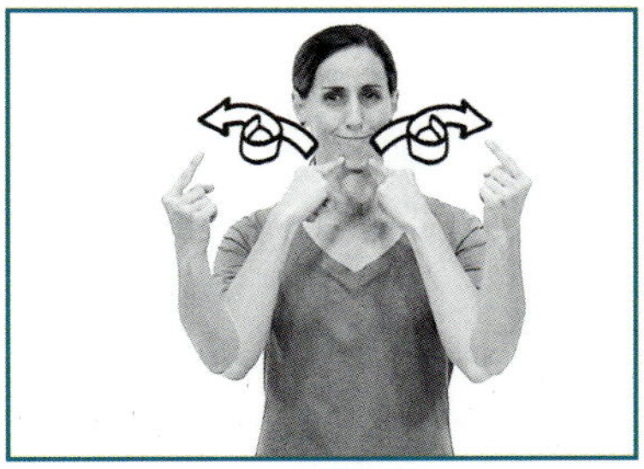

11. famous, well-known, prominent

12. to name or identify by name

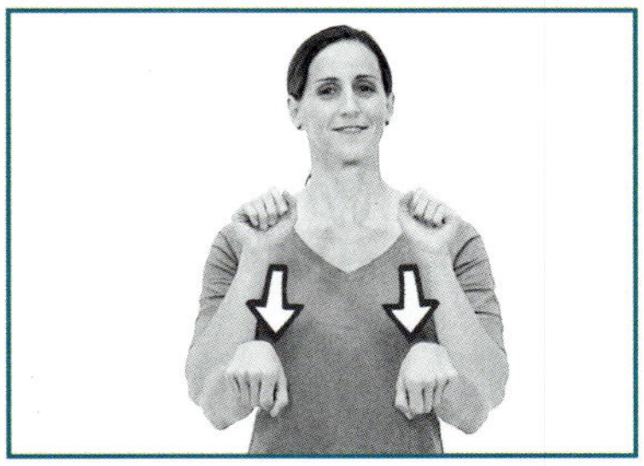

13. able to; can

Homework 9:13

CULTURAL

KEEPING OTHERS INFORMED

If you were late to your history class, what would you do when you entered the classroom? Most people would enter and quietly take a seat. That would be considered courteous behavior.

In an ASL class, however, that would not be viewed as courteous. In an ASL classroom, upon entering quietly you wait until the teacher acknowledges you, then you take a moment to explain your lateness before taking your seat. Explanations should not to be viewed as giving excuses but rather viewed as appropriate sharing of information.

Why is this? Deaf people have a cohesive and mutually supportive community. This close-knit community encourages a greater sense of familiarity, as evidenced by the kind of and amount of information shared. Deaf people in everyday conversations share information about their day-to-day lives talking about family, friends, what they've been doing, problems they are having, community news and events, with those around them.

As you become more proficient in ASL, you will begin to appreciate how your ability to share information about yourself and your community affects how well you get to know Deaf people and how much of the their community you will experience.

Begin by developing the following information sharing habits:

- if you are late or need to leave early, inform others and include a brief explanation
- if you're leaving only for a short while, tell someone why you are leaving and when you'll be back
- if you leave a group conversation, even if you were not directly involved, someone in the group may ask about you. If you've told someone, that person is able to inform the group and the conversation will continue normally.

In this way the expected level of information sharing is maintained.

Situations 1–4

Watch these situations showing how to keep others informed.

Situation 1. Amber explains her absence from the previous class (family problem came up). Notice:

- attention getting behaviors Amber uses to get Melvin's (teacher's) attention.
- Amber walking to her seat only after getting acknowledgment from the teacher.

Situation 2. Lauren tells the teacher why she needs to leave class early (she has a doctor appointment). Notice:

- attention getting behaviors Lauren uses when approaching Melvin (teacher)
- Lauren thanking Melvin for allowing her to leave class early.

Situation 3. JT apologizes then tells the teacher why he is late to class (he overslept because the alarm was set up wrong). Notice:

- JT not wanting to interrupt Melvin (teacher) talking to the class, instead keeping his eyes on the teacher as he takes his seat, in the event Melvin notices him, he will be ready to give an explanation.

Situation 4. Suzanne explains why she cannot come to the next class (she has to attend a funeral). Notice:

- as soon as Melvin looks up, Suzanne begins her explanation.

VOCABULARY REVIEW

Review the vocabulary on the video.

1. to apologize, to say you're sorry

2. to be late

3. to miss or be absent from a class

Homework 9:14

STORY: THE HITCHHIKER

View the story **The Hitchhiker**, then answer the questions below.

1. Describe the hitchhiker.

2. Describe the driver.

3. How do the hitchhiker and the driver communicate with each other?

4. Where does the hitchhiker want to go?

5. What does the driver see in the rearview mirror?

6. Why is he pulled over?

7. How do the driver and cop communicate?

8. What do the driver and the cop say to each other?

9. What is the hitchhiker's reaction?

10. Why do the two switch places?

11. How fast is the second driver going when stopped by the policeman?

12. When the second driver is stopped by the police, what does he plan to do?

13. Why does his plan not work?

14. What does he get?

15. What can we learn from this story?

Answers given in class.

NEW SIGNS

Use these definitions to help your understanding of the story.

1. to hitchhike

2. to speak

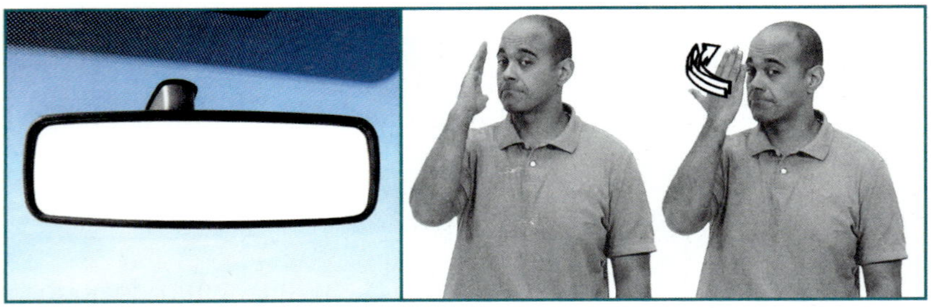

3.

4. classifier sign meaning (patrol) car following another car

5. to go very fast

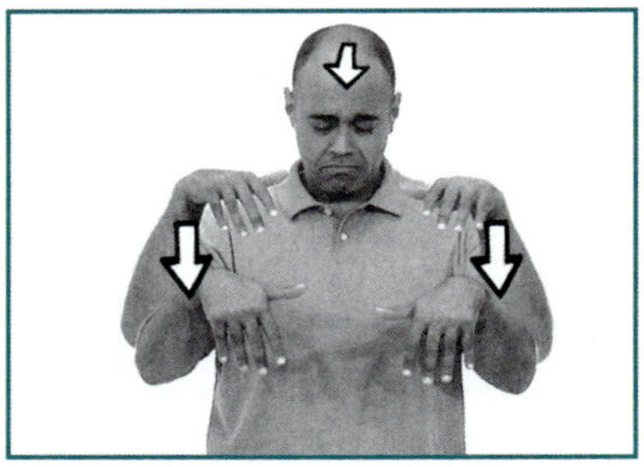

6. to be stumped; be at a loss

ERIC MALZKUHN (1922–2008)

"I was influenced by others, influenced others, who will go on to influence still others, and that will continue."

Eric Malzkuhn was a celebrated teacher, storyteller, playwright, poet and sign master who made a lasting mark on the Deaf community.

Eric "Malz" Malzkuhn was born in Vallejo, California. Malz became Deaf from spinal meningitis at the age of 10. He quickly embraced the Deaf community as his home, and ASL as his language.

Malz was a gifted writer, becoming editor of the student paper at the California School for the Deaf, Berkeley (now Fremont) in the 8th grade. Over the summers, he wrote sports columns for a local daily and was paid $.10 for each inch of print, good money during the Great Depression. Later, he wrote for the Buff and Blue during his time at Gallaudet University.

Malz said that in many ways his years at Gallaudet were the best years of his life. He was a passionate participant in school activities and events. He was the team manager for the legendary basketball team the "Five Iron Men,"[1] and an active member of the Gallaudet Dramatics Club. During this time, he developed the now famous ASL translation of Carroll Lewis's classic poem "Jabberwocky" and he brought an ASL version of "Arsenic and Old Lace" onto Broadway.

In an interview with Malz, he said his translation of Jabberwocky "changed [that type] of signing overnight." Malz had broken away from the traditional style of signed poetry, which was usually a literal translation of the original poem with very little expression. In translating Lewis Carroll's nonsense poem, Malz invented a succession of "nonsense" animal signs that incorporated the use of his whole body, and intense facial expressions. He presented Jabberwocky at the annual poetry contest and even though he took second place, the performance inspired Deaf poets to explore and express the poetic capacity of ASL.

---

[1] To read more about the "Five Iron Men," see page 68.

Another historical success came when a 19-year-old Malz convinced the producers of "Arsenic and Old Lace," then playing on Broadway to allow the Gallaudet Dramatics Club perform the play with the "best sign language actors in the world." So, for one night in May 1942, Gallaudet performers walked the boards on Broadway using the same stage and even some costumes from the Broadway show. Even though Malz had translated, directed, and acted in many plays over the years, this one was his most memorable.

After graduating from Gallaudet, Malz was a teacher at the Michigan School for the Deaf. Eventually he left teaching and worked in printing for over a decade. During this time he contracted polio. He had to learn everything again, even walking. He moved back to California to avoid harsh winters and slippery ice. While working a union job as a printer in his hometown, he decided he wanted to teach again. He spent several happy years teaching at the California School for the Deaf in Berkeley before moving east to accept a full time English and Drama teaching position at the Model Secondary School for the Deaf (MSSD) in Washington, D.C., where he stayed for 18 years, eventually retiring in 1988.

While Malz's many accomplishments are too vast to include here, some that should be mentioned are encouraging Andrew J. Foster[2] to apply to Gallaudet, where Foster became the first Black Deaf graduate. Another enduring contribution happened when Malz collaborated with others to translate and adapt classical works of poetry for the National Theatre of the Deaf's first national tour.

Malz listed three awards of his many honors as most dear to him: being named to the Gallaudet Sports Hall of Fame for sports writing, being awarded the degree of Doctor of Fine Arts from Gallaudet, and having the MSSD theatre renamed "Theatre Malz" in his honor.

Malz was always interested in new challenges and ended up breaking through many barriers. While he acknowledged that he influenced many others during his long career, he said "I was influenced by others, influenced others, who will go on to influence still others, and that will continue."

---

[2] To read more about Andrew Foster, see pages 14–15 in *Signing Naturally Student Workbook* Units 1–6.

INSIGHT

What does it take to learn a language well?

Language is a complex communication system governed by the culture of its users. So it is not enough to learn words and phrases and a set of rules. Language learning takes time and the less similar the language is to your native language, the more time it takes. In a typical semester course in college, you have fewer than 100 hours of contact with the language. In U.S. government language schools, where languages are taught for real proficiency, none of the courses meet for less than 600 hours of full time study.

After puberty it becomes more difficult to achieve fluency when learning another language. Most of us need classroom work to create a framework for figuring out how the language works and the cultural context. Adults that pick up language without this framework often end up with a kind of skewed fluency—a lot of words but typically mangled grammar and not much sensitivity to how the words are used. So you need the classroom but in and of itself, it is not enough! You also need prolonged contact with people that speak the language. You can achieve this by signing more outside the classroom with more advanced students, setting up regular study groups, attending ASL immersion weekends or camps, attending community sponsored events like ASL Coffee Social, making Deaf friends or chatting with native signers over the internet.

Without the contact, and without passing the threshold of confidence and comfort with the language, what you learn in class will probably fade away. But, once you cross the threshold, like learning to ride a bike, the language will be with you a long, long, time.

Unit 9 Review: Self-Assessment

Write the number of: classes you missed: _____
homework assignments not completed for class: ____
hours you practiced/used signs outside of the classroom per week: _____

Now that you are done with this unit, rate yourself using the list below: **5** indicates feeling the most comfortable and confident about your skill in that area and **1** indicates feeling the least confident.

NOTE: If you marked **3** or lower, you should review that portion of the workbook and write down steps you plan to take to improve your skills in that area.

1. I can describe my neighborhood by following the narrative structure and using rhetorical questions as transitions.	5	4	3	2	1
2. I can tell time using clock number patterns.	5	4	3	2	1
3. I can give directions to a location in the neighborhood by using horizontal map orientation, reference points and perspective shifts.	5	4	3	2	1
4. I know the word order to follow when translating yes-no questions.	5	4	3	2	1
5. I can describe a restaurant using descriptive, locative and element classifiers, use listing skills to name the foods served, and give opinions about the food and cost.	5	4	3	2	1
6. When asked for advice, I can suggest a place to eat and name a potential drawback for that place.	5	4	3	2	1
7. I understand the role of "information sharing" in the culture and how to share with the teacher about my absence, tardiness or leaving early.	5	4	3	2	1
8. When viewing **The Hitchhiker**, I'm able to figure out the meaning of what is signed even though I don't know every sign used.	5	4	3	2	1

Steps I will take: ______________________________

____

Spirtuality of De'VIA
Ellen Mansfield

Ceramic
21" round
2012

UNIT 10

Giving Opinions About Others

Homework 10:1

CONVERSATION 1

JT (A) and Justin (B) demonstrate this dialogue in which they discuss their school work.

A: tell about your tendency, ask if it is the same for B
B: respond
- **affirm, tell that it is the same for you**
- **negate, tell how you are different**

Key Grammar

TEMPORAL ASPECT

To explain a person's tendency or habit in English, the present simple tense is used, and often adverbs are added to show the frequency. For example, in these sentences, "Pat showers twice daily," and, "Pat always cries at sad movies," the adverbs "twice daily" and "always" are added to indicate the actions are a habit or tendency. However, in ASL, to explain a person's tendency or habit, the movement of the verb (or predicate) is modified, usually by repeating the movement. When the movement is modified it indicates that a habit or behavior is continually or regularly done. This is called temporal aspect. For example, if you want to say a person is always punctual, you would use the sign for "on time" and repeat the sign's movement to indicate the person is "always on time" (see below).

"on time"
(single movement)

"always on time"
(repeated movement)

When rehearsing this lesson's vocabulary, pay attention to whether or not the movement of the sign is repeated.

Certain facial expressions add meaning to the sign and helps convey more specifically the attitude and intention of the person described. For example, the facial expression in the picture above adds the idea that the person described is also serious about being consistently punctual.

View. Watch how JT and Justin use temporal aspect to describe their tendencies that resulted in JT getting an A and Justin getting a B. Notice how their facial expressions add information to the tendencies described.

facial expression: serious

facial expression: focused

facial expression: neutral

facial expression: not focused

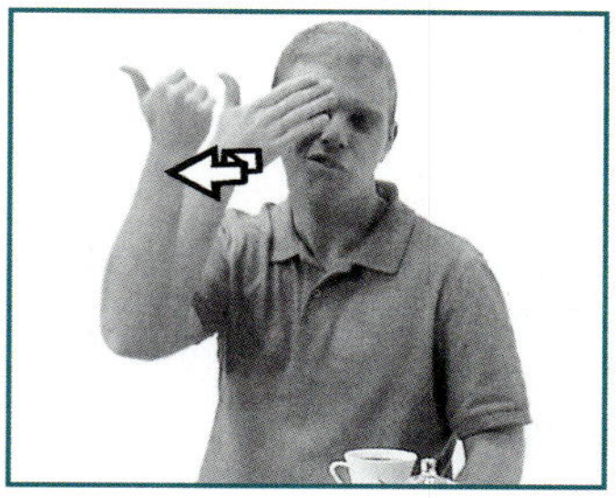

facial expression: careless, irresponsible

MINIDIALOGUES

Minidialogue 1

1. Why does John suggest to David they trade roommates?

2. Why do you think David responds the way he does?

Minidialogue 2

1. What is it about their bosses that causes Ursula to suggest she and Tonique find a new job?

2. What other complaint about their jobs is implied at the end of the conversation?

New Sign

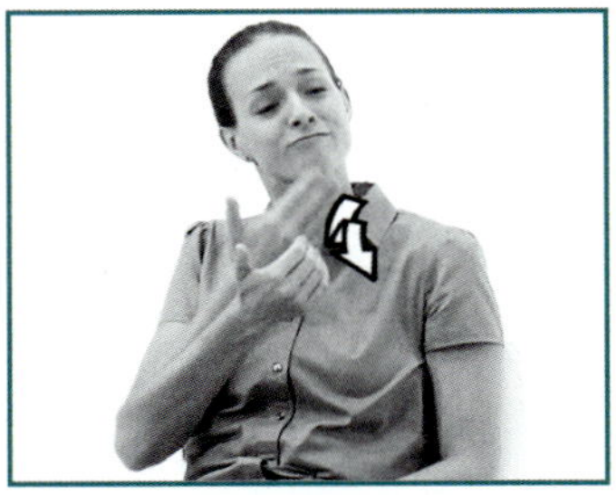

to be kind; sweet; nice

Minidialogue 3

1. Describe David and Iva's children.

   David's son ***Iva's son***

2. Compare the children's teachers.

New Signs

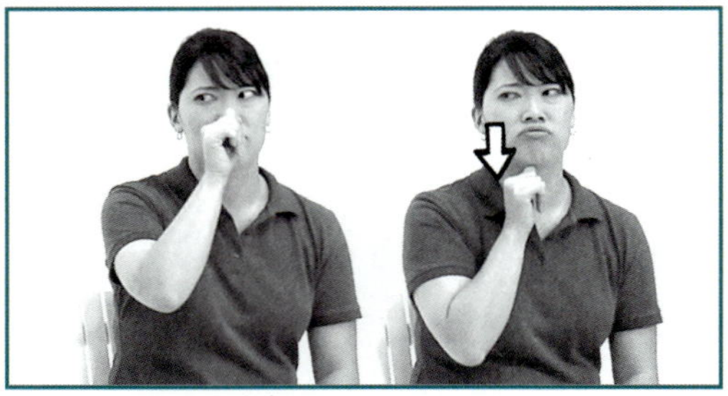

uncomplaining; patient

to be enthusiastic, eager, or excited

to truly like or enjoy

Answers given in class.

GIVE THE OPPOSITE 1–15

Melvin and Terrylene will give a sign and ask what is the opposite. After a pause of a few seconds, they will give the opposite sign so you can confirm your answer.

Assignment

DEFINE THESE WORDS

For next class, you are to define these English words.

1. cautious
2. unreliable
3. friendly
4. trustworthy
5. tidy
6. bashful

Strategies to use:

- explain the meaning of the word by using signs you have learned
- use opposite signs to emphasize what it is not
- describe behavior and situation to illustrate the tendency.

VOCABULARY REVIEW

Review the vocabulary on the video.

Punctuality

Being on Time

1. to be punctual; always on time

2. to always be late

Attendance

3. to attend regularly

4. to intentionally miss class or work

Approach to Work

Hardworking (Diligent)

5. to be hard-working or diligent

6. to play around; not working hard; goof off

Completion of Tasks

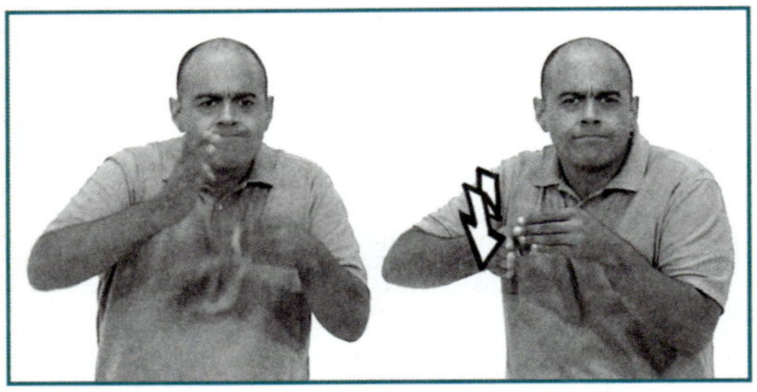

7. to complete tasks in a timely manner

8. to procrastinate; to put off tasks until the last minute

Focused

9. to pay close attention; attentive

10. to not pay attention; be unfocused

Level of Accountability

Responsibility

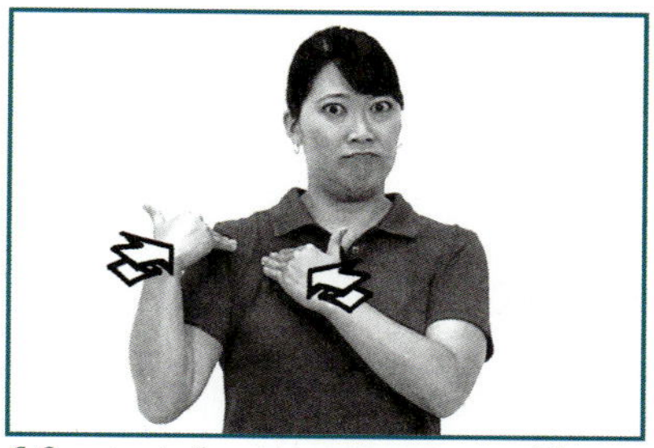

11. to take it upon oneself to complete tasks, follow instructions, and meet deadlines; to be responsible

12. not being responsible

Carefulness

13. to give careful attention; be careful

14. to be unconcerned or careless

Organized or Orderly

15. to be well-organized or efficient

16. to be untidy, disorganized, or messy

Money Matters

17. to be good with money management

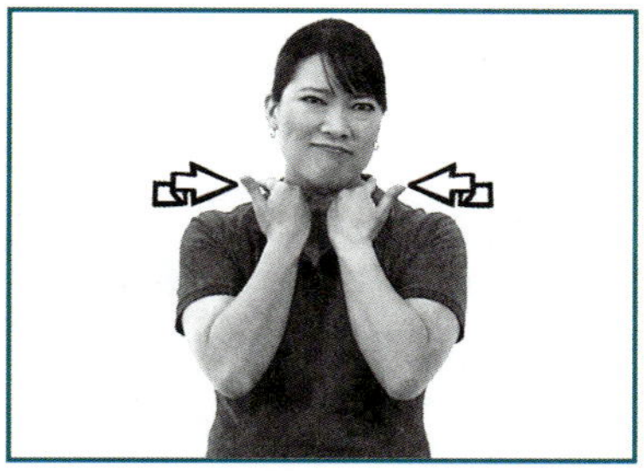

18. to be often run out of money; constantly be broke

Relating to Others

Extrovert or Introvert

19. to be gregarious; to enjoy meeting people

20. having a quiet nature; not talkative

21. being timid around other people: bashful; shy

Supportive

22. to be supportive or reassuring

23. to find fault with someone; to criticize

Encouraging

24. to be encouraging or supportive

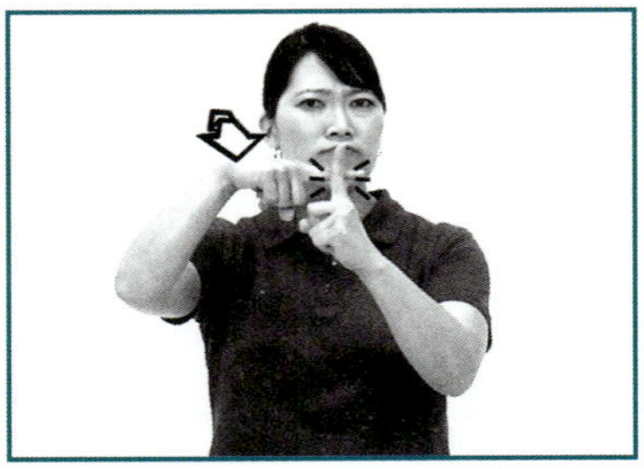

25. to have a positive attitude; to say positive things about others

26. to speak to (someone) with disrespect; to insult

27. having a negative attitude; pessimistic

Honesty

28. to be honest; to be trustworthy

29. to be dishonest; to have a tendency to lie

Directness

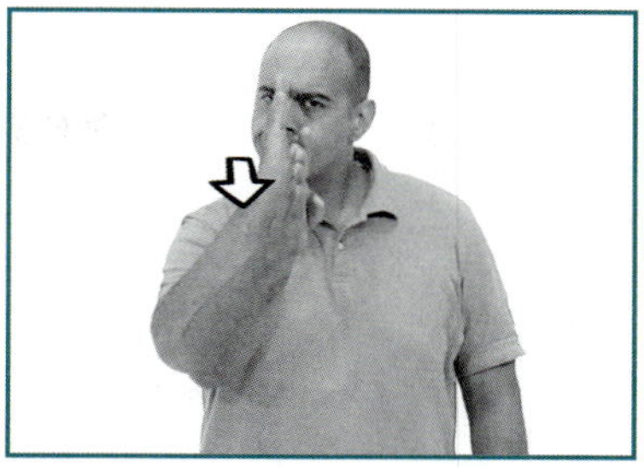

30. to be straightforward; to be frank; to be candid

31. to talk in a vague way; to be indirect

Amiable or Agreeable

32. to get along with others easily; affable

33. to be accommodating; to be receptive to others; to be agreeable

34. to complain or gripe about something

35. to disagree, quarrel or argue with someone

Sharing

36. to be willing to give or share with others; to be unselfish

37. to be concerned primarily with one's own needs, interest, welfare; to be selfish

Respect One's Privacy

or

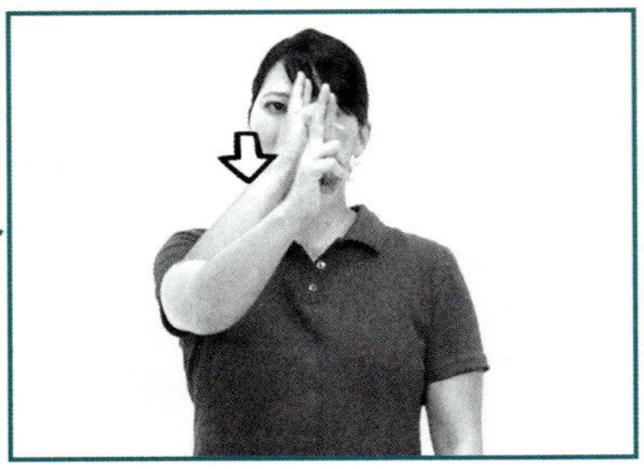

38. to show deference and respect

39. to butt in; to be nosy

Respect One's Things

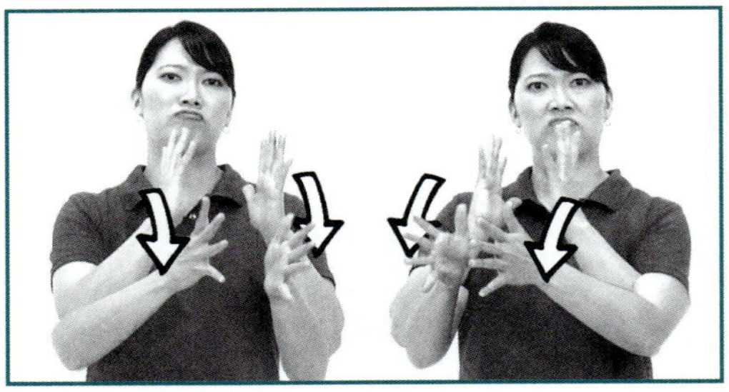

40. to show respect for other's personal belongings by not touching or using them

41. to use, handle or touch another's things without permission

Others

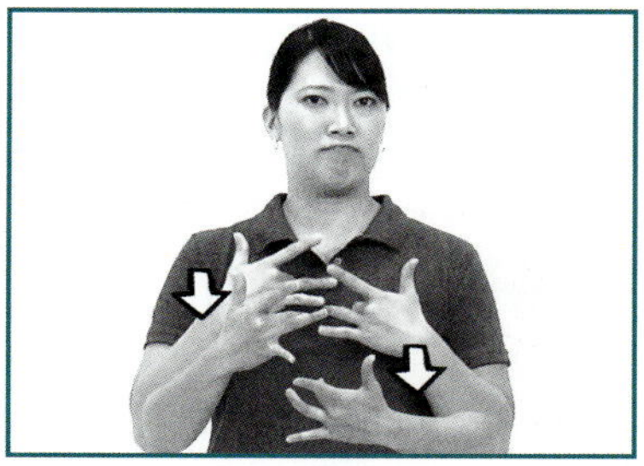

42. have a tendency to

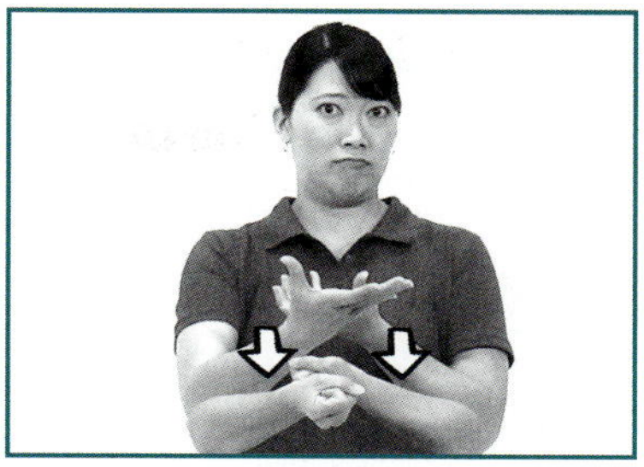

43. to believe that someone is honest or reliable; to trust someone

44. to avoid or evade tasks

45. to shirk responsibility or involvement

46. to be very clean or neat

47. not fussy or strict; to be lax

48. to socialize; to mingle

Homework 10:2

TELLING THE PRICE 1

Cents

When giving the cost of something in cents, the number is incorporated with the sign for cent. The cent sign starts with either the tip or the side of the index finger contacting the forehead and moves outward.

1–5 Cents

Iva demonstrates the forms for 1–5 cents. Notice the handshape for the number is formed at the forehead with the palm facing in and remains the same as the hand moves outward.

5 cents

6–9 Cents

Iva demonstrates the forms for 6–9 cents. Notice the handshape for the number is formed with the palm facing out and remains the same as the hand moves outward. For 9 cents, the handshape for the number is modified at the beginning in order for the side of the index finger to contact the forehead.

7 cents

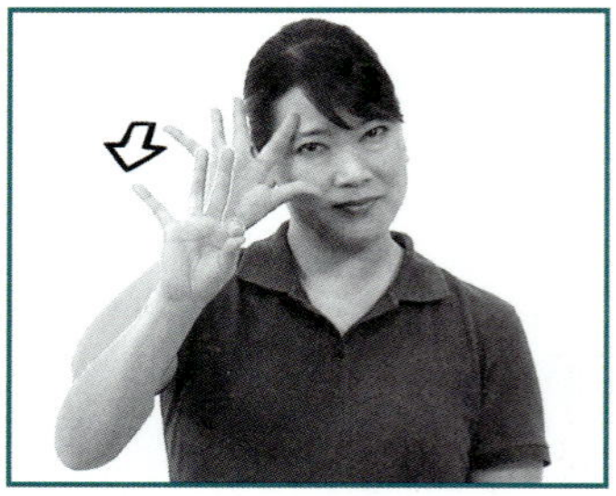

9 cents

10–15 Cents

Iva demonstrates the forms for 10–15 cents. Notice for 10 cents, the "L" handshape begins at the forehead with the palm facing in, and ends with the number 10 as the hand moves outward. Notice for 11–15 cents, the tips of the fingers that form the numbers 11–15 touch the forehead.

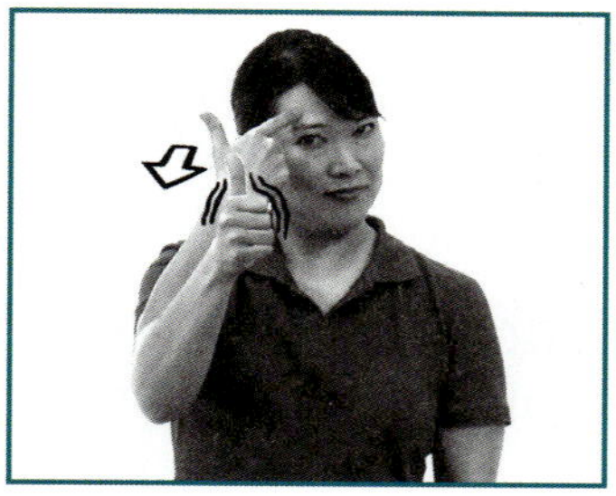
10 cents

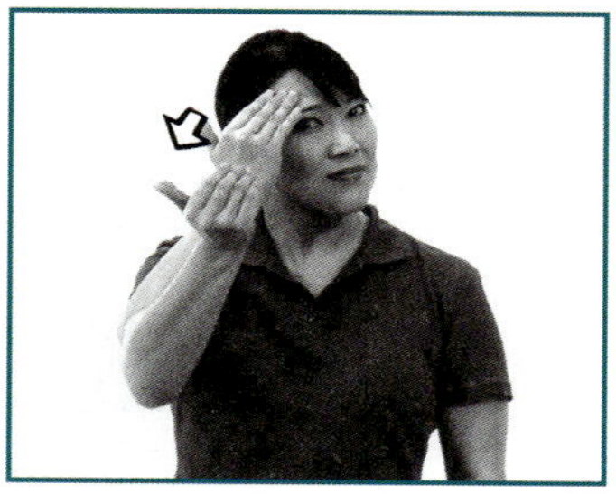
15 cents

16–19 Cents

Iva demonstrates the forms for 16–19 cents. Notice the "L" handshape begins at the forehead with the palm facing in. Then, the hand twists and ends with the palm facing out to form the number 16–19.

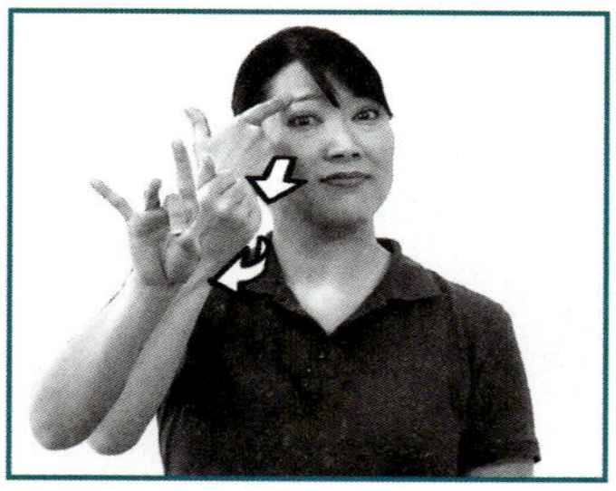
18 cents

20–25 Cents

Iva demonstrates the forms for 20–25 cents. Notice the "L" handshape begins at the forehead with the palm facing out and the hand moves outward to form the number 20–25. For 22 cents, the "2" handshape is used at the beginning.

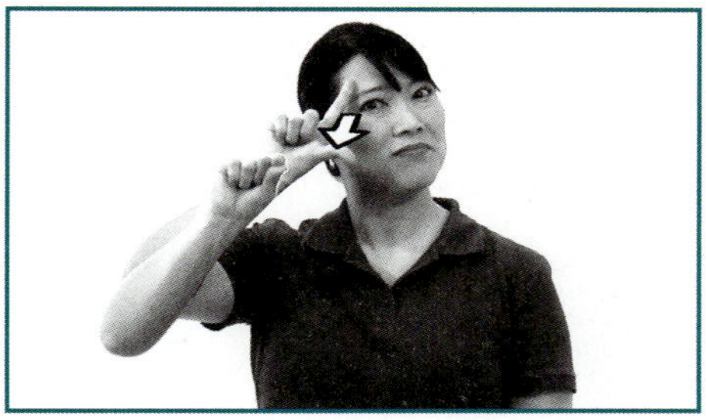
20 cents (number 20 is repeated)

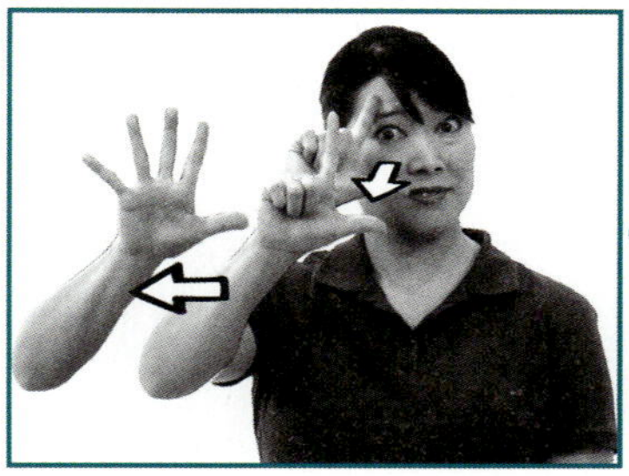
25 cents

or

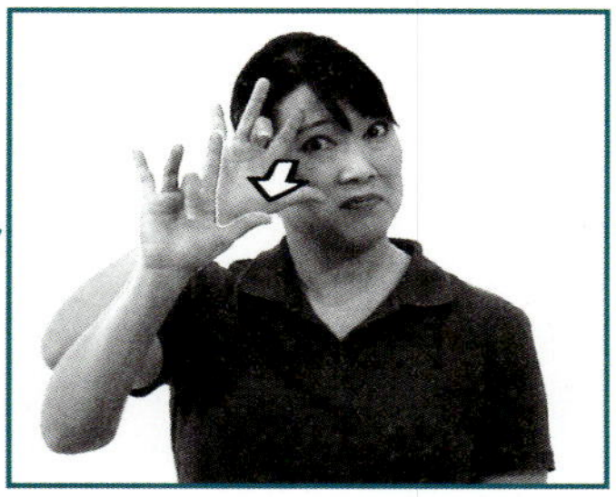
25 cents

For 26–99 cents, follow the same principles. Remember:

- for multiples of 10, the extended fingers and thumb for the numbers 30, 40, and 50 cents close repeatedly. For numbers 60, 70, 80 and 90 cents, the thumb and pinkly fingers remain in contact while the extended fingers close repeatedly.
- for "rocking numbers," the smaller number twists up to the larger number for 67–89 cents and the larger number twists down to the smaller number for 76–98 cents.

Dollars

When telling the cost of something in dollars, the number is given followed by the sign for dollar. However, for $1–9, a twisting movement is added to the number and the sign for dollar is not needed.

1–10 Dollars

Iva demonstrates the forms for 1–10 dollars.

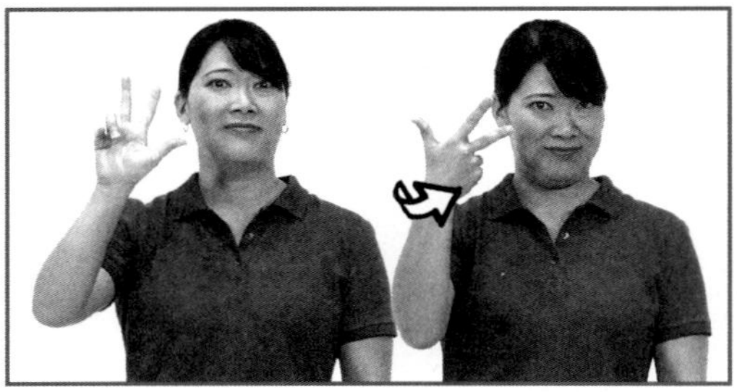

3 dollars

For dollars 1–9, the handshape for the number is formed with the palm facing out and remains the same as the hand twists in a sweeping arc, ending with the palm facing in.

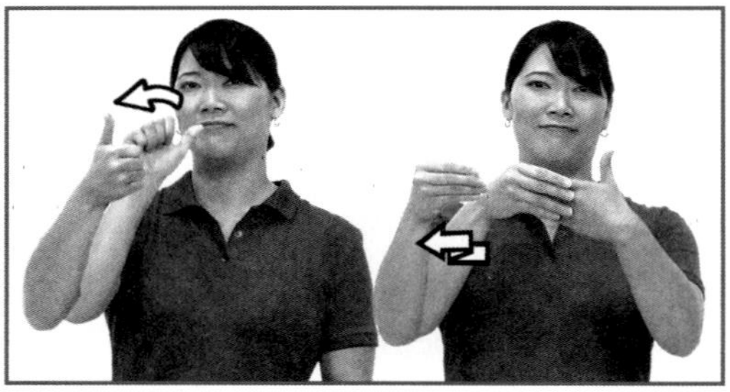

10 dollars

For 10 dollars, the number is formed with a single movement and ends with the sign for dollar.

WRITE THE AMOUNT

Write the money amount Iva gives.

1.	______	13.	______
2.	______	14.	______
3.	______	15.	______
4.	______	16.	______
5.	______	17.	______
6.	______	18.	______
7.	______	19.	______
8.	______	20.	______
9.	______	21.	______
10.	______	22.	______
11.	______	23.	______
12.	______	24.	______

Answers on page 519.

Challenge Yourself

After you correct your answers, go back and practice signing the numbers by replaying the video and signing along or you can film yourself and compare your number forms with Iva's.

HOW MUCH

Ursula, John, Derrick, Terrylene, Melvin and Amber describe an item, then give its price. Write the information in the blanks below.

	Item	*Amount*		*Item*	*Amount*
1.	______	______	7.	______	______
2.	______	______	8.	______	______
3.	______	______	9.	______	______
4.	______	______	10.	______	______
5.	______	______	11.	______	______
6.	______	______	12.	______	______

Answers given in class.

VOCABULARY REVIEW

Review the vocabulary on the video.

1.

2.

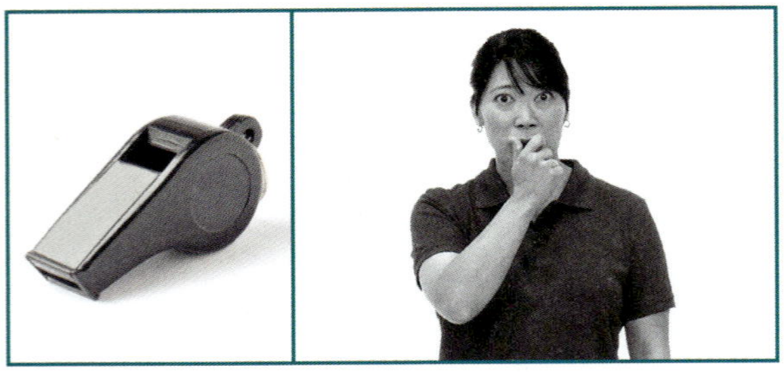

3.

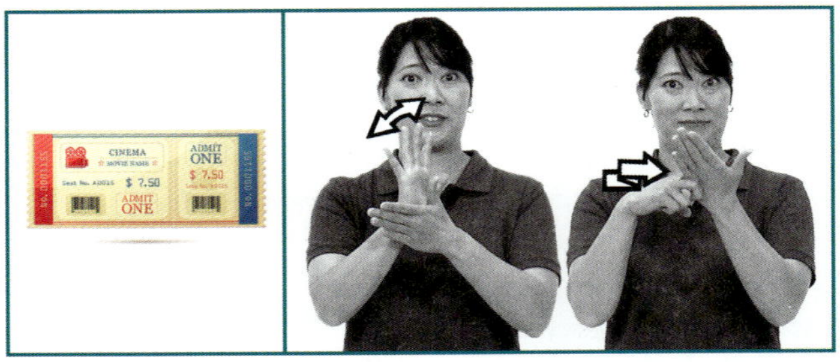

4.

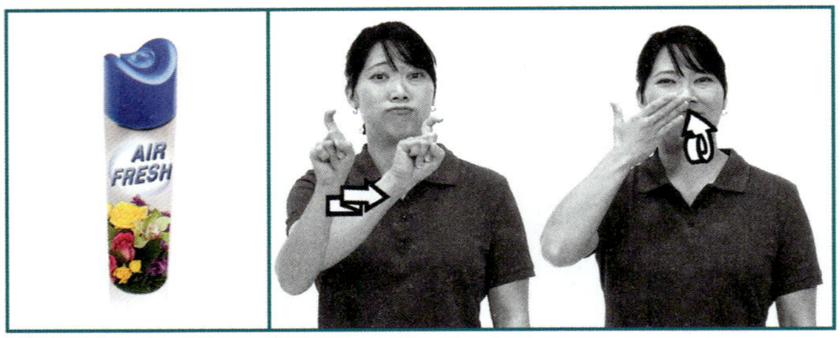

5.

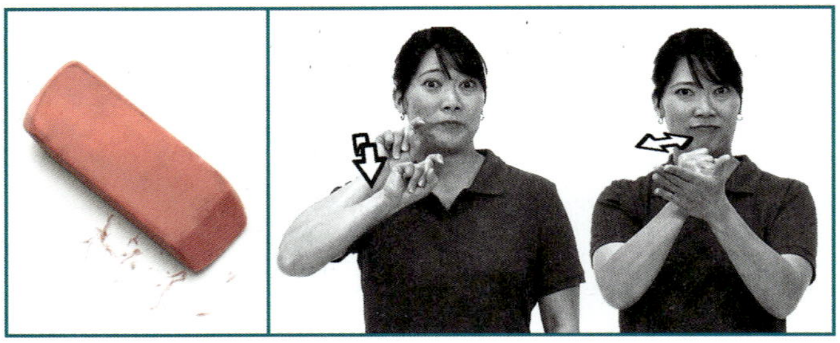

6.

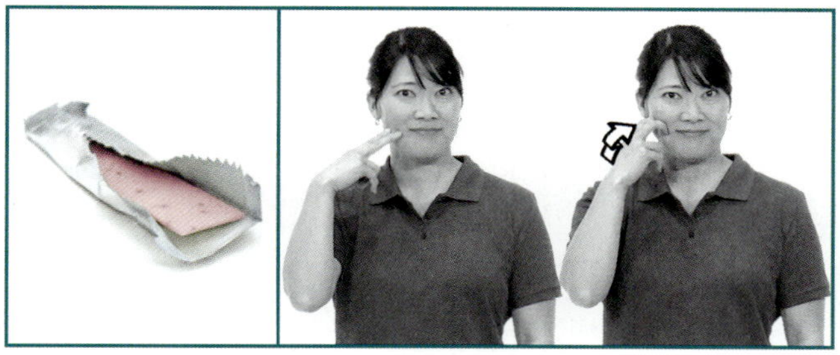

7.

8.

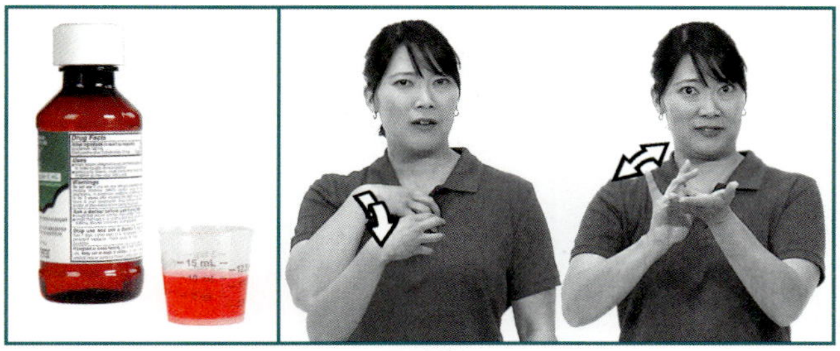

9.

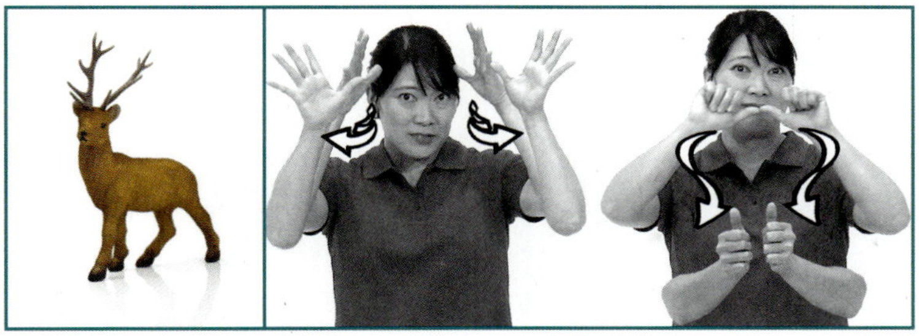

10.

Fingerspell CHIPS

11.

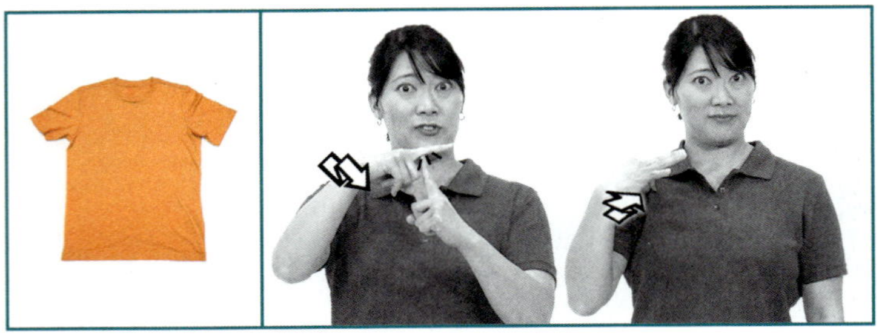

12.

13.

14.

15.

16.

Money-related

17. be priced at; to cost an amount

18. monetary unit equal to 100 cents; dollar

SIGNING NATURALLY

Homework 10:3

WH-WORD QUESTIONS 1

Underline the topic of each question.

1. How much does a baseball hat cost?
2. What is the number that comes after 67?
3. What activities do you have to do in the next few days?
4. Why is talking not allowed in class?
5. How do you get money from an ATM?
6. Who are you closer to—your mom or your dad?
7. Who invented the light bulb?
8. What happened when Gallaudet and Clerc arrived in America?
9. What two colors make green?
10. Which day of the week do you like best?

To translate wh-word questions, follow this structure:

- establish time if specified (raise brows)
- establish location if specified (raise brows)
- name the topic (raise brows)
- end with a wh-word question (furrow brows, tilt head forward, hold last sign)

Example: 1. How much does a baseball hat cost?

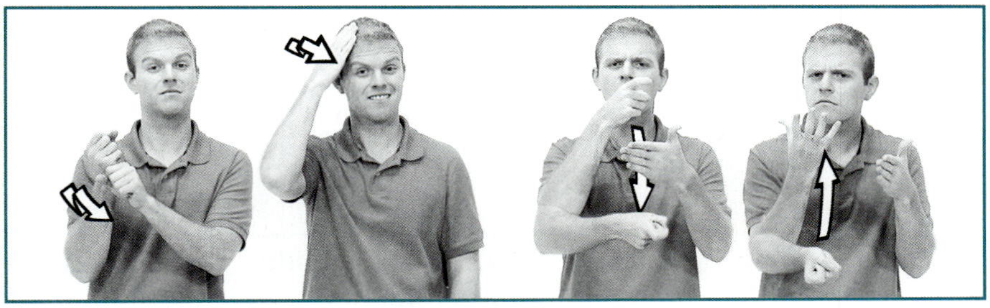

name the topic, end with a wh-word question

View. Justin signs translations of the questions above. Review the notes associated with some of the questions.

Question 2

"after 67" functions like a location, so it is signed in the beginning.

Question 3

"next few days" specifies a time frame, so it is signed in the beginning. There is no specific sign for the English word "activities" but the translation for the phrase "have to do" implies activities so it functions as the topic of the sentence.

Question 4

"in class" specifies a location, so it is signed in the beginning.

Question 5

"an ATM" specifies a location, so it is signed in the beginning.

Question 8

even though ***"America"*** is a location, it is not signed first because it is embedded in a "when" clause. However, you can sign it first as a location if you want to.

Practice. Now practice the questions—be mindful of the phrasing of the signs and the facial expressions. Be prepared to sign the questions in class.

VOCABULARY REVIEW

Review the vocabulary on the video.

1. to invent; to create something new, like for a patent

2. wh-word question used to ask "what happened"

Homework 10:4

CONVERSATION 2

Ursula (A) explains to John (B) why she thinks David (C, as Zack) is mean. John tells David (Zack) what he has heard and David (Zack) corrects the misperception.

Scene 1	A: (to B) tell about C B: ask why A thinks that way A: describe situation to support opinion B: respond, state she or he will check with C
Scene 2	B: (to C) repeat what A told you about C C: respond, ask why B: repeat A's situation C: correct information B: respond
Scene 3	B: (to A) tell what you found out A: respond

New Signs

to cry one's eyes out; to bawl

to misunderstand; to misinterpret; to get the wrong idea or impression

Key Grammar

PREDICATIVE ADJECTIVES

In English, either an attributive adjective or a predicative adjective can be used to describe someone's personal qualities. For example:

- "I like the *friendly* dog." The adjective "friendly" is an attributive adjective and comes before the noun.
- "The dog is *friendly*." The adjective "friendly" is a predicative adjective, functioning similarly to a verb, and comes after the subject of the sentence.

However, in ASL, to describe a personal quality, only predicative adjectives can be used. This means the subject is named before signing the adjective.

View. Watch Ursula using a predicative adjective to describe Zack (David) and uses temporal aspect to describe Zack's actions and his friend's reactions.

using a predicative adjective

using verb signs with temporal aspect

MINIDIALOGUES

Minidialogue 1

1. What was Iva's initial opinion about John and what situation does she describe to support the opinion?

2. What explanation does John give to Tonique that corrects Iva's misperception of him?

New Sign

expression meaning
"Are you all right?"

Minidialogue 2

1. How are Melvin's partner and Derrick's girlfriend different when they are traveling?

2. What situations do Melvin and Derrick describe to support their opinions?

3. Where is Derrick flying to?

Minidialogue 3

1. What have others told Amber about the LSF (Langue des Signes Francaise) teacher, LaRue?

2. What opinion does Lauren have about the teacher? How does she describe the class experience?

3. What is Amber's decision about taking the class?

Answers given in class.

GIVE THE OPPOSITE 1–16

Justin and Lauren will give a sign and ask what is the opposite. Then, after a short pause, they will give the opposite sign so you can confirm your answer.

VOCABULARY REVIEW

Review the vocabulary on the video.

Disposition

Pleasant

1. to be cheerful, pleasant, friendly

2. to feel superior to others; to be stuck up; snobbish

Polite

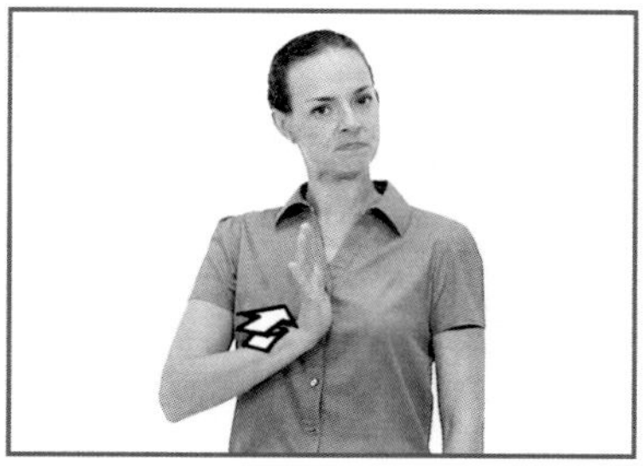

3. to be courteous; to be polite

4. to be discourteous; to be rude

Kind

5. to be generous; to be sweet

6. to be insensitive; to be mean

Temperament

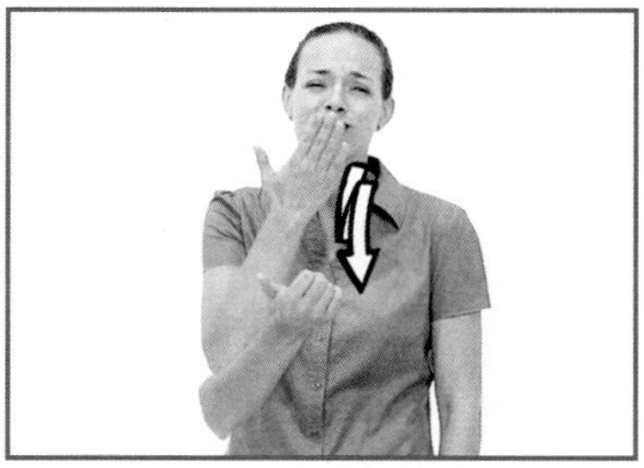

7. to be positive and loving; to be very sweet

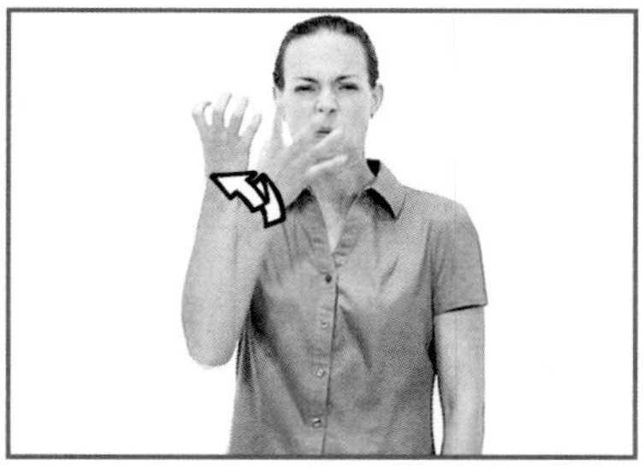

8. to be grouchy, crabby or cranky

Modest

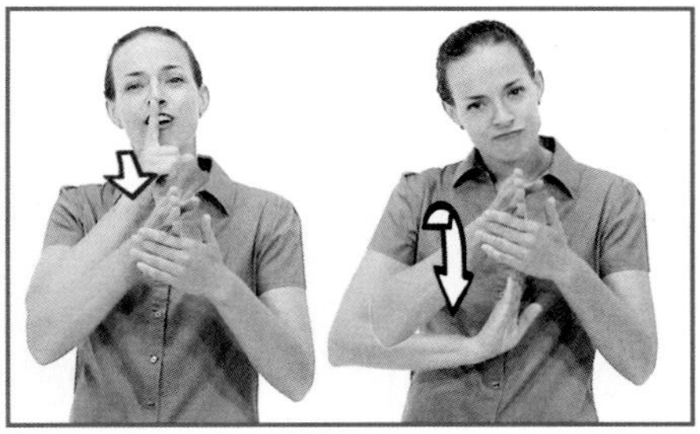

9. to be modest; to be humble

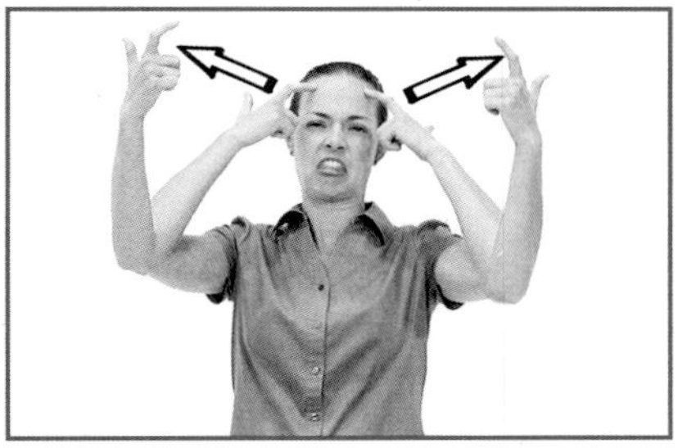

10. to think oneself is better than others; to be arrogant

11. to be a "big talker"

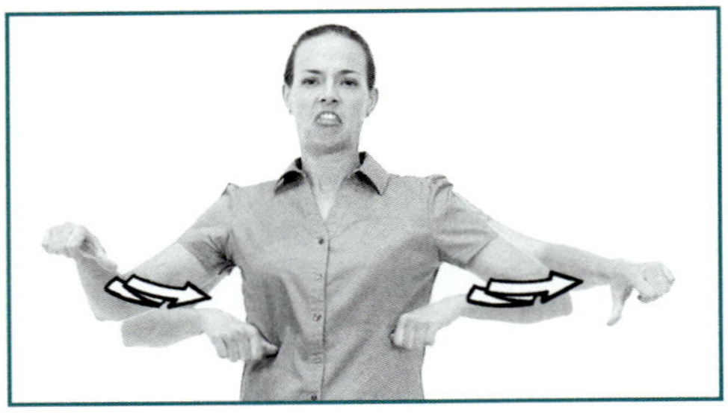

12. to be boastful, bragging, showing off

Goody-Goody

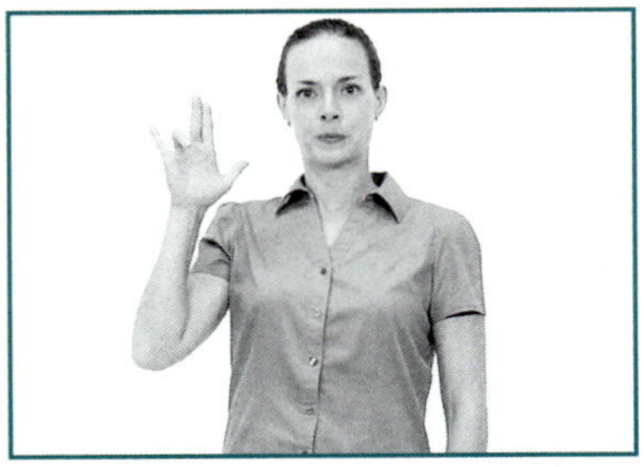

13. to behave in a way that makes the person appear virtuous: not willing to get into any mischief; being a goody-goody

14. to have the tendency to cause trouble, or get into trouble

15. to have the tendency to be mischievous in a playful way

Humor

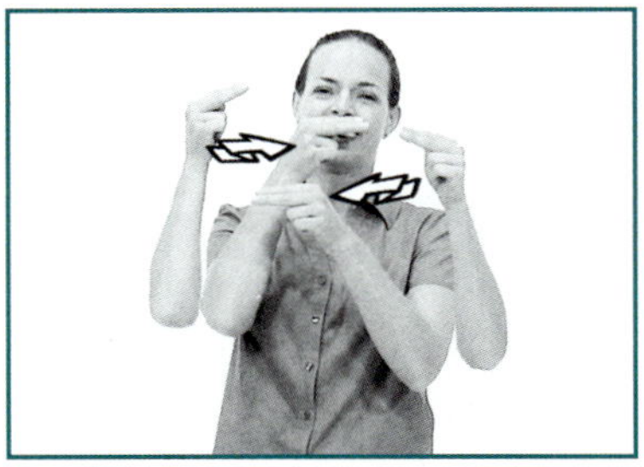

16. to be funny, amusing, humorous

17. to have a quiet nature; not talkative

Imposing Discipline

18. to be firm, strict; to demand one follows the rules, or meets expectations

19. to be lenient, soft, not demanding

Cool

20. to be hip, cool, trendy

21. to be strange; to be odd; to act peculiar

Active

22. to be always on the go; tendency to keep oneself occupied all the time

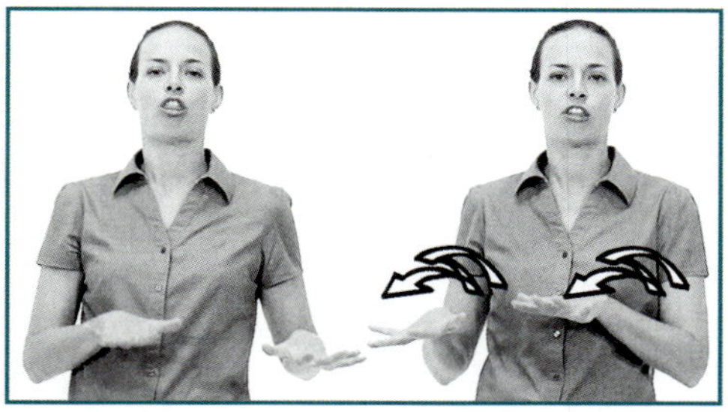

23. to be laid back; lacking effort

Anxious or Carefree

24. to feel anxious; to be worried

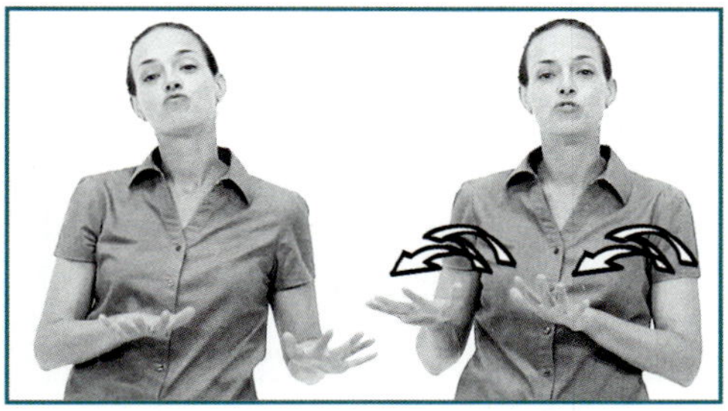

25. to be carefree or unruffled, to have an easygoing nature

Dealing with Others

Tolerance

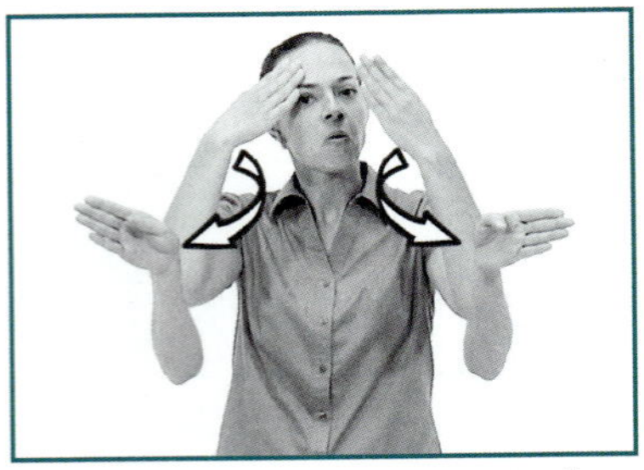

26. to keep an open mind; to be broad-minded

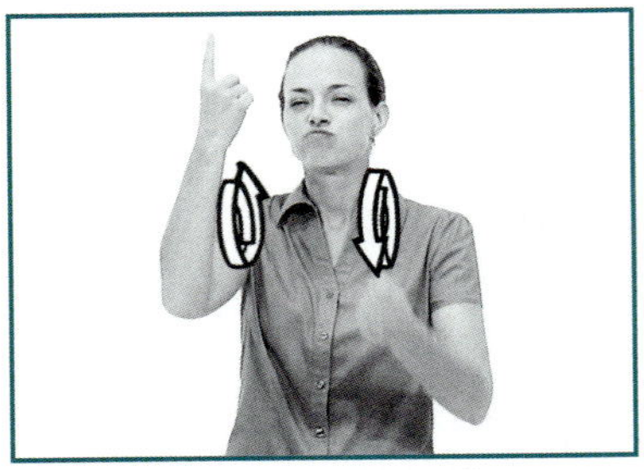

27. to be understanding; showing compassion and sensitivity

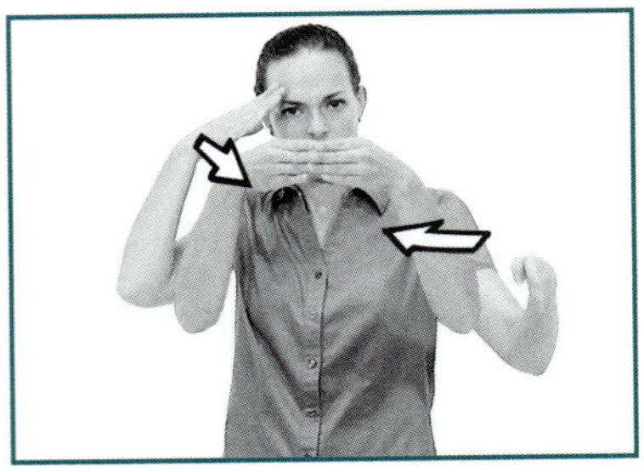

28. to be small minded; to be intolerant

29. to be headstrong; to be stubborn

30. to be able to adapt to change or different circumstances; flexible

31. to allow, to tolerate, to accept

Affections

32. to be affectionate; to be warm

33. to be indifferent; not affectionate; cold

Patience

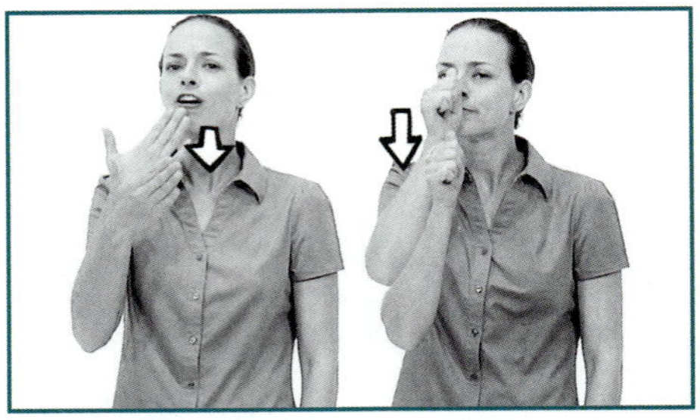

34. to be uncomplaining; patient

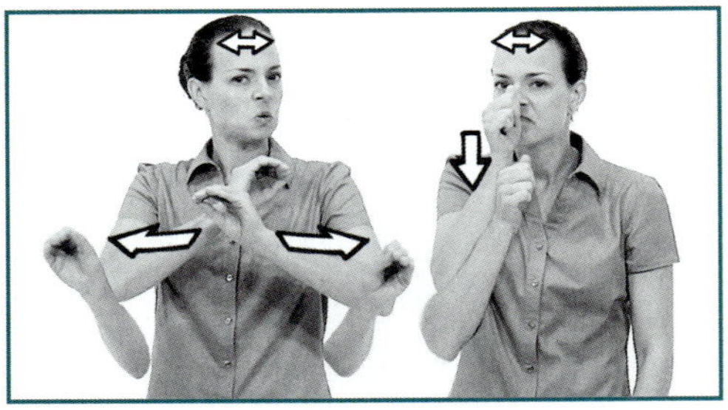

35. to be impatient; to become irritated easily

Intellectual Ability

36. to be smart or intelligent; to be clever

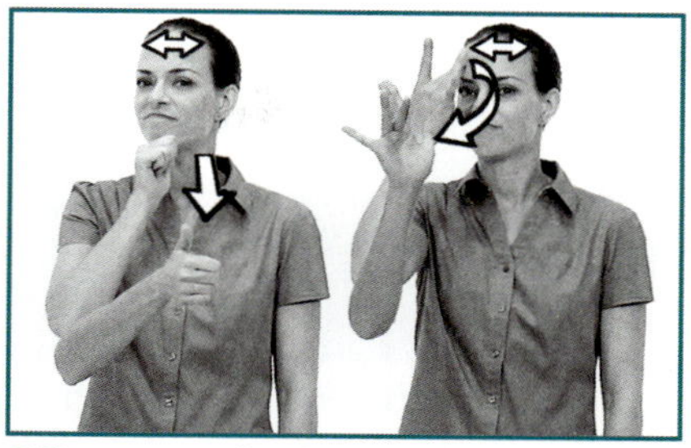

37. to not be bright; to not be smart

Good Sense or Foolish

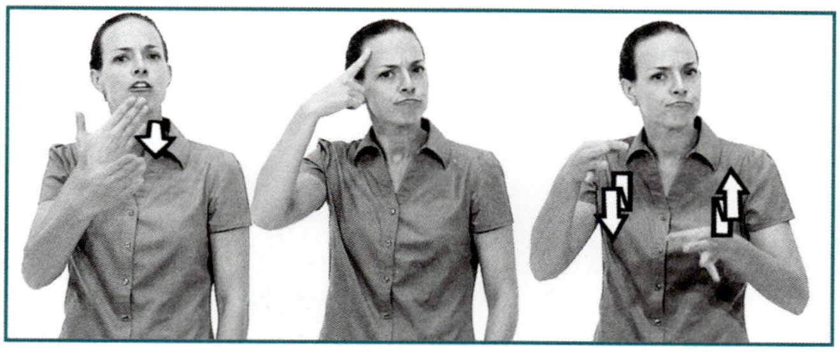

38. to have good sense; to be capable of making good judgements

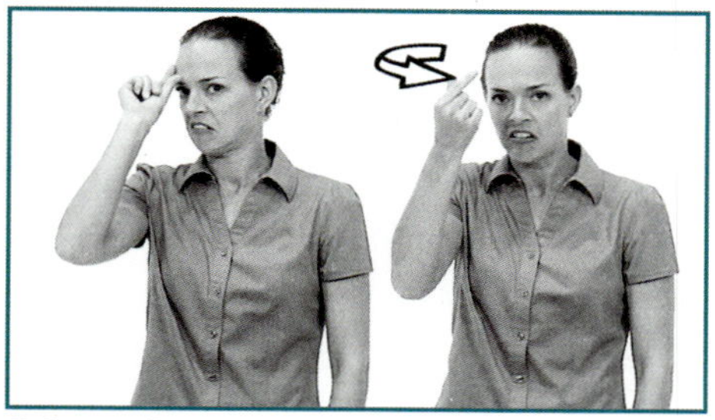

39. to be foolish; to make an unwise or stupid choice

Courageous

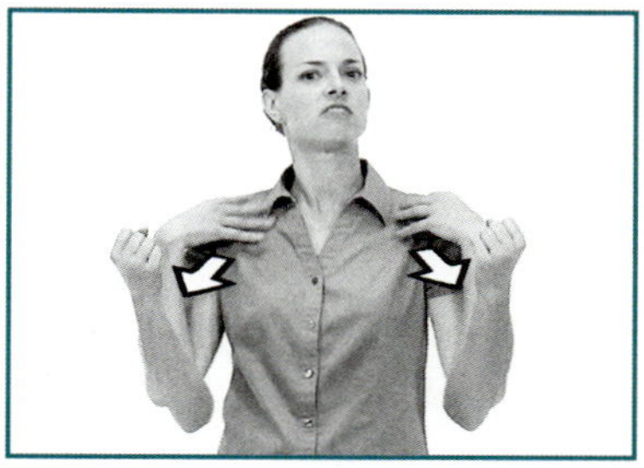

40. to be fearless; to be bold; to take risks

41. to be timid; to be apprehensive; to be fearful

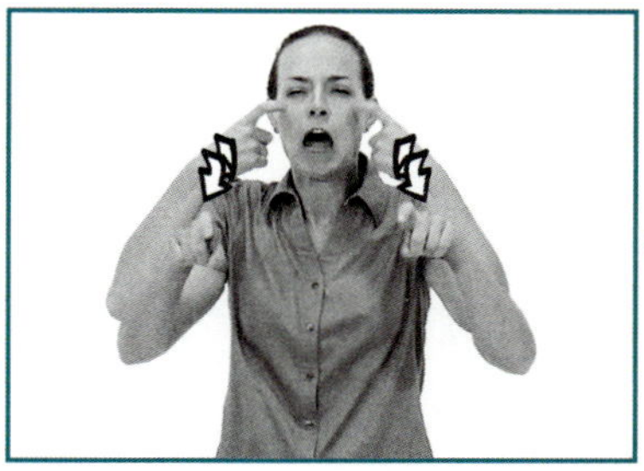

or

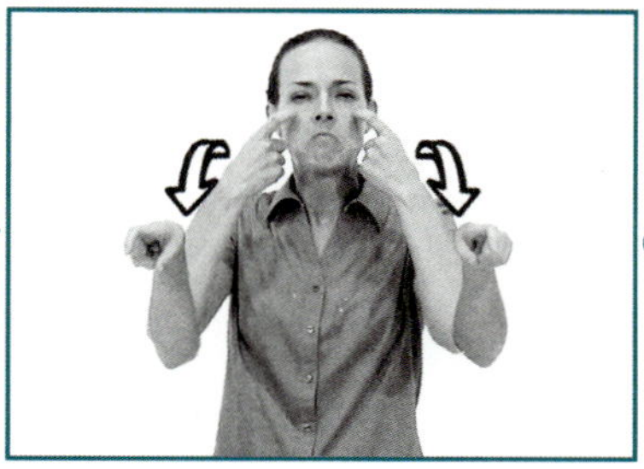

or

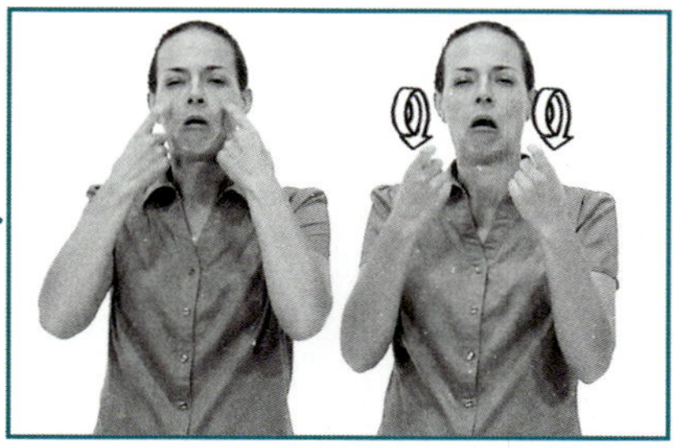

42. to cry one's eyes out; to bawl

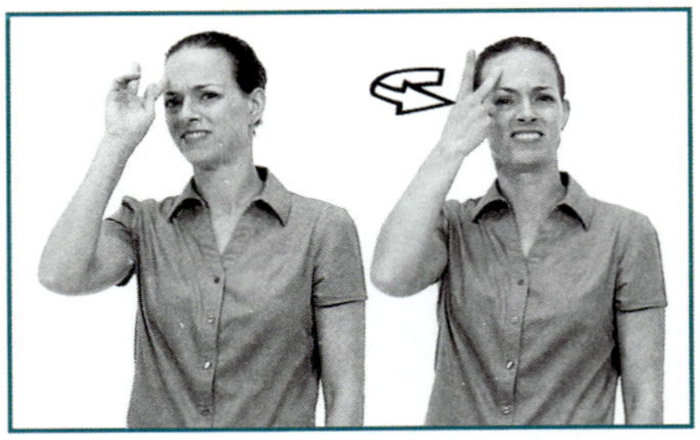

43. to get the wrong idea; to misunderstand or misinterpret

44. to burst into laughter; to laugh out loud

Homework 10:5

NUMBERS: TELLING THE PRICE 2

To express money numbers in dollars and cents, like $1.75, $3.99, $7.05, make a twisting motion with the hand for the dollar number, then give the cent number. There is no need to give the sign for dollar or to touch the forehead with the index finger for the cent number.

Combining Dollars and Cents

Iva demonstrates how to form these dollar and cent combinations.

$1.75

$2.05 *(the palm for both the zero and the 5 faces out)*

$3.50 *(the 50 is signed with a singular movement, and the palm faces either in or out)*

$4.15 *(the 15 is signed with a singular movement)*

$5.59

$6.89

$7.25 *(the 25 is signed with a singular movement, and the palm faces either in or out)*

$8.95

$9.70 *(the 70 is signed with a singular movement)*

WRITE THE AMOUNT

Write the money amount Iva gives.

1. ______________	**9.** ______________	**17.** ______________
2. ______________	**10.** ______________	**18.** ______________
3. ______________	**11.** ______________	**19.** ______________
4. ______________	**12.** ______________	**20.** ______________
5. ______________	**13.** ______________	**21.** ______________
6. ______________	**14.** ______________	**22.** ______________
7. ______________	**15.** ______________	**23.** ______________
8. ______________	**16.** ______________	**24.** ______________

Answers on page 519.

HOW MUCH

Tonique, John, Iva, David, and Ursula give prices for each item. Write the prices in the blanks below.

Answers given in class.

Assignment

BRING SIX ITEMS

Bring to class six (6) items all under the price of $10.00. Be sure you have the actual prices. If not, determine the price(s) before class.

VOCABULARY REVIEW

Review the vocabulary on the video.

1.

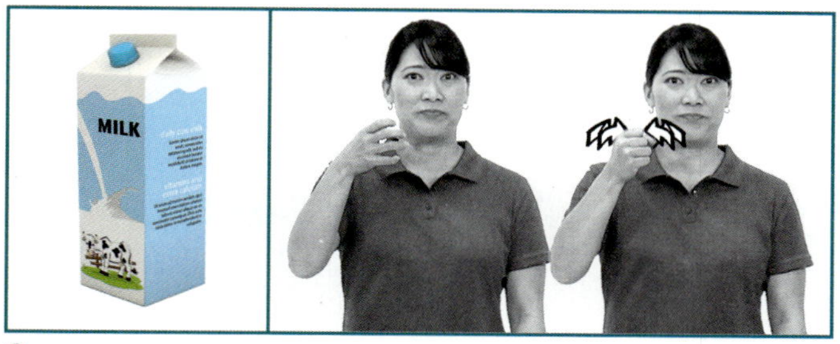

2.

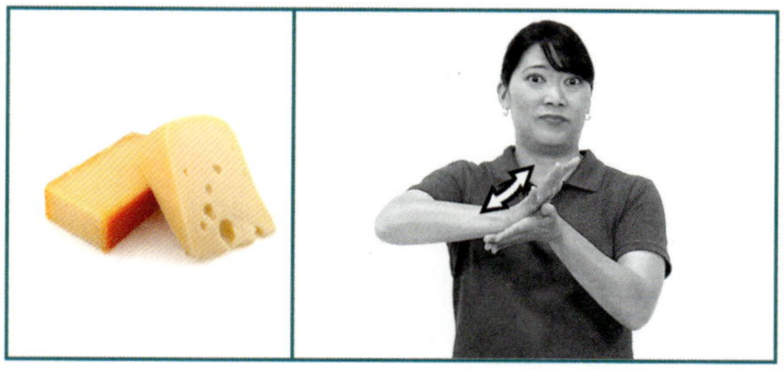

3.

4.

5.

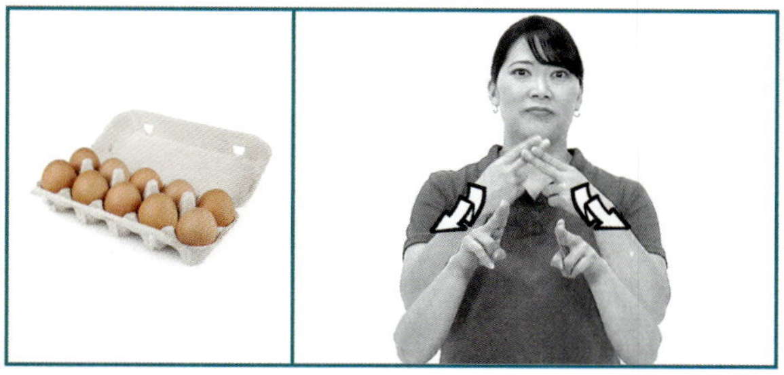

6.

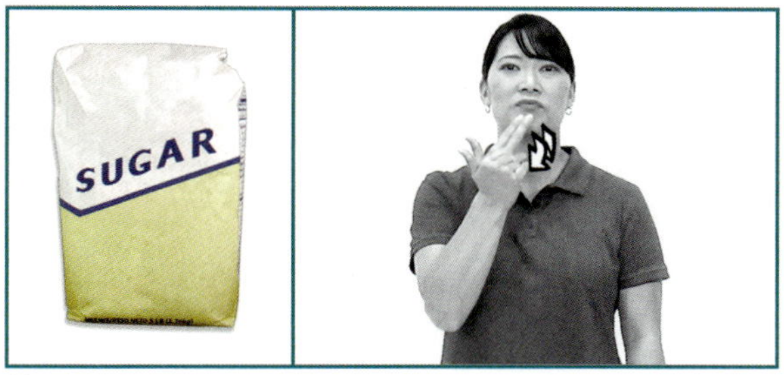

7.

8.

9.

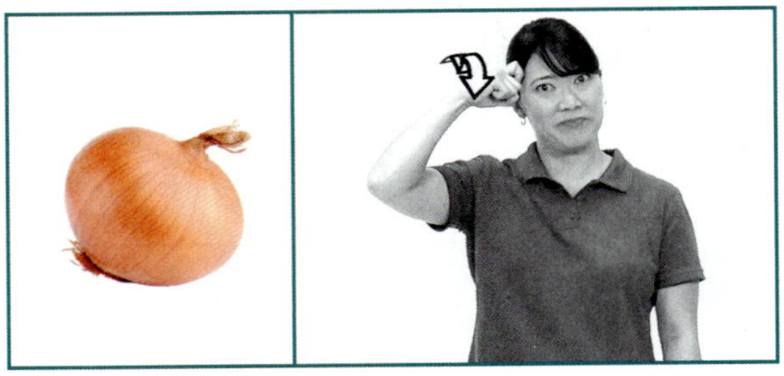

10.

or

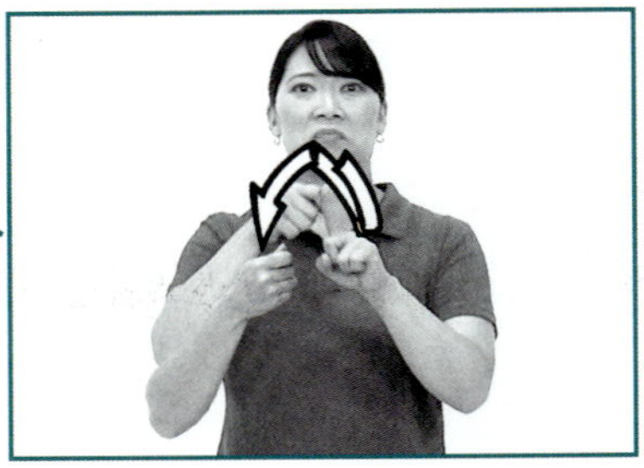

11.

12.

13.

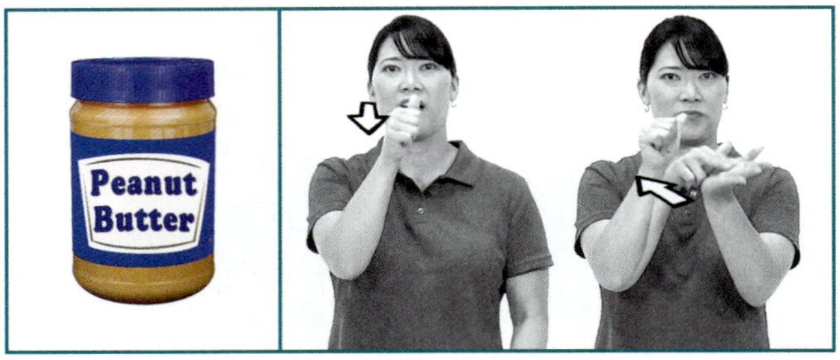

14.

15.

Fingerspell
MAYO

16.

17.

18.

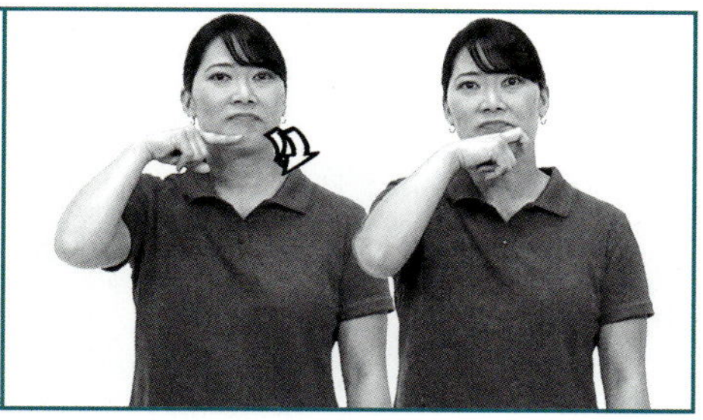

19.

Fingerspell
YOGURT

20.

21.

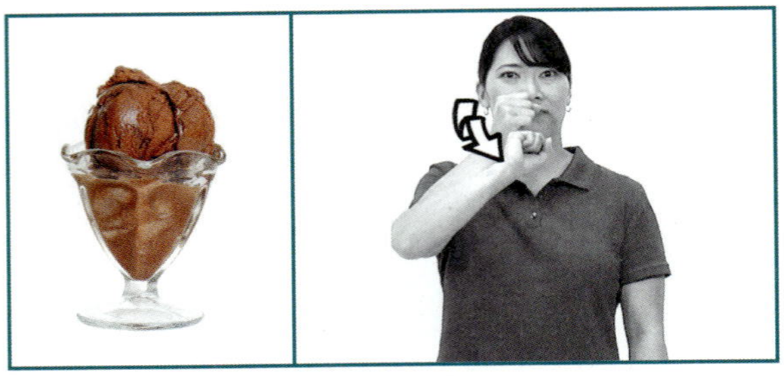

22.

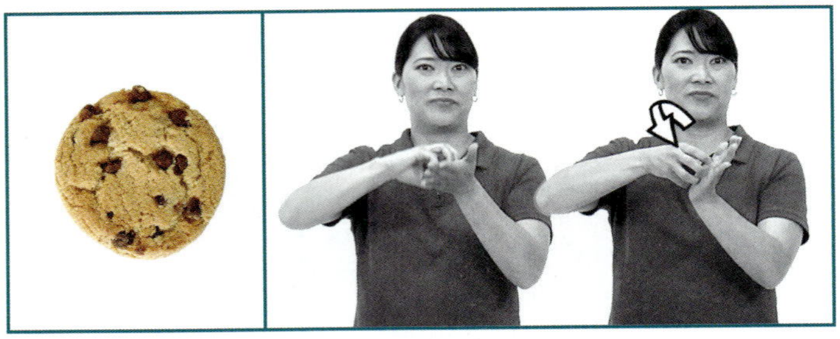

23.

24.

25.

Homework 10:6

CONVERSATION 3

Suzanne (A) asks Lauren (B) how she likes her sister's new boyfriend.

A: ask if B has met person
B: explain relationship and how met him
A: ask if B likes him, [ask why]
B: reply, describe person
- use at least three personal quality signs
- use role shift to describe situation(s)

A: comment and ask further questions
B: reply

Key Grammar

USING ROLE SHIFT TO DESCRIBE SITUATION

Describing a person's qualities requires more than just stating an opinion. Usually when a signer tells what she or he thinks of a person, she or he substantiates it by elaborating on something that happened that led them to form the opinion. This gives the listener a better idea of how one came to form such an opinion. Role shifting is key to successfully describing a situation or illustrating a behavior. It allows you to "become" the person you are describing, taking on his or her actions, manner and feelings to further support the opinion given.

View. Observe Lauren using role shift to describe a situation involving her sister's boyfriend to illustrate he is not good with money and cannot be trusted.

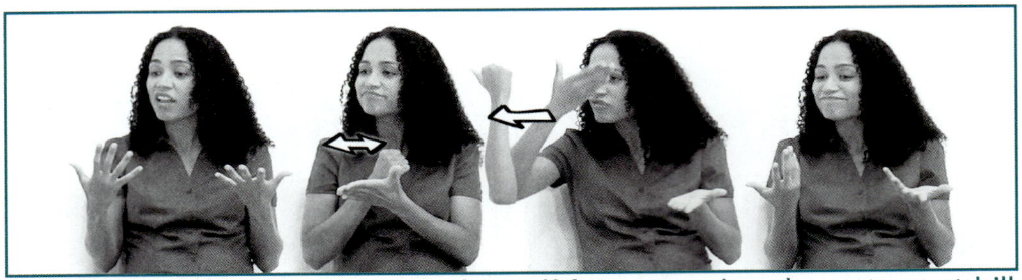

role shift the boyfriend excusing himself for not paying the restaurant bill

CIRCLE THE NUMBER

For each situation below, the signer will first list three different signs, followed by a description of a situation using role shift. Of the three signs, choose the one the best matches the description given.

A.	1	2	3
B.	1	2	3
C.	1	2	3
D.	1	2	3
E.	1	2	3
F.	1	2	3
G.	1	2	3
H.	1	2	3

Answers on page 519.

PERSONAL QUALITY 1–4

View the following demonstrations. See how Justin and Suzanne follow this narrative sequence to describe a person:

- give name of person
- tell how you know this person
- tell if you like or don't like the person
- tell why, describe the person
  - use at least three additional personal quality signs
  - use role shift to describe situation(s)

Personal Quality 1

Personal Quality 2

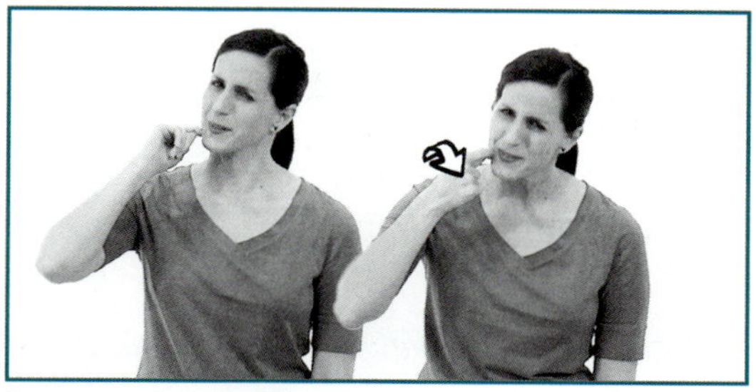

Personal Quality 3

Personal Quality 4

Assignment

TWO PEOPLE YOU KNOW

Select two people you know, each having one of the four personal qualities signed below.

1.

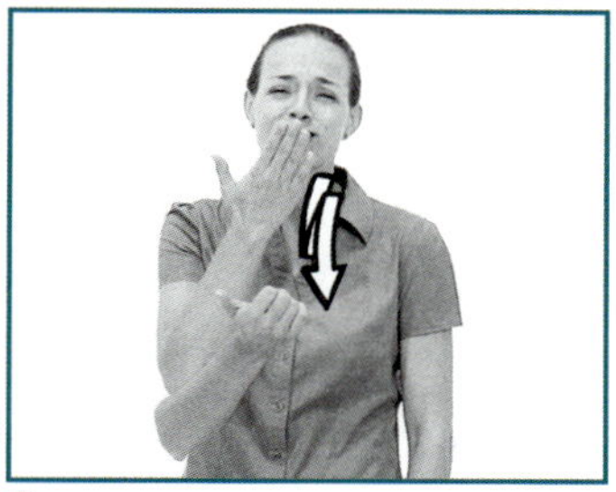

2.

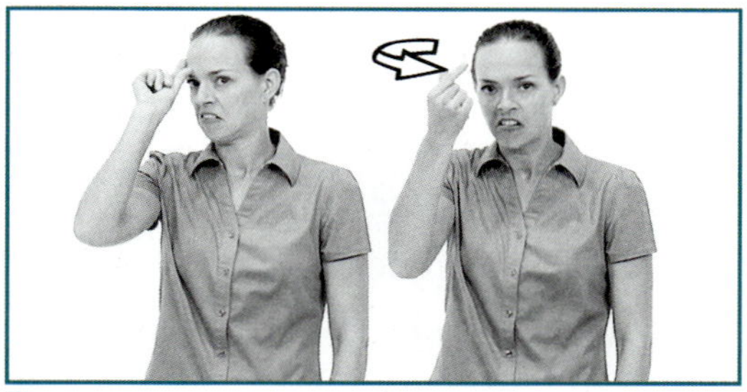

3.

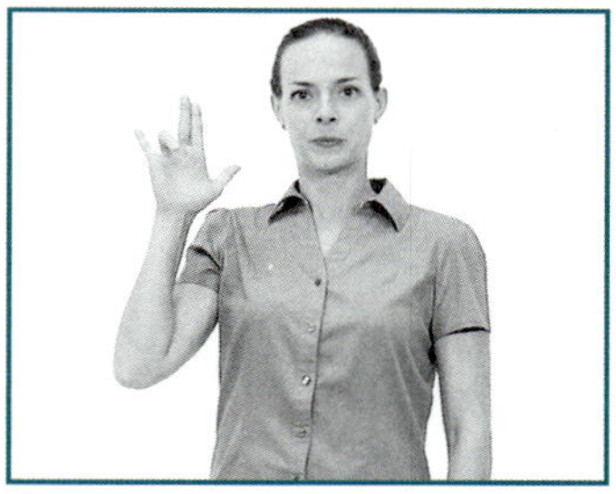

4.

Use the following narrative sequence to describe each person.

- give name of person
- tell how you know this person
- tell if you like or don't like the person
- tell why, describe the person
  - use at least three additional personal quality signs
  - use role shift to describe situation(s)

Be prepared to sign the information in class.

INSIGHT

Nikki, a Deaf woman recounts an all-too-familiar incident at a store that left her feeling upset. This is what she said:

Something happened to me recently that was very upsetting. It reminded me of how different it is to be in public with a hearing person, than to be by myself or with another Deaf person. Typically, if I'm by myself and need to buy something, order food, or deal with someone at the bank, hearing people find ways to communicate with me directly.

That changes when I am with a hearing person. Automatically, the people ignore or bypass me and go straight to the hearing person, like I'm invisible and don't even exist.

Well, yesterday, I went into an express mail store with a hearing friend to mail a package. I asked the clerk at the counter for a pen and paper so we could communicate. She turned, looked past me, she spoke only to my hearing friend, asking her questions, completely ignoring me. She never dealt with me again.

I barely made it out of the store before I was in tears. My very existence was ignored, my self-sufficiency taken away, my ability to communicate disregarded. It was humiliating.

What's the take away?

The clerk may have been nervous and unsure of how to handle the situation of the clerk might have decided it was easier and more efficient to speak to the friend instead of Nikki. It is difficult to constantly be invisible. The perception about disability continues to have a powerful hold on the general public's perception of Deaf people and continues to create obstacles between the hearing person and the Deaf person developing mutually respectful experiences.

If you ever find yourself in such a situation where another hearing person chooses to talk to you rather than directly engage a Deaf person, challenge yourself to find a way to redirect the conversation back to the Deaf person. In this way, you support your Deaf friend's autonomy and personhood as well as gently teach the hearing person that the communication solution is not to marginalize or ignore the Deaf person, but to find ways to understand each other.

Homework 10:7

TELLING WHERE ITEMS ARE LOCATED

When telling where items are located in a room, follow this sequence:

- name the room (raise brows)
- name furniture or appliance, or part of room (raise brows)
- specify location of item (use reference point)

View. Terrylene follows the sequence to locate where items are or should be. Pay particular attention to how she uses a reference point to help specify the location.

Dialogue 1

Terrylene asks Iva to go get some candles and tells her where they are located.

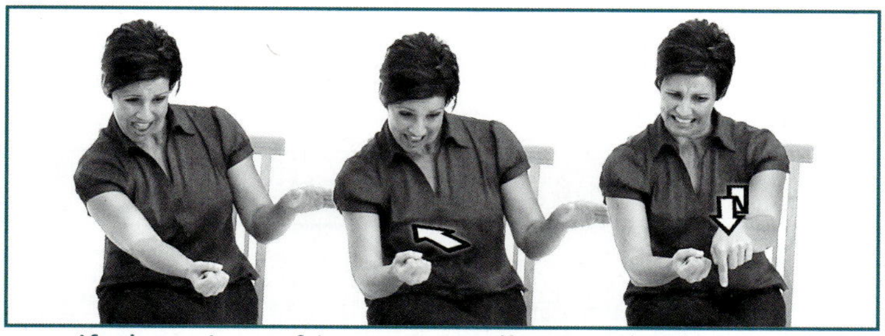

specify location of item—candles inside the 3rd drawer (use reference point "3rd drawer")

Dialogue 2

Terrylene asks Iva to put away the scissors she forgot to put in their proper location. Terrylene tells the specific location when Iva asks where to put the scissors.

specify location of item—scissors in the box
(use reference point "box")

ASK FAVOR 1–6

Tonique and Derrick tell where to locate items. Write the name of the item and the reason for their requests, then place the corresponding number in the picture of the kitchen to indicate the item's location.

	Item	*Reason for the Request*
1.	______________	______________________
2.	______________	______________________
3.	______________	______________________
4.	______________	______________________
5.	______________	______________________
6.	______________	______________________

Answers on page 520.

VOCABULARY REVIEW

Review the vocabulary on the video.

Household Items

1.

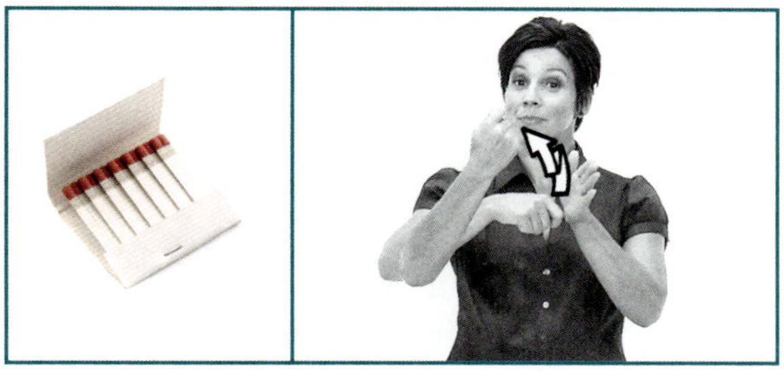

2.

3.

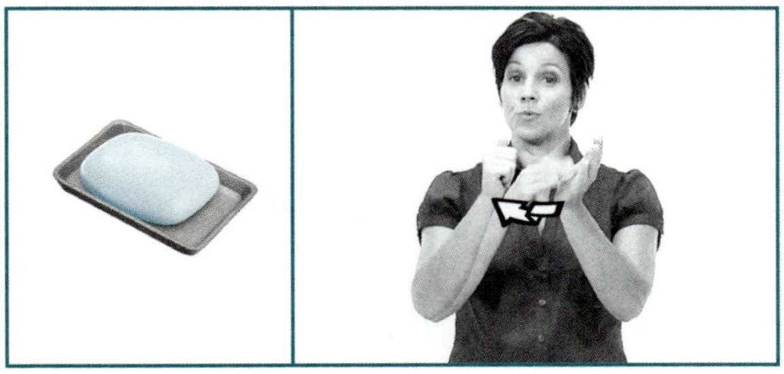

4.

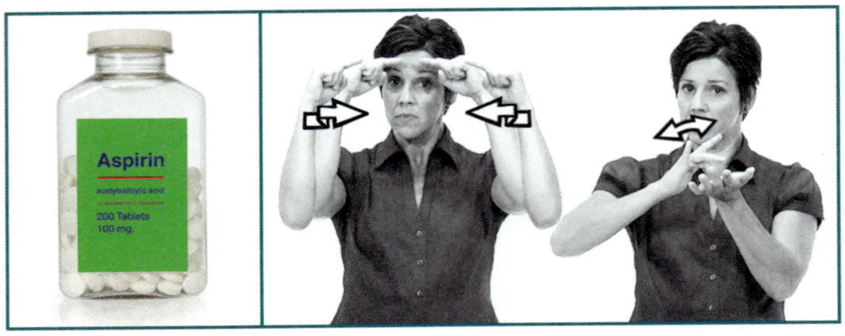

5.

6.

7.

8.

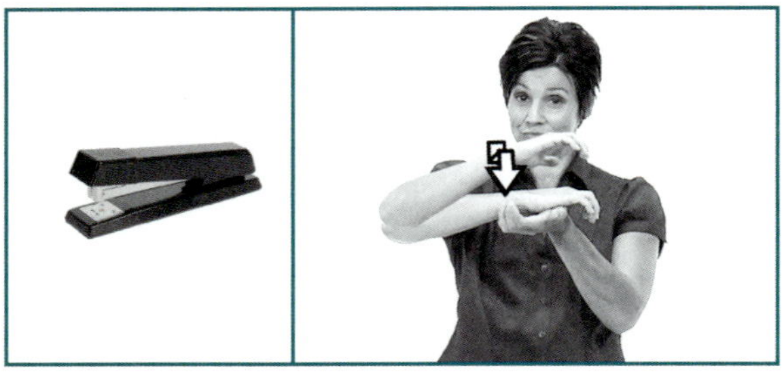

9.

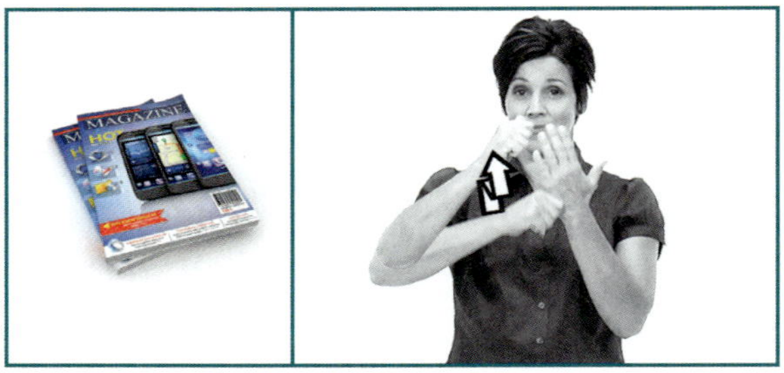

10.

11.

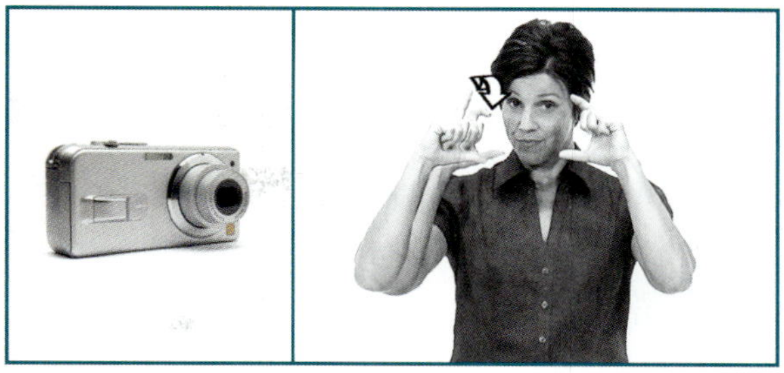

12.

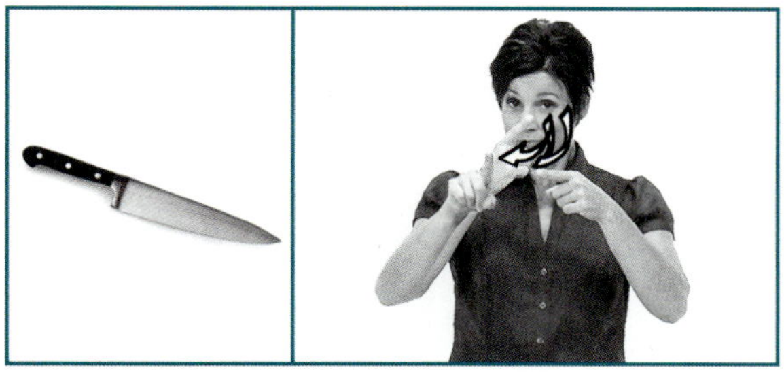

13.

14.

15.

16.

Kitchen Appliances

Fingerspell STOVE

17.

Fingerspell SINK

18.

Fingerspell OVEN

19.

Fingerspell REF

20.

or

Fingerspell DW

21.

Homework 10:8

WH-WORD QUESTIONS 2

Circle the topic and underline the choices listed in each question.

1. Do you prefer cool or warm weather?
2. Do you prefer cats or dogs?
3. Do you prefer comedy, romance or action films?
4. Do you prefer to eat at a table or in front of the TV?
5. Do you prefer to sleep on your back or on your side?
6. Do you prefer to get in touch with Deaf people by email or by videophone?
7. Do you prefer to save or spend money?
8. Do you prefer to work at a job you hate but get paid a lot of money or a job that's fun but doesn't pay well?
9. Do you prefer to be with a person who is kind, intelligent or beautiful?

To translate the questions, follow this word order:

- name the topic (raise brows)
- name the choices
  - contrastive structure (for 2 choices)
  - listing in neutral space in front (for 3 choices)
- end with wh-word question (furrow brows, tilt head forward, hold last sign)

Example—2 choices. 1. Do you prefer cool or warm weather?

name topic, name choices using contrastive structure,* end with wh-word question

* Remember with contrastive structure you begin on your non-dominant side.

Example—3 choices. 3. Do you prefer comedy, romance or action films?

name topic, name choices—list in neutral space*, end with wh-word question

Questions 1–9

View. Tonique signs translations of the questions above.

Practice. Now practice the questions and be prepared to sign them in class.

VOCABULARY REVIEW

Review the vocabulary on the video.

1. conditions in the atmosphere such as being rainy, sunny, cloudy; weather

2. cool (weather)

* Put the choices in sequence space in front of your body—begin on your non-dominant side.

3. neither cold or hot; warm

4. romance; associated with love

5. full of action and, or suspense

6. shooting off automatic weapons as in a gunfight

7. to send (something) electronically

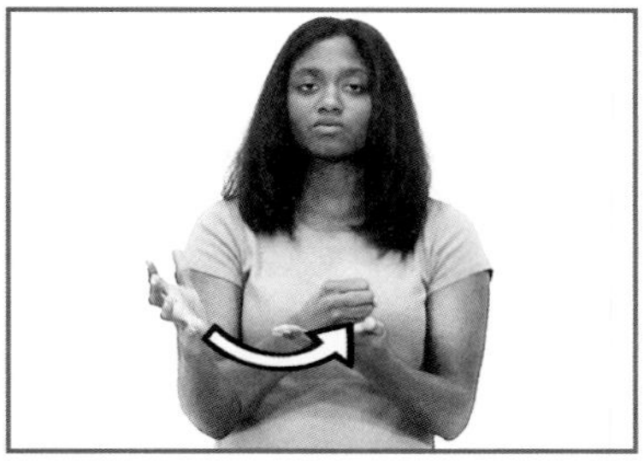

8. to get or earn money in return for work

9. to make good money; to make lots of money

Homework 10:9

INTERVIEW

In class, you will be doing this interview with your partner.

Part 1 A: ask who are the two people B chose
B: name two people you know well and describe them:
- their names
- how they are related to you
- what they look like
- what they do
- their ages
- etc.

Part 2 A: ask "which" questions
"which is more..."
"which is better..."
B: reply, give reasons and give examples

Part 3 A: give a hypothetical situation, ask who B would pick or prefer
B: reply, explain why
A: respond

Learn the Interview

Review the key language elements needed for the interview.

View. In **Interview Part 1**, observe how Ursula and Iva introduce the two people being compared:

For **"A: ask who are the two people B chose"**

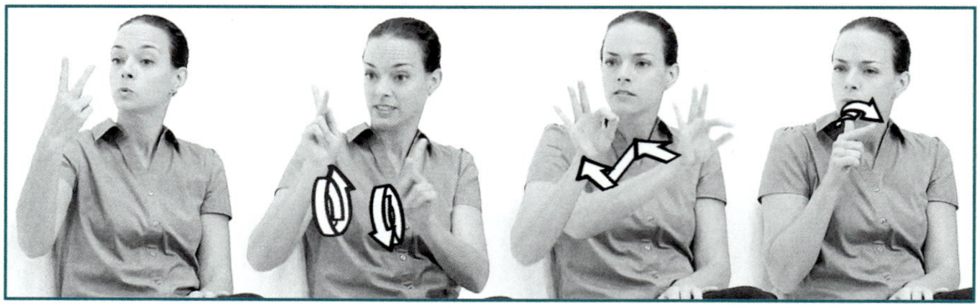

For **"B. name two people you know well"**

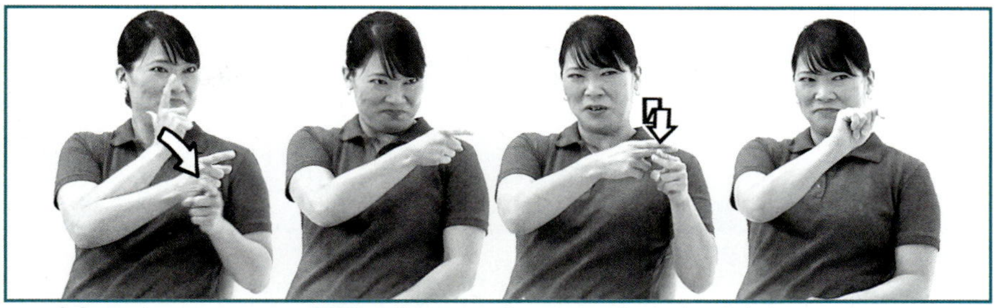

...older sister named Tia (located on Iva's left side)

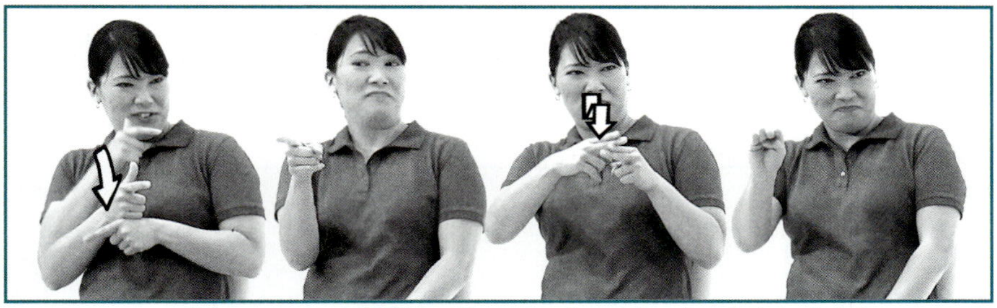

...younger sister named Kim (located on Iva's right side)

NOTE: To compare two people, use contrastive structure. Establish the first person on your non-dominant side and the other person on your dominant side. As you share information about each person, orient your signs and body in the direction where the person you are talking about was established.

View. In **Interview Part 2**, observe how Ursula asks two kinds of "which" questions and how Iva responds.

A: ask "which" questions

B: reply, give reasons and give examples

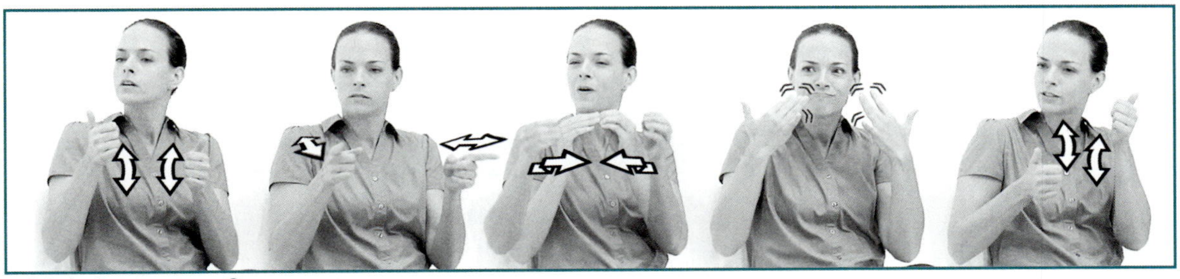

which is more...?

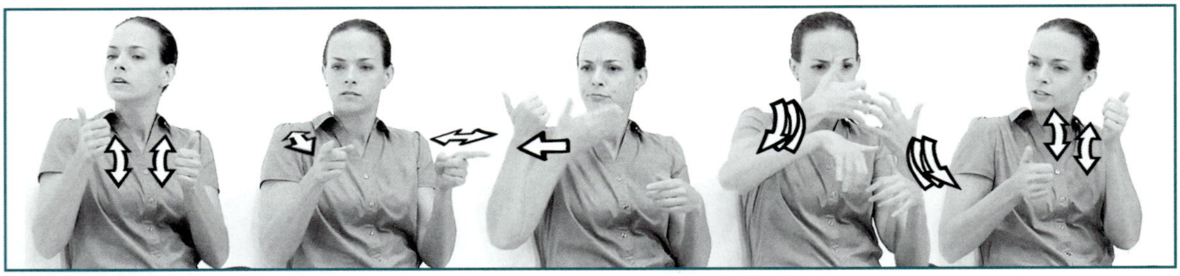

which is better...?

NOTE: The sign "being organized" shown above, and the two other signs (shown below) are the only signs that can be used with the phrase "which is better...?"

having good judgement

manage money well

- to reply, point to the location designated for the person (on left or right), then give reasons and examples of why you choose him or her. Then, point to the other person's location, shake head to indicate she or he is not the same and describe the differences.
- if both are the same, begin your reply with the sign below, then give the reasons and examples.

the two of them are the same; both

View. In **Interview Part 3**, observe how Ursula signed the following:

A: give a hypothetical situation, ask who B would pick or prefer

Assignment

INTERVIEWS

You may have been assigned to be either **Interviewer 1** (page 294) or **Interviewer 2** (page 295). Follow the instructions on that page to prepare to be Signer A when you are the interviewer, and Signer B when you are the interviewee. Review **Learn the Interview** (page 290–293) to help you develop your questions as Signer A and to structure your reply as Signer B

INTERVIEWER 1

Follow this dialogue.

Part 1	A:	ask about the two people B chose
	B:	name two people you know well and describe them (fill out chart below)
Part 2	A:	ask 6–8 "which" questions to compare the two people (see categories below)
	B:	reply, give reasons and examples
Part 3	A:	give a hypothetical situation, ask who B would pick or prefer
	B:	reply, explain why
	A:	respond

As Signer A (interviewer). For **Part 2** develop 6–8 questions from the categories below.

approach to work (page 246) • **hardworking** • **focused** **level of accountability** (page 247) • **responsibility** • **money matters** **relating to others** (page 248) • **extrovert or introvert** • **direct** • **sharing**	**disposition** (page 264) • **pleasant** • **kind** • **modest** • **humor** • **cool** • **anxious or carefree** **dealing with others** (page 268) • **tolerance** • **patience** **intellectual ability** (page 269)

Think of a hypothetical situation for the question in **Part 3**.

As Signer B (interviewee). For **Part 1**, prepare to give information about the two people you have chosen. Fill in the chart below and rehearse the information.

personal information	person 1	person 2
names		
relationship		
ages		
marital status		
occupation		
appearance		

During the interview, when telling who is "more" or "better," elaborate on your answers and include how the second person differs.

INTERVIEWER 2

Follow this dialogue.

Part 1	A:	ask about the two people B chose
	B:	name two people you know well and describe them (fill out chart below)
Part 2	A:	ask 6–8 "which" questions to compare the two people (see categories below)
	B:	reply, give reasons and examples
Part 3	A:	give a hypothetical situation, ask who B would pick or prefer
	B:	reply, explain why
	A:	respond

As Signer A (interviewer). For **Part 2** develop 6–8 questions from the categories below.

approach to work (page 246) • **completion of tasks** **level of accountability** (page 247) • **careful** • **organized or orderly** **relating to others** (page 248) • **supportive** • **honest** • **amiable or agreeable** • **respecting one's privacy**	**disposition** (page 264) • **polite** • **temperament** • **goody-goody** • **imposing discipline** • **active** **dealing with others** (page 268) • **affectionate** **good sense or foolish** (page 269) **courageous** (page 269)

Think of a hypothetical situation for the question in **Part 3**.

As Signer B (interviewee). For **Part 1**, prepare to give information about the two people you have chosen. Fill in the chart below and rehearse the information.

personal information	person 1	person 2
names		
relationship		
ages		
marital status		
occupation		
appearance		

During the interview, when telling who is "more" or "better," elaborate on your answers and include how the second person differs.

VOCABULARY REVIEW

Review the vocabulary on the video.

1. to debate or argue the point(s)

2. to hire or employ someone

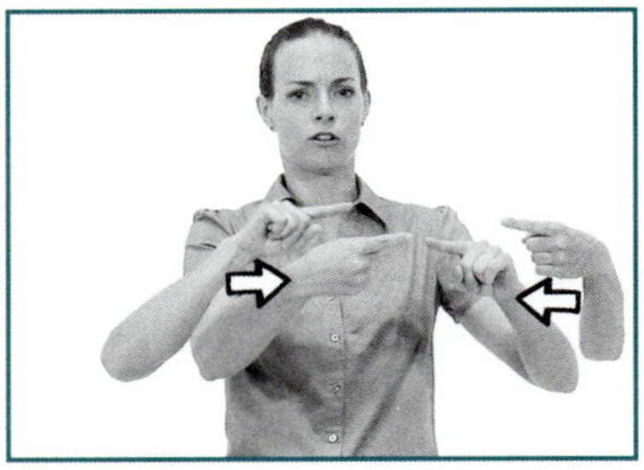

3. to cause pain or hurt one's feelings

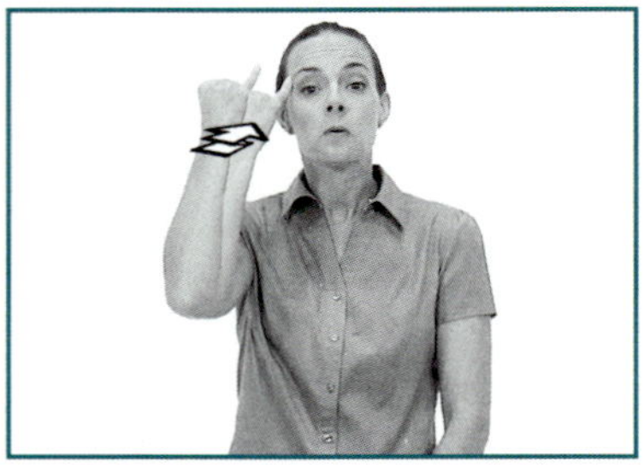

4. a sign that begins a hypothetical situation, for example, "What if…" or "Let's suppose…"

5. a continent which includes the British Isles, France, Spain, Germany, Italy, Greece; in other words Europe

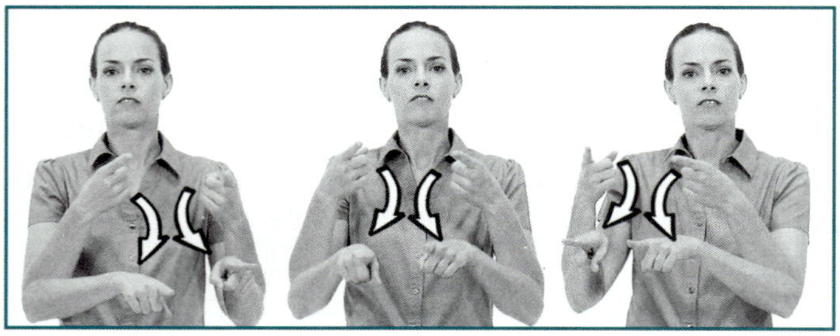

6. a series of incidents or occurrences

Homework 10:10

CULTURAL

INTERRUPTING OTHERS

Maintaining eye contact while conversing is essential to a culturally successful interaction in ASL. However, there are times when you need to interrupt a conversation, yours or someone else's, that requires breaking eye contact. How do you do it without appearing rude?

Interrupting Others' Conversations

Approach the people in the conversation and get the attention of at least one person. Once the person acknowledges you, indicate the reason for the interruption and apologize.

Interrupt to Deliver a Message 1: Observe Derrick approaching slightly hunched over and waving his hand to indicate he needs to interrupt Terrylene and Melvin's conversation. Once acknowledged, he delivers the message to Melvin. Then he apologizes to Terrylene for the interruption.

If the conversation looks serious (rapid overlapping turn-takings and intense expressions on the peoples' faces), approach and stand at a polite distance and wave your hand slightly to indicate that you need to interrupt. If you are not acknowledged right away, continue moving closer and waving your hand slightly, until you get their attention.

Interrupt to Deliver a Message 2: Observe when Lauren realizes the seriousness of Melvin and Terrylene's conversation, she makes three attempts, each time moving closer and waving her hand slightly, to get their attention. Once she is acknowledged, she apologizes for the interruption before delivering the message.

Interrupting Someone Signing to You

It is important to develop your ability in handling distractions, as they may occur while you interact with Deaf people. For example, if you are distracted by the phone ringing or someone calling your name while a Deaf person is signing to you, you should ask him or her to briefly hold on. Once she or he acknowledges or agrees to hold on, you may now explain the distraction and break eye contact to check the distraction. Breaking eye contact without your partner's acknowledgement is considered rude.

Ask to Hold On 1 and 2: Observe Lauren in both conversations asking her partner to briefly hold on before looking away to check the source of the distraction. Then she explains the distraction.

ask to hold on

Resuming Conversation

Lauren's conversation with JT occurred in her home. After checking the distraction, Lauren used the phrase (below) to ask JT to resume signing:

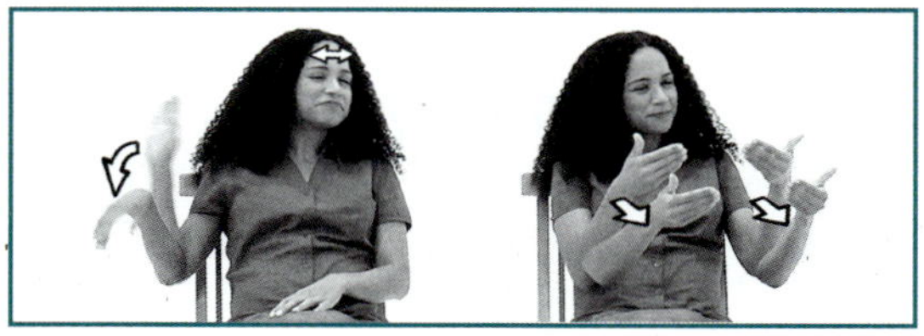

disregard distraction, ask to resume conversation

VOCABULARY REVIEW

Review the vocabulary on the video.

Interrupting

1. expression asking for forgiveness; like "excuse me"

2. to interrupt or stop a conversation or activity

3. expression used to apologize; like "I'm sorry"

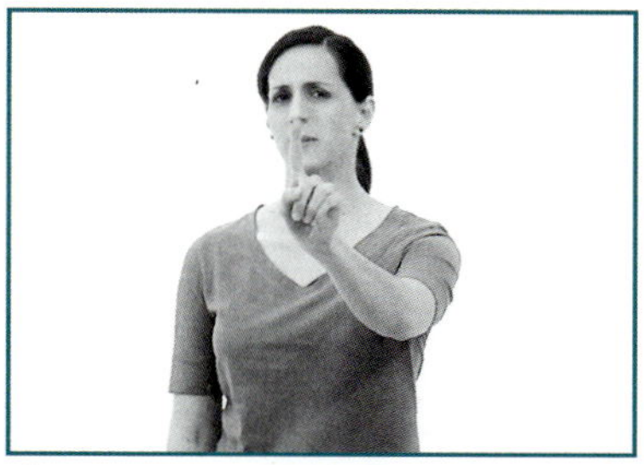

4. expression asking to hold on; like "Wait a minute"

Resume Conversation

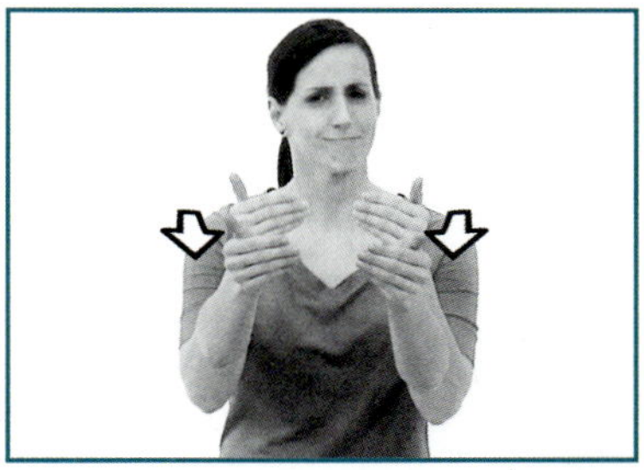

5. expression used to tell someone to resume signing

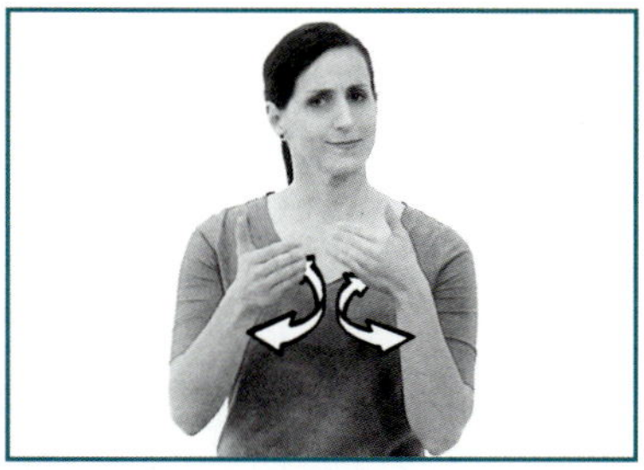

6. sign indicating the signer will resume where she or he left off

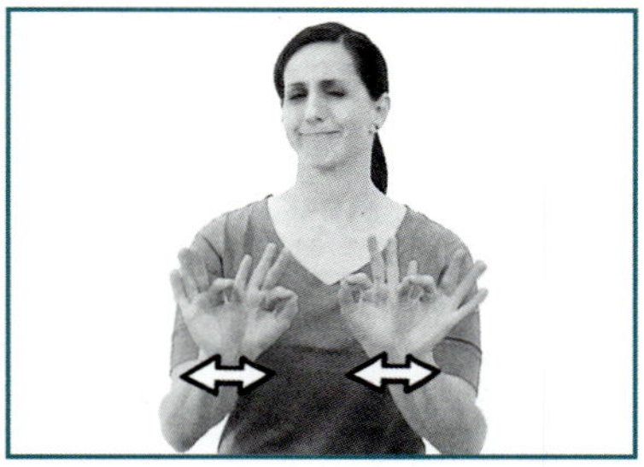

7. having no or very little importance; not worth attending to; it's nothing

Distractions

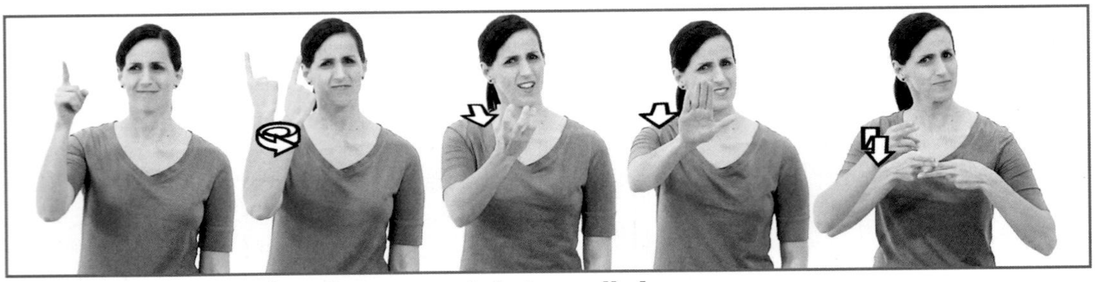

8. telling someone that their name is being called

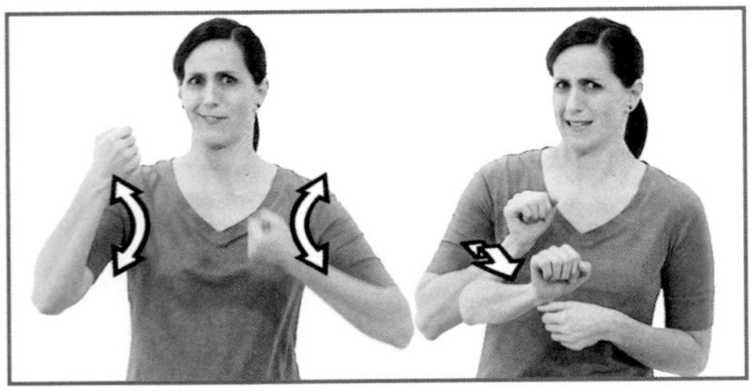

9. informing someone that a car is honking

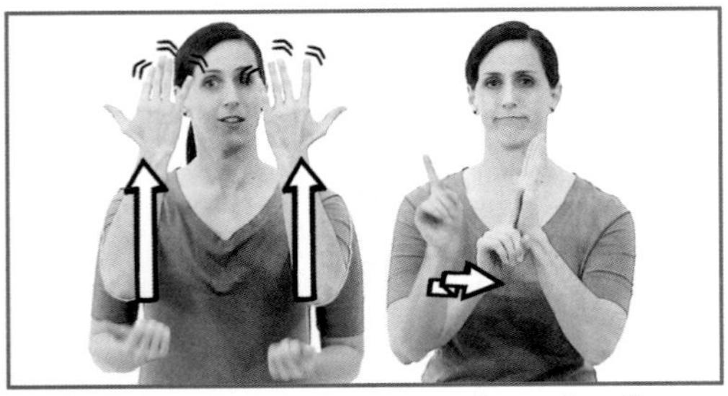

10. informing someone that the fire alarm is ringing

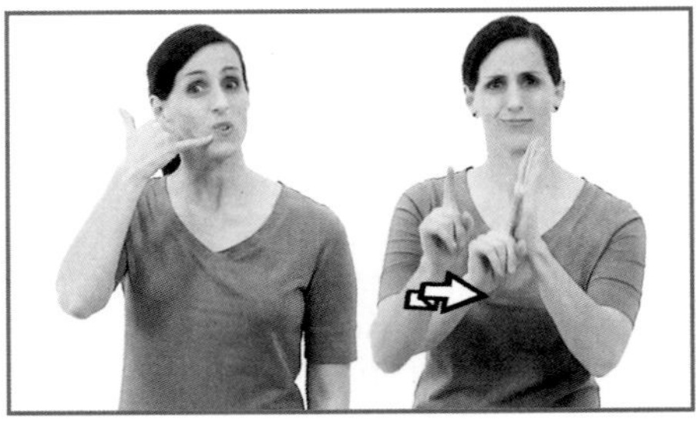

11. telling someone that the phone is ringing

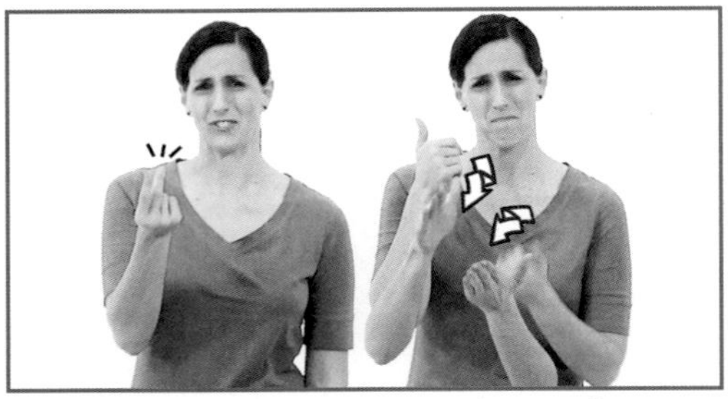

12. informing someone that a dog is barking

13. informing someone that a baby is crying

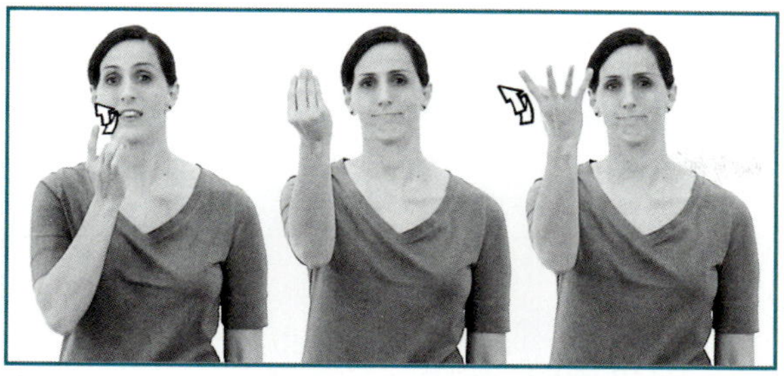

14. telling someone that a light is flashing

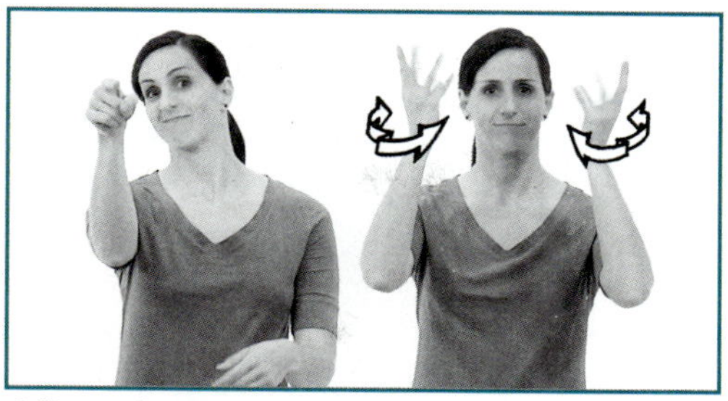

15. informing someone that sirens are blaring

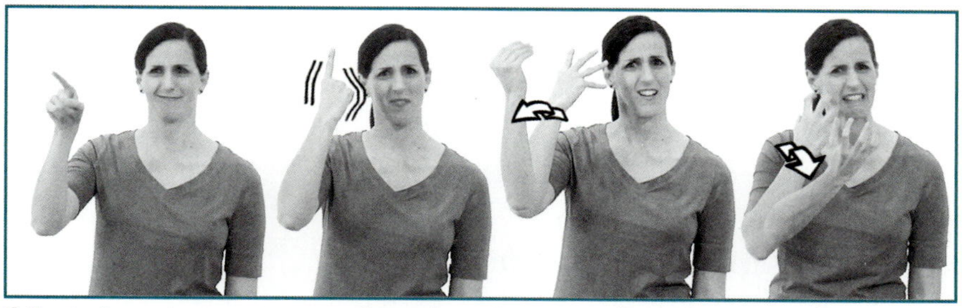

16. informing someone that there's some shouting outside

17. telling someone about an announcement of a delayed flight

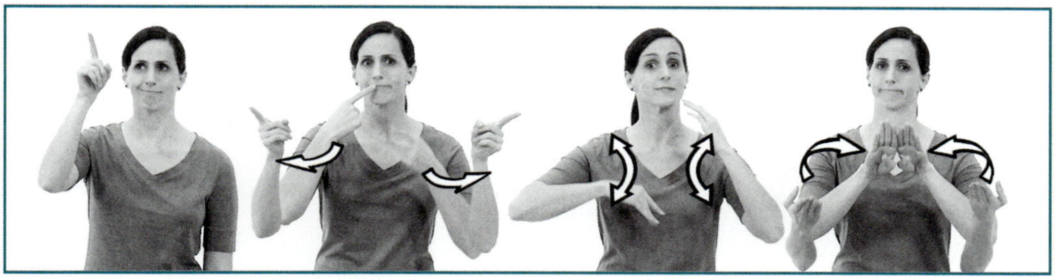

18. telling someone about an announcement that the building is about to close

SIGNING NATURALLY

Homework 10:11

STORY: A LESSON LEARNED

View the story **A Lesson Learned**, then answer the questions below.

1. Describe the family.

2. Why did the father ask Melvin to babysit?

3. What did Melvin teach the little girl and why?

4. After Melvin left, what happened during the night?

5. Why is the title **A Lesson Learned** appropriate for this story?

Answers given in class.

New Signs

1. to be enthusiastic, eager, or excited

2. to be thrilled about; to be delighted

DEAF PROFILE

ALICE TAYLOR TERRY (1878–1950)

"The happy expression on the faces of the sign-users told me more powerful than words have ever told me, that it, this sign-language, is the one reliable means in the world to drive away the sense of isolation."

Like many of her generation, Alice Taylor Terry attended a residential school for the Deaf, married a Deaf man, and was an active member of local Deaf organizations. Yet, she stood out among her peers because she was one of the few women who attended college, was an accomplished writer, an outspoken advocate for using Sign Language in schools for the Deaf, and a recognized leader on both the local and national stages.

Alice Taylor was born in 1878 on a Missouri farm, the youngest of several children. She became Deaf at the age of 9, and enrolled in the Missouri School for the Deaf, where she thrived. She wrote about her arrival at the school, "The happy expression on the faces of the sign-users told me more powerful than words have ever told me, that it, this sign-language, is the one reliable means in the world to drive away the sense of isolation." (*Silent Worker*, vol 33, no 2, p. 48). After graduation in 1895, she enrolled at Gallaudet College (later renamed Gallaudet University) for one year, then continued her education at Marionville College in Missouri. In 1901, she married Howard Terry, who like Alice, was a Missouri native and a Gallaudet alumnus. Several years later, they moved to Santa Monica, California, where they raised their three children.

Many of Alice Terry's works were published in national Deaf publications like the *Silent Worker*, *Silent Broadcaster*, and the *Jewish Deaf*. Some of her popular themes were the issues of eugenics, the benefits of Sign Language, driving rights for Deaf people, the importance of Deaf social life, and the need for Deaf people to organize, educate and contribute to their own communities and to the welfare of "our thousands of little deaf children across the United States." Reaching out to Deaf people through her writings, Terry pointed out the important role Deaf women played in Deaf history and praised Deaf women for their superior service to their families as wives and as mothers.

Like many others in the Deaf community, she belonged to a local deaf club, the Los Angeles Silent Club (LASC), which provided an important social outlet. In 1920 she was elected president of the association (LASC). During her tenure, the LASC passed a resolution in support of sign language and decrying the misleading propaganda promoting "pure" oralism[1] in schools. Three years later, Terry went on to serve as the first woman president of the California Association of the Deaf (from 1923 to 1926).

On the national level, Alice Terry was a member of the National Association of the Deaf (NAD) but she was not allowed to vote due to her gender. Instead she used her columns as a forum to express her ideas. She warned of the dangerous infiltration of "pure" oralism during that time. In a speech at the 1915 NAD Convention, Terry pointed out, "It may be argued that the amazing growth of Pure Oralism is a sign of progress. It cannot be, because the results do not justify the sinful waste of time and labor spent. Any system of teaching before it can be called *progressive* must be able to show widespread and lasting results. As a rule these orally taught pupils, when through [with] school, seek the other deaf to learn their sign language, fall in love with them, marry them and forget what they learned in articulation. This need surprise no one, for it is only natural."

Terry believed that the general world could be educated to see what was already true, that Deaf people's lives are good, despite, "The fierce battles we have already fought alone; the prejudice of deafness we have had to overcome also alone; the ceaseless struggle to prove to a cold, callous world that we are just like other people...!"

Alice Terry will long be remembered as an articulate and forceful figure in promoting the importance of Sign Language in educating Deaf children, and the rights of Deaf people to achieve full citizenship status. She died just short of her 72nd birthday in April 1950.

---

[1] Oralism is the belief that deaf children should be taught exclusively by lipreading and speech, without the use of sign language. Oralism in the United States dates back to 1867 when the Clarke Institution for Deaf Mutes in Massachusetts, and the Institution for the Improved Instruction of Deaf Mutes in New York City, known as Lexington School, opened. Oralism established wide and deep roots in education of Deaf children, after the overwhelming vote to ban Sign Language from the education of Deaf children at the 1880 International Congress on Education of the Deaf in Milan. Another powerful boost to oralism was when Alexander Graham Bell used his fame and wealth to advocate for speech training, and not sign language, as essential to Deaf people's personal and professional advancement.

Homework 10:12

LOOKING FOR A MISPLACED ITEM

View **The Missing Sandwich** story. See how Tonique tells her story according to the storyboard below. A storyboard is a series of pictures that represent the sequence of events that takes place in the story.

I. Background

II. Body

I. III. Conclusion

LANGUAGE ELEMENTS

Review the following language elements to describe searching for a missing item.

The Search

For each of the three (or more) searches incorporate these language elements.

- ***Rationale for Search (transition)***

  To begin the search in a particular location, explain the thought that led you to look in that location. Be sure to use this sign.

"it occurred to me"

- ***Spatial Agreement***

  Set up locations in your signing space in a way that resembles the real locations from your experience. Be sure the locations remain constant throughout the story. Then, have your movement verbs, including classifiers, match the locations.

Examples from Tonique's story:

from the kitchen to the office

from the office to the kitchen

from the kitchen to the car

entering the bathroom

going from the bathroom to the kitchen

from the office to the front door

from the front door to the office

- ***Word Order***
  Name the object before using an instrument classifier (ICL) to show how you handled it.

Examples from Tonique's story:

name object: sandwich — use ICL: put inside purse

name object: refrigerator — use ICL: open refrigerator door

name object: car — use ICL: open car trunk

name object: money use ICL: give money to newspaper boy

- ***Role Shift***
  When you describe the action of yourself searching for the item, be sure to use the sign for "look at," moving the hand to indicate where you are searching. Be sure your head and eye gaze move in a way that matches the movement of that sign.

Examples from Tonique's story (notice the head and eye gaze move together with the sign for "look at"):

looking through the refrigerator

looking over the counter

looking inside the car trunk

looking inside the upper cabinet

looking inside the lower cabinet

- *End the Search*
  Be sure to end each unsuccessful search with this sign.

not present, not there

Assignment

MISPLACED ITEM

Develop your own story about looking for something you lost or misplaced.

Storyboard

Develop your storyboard following the narrative structure below. A storyboard is a series of pictures (photographed or drawn) to represent the sequence of events (see Tonique's storyboard on page 305). Use the storyboard to help you visualize and remember the details in the story.

Narrative Structure

I. Background
II. Body
   a. the search (at least three searches)
   b. the discovery
III. Conclusion

Language Elements

Incorporate the language elements when describing each search (pages 306–309). For the Conclusion, use one of these signs below to indicate how you felt about finding the item.

to feel annoyed after realizing you should have known better

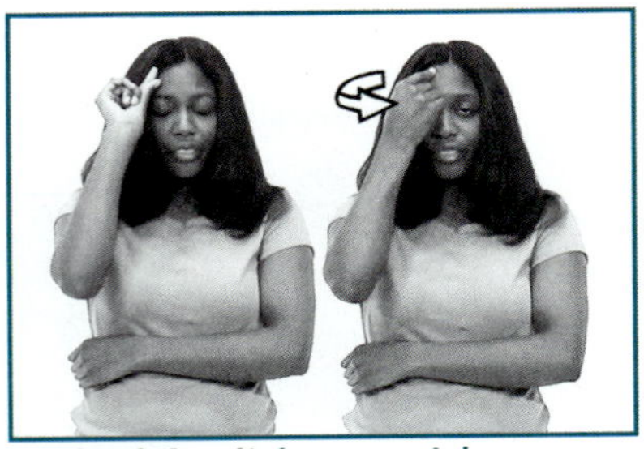

to feel foolish; stupid

Rehearse your story until you do not need to look at the storyboard to tell the story. Be prepared to turn in your storyboard at the time you tell your story.

Unit 10 Review: Self-Assessment

Write the number of: classes you missed: _____
homework assignments not completed for class: ____
hours you practiced/used signs outside of the classroom per week: _____

Now that you are done with this unit, rate yourself using the list below: **5** indicates feeling the most comfortable and confident about your skill in that area and **1** indicates feeling the least confident.

NOTE: If you marked **3** or lower, you should review that portion of the workbook and write down steps you plan to take to improve your skills in that area.

1. I know how to use the temporal aspect to describe a person's tendency.	5	4	3	2	1
2. I know to use predicative adjectives, and not attributive adjectives, to describe someone's personal qualities.	5	4	3	2	1
3. I know the structure to follow when translating wh-word questions.	5	4	3	2	1
4. I can tell a price or a cost using dollar and cent number patterns.	5	4	3	2	1
5. I can elaborate on a situation using role shift to support my opinion(s) about someone.	5	4	3	2	1
6. I can follow the sequence to tell where an item is located in a room.	5	4	3	2	1
7. I know to use contrastive structure when translating "which" questions.	5	4	3	2	1
8. I can compare two people's personal qualities using the contrastive structure.	5	4	3	2	1
9. I know how to politely interrupt a conversation to deliver a message.	5	4	3	2	1
10. I know how to politely interrupt someone talking to me and to resume the conversation.	5	4	3	2	1
11. When viewing the story "A Lesson Learned," I'm able to figure out the meaning of what is signed even though I don't know every sign Melvin used.	5	4	3	2	1
12. I can tell a story about an item I have misplaced by following the narrative structure and incorporating the language elements to describe the search.	5	4	3	2	1

Steps I will take: ______________________________

____

NOTES:

untitled 1
Tony Fowler

Digital Painting

UNIT 11

Discussing Plans and Goals

SIGNING NATURALLY

Homework 11:1

DISCUSSING ONE'S KNOWLEDGE AND ABILITIES

The signs below are used to discuss types and levels of knowledge and abilities a person may have. Review the signs and their definitions before beginning the activity.

A. being well-informed about a subject

B. having the ability or training to perform a certain task well; to be skilled in

C. having a talent or unusual ability to perform tasks

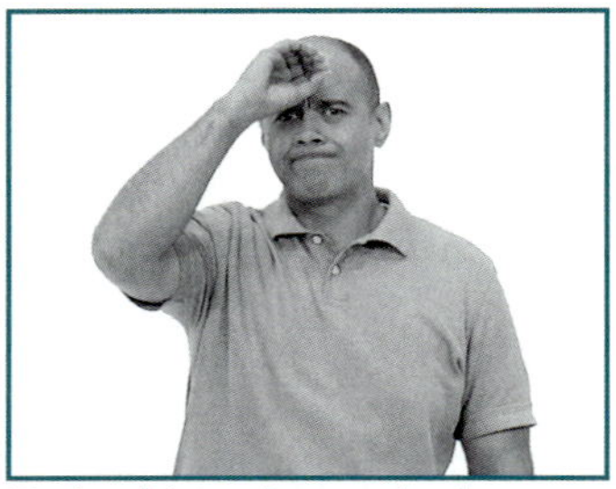

D. lacking knowledge or awareness

E. not knowing how to

F. do something without skill or elegance; clumsy

G. not having the necessary training or skills; inept

H. not able to; can't due to some type of obstacle

MINIDIALOGUES

Watch the mini-dialogues and answer the questions below.

Minidialogue 1

1. Summarize the information shared in the dialogue.

2. Which sign(s) from above were are to describe each person's familiarity with the topic. Circle the letter(s):

   Ursula: **A B C D E F G H**

   The person off screen (K on forehead):

   A B C D E F G H

Minidialogue 2

1. Summarize the information shared in the dialogue.

2. Which sign(s) are used to describe each person's abilities? Circle the letter(s):

   John: **A B C D E F G H**

   David: **A B C D E F G H**

Minidialogue 3

1. Which sign(s) are used to describe each person's abilities? Circle the letter(s) and write what each person could do in how much time.

   JT: **A B C D E F G H**

   What can he do? In how much time?

   Justin: **A B C D E F G H**

   What can he do? In how much time?

   Melvin: **A B C D E F G H**

   What can he do? In how much time?

Minidialogue 4

1. Circle the letter(s) for the sign(s) that describe Terrylene's ability.

   Sign(s) Terrylene uses to describe herself:

   A B C D E F G H

   Sign(s) Iva uses to describe Terrylene:

   A B C D E F G H

2. List the steps Iva recommends Terrylene take to pursue her dream.

a.

b.

c.

3. Circle the letters for the sign(s) Iva uses at the end of each step.

A B C D E F G H

Answers on page 521–522.

VOCABULARY REVIEW

Review the vocabulary on the video.

Having Knowledge or Ability

1. being well-informed about a subject

2. having a talent or unusual ability to perform tasks well

3. having the ability or training to perform a certain task well; to be skilled in

Lacking Knowledge

4. lacking knowledge or awareness

5. not knowing how to

Lacking Ability

or

6. not having the necessary training or skills; inept

7. do something without skill or elegance; clumsy

8. not able to; can't due to some type of obstacle

Areas of Study

9.

10.

11.

12.

13.

14.

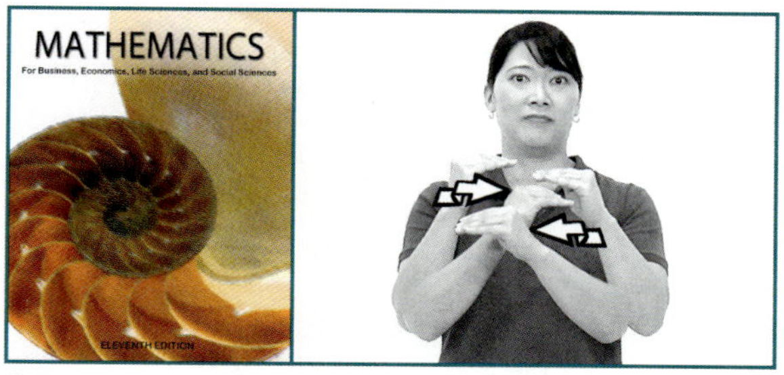

15.

16.

17.

18.

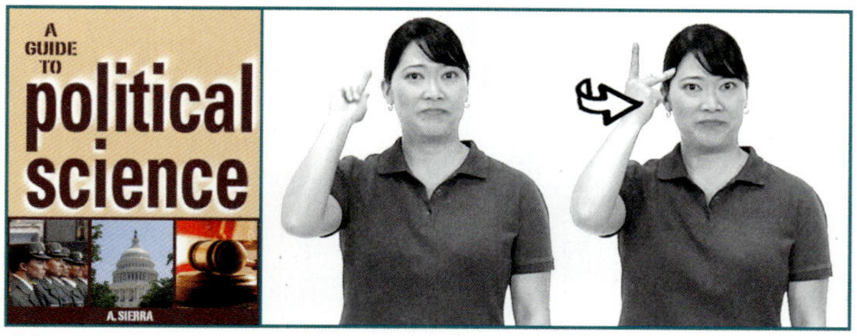

19.

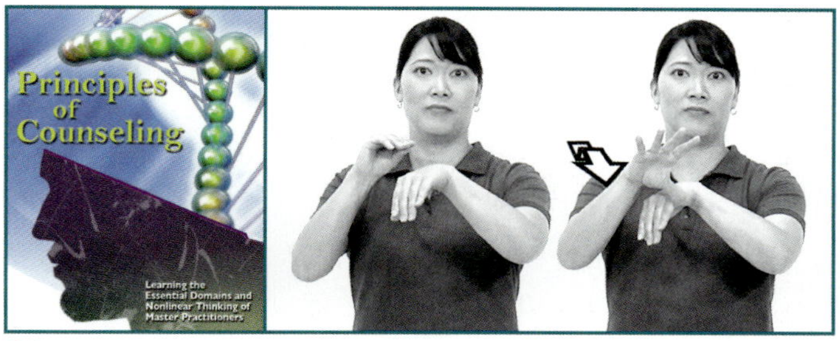

20.

21.

22.

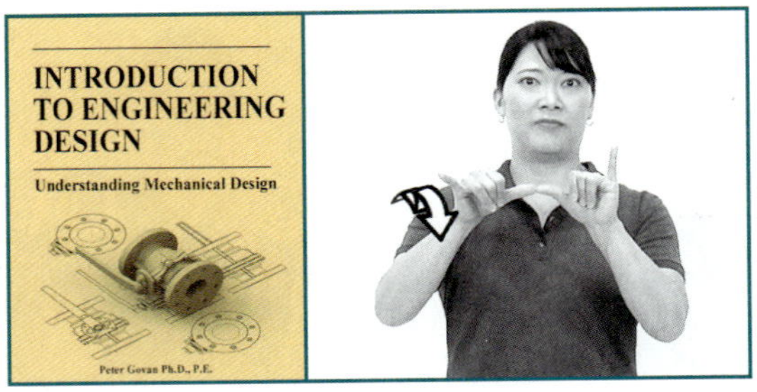

23.

24.

or

Fingerspell IT

25.

Others

26.

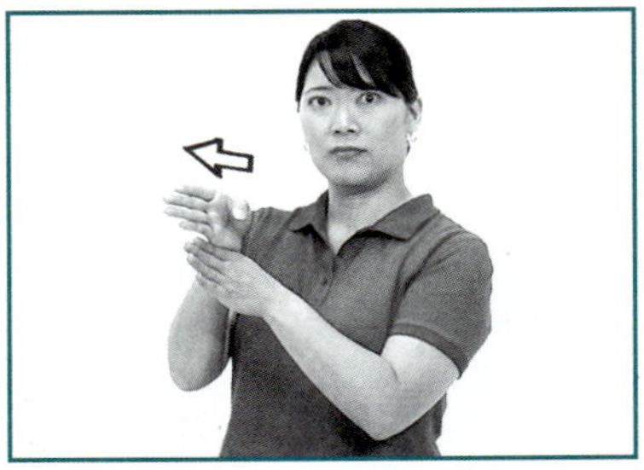

27. a field of study chosen by a student to represent their area of interest or concentration; to major in

Homework 11:2

NUMBERS REVIEW

Number Types

Iva reviews these number types using the number 3. Observe the palm orientation and movement associated with each type of number.

- cardinal
- age
- dollars
- cents
- clock
- minutes
- hours
- days
- weeks
- months

Number Combinations

Iva reviews number combinations, using the number 3. Observe the palm orientation and movement of the number 3.

- year (2003, 1903)
- money ($3.03)
- clock (3:03)

Write the Number

Iva will sign a number. Write the number and the number type in the blanks below.

	number	*type*		*number*	*type*
1.	______	______________	11.	______	______________
2.	______	______________	12.	______	______________
3.	______	______________	13.	______	______________
4.	______	______________	14.	______	______________
5.	______	______________	15.	______	______________
6.	______	______________	16.	______	______________
7.	______	______________	17.	______	______________
8.	______	______________	18.	______	______________
9.	______	______________	19.	______	______________
10.	______	______________	20.	______	______________

Answers on page 523.

EXPLAIN THE NUMBER

Melvin, Terrylene, Derrick and Amber will sign sentences using a money, year, or clock number. In the blanks below, write the number, the type and to what it refers.

	number	*type*	*what it refers to*
1.	______	________	______________________________
2.	______	________	______________________________
3.	______	________	______________________________
4.	______	________	______________________________
5.	______	________	______________________________
6.	______	________	______________________________
7.	______	________	______________________________
8.	______	________	______________________________
9.	______	________	______________________________
10.	______	________	______________________________
11.	______	________	______________________________
12.	______	________	______________________________
13.	______	________	______________________________
14.	______	________	______________________________
15.	______	________	______________________________
16.	______	________	______________________________
17.	______	________	______________________________
18.	______	________	______________________________
19.	______	________	______________________________
20.	______	________	______________________________

Answers on page 524.

SIGNING NATURALLY

Homework 11:3

ASKING FOR OPINION ABOUT SOMEONE

In the five minidialogues below, observe:

- Signer A explaining his or her need and asking for opinions about the person;
- Signer B, giving his or her opinion, including descriptions of the person's qualities along with examples to support the opinion, and offering possible drawbacks to having the person in the given "role";
- and finally, Signer A explaining what he or she plans to do.

Minidialogue 1

Lauren is looking for a travel companion and asks Justin about Rose.

1. What is Justin's relationship with Rose?

2. How does Justin describe Rose ?

3. What are the two possible drawbacks of traveling with Rose?

New Signs

former spouse or partner in a relationship

ordinary, nothing special

to move from place to place

a brief amount of time (at each place)

Minidialogue 2

Tonique asks Iva if Renee would be a good potential roommate.

1. What is Iva's relationship with Renee?

2. How does Iva describe Renee?

3. What are possible drawbacks of rooming with Renee?

New Sign

every month, monthly

Minidialogue 3

Melvin checks with Terrylene about the idea of hiring Gerri to work with him.

1. What is Terrylene's relationship with Gerri?

2. How does Terrylene describe Gerri?

3. What are possible drawbacks of working with Gerri?

Minidialogue 4

Amber asks Justin about David, a guy she is considering a date with.

1. What is Justin's relationship with David?

2. How does Justin describe David?

3. What are the possible drawbacks of dating David?

New Sign

have no interest in; not fond of; to not care for

Minidialogue 5

Melvin needs a babysitter and asks Terrylene about Erin.

1. What is Terrylene's relationship with Erin?

2. How does Terrylene describe Erin?

3. What are the possible drawbacks of hiring Erin?

New Signs

to behave or conduct oneself in an acceptable way

full of ideas; imaginative

to be affectionate; to love or adore someone

to be marvelous, amazing, wonderful

Answers given in class.

Learn the Dialogue

Practice the key phrases used in the dialogue.

A: give name; ask who
B: explain relationship
A: explain need, ask opinion about person as a potential...

- travel companion
- roommate
- employee
- date
- babysitter

B: give opinion about him or her

- at least three personal quality signs
- example(s) to support your opinion
- at least one drawback about this person

A: ask follow-up questions if necessary
B: reply
A: tell what you plan to do

For *"A: explain need, ask opinion about person as a potential..."*

- travel companion

For *"A: tell what you plan to do"*

For ***"A: explain need, ask opinion about person as a potential..."***

- roommate

For ***"A: tell what you plan to do"***

For ***"A: explain need, ask opinion about person as a potential..."***

- employee

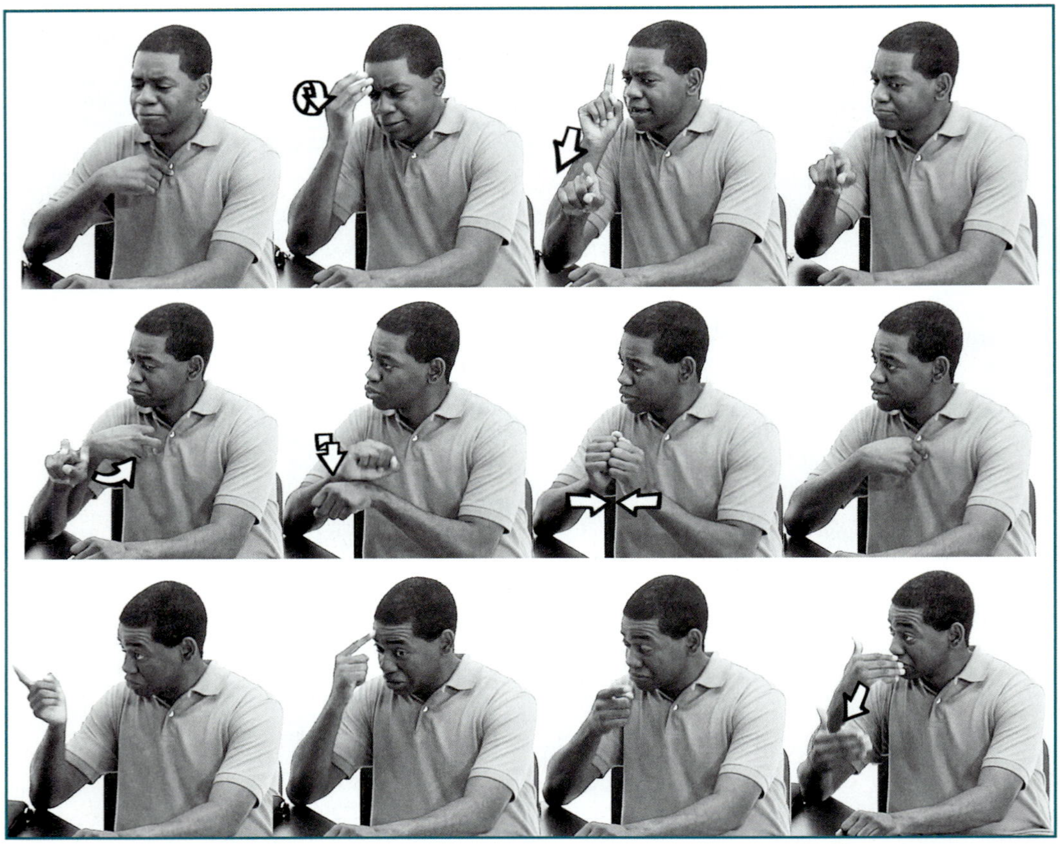

For ***"A: tell what you plan to do"***

For ***"A: explain need, ask opinion about person as a potential..."***

- date

For ***"A: tell what you plan to do"***

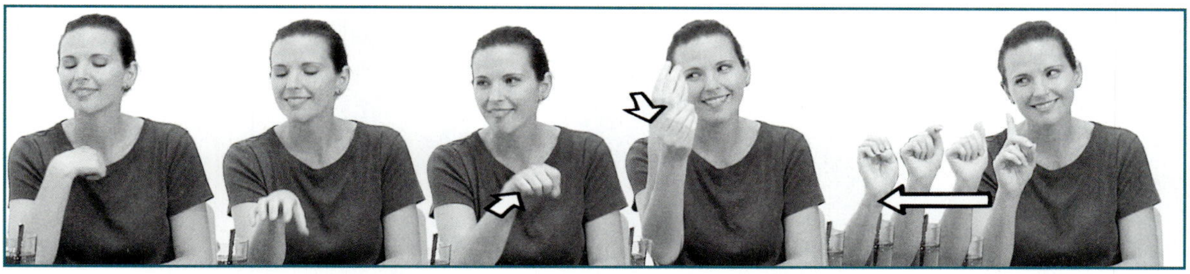

For ***"A: explain need, ask opinion about person as a potential..."***

- babysitter

For ***"A: tell what you plan to do"***

VOCABULARY REVIEW

Review the vocabulary on the video.

Verbs

1. to get in contact with

2. to hire someone

3. to catch on quite easily

4. to flirt with

5. having a creative mind

6. to transfer from here to there

7. to have experience with

Homework 11:4

REACTIONS

This group of signs are used to describe one's reaction to situations. These signs function as predicative adjectives. They are not used to describe the effect one has on someone else. For example, we can use **Reaction 13** to say "I'm embarrassed" but not to say "She embarrassed me." Review the signs and their definitions.

1. a sentimental reaction to something heartwarming or heartbreaking

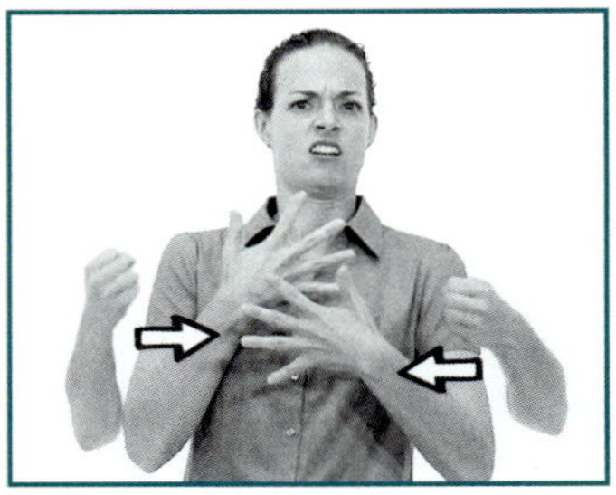

2. a frightened or alarmed reaction; to be scared

3. a joyful reaction upon learning good news; to be thrilled

4. a disheartened reaction; to feel let down

5. a reaction to something that failed to meet one's expectations; to be disappointed

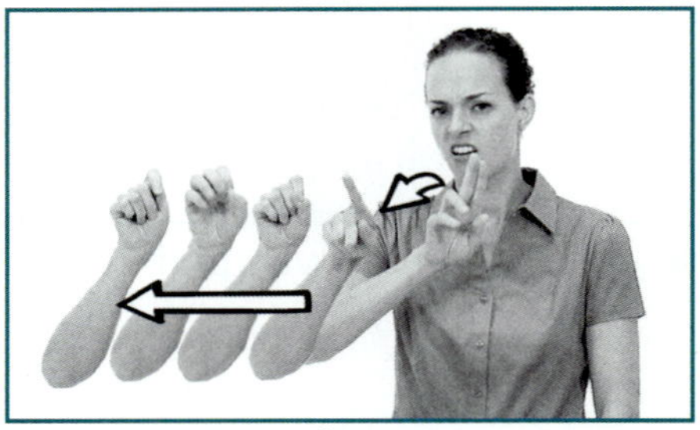

6. a reaction of anxious uneasiness or worry; to be disturbed or upset

7. an angry or furious reaction

8. a puzzled reaction; uncertain of what's going on

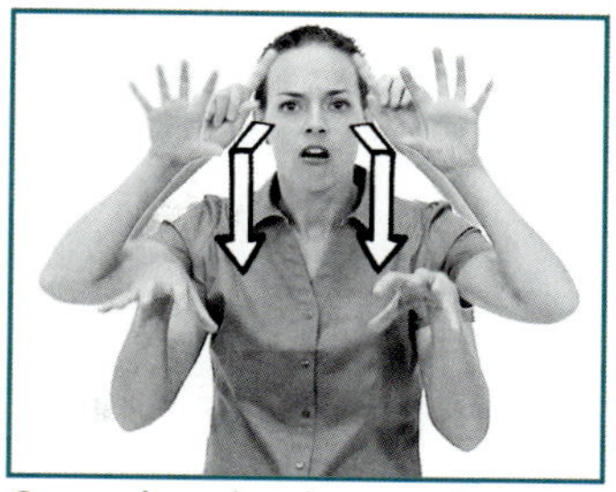

9. a shocked reaction; temporarily unable to react upon seeing or learning something surprising or tragic

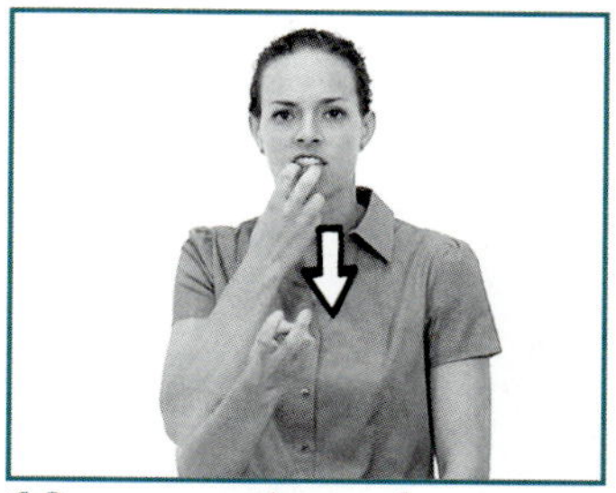

10. a reaction of astonishment to something that is hard to believe

11. a sheepish reaction after learning you made a fool of yourself

12. an annoyed reaction toward yourself after realizing you should have known better

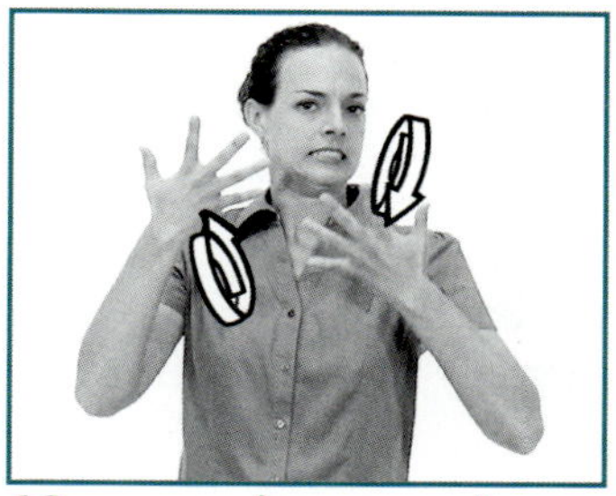

13. an embarrassed reaction upon realizing others have witnessed your predicament

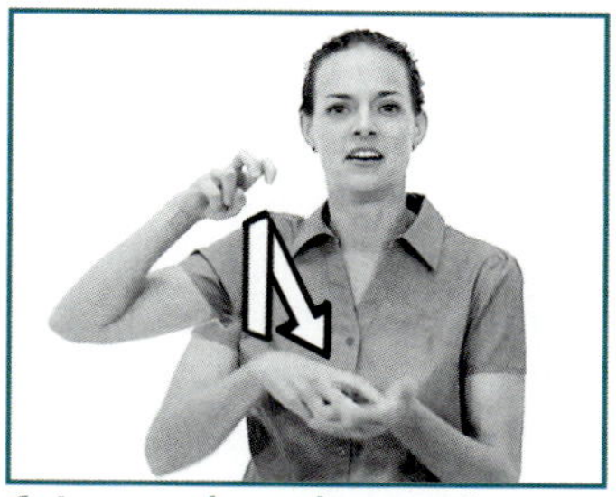

14. an elated reaction; with great joy

15. a relieved reaction; being freed from fear or worry

ASKING HYPOTHETICAL QUESTIONS

One way to elicit reaction signs is to present a hypothetical question asking how one would feel or react to a given situation.

To ask a hypothetical question,
- **use hypothetical sign**
- **state sequence of events**
- **ask the question**

For "• *use hypothetical sign*"—be sure to raise brows and tilt head up slightly to signal it's a conditional clause.

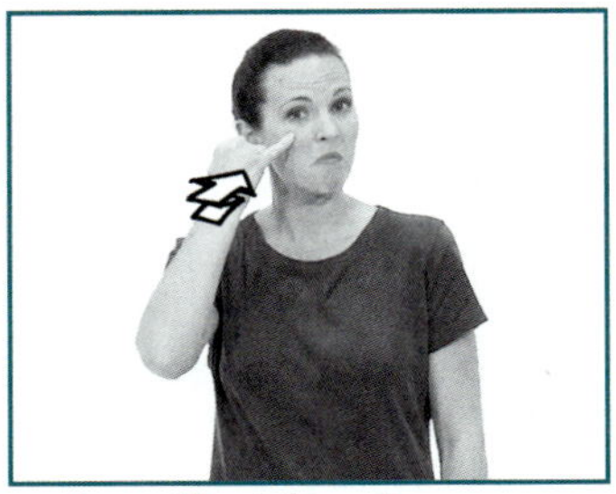

a sign that begins a hypothetical question

For "• *state sequence of events*"—when describing a situation that involves several actions, be sure to arrange the information sequentially.

For "• *ask the question*"—use either phrase below. Be sure to furrow brows, drop head forward slightly and hold the last sign.

ask how one would react

ask how one would feel

MINIDIALOGUES

Watch the following minidialogues where a person will present hypothetical questions and two people give their reactions. Write the situation and choose which reaction is more appropriate for the situation and explain why.

Minidialogue 1

Situation: ____

____

____

Whose reaction is more appropriate? ❑ John's ❑ David's

Why? ____

Minidialogue 2

Situation: ____

____

____

Whose reaction is more appropriate? ❑ David's ❑ Ursula's

Why? ____

Minidialogue 3

Situation: ____

____

____

Whose reaction is more appropriate? ❑ Ursula's ❑ Tonique's

Why? ____

New Signs

publishing company

to publish or print

Minidialogue 4

Situation: ____

____

____

Whose reaction is more appropriate? ❑ Tonique's ❑ John's

Why? ____

Minidialogue 5

Situation: ____

____

____

Whose reaction is more appropriate? ❑ Amber's ❑ Derrick's

Why? ____

Minidialogue 6

Situation: ______________________________

____

____

Whose reaction is more appropriate? ❑ Derrick's ❑ Terrylene's

Why? ______________________________

New Sign

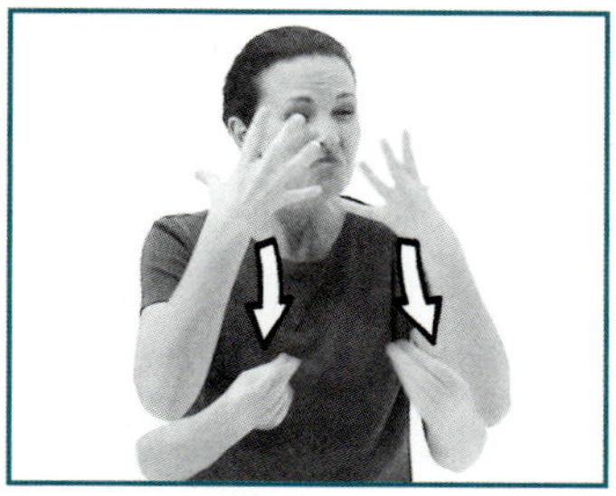

to get soaked or wet

Minidialogue 7

Situation: ______________________________

____

____

Whose reaction is more appropriate? ❑ Terrylene's ❑ Amber's

Why? ______________________________

Answers on page 525–526.

VOCABULARY REVIEW

Review the vocabulary on the video.

Reactions

1. a sentimental reaction to something heartwarming or heartbreaking

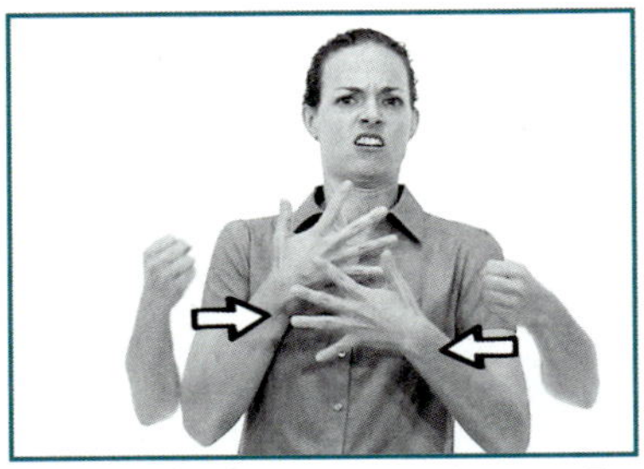

2. a frightened or alarmed reaction; to be scared

3. a joyful reaction upon learning good news; to be thrilled

4. a disheartened reaction; to feel let down

5. a reaction to something that failed to meet one's expectations, to be disappointed

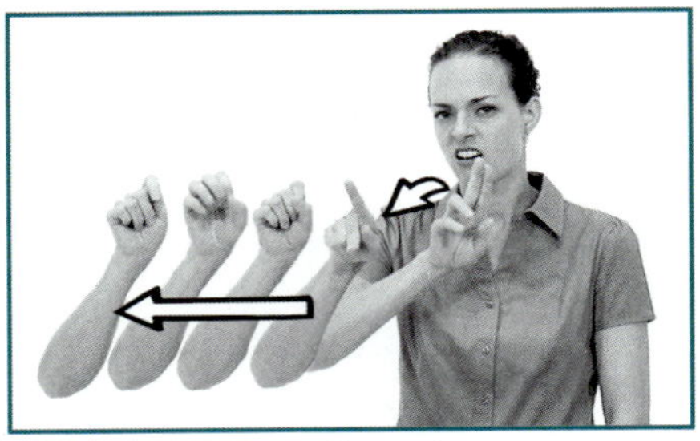

6. a reaction of anxious uneasiness or worry; to be disturbed or upset

7. an angry or furious reaction

8. a puzzled reaction; uncertain of what's going on

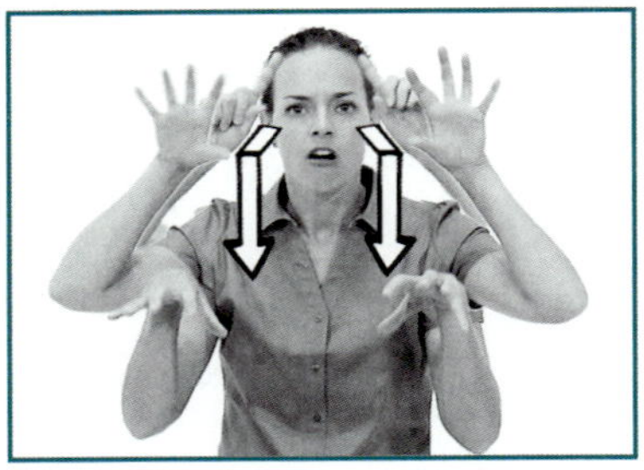

9. a shocked reaction; temporarily unable to react upon seeing or learning something surprising or tragic

10. a reaction of astonishment to something that is hard to believe

11. a sheepish reaction after learning you made a fool of yourself

12. an annoyed reaction toward yourself after realizing you should have known better

13. an embarrassed reaction upon realizing others have witnessed your predicament

14. an elated reaction; with great joy

15. a relieved reaction; being freed from fear or worry

Nouns

16.

17.

18.

19.

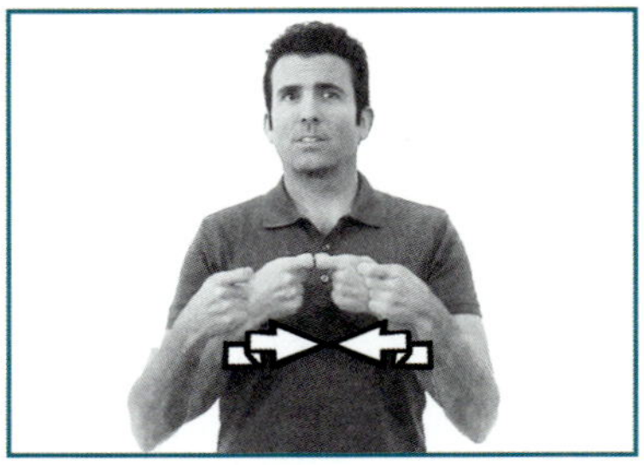

20. a form of energy carried through wires; electricity

Verbs

21. to run out of; to be all out of

22. to be permanently erased or deleted

23. to request or apply for admission to a university

Others

24. feeling sad or lonely because one has no friends or company

25. at the very end of

26. to be full; no vacancy

Homework 11:5

STATES AND PROVINCES 1

ASL is used in the United States and Canada. How do ASL users name the states and provinces? Some are signed, but many are fingerspelled.

There are four kinds of fingerspelling forms used—the full name is fingerspelled, the first few letters are fingerspelled, the first and last letters are fingerspelled, or the initials are fingerspelled.

The U.S. States

View. John demonstrates how to name all fifty states. Pay attention to the movement and palm orientation of the fingerspelled forms.

Alabama	fingerspell first few letters (ALA)
Alaska	signed, or fingerspelled in full
Arizona	signed, or fingerspelled in full
Arkansas	fingerspell first few letters (ARK)
California	signed
Colorado	signed (sign for "color," then fingerspell "ADO"), fingerspelled in full, or first few letters (COLO)
Connecticut	fingerspell first few letters (CONN)
Delaware	fingerspell first few letters (DEL)
Florida	fingerspell first few letters (FLA)
Georgia	fingerspell the first and last letters (GA)
Hawaii	signed, or fingerspelled in full
Idaho	fingerspelled in full
Illinois	fingerspell first few letters (ILL)
Indiana	fingerspell first few letters (IND)
Iowa	fingerspelled in full
Kansas	fingerspelled in full, or the first few letters (KAN)
Kentucky	fingerspell the first and last letters (KY)
Louisiana	fingerspell the first and last letters (LA)
Maine	signed, or fingerspelled in full

Maryland	fingerspell the first and last letters (MD)
Massachusetts	fingerspell first few letters (MASS)
Michigan	fingerspell first few letters (MICH)
Minnesota	fingerspell first few letters (MINN)
Mississippi	fingerspell first few letters (MISS)
Missouri	fingerspell the first and last letters (MO)*
Montana	signed, or fingerspelled in full
Nebraska	fingerspell first few letters (NEB)
Nevada	fingerspelled in full, or the first few letters (NEV)
New Hampshire	fingerspell initials (NH)
New Jersey	fingerspell initials (NJ)
New Mexico	fingerspell initials (NM)
New York	signed
North Carolina	fingerspell initials (NC)
North Dakota	fingerspell initials (ND)
Ohio	fingerspelled in full
Oklahoma	fingerspell first few letters (OKLA)
Oregon	signed, or fingerspelled in full
Pennsylvania	fingerspell the first and last letters (PA)
Rhode Island	fingerspell initials (RI)
South Carolina	fingerspell initials (SC)
South Dakota	fingerspell initials (SD)
Tennessee	fingerspell first few letters (TENN)
Texas	signed
Utah	fingerspelled in full
Vermont	fingerspell the first and last letters (VT)
Virginia	fingerspell initials (VA)
Washington	signed
West Virginia	signed (sign for "west," then fingerspell first and last letters VA)
Wisconsin	fingerspell first few letters (WIS or WISC)
Wyoming	fingerspell first few letters (WYO)

* This is an exception because the "O" is not the last letter in "Missouri," but the fourth from last.

The Canadian Provinces

View. Ursula demonstrates how to name the 10 Canadian provinces. Pay attention to the movement and palm orientation of the fingerspelled forms.

Alberta	signed
British Colombia	fingerspell initials (BC)
Manitoba	signed, or fingerspelled in full
New Brunswick	fingerspell initials (NB)
Newfoundland*	signed
Nova Scotia	fingerspell initials (NS) (2 variations)
Ontario	signed (2 variations)
Prince Edward Island	fingerspell initials (PEI)
Quebec	signed (2 variations)
Saskatchewan	fingerspell first few letters (SASK) (2 variations)

CIRCLE THE STATE

Circle the state that John or Ursula names.

1.	Minnesota	Tennessee	Connecticut
2.	North Dakota	South Dakota	Maryland
3.	Utah	New Hampshire	Ohio
4.	Virginia	Pennsylvania	Vermont
5.	North Carolina	New Jersey	New Mexico
6.	South Carolina	South Dakota	North Carolina
7.	Georgia	New Mexico	Missouri
8.	Iowa	Idaho	Ohio
9.	New Brunswick	Nebraska	Nevada

Answers on page 526.

* In 2001 the Constitution of Canada was amended to officially change the name of the province to Newfoundland and Labrador. In day-to-day communication, the sign shown on video is used to refer to the island of Newfoundland, or, less commonly, the entire province. You may also see the sign, plus fingerspell LAB, or less frequently the initials NL.

WRITE THE STATE

Write the state that Ursula or John names.

1. ________	13. ________
2. ________	14. ________
3. ________	15. ________
4. ________	16. ________
5. ________	17. ________
6. ________	18. ________
7. ________	19. ________
8. ________	20. ________
9. ________	21. ________
10. ________	22. ________
11. ________	23. ________
12. ________	24. ________

Answers on page 527.

WRITE THE PROVINCE

Write the province that Ursula or John names.

1. ________	4. ________
2. ________	5. ________
3. ________	6. ________

Answers on page 527.

VOCABULARY REVIEW

Review the vocabulary on the video.

States that Are Signed

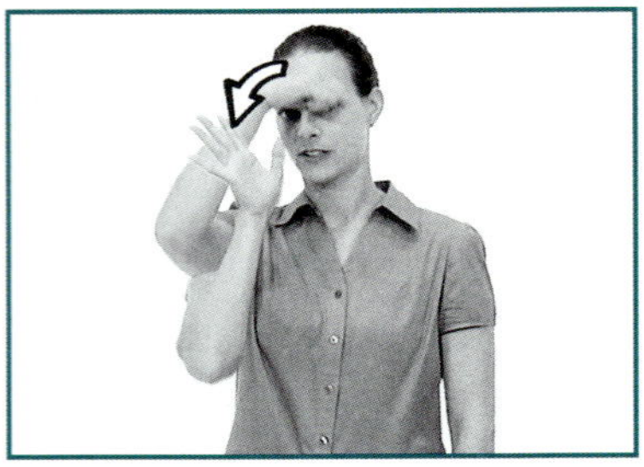
1. Alaska

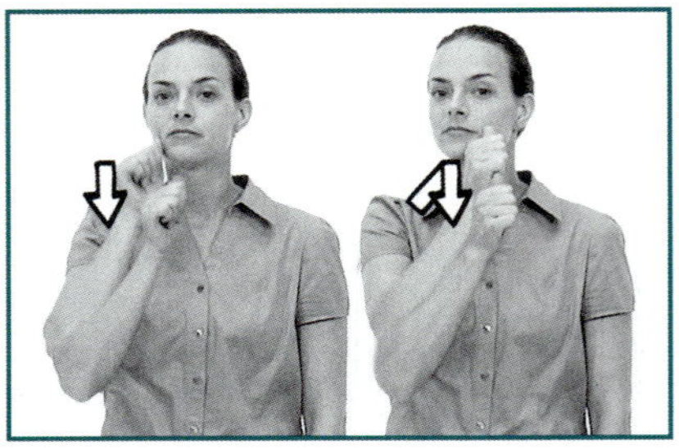
2. Arizona

3. California

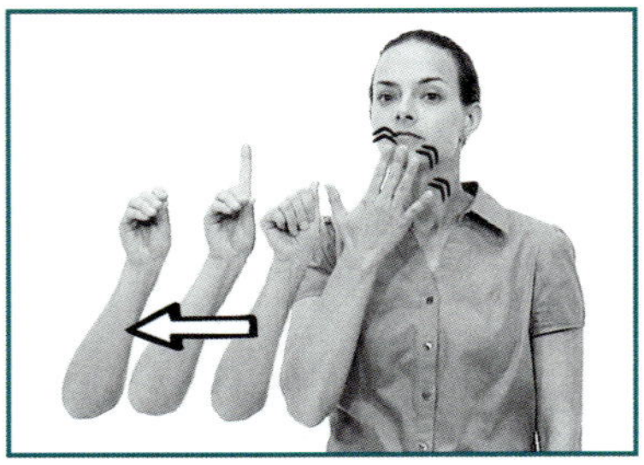
4. Colorado

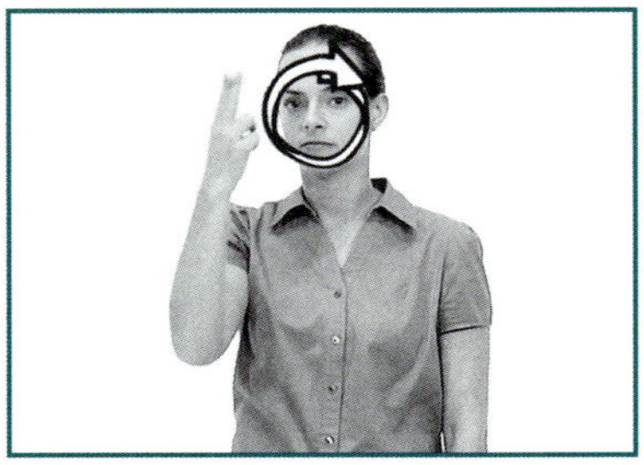
5. Hawaii

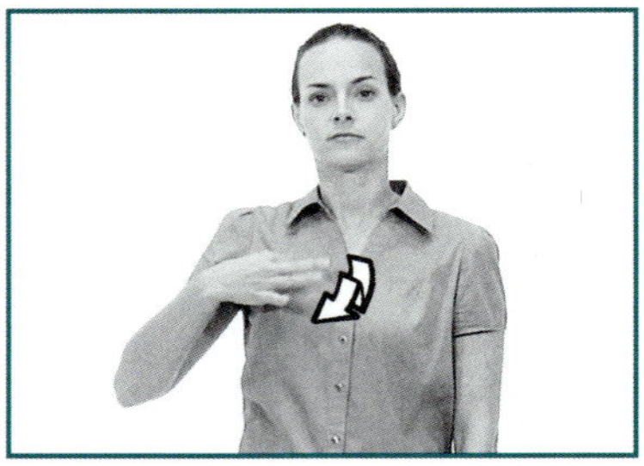
6. Maine

7. Montana

8. New York

9. Oregon

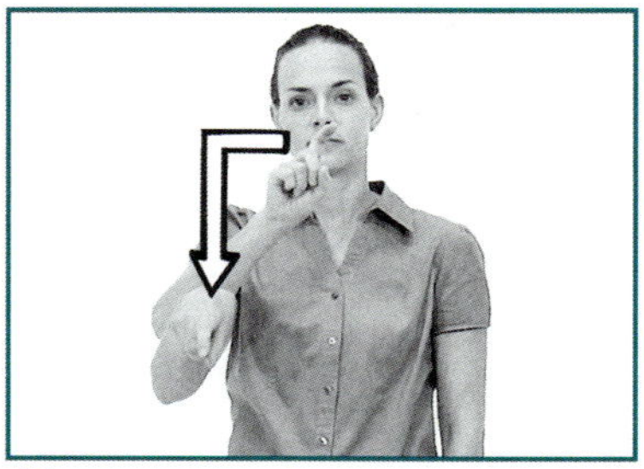
10. Texas

11. Washington

Provinces that Are Signed

12. Alberta

13. Manitoba

14. Newfoundland

or

15. Ontario

or

16. Quebec

Others

or

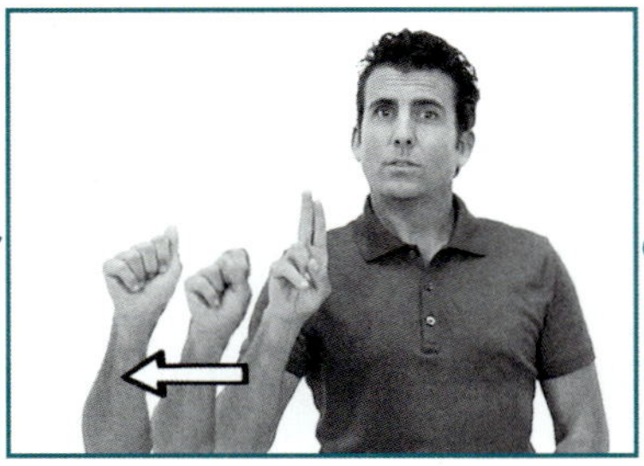

or

17. United States

or

Fingerspell STATE

18. state

19. Canada

or

20. province

SIGNING NATURALLY

Homework 11:6

CONVERSATION 2

Suzanne (A) and Lauren (B) demonstrate this dialogue in which they make plans to take their families to the Apple Festival.

Signer A: invite B to join him or her
B: respond
- accept invitation
- state problem with date
- decline invitation

A and B: finalize plans if B accepts
A and B: close conversation

New Signs

to select a course of action; to make a decision

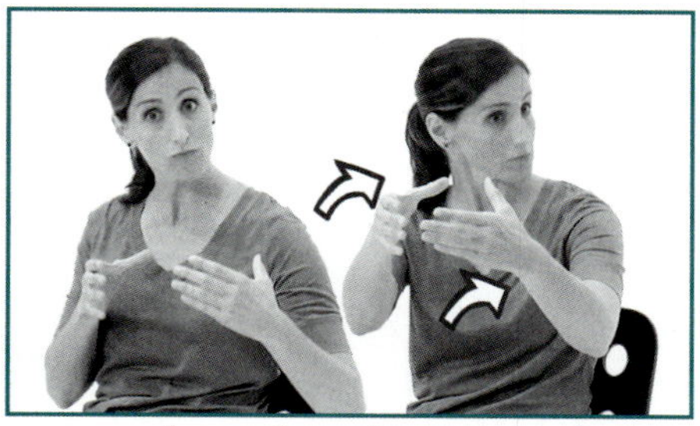

group of people going someplace together

performance or show

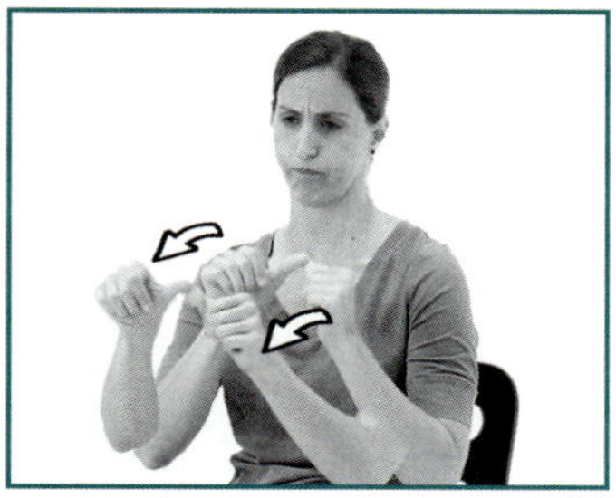

to last until; to go on or continue

CONVERSATION 3

Suzanne (A) and Lauren (B) demonstrate this dialogue taking place a few days later when Suzanne has to cancel their plan.

A: refer to the plan you made together (use relative clause)
B: acknowledge
A: tell you must cancel the plans; explain why
A and B: close conversation

New Signs

to give assurance; to promise

to proceed or carry on with plans

Key Grammar

RELATIVE CLAUSE

One way to raise a topic is to use a relative clause. A relative clause gives additional information about the noun to which it refers. For instance, in the sentence "I have to cancel the plan *that we made to go skiing next weekend*," the clause "that we made to go skiing next weekend" specifies of which plan (the noun) the signer is speaking. To sign a relative clause, the signer needs to raise brows, cheek and upper lip, and nod head.

View. Watch Suzanne use a relative clause (raised brows, cheeks and upper lip, and nodding) to refer to the plan she and Lauren made. Once Lauren indicates she remembers, Suzanne transitions into explaining she has to cancel the plan.

MINIDIALOGUES

Watch the three video minidialogues and fill in the information below.

Minidialogue 1

1. What plans were made previously?

2. Why must the plans be canceled?

Minidialogue 2

1. What plans were made previously?

2. Why must the plan be canceled?

3. What does Derrick suggest they do instead?

New Signs

a large outdoor area with rides, food stands and entertainment

public event where something new is officially put into operation; opening ceremony

the building or construction of something

Minidialogue 3

1. What is the intended plan?

2. What is the hitch in the plan?

3. What does Amber suggest?

4. What does Lauren say she will do?

Answers given in class.

NARRATING ABOUT CANCELED PLANS

Watch Suzanne utilize the sequence below to narrate about her canceled plans.

1. **tell what was planned with the other person**
   - **tell when (date and time)**
   - **tell who (use plural pronoun)**
   - **tell about activity planned**
2. **tell what came up that caused you to cancel (use conjunction)**
3. **tell that you informed the other person and describe their reaction**
4. **close with your reaction**

Assignment

YOUR CANCELED PLAN

Pick one of your canceled plans and develop a narrative following the sequence above.

Be sure to incorporate the following in your narrative:

For ***"2. (conjunction) tell what came up that caused you to cancel,"*** use this conjunction sign to transition into telling why plans must be canceled.

For ***"3. tell you informed the other person,"*** use this agreement verb. Be sure the verb ends at the location established for the other person.

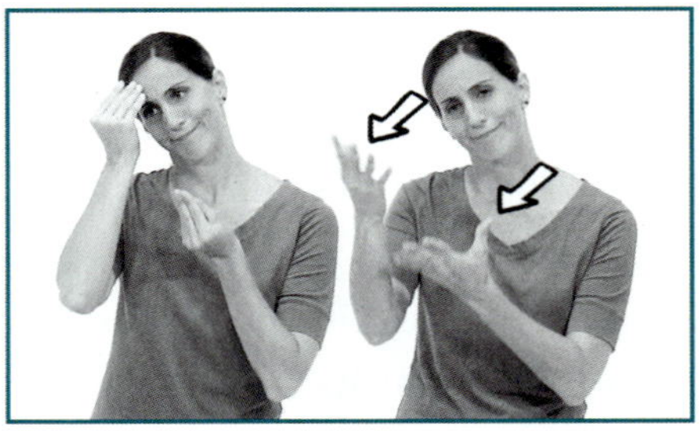

Be prepared to sign your narrative next class.

Assignment

SIGNS FOR THINKING

JT signs a narrative using all four signs below. Watch the narrative and see how the signs are used in context.

A.

- **to ponder**
- **to weigh mentally**
- **to use mind to arrive at conclusion, to make decision, to draw inferences**

B.

- **to think over**
- **to mull over**
- **to give thought or consideration to**

C.

- to suddenly remember
- to bring to mind; to recall
- a thought or idea comes to mind

D.

- an idea
- a mental image or concept conceived in the mind

Identify the best sign(s) to use (A, B, C, or D) to translate the sentences below. Put the corresponding letter next to the sentence. Be prepared to translate the sentences in class.

1. _______ I just remembered, I forgot to turn off the water.
2. _______ I wonder if she will come.
3. _______ We are considering adopting a baby.
4. _______ It occurred to me that I have not paid my bills.
5. _______ I just realized I have no money. I have to stop at an ATM to get some money.
6. _______ I like her idea.
7. _______ I just remembered I have a doctor's appointment at 3 o'clock.
8. _______ I have an idea! Why don't we go camping?
9. _______ I'm thinking about going to the beach this Saturday.
10. _______ I am still thinking about the movie I saw last night.

Answers given in class.

VOCABULARY REVIEW

Review the vocabulary on the video.

Inviting

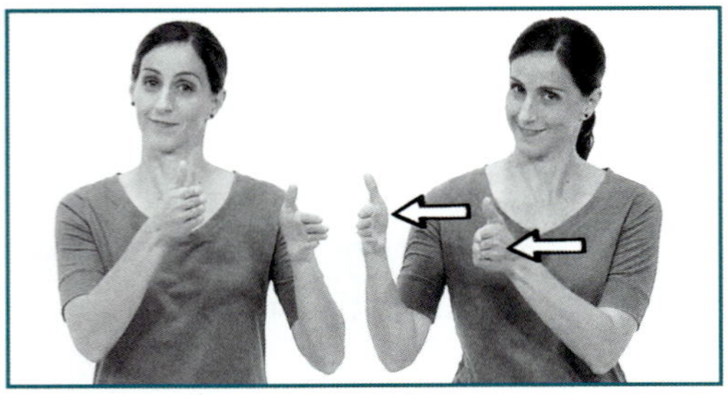

1. to make or have plans

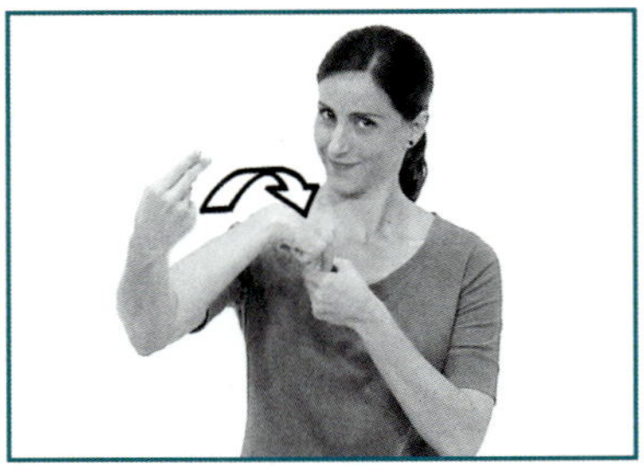

2. to participate or join in something (with me)

Declining Invitation

3. to be prevented from

4. conflict with another activity; to have a scheduling conflict

5. have no interest in; not fond of; to not care for

Canceling

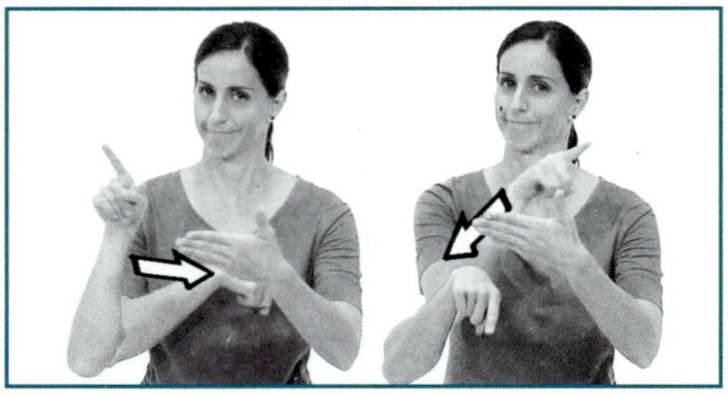

6. to call off or cancel a plan

Comments ____

7. to say "sorry"

8. gesture meaning "aww shucks" or "darn it"

9. gesture meaning "fantastic" or "perfect"

10. to look forward to

Homework 11:7

FIRST AND LAST TIME YOU DID SOMETHING

Use this dialogue to ask others about the last time they did something.

A: ask when was the last time B did something
B: tell when, explain (what, with whom, why)

Repeat Information

Observe how Justin asks Amber about the last time she rode a train, and then repeats the information to Suzanne. Notice he orients his glances and his signs "to ask" and "to tell" to reference Amber's location.

glances at Amber with the sign "to ask" then back to Suzanne

glances at Amber with the sign "to tell" then back to Suzanne

Use this dialogue to ask others your question and develop a summary using horizontal listing.

A: ask how old B was the first time she or he did something
B: tell how old

Using Horizontal Listing

Observe Suzanne surveying several people about the first time they earned money working, then sharing the results of the survey by using horizontal listing to present the information.

Notice she begins with the largest group on her non-dominant side and ends with the smallest group on her dominant side. Note her brows raise when she gives the numbers.

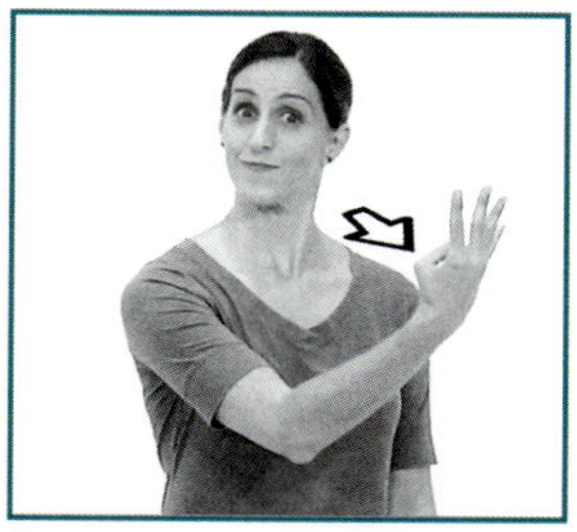

1st group (largest) (non-dominant side)

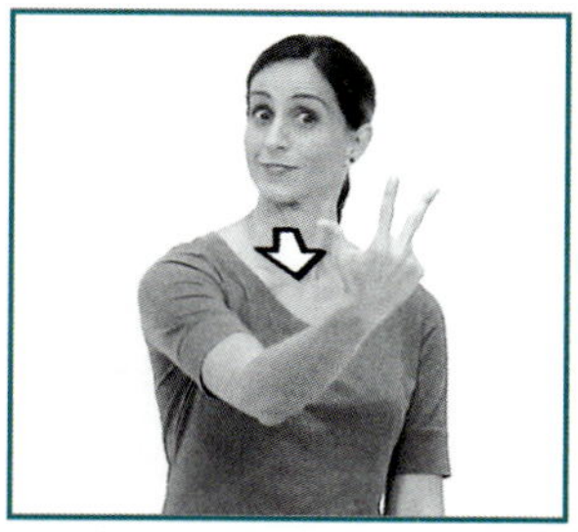

2nd group

3rd group

4th group (smallest) (dominant side)

Assignment

CONDUCT A SURVEY

Think of a question asking how old someone was the first time they did something. Ask 10 people your question, then organize the information into four groups. Be prepared to present a summary of the survey results in class. Organize your summary as follows:

- tell you surveyed 10 people
- repeat the question you asked
- tell results (arrange data into 4 groups using horizontal listing, starting with the largest group on your non-dominant side and ending with the smallest group on your dominant side).

Be sure to raise your brows when giving the number for each group.

VOCABULARY REVIEW

Review the vocabulary on the video.

1. the first time

2. the last time

3. wh-word meaning "when"

Homework 11:8

Numbers Review

David, Iva, Tonique, John and Ursula will sign sentences using money, year, or clock numbers. In the blanks below, write the number and tell to what it refers.

	number	*what it refers to*
1.	__________	__________
2.	__________	__________
3.	__________	__________
4.	__________	__________
5.	__________	__________
6.	__________	__________
7.	__________	__________
8.	__________	__________
9.	__________	__________
10.	__________	__________
11.	__________	__________
12.	__________	__________
13.	__________	__________
14.	__________	__________
15.	__________	__________

Answers on page 527.

Homework 11:9

DISCUSSING PERSONAL GOALS

Derrick's Bucket List

Derrick tells about his five goals using this narrative structure.

1. **Broach subject**
2. **State five goals**
   - **personal**
   - **lifelong learning**
   - **travel**
   - **community service**
   - **adventure**
3. **Conclude**

Key Grammar

REPEATING FOR EMPHASIS

The phrase used at the beginning of the sentence is repeated at the end of the sentence to give the information special prominence. Derrick demonstrates this technique throughout his narrative.

View. Observe how Derrick repeats these phrases at the beginning and end of the sentence for emphasis.

Repeat for emphasis 1

Repeat for emphasis 2

John's Bucket List

Name five goals John would like to accomplish before he dies.

1. ______________________
2. ______________________
3. ______________________
4. ______________________
5. ______________________

Tonique's Bucket List

Name five goals Tonique would like to accomplish before she dies.

1. ______________________
2. ______________________
3. ______________________
4. ______________________
5. ______________________

New Signs

to publish (DVDs)

to gather or collect

the layer of earth in which plants grow; soil

Suzanne's Bucket List

Name five goals Suzanne would like to accomplish before she dies.

1. ______________________________
2. ______________________________
3. ______________________________
4. ______________________________
5. ______________________________

New Signs

to lose interest in; to get bored with

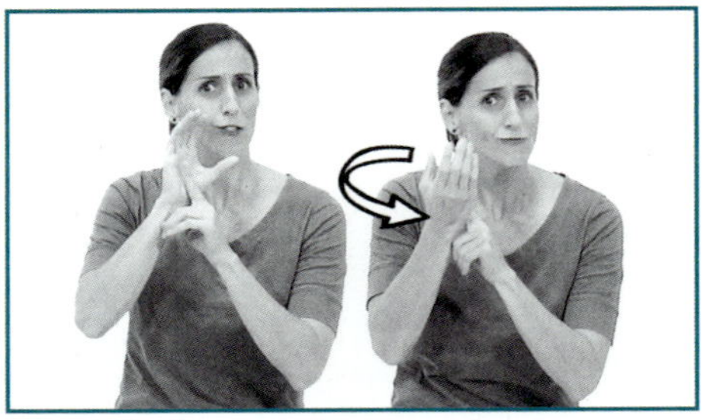

the system of values and customs that the members of a society share and use; culture

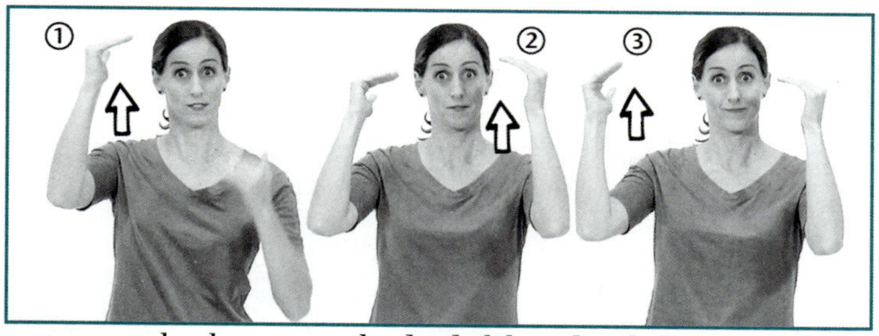

persons who have reached adulthood; adults

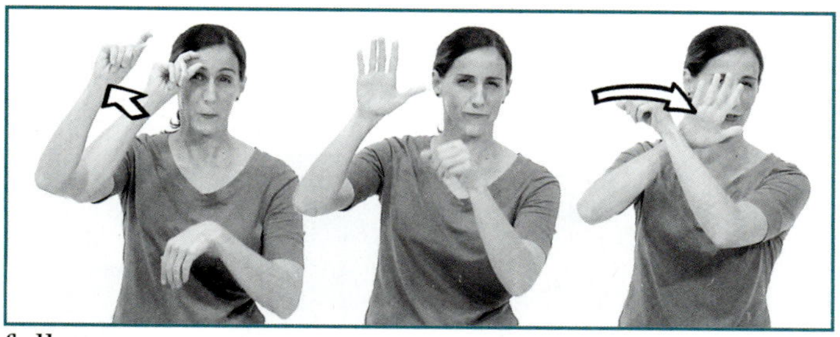
full moon

Answers are on page 528.

Learn the Narrative

Practice the key phrases used in the narrative.

Narrative Structure

1. Broach subject
2. State five goals
3. Conclude

For *"1. Broach subject"*

Use this phrase to begin the narrative.

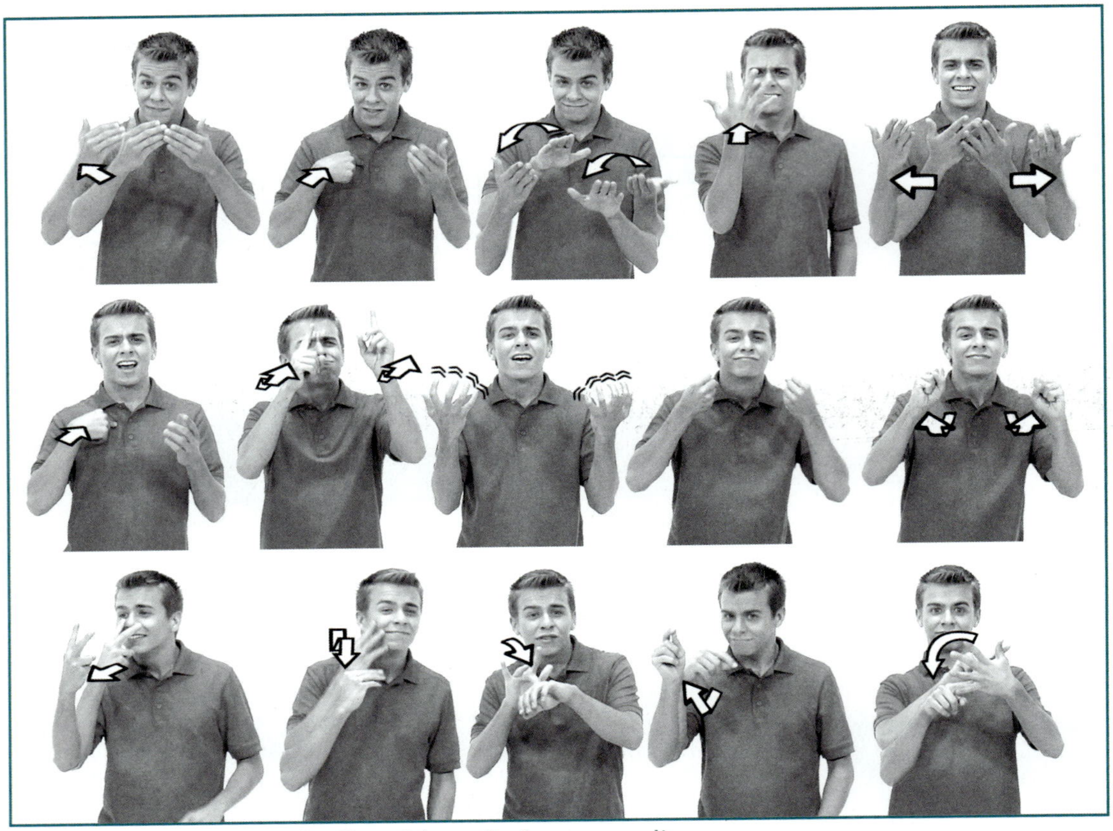

explain you want to do five things before you die

NOTE: The three signs below can be used interchangeably to mean "to die."

For "2. *State Five Goals*"

Be sure to repeat the phrase in the beginning, and at the end of each goal. See **Repeating for Emphasis** on pages 366–367 for the phrases.

Also, be sure to use your weak hand to list the five goals.

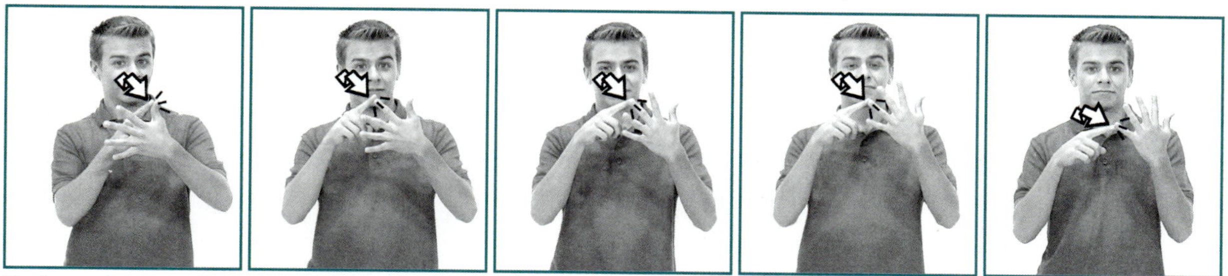

listing the goals on weak hand

For "3. *Conclude*"

Use this phrase to conclude the narrative.

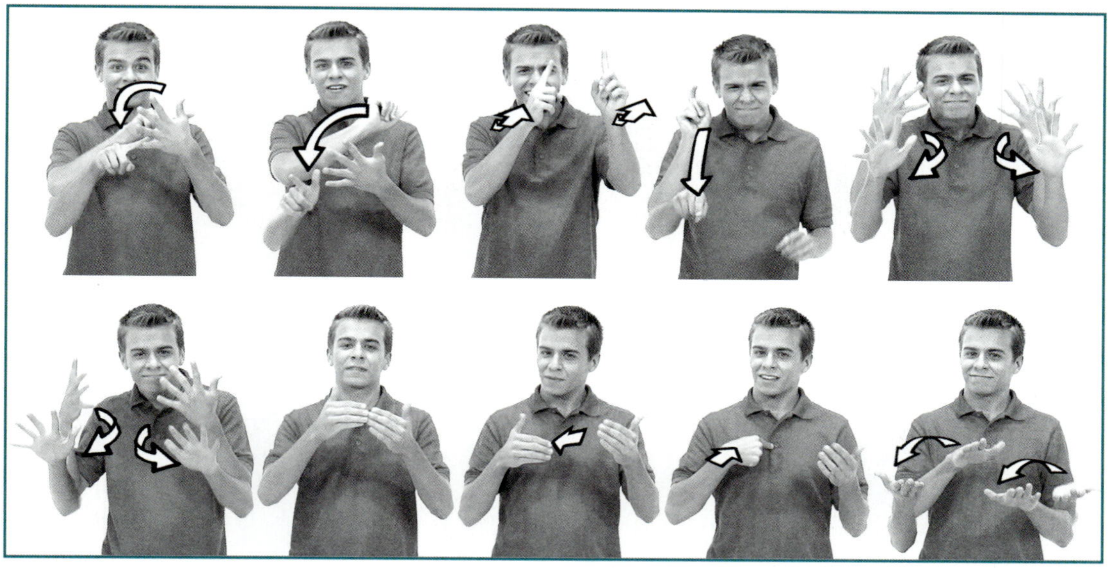

Assignment

YOUR BUCKET LIST

Develop a narrative about your own bucket list.

Follow the narrative structure and incorporate the phrases reviewed in the **Learn the Narrative** section above. Be sure to include one goal from each of these categories below:

- travel
- personal
- lifelong learning
- adventure
- community service

Review Derrick's, John's, Tonique's and Suzanne's Bucket Lists as examples. Practice your narrative until you can sign the information without referring to notes. Be prepared to present your narrative in class.

VOCABULARY REVIEW

Review the vocabulary on the video.

Time-Related

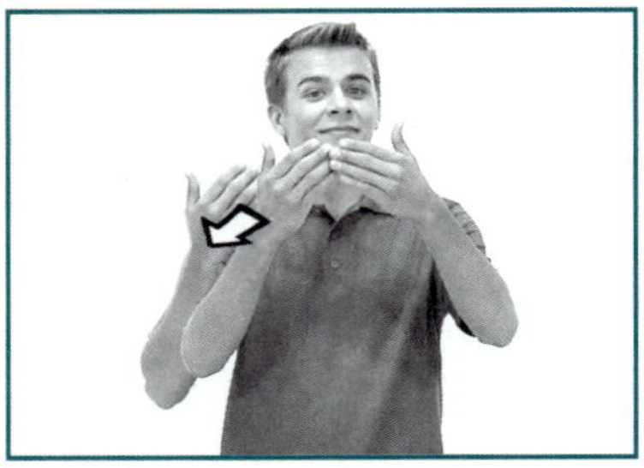

1. previous to a particular time, date or event; before (event)

Nouns

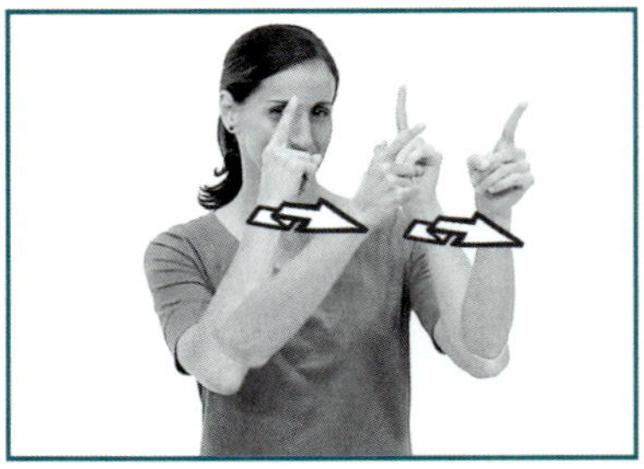

2. an aim or desired outcome; goal

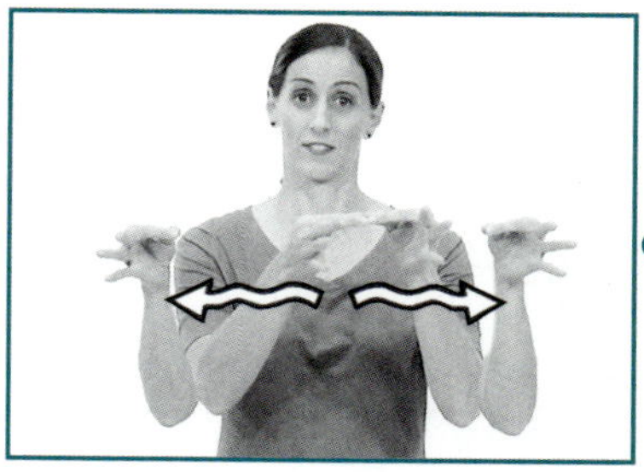

or

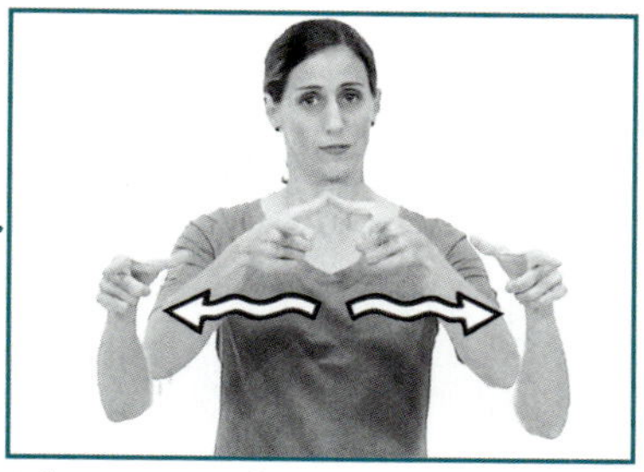

3. system of communication, either signed or spoken; language

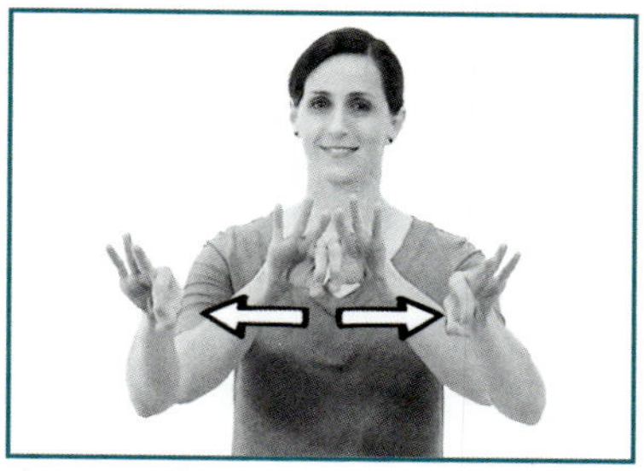

4. academic title conferred by a college or university; college degree

Verbs

5. used to refer to activities, events or situations without specifying what; things

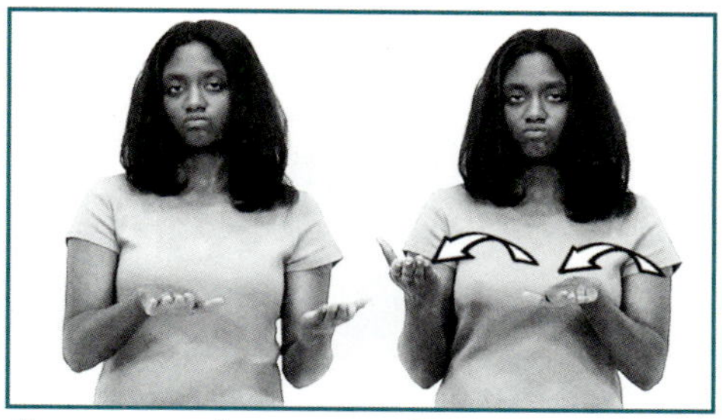

6. to stop living; to die

7. euphemism meaning "to die"

8. euphemism meaning "to die"

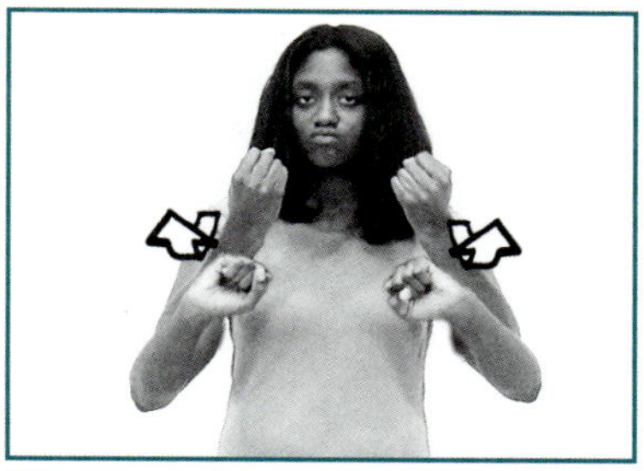

9. to make an attempt to do something

10. to mark or check off

11. to experience something

12. to have been to a place

13. to serve or work for an organization without being paid; to volunteer

14. to study or examine areas related to a subject

15. to make something look more attractive; to decorate

16. to come to be; to turn into; to become

Continents

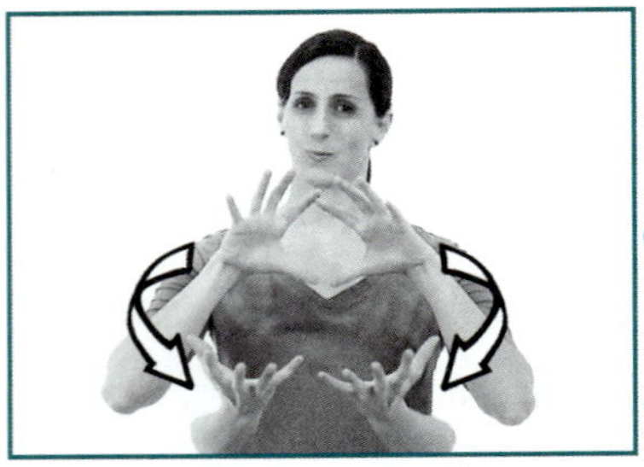

or

17. the earth with all the countries and their inhabitants; world

18. Europe

or

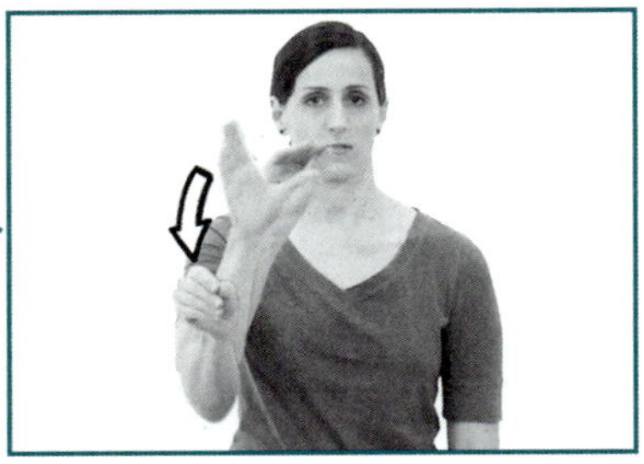

19. Africa

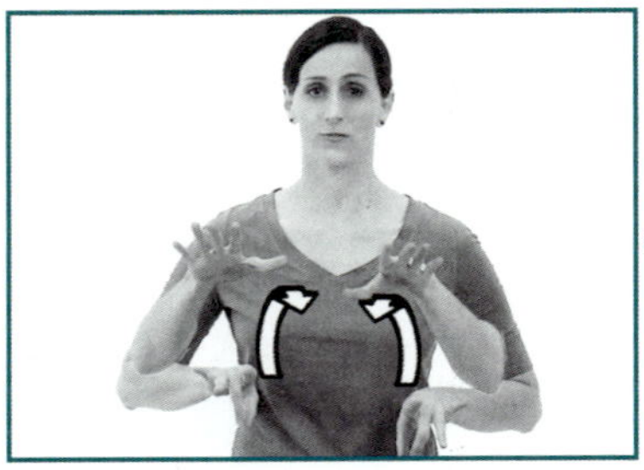

or

20. Australia

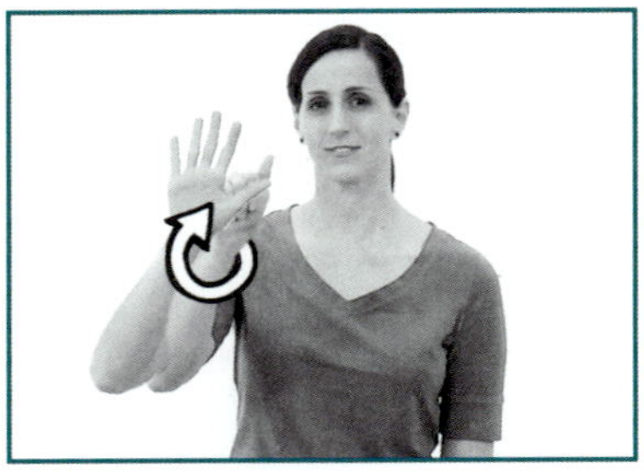

21. Asia

22. South America

23. North America

Countries

or

24. the territory of a nation; country

25. England

26. France

or

or

27. Spain

or

28. Mexico

or

29. Italy

or

30. Germany

31. China

32. Japan

or

33. India

or

34. Egypt

Homework 11:10

STATES AND PROVINCES 2

Trivia

Suzanne, JT, Lauren, Justin and Amber sign information about a state or province. Write the information below.

state or province	*information*
1. ____________	____________
2. ____________	____________
3. ____________	____________
4. ____________	____________
5. ____________	____________
6. ____________	____________
7. ____________	____________
8. ____________	____________
9. ____________	____________
10. ____________	____________
11. ____________	____________
12. ____________	____________
13. ____________	____________
14. ____________	____________
15. ____________	____________

Answers on page 528.

Homework 11:11

STORY: BUSTED!

Watch the story **Busted!** Write answers to the following questions:

1. What does Lauren say about her father?

2. What did she get when she turned 16 years old?

3. What did Lauren and her sister want to do?

4. Why did Lauren's father say they can't use the car?

5. What did Lauren and her sister do after their parents went to bed?

6. How did their father know they were taking the car?

7. What happened the night the parents went to church?

8. How did the father know the girls had been out?

9. What did Lauren resolve to be from now on?

Answers given in class.

NEW VOCABULARY

Use these definitions to help your understanding of the story.

1. to find (out) things

2. a permit or license (to drive)

3. throughout the duration of; during

4. cars cruising up and down

5. to say nothing

6. exclamation of excitement (similar to "woo hoo")

7. car engine starting up

8. all night and into the morning

9. fumes coming out of exhaust pipe

10. fumes in the air

11. to smell

12. not quite; almost

13. to move or act quickly; hurry

14. to exchange one set of clothes for another

15. sleepwear; pajamas

16. having a high temperature; hot

Homework 11:12

CULTURAL

ASL STUDENT IN THE COMMUNITY

By now, you have learned enough ASL to carry on a conversation outside the classroom with people from the community. Congratulations! However, with opportunity comes challenges. You may encounter situations where you may feel awkward and unsure of what is culturally appropriate to do. So let's review the examples shown in class, to remind you of ways to navigate situations appropriately.

At the Cafe

Observe Lauren (as an ASL student) notice the barista having difficulty understanding Justin, who is Deaf. Lauren asks him if he needs help with his order rather than going ahead and interpret what Justin signed to the barista.

TIP: Check with the Deaf person to offer help. Let the Deaf person know you sign and they will decide whether to involve you in their interaction or not.

Lauren showed respect for Justin in two important ways: 1) by not presuming he needs help and 2) by deferring to Justin's decision to handle the situation himself.

If Lauren had assumed Justin would welcome her help and proceeded to interpret for him, it would have been patronizing, and worse yet, it would have marginalized him in that situation.

Deaf people are experienced and adept at communicating with people who do not sign. In this example, you see Justin using a variety of communication strategies with the barista, first signing directly, then switching to gestures and finally to writing to successfully place the order.

It is important to understand that the Deaf community is a linguistic and cultural minority. Achieving equality in everyday situations is what everyone expects, including Deaf people.

At the Gallery

Observe two ASL students (Derrick and Terrylene) signing with each other at a Deaf Art gallery instead of standing off and talking by themselves.

These two ASL students continually sign while they are in presence of Deaf people and other signers. Their behavior implies "total inclusion" and provides opportunities for Deaf people to approach them and chat should they be interested. Signing to the best of one's ability in a Deaf environment (school, event, gathering, etc.) shows respect and courtesy to Deaf people.

TIP: When you are in a Deaf space, use ASL to the best of your ability.

If the students had thought it were polite if they stood off to the side and used spoken language softly, like they would in a hearing environment, they would be mistaken. By not signing, it would appear just as rude to Deaf people as if they had been standing right in the midst of the gathering.

What if the students felt their signing abilities were inadequate to communicate their needs? Politeness dictates they find a place visually away from the signing environment to talk.

A SIGN OF CAUTION:

In case you attend a signing event with Deaf people present, and you do not have any choice but to bring a non-signing friend or family member, what do you do to avoid cultural faux pas?

We recommend that you explain to your companion the following prior to attending the event:

- it is considered rude to use voice only in a Deaf environment
- even when talking with each other, you both should use voice sparingly and only when necessary
- if you need to approach a Deaf person or ASL user, to buy a ticket, to order refreshments, or to ask for information, use ASL to relay information to both parties to the best of your ability. Your companion should be patient with the process since you will not be talking and signing at the same time as it compromises both languages
- there may be times when you may be engaged in an extended conversation in ASL with someone else. In this case, your companion should not consider it rude if the information isn't relayed immediately.

Assignment

DISCUSS SITUATION

In the Classroom

View. Watch this video and determine how Justin, as an ASL student, should have handled the situation with the AV technician to make it more acceptable to Melvin, the Deaf teacher.

Be prepared to discuss your ideas or suggestions in class.

INSIGHT

CAN LOVING LANGUAGE MAKE YOU A LIVING?

When thinking about careers in languages the first thing that comes to mind is teaching in schools or colleges and interpreting, which requires additional training and certification. If you like variety, then both fields offer plenty. There is also language in other careers. Some professionals, such as nurses, librarians, secretaries, social workers or police officers can receive, in addition to their salary, bilingual pay for possessing fluency in another language. Knowing another language gives you more options and makes you more effective at whatever job you pursue. If you love language, give it the time it takes to learn it well and it will pay off.

What does it take to be an interpreter? It's always impressive to see an interpreter working. What talent it takes to translate one language into another—expressing in one language while listening to another language, all simultaneously. An interpreter cannot throw out the first word that comes to mind. The interpreter's job is to convey meaning. This requires careful analysis of words and phrases and their nuances to uncover the meaning and provide the correct translation. Knowing two languages is just the starting point. Beyond skills in the second language, the interpreter must know and understand the two cultures involved, and the subject matter being interpreted. If she or he is good at it, they will have an exceptional memory and a lot of training in the art of interpreting.*

* See Commission of Collegiate Interpreting Education (CCIE) and the Registry of Interpreters for the Deaf (RID) for a list of interpreter training programs in your area.

Homework 11:13

DEAF PROFILE

CHUCK BAIRD (1947–2012)

"Deaf art expresses the values of Deaf culture— the beauty of sign language and its painful oppression, the joys of Deaf bonding,..."

Chuck Baird, one of the founding artists of the De'VIA movement was a painter, storyteller, actor and teacher whose long career centered on expressing the Deaf experience.

Chuck Baird was born Deaf in Kansas City, Missouri in 1947. He was the youngest of five children, and had three Deaf older sisters. Like his sisters, Baird attended the Kansas School for the Deaf (KSD) where he showed his interest and talent as an artist. He submitted his first award-winning painting at age 13, and the work eventually won a National Scholastic Art Award. Through his years at KSD, Baird was a national finalist in the categories of oil, watercolor and drawing.

After KSD, Baird attended Gallaudet University for two years, eventually graduating from the National Technical Institute for the Deaf (NTID) in 1974 with a B.F.A. in Studio Painting. In 1975 Baird was invited to participate in SPECTRUM: Focus on Deaf Artists in Austin, Texas. SPECTRUM was an art colony that drew 22 Deaf artists from different fields. Baird was hired as a staff photographer, and eventually became the group's Visual Coordinator. During this time Baird worked summers for the National Theatre of the Deaf (NTD) designing and building their sets and taught art at several schools for the Deaf.

Baird joined NTD full time in 1980. He designed sets and acted, most notably in the 1989 staging of *King of Hearts*, where as the Painter, Baird created backdrops from scratch every night in front of amazed audiences. Of his acting experience, Baird said, "I've noticed my signing as a storyteller has become more confident and graceful; I feel as if I paint the words in the air as though they were images on canvas. My painting skills have helped me in my work as an actor— each craft gives the other more strength."

The year 1989 was also the year the De'VIA manifesto was created. Baird was one of eight Deaf artists who gathered for a four-day workshop before The Deaf Way International Conference on Deaf Culture held at Gallaudet University in the summer of 1989. At this workshop, led by Betty G. Miller and Paul Johnston, a manifesto was developed that defined Deaf Culture Art, called De'VIA, short for Deaf View/Image Art (see next page). Baird said about this type of art, "Deaf art expresses the values of Deaf culture—the beauty of sign language and its painful oppression, the joys of Deaf bonding, communication breakdowns between signers and non-signers, the discovery of language and community, and the history of Deaf people."

After leaving NTD, Baird was commissioned to do a collection of De'VIA art for his book *Chuck Baird: 35 Plates* published by DawnSignPress and to create murals for Gallaudet University, The Learning Center for Deaf Children in Framingham, Massachusetts and the Kentucky Commission on the Deaf and Hard of Hearing. In the next decade Baird would be artist-in-residence at several Deaf schools, and especially enjoyed working with children to inspire positive growth in De'VIA art.

TAKE A LOOK!
In the video segment "At the Gallery" in **Homework 11:12** Chuck Baird's paintings are displayed in the background.

Baird was a role model for many, and always a warm and optimistic force in the lives of those around him. He was encouraged by the progress made by De'VIA artists that he witnessed throughout his life, but dreamed for more. On his personal blog, he worried about the general cultural reduction in focus on the arts. Baird said of De'VIA, "I am confident that if more people know about De'VIA, recognize the immense importance of supporting Deaf artists through collecting their works and exhibiting their works, and are educated on the impact of De'VIA on Deaf culture, there would be a rapid progression in the professionalization of De'VIA."

REFERENCES:

http://www.gallaudet.edu/clerc_center/chuck_baird_shares_his_vision_of_deaf_art_and_culture.html (retrieved 4/25/14).

Chuck Baird: 35 Plates.
http://chuck-baird.blogspot.com/2010/04/letter-from-chuck-baird_1222.html.

THE DE'VIA MANIFESTO, DEAF VIEW/IMAGE ART

De'VIA represents Deaf artists and perceptions based on their Deaf experiences. It uses formal art elements with the intention of expressing innate cultural or physical Deaf experience. These experiences may include Deaf metaphors, Deaf perspectives, and Deaf insight in relationship with the environment (both the natural world and Deaf cultural environment), spiritual and everyday life.

De'VIA can be identified by formal elements such as Deaf artists' possible tendency to use contrasting colors and values, intense colors, contrasting textures. It may also most often include a centralized focus, with exaggeration or emphasis on facial features, especially eyes, mouths, ears, and hands. Currently, Deaf artists tend to work in human scale with these exaggerations, and not exaggerate the space around these elements.

There is a difference between Deaf artists and De'VIA. Deaf artists are those who use art in any form, media, or subject matter, and who are held to the same artistic standards as other artists. De'VIA is created when the artist intends to express their Deaf experience through visual art. De'VIA may also be created by deafened or hearing artists, if the intention is to create work that is born of their Deaf experience (a possible example would be a hearing child of Deaf parents). It is clearly possible for Deaf artists not to work in the area of De'VIA.

While applied and decorative arts may also use the qualities of De'VIA (high contrast, centralized focus, exaggeration of specific features), this manifesto is specifically written to cover the traditional fields of visual fine arts (painting, sculpture, drawing, photography, printmaking) as well as alternative media when used as fine arts such as fiber arts, ceramics, neon, and collage.

Created in May, 1989, at The Deaf Way.

The signatories were: Dr. Betty G. Miller, painter; Dr. Paul Johnston, sculptor; Dr. Deborah M. Sonnenstrahl, art historian; Chuck Baird, painter; Guy Wonder, sculptor; Alex Wilhite, painter; Sandi Inches Vasnick, fiber artist; Nancy Creighton, fiber artist; and Lai-Yok Ho, video artist.

Assignment

DE'VIA ARTIST REPORT

Report on a De'VIA artist. Choose one of the De'VIA artists from the list below, select a piece of artwork by that artist, and describe how that artwork meets the following De'VIA criteria:

- visual fine arts intended to express cultural or physical Deaf experience
- centralized focus on facial features or on the hands
- may incorporate contrasting or intense colors and values.

Check with your teacher if your report is to be written or signed.

Make sure you include a copy of the artwork or at least a link to the site that shows that artwork.

De'VIA Artists

Mary J. Thornley	Kendra Harness	Nancy Rourke
Betty G. Miller	Lee Ivey	Ann Silver Morris
Broderson	Paul Johnston	Robin Taylor
David Call	Ellen Mansfield	Paia Schroeder
Susan Dupor	Warren Miller	Guy Wonder
Uzi Buzgalo	Harry Williams	Alex Wilhite

SUGGESTED RESOURCES

- *Deaf Artists of America: Colonial to Contemporary* by Debbie Sonnenstrahl
- The HeART of Deaf Culture: Literary & Artistic Expressions of Deafhood,
  produced and edited by Karen Christie and Patti Durr (DVD)
- http://infoguides.rit.edu/deafart
- http://www.deafart.org

Unit 11 Review: Self-Assessment

Write the number of: classes you missed: _____
homework assignments not completed for class: ____
hours you practiced/used signs outside of the classroom per week: _____

Now that you are done with this unit, rate yourself using the list below: **5** indicates feeling the most comfortable and confident about your skill in that area and **1** indicates feeling the least confident.

NOTE: If you marked **3** or lower, you should review that portion of the workbook and write down steps you plan to take to improve your skills in that area.

1. I know how to discuss a person's level of knowledge and ability or their lack thereof.	5	4	3	2	1
2. I can name the different areas of study and tell what is my major.	5	4	3	2	1
3. I can use the correct forms and movements associated with different number types.	5	4	3	2	1
4. I know how to use reaction signs as predictive adjectives.	5	4	3	2	1
5. I know how to ask a hypothetical question to find out how one would react to a situation.	5	4	3	2	1
6. I know the correct signs or fingerspelling forms to use to name the U.S. states and Canadian provinces.	5	4	3	2	1
7. I can invite others, accept and decline invitations, cancel plans and narrate about the canceled plans.	5	4	3	2	1
8. I know how the four "Signs for Thinking" differ from each other in meaning and usage.	5	4	3	2	1
9. I can ask a person when was the first or last time they did something.	5	4	3	2	1
10. I can summarize the results of a survey using horizontal listing.	5	4	3	2	1
11. I can talk about my "bucket list" by following the narrative structure and incorporating key phrases for emphasis.	5	4	3	2	1
12. When viewing "Busted!" I'm able to figure out the meaning of what is signed even though I don't know every sign used.	5	4	3	2	1

13. I know how to conduct myself when I'm in the general public and see communication issues arise between a Deaf person and a non-signing hearing person; and I understand how to conduct myself when I'm in a space designated as "Deaf space."	5	4	3	2	1
14. I know what De'VIA art is and by using the De'VIA criteria I can explain how a piece of art work is of that genre.	5	4	3	2	1

Steps I will take: ______________________________

____

____

NOTES:

Storytelling

UNIT 12

Storytelling and Fables

Homework 12:1

THE TAILOR

Watch Lauren tell this story, then complete activity below.

Draw how the clothing item changed throughout the story and explain the reason for each change.

Change 1

reason for change

Change 2

reason for change

Change 3

reason for change

Answers given in class.

NEW VOCABULARY

1. to select as a course of action; to decide

2. at a low temperature; cold weather

3. reflexive pronoun meaning "him/herself"

4. smooth and silky texture

5. to sew by hand

6. to wear; to use

7. to appear shabby as a result of much use: to wear out

8.

9. to feel comfortable

MY FAVORITE LEATHER JACKET

Watch Justin's tell his story, then fill in the following with your answers.

1. Explain why Justin rejected the first two jackets before finding the one he liked.

2. Describe the coat he bought.

3. Describe or draw the first change and tell why change was made.

4. Describe or draw the second change and tell why change was made.

5. Describe or draw the third change and tell why change was made.

Answers given in class.

Homework 12:2

GUIDELINES: YOUR VERSION

Use the narrative outline to construct your own version about changes made to a clothing item. Use **The Tailor** by Lauren and **My Favorite Leather Jacket** by Justin as guides.

NARRATIVE STRUCTURE

I. Background
- give relevant background – who, when, where
- tell how you got the clothing item
- describe the item (include those parts that you will make changes to in the story)

II. Body
- first change
  1. tell problem and reason for change
  2. (transition) what change was made
  3. tell how feel about the change
- second change
  1. tell problem and reason for change
  2. (transition) what change was made
  3. tell how feel about the change
- third change
  1. tell problem and reason for change
  2. (transition) what change was made
  3. tell how feel about the change

III. Conclusion

KEY LANGUAGE ELEMENTS

The following language elements will help your narrative.

Describing Changes

Use the following signs to describe changes to the clothing item. Be sure to sign them in the location where the change is made.

- **Removing**

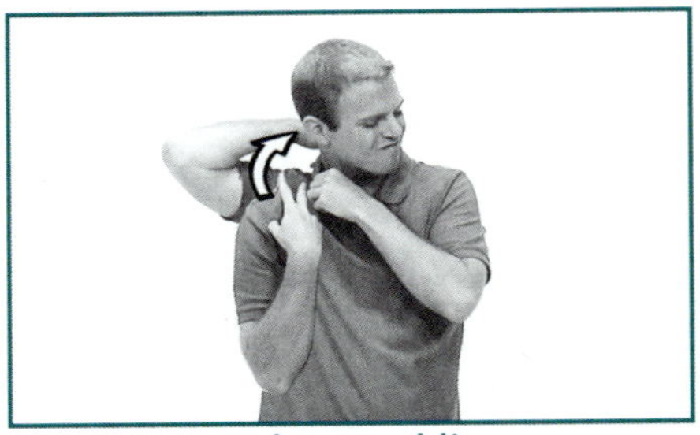

location: at the neckline
method: scissors

location: at the waistline
method: scissors

location: at the shoulders
method: scissors

location: from the front
method: not specified

- **Adding or Replacing**

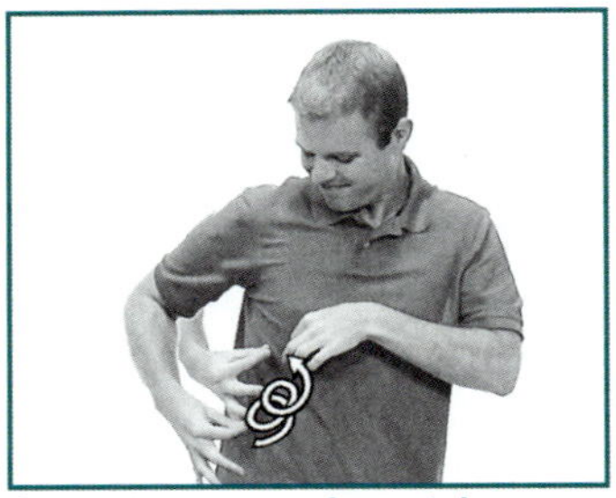

location: on the side
method: sewing

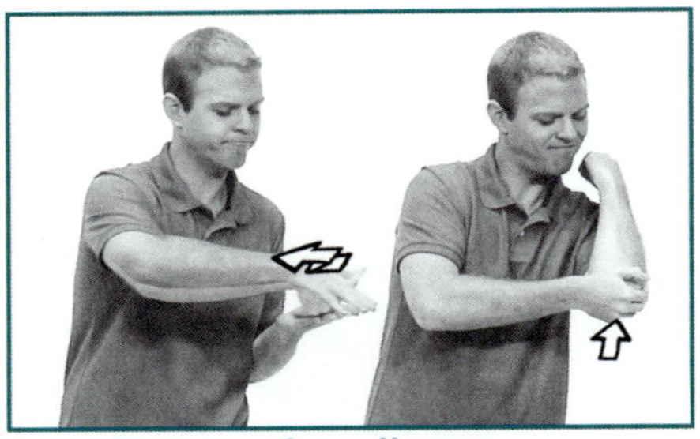

location: on the elbow
method: glueing (the patch) on

location: on the elbow
method: not specified

location: not specified
method: not specified

Transitions 1–6

View how Lauren and Justin use negative expression or headshaking when indicating the problem then use nodding to transition into telling about the change.

VOCABULARY REVIEW

Review the vocabulary on the video.

Removing

1. to remove and discard (from the shirt front)

2. to cut off (the shirt cuff)

Adding

3. to add to

4. to put on (the shirt front)

5. to sew onto (the sleeve)

Reasons for Change

6. too long (for length of coat, robe, dress, pants, skirt, and so on)

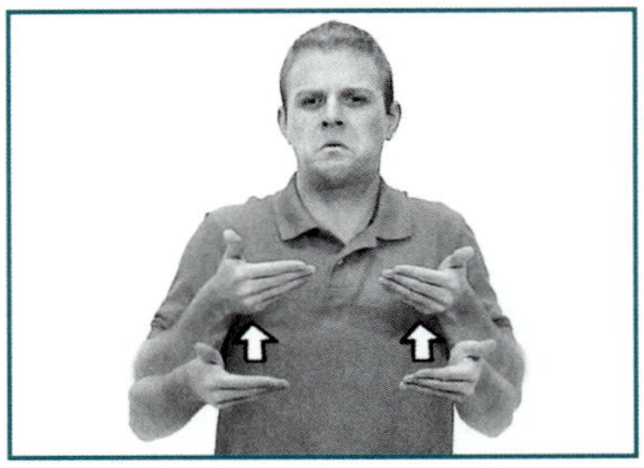

7. too short (for length of coat, robe, dress, pants, skirt, and so on)

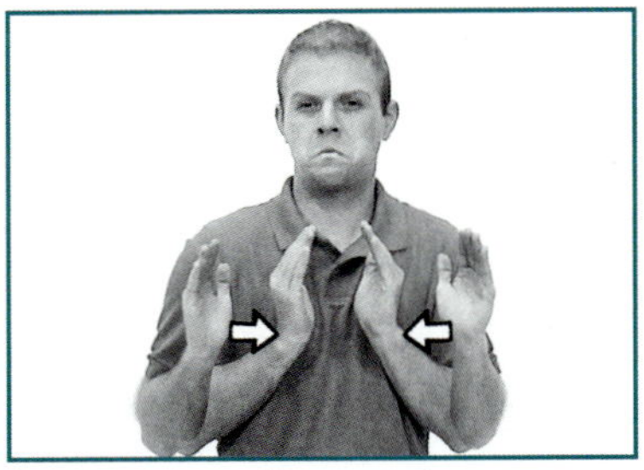

8. too small or tight (for size of jacket, shirt, blouse, vest, and so on)

9. too big or loose (for size of jacket, shirt, blouse, vest, and so on)

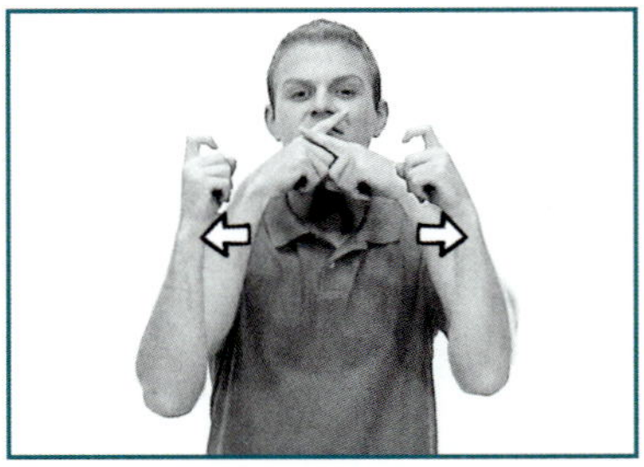

10. not pretty; unattractive, ugly

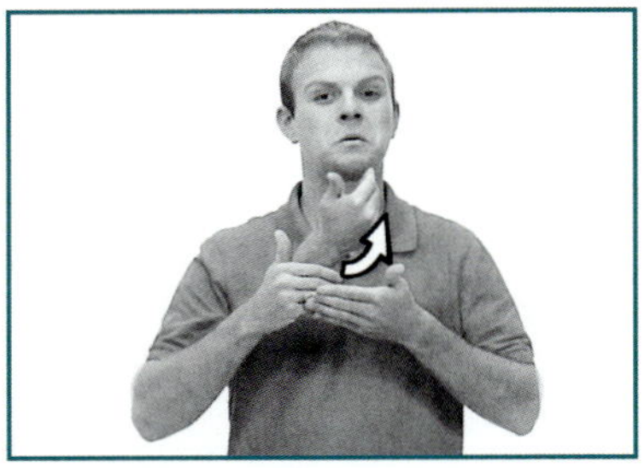

11. brand new

12. old-fashioned; not in style

Fingerspell
STYLE

13. in vogue; in style

14. simple; plain

15. frilly, fancy

How Feel about the Change ___

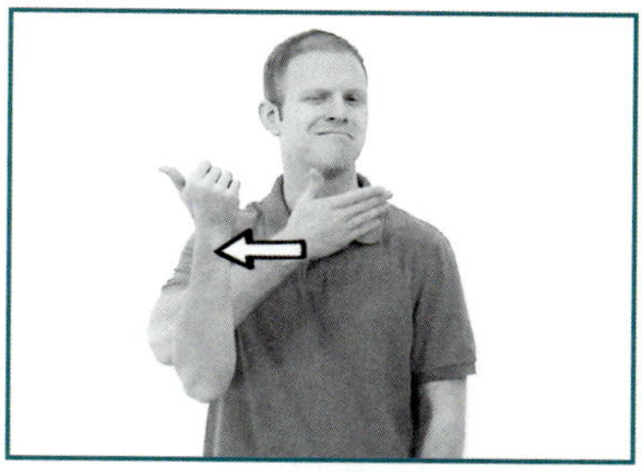

16. to state something is better or is an improvement

17. to state something is just right or perfect

18. to state something is pretty or beautiful

Homework 12:3

ONE FINE DAY

Melvin tells an abbreviated version of **One Fine Day**, a story based on the popular children's story (by Nonny Hogrogian) about a fox who, after being caught drinking milk from a woman's pail, meets a number of characters in a search for milk to repay the woman. This type of story, where events are cumulative and the language is repeated, is a good way to practice and internalize grammar structures, phrases and vocabulary in a meaningful way.

Write the number for the character in the box matching the location of the characters in the story. Use the fox's perspective.

1. 

2. 

3. 

4. 

5. 

Answers given in class.

VOCABULARY REVIEW

Review the vocabulary on the video.

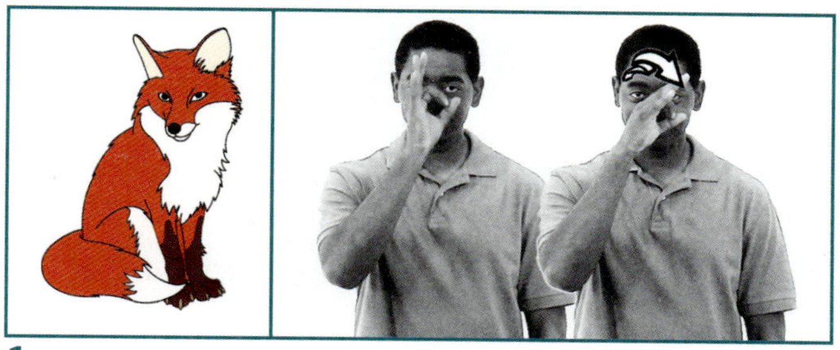

1.

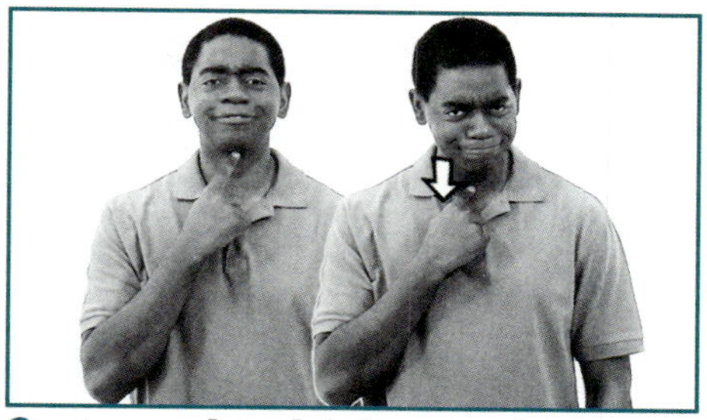

2. to need to drink something; be thirsty

3. to be filled up (refers to container)

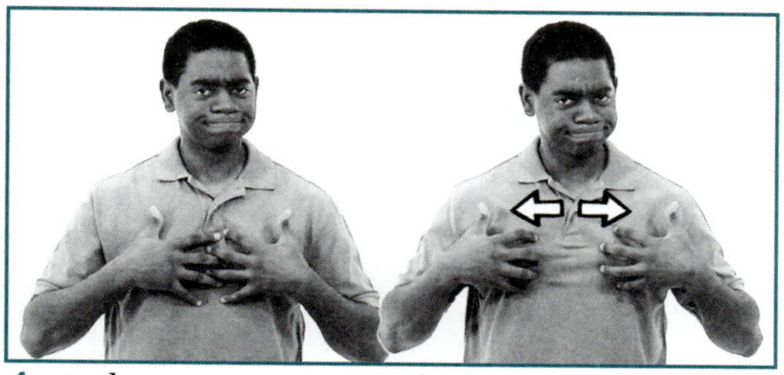

4. to become angry or furious

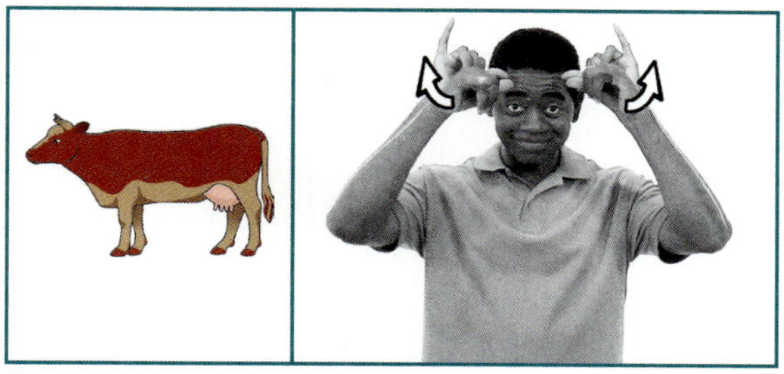

5.

6. to chomp; to chew

7.

8. to express gratitude

9. to ask if ready

10. time sign meaning
"from that point on"

Homework 12:4

Character Placement

In **One Fine Day**, placing characters alternatively on the left and right sides and consistently referring to them in their established locations is essential for maintaining story cohesion. In addition, signs that refer to the character need to be oriented to match the location and height of the characters.

Placements 1–4

Melvin orients his eye gaze and signs according to the location and height of the characters. Observe how he:

- reacts first, then points to the location of the character (cow, grass, water, girl and jug)
- tilts his head when he points to show distance and location
- looks at his audience when he names the character
- shifts his eye gaze and signs to match the height and location of the character.

Take the fox's perspective and rehearse these segments.

The Fox and the Cow

When describing the fox approaching the cow be sure to:

- react first before signing "see"
- tilt your head back when pointing out the cow down the road on your right
- shift your eye gaze back to your audience when signing "cow"
- shift your eye gaze and signs upward to your right when signing "meet" and waving to get the cow's attention.

The Fox and the Grass

When describing the fox approaching the grass be sure to:

- react first before signing "see"
- tilt your head back when pointing out the grass down the road on your left
- shift your eye gaze back to the audience when signing "grass"
- shift your eye gaze and signs downward to the left when signing "meet" and waving to get the grass' attention.

The Fox and the Stream

When describing the fox approaching the stream be sure to:

- react first before signing "hear"
- tilt your head back when pointing out the stream down the road on your right
- shift your eye gaze back to the audience when signing "stream"
- shift your eye gaze and signs downward to the right when signing "meet" and waving to get the stream's attention.

The Fox and the Girl

When describing the fox approaching the girl be sure to:

- point to the left, with raised brows, at the location of the tree
- shift your eye gaze back to the audience when signing "tree"
- shift your eye gaze back to the tree to sign "girl in the tree"
- look down to base of the tree, react, and point to the jug
- shift your eye gaze back to the audience when describing the jug
- shift your eye gaze and signs upward to the left when signing "meet" and waving to get the girl's attention.

Homework 12:5

CONDITIONAL SENTENCES AND AGREEMENT VERBS WITH ROLE SHIFT

Conditional Sentences with Role Shift

Conditional sentences can present a "condition" that must happen before an action can ensue. In **One Fine Day**, characters present a condition for the fox to get them something they want before they give the fox what he needs.

To sign a conditional sentence raise brows for the condition ("what must happen first") then nod when telling what the character will do if the condition is met.

Conditionals 1–4

Observe how Melvin presents each character's condition by:

- reacting to the fox's request
- raising brows to state the condition—what must happen first
- nodding to tell what she or he wants in return.

Rehearse these segments.

The Fox and the Woman

When role shifting between the fox and the woman be sure:

- as the fox, to look up and orient your signs up to the left to the woman with the request
- as the woman, to look down and orient your signs down to the right when responding to the fox.

The Fox and the Cow

When role shifting between the fox and the cow be sure:

- as the fox, to look up and orient your signs up to the right to the cow with the request
- as the cow, to look down and orient your signs down to the left when responding to the fox.

The Fox and the Grass

When role shifting between the fox and the grass be sure:

- as the fox, to look down and orient your signs down to the left to the grass with the request
- as the grass, to look up and orient your signs up to the right when responding to the fox.

The Fox and the Stream

When role shifting between the fox and the stream be sure:

- as the fox, to look down and orient your signs down to the right to the stream when making the request
- as the stream, to look up and orient your signs up to the left when responding to the fox.

Agreement Verbs with Role Shift

In **One Fine Day**, when the fox presents his request of each character to get his tail back, he uses the agreement verb "to give." Since the movement of the verb indicates the "giver" and the "receiver," the verb's movement must correctly refer to the characters' locations.

Agreement Verb

In the story, Melvin presents the fox's requests using the verb "to give." Observe how he as the fox:

- maintains eye contact with the character he is addressing
- except to glance left or right when he signs the verb "to give"
- orients the verb "to give" to match the locations and heights of the other characters
- ends the request by looking directly at the character being addressed.

Rehearse the segment and be prepared to sign it in class.

The Fox and the Girl. When role shifting the fox explaining to the girl why he needs the "jug" be sure to:

- maintain eye contact with the girl on your left
- except to glance right to the stream, left to the grass, right to the cow and then left to the woman when signing the verb "to give"
- orient the verb "to give" downward and upward to match the stream's, the grass', the cow's and the woman's heights
- end the request by looking directly at the girl.

Homework 12:6

INSTRUMENT CLASSIFIERS WITH ROLE SHIFT

In this part of **One Fine Day**, instrument classifiers (ICLs) are essential language elements needed to show how the characters handle objects, such as the fox picking up the jug, pouring the water on the grass, gathering up an armful of grass, setting the pail and stool under the cow, milking the cow, and taking the pail of milk to the woman's house.

The Exchanges

For each exchange, observe how Melvin role shifts and uses instrument classifiers to show how objects are handled. For each exchange this sequence is followed:

- first, he shows the fox getting permission to begin the exchange (except with the girl and woman)
- then, with instrument classifiers, he shows how the object(s) are handled
- finally, as the fox, he thanks the other character while holding the object in his other hand.

Rehearse these segments and be prepared to sign them in class.

The Fox and the Girl

When describing the exchange between the fox and the girl be sure to:

- role shift to show girl permitting the fox to take the jug
- use instrument classifier (ICL*"hold jug"*) to show the fox picking up the jug and holding it while thanking the girl

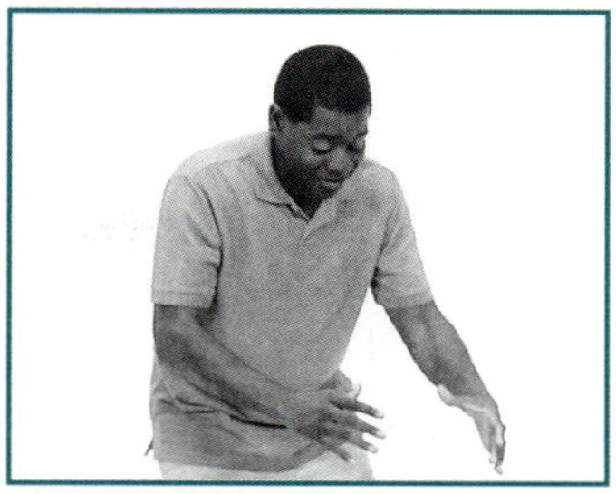
ICL *"hold jug"*

ICL *"hold jug"*(while thanking the girl)

- show the fox running to the right side (toward the stream).

The Fox and the Stream

When describing the exchange between the fox and the stream be sure to:

- role shift to show the fox greeting the stream; then role shift to show the stream giving permission for the fox to proceed
- role shift to show the fox scooping up water with jug with instrument classifier (ICL*"hold jug"*) and holding the jug while thanking the stream

ICL *"hold jug"* (while scooping up water)

ICL *"hold jug"* (while thanking the stream)

- show the fox running to the left side (toward the grass).

The Fox and the Grass

When describing the exchange between the fox and the grass be sure to:

- role shift to show the fox greeting the grass; then role shift to show the grass giving permission for the fox to proceed
- role shift to show the fox pouring water on the grass with instrument classifier (ICL*"hold jug"*)
- role shift to show the grass growing, then telling the fox it is ready for cutting

- role shift to show the fox cutting the grass with instrument classifier (ICL*"use blade"*)
- role shift to show the fox gathering and holding the cuttings while thanking the grass with instrument classifier (ICL*"hold grass"*)

ICL*"hold jug"*

ICL*"use blade"* (to cut grass)

ICL*"hold grass"* (while thanking the grass)

- show the fox running to the right side (toward the cow).

The Fox and the Cow

When describing the exchange between the fox and the cow be sure to:

- role shift to show the cow giving permission for the fox to proceed
- role shift to show the fox spreading out the grass in front of the cow with instrument classifier (ICL*"spread grass"*)
- role shift to show the fox asking the cow if it's ready, and role shift to show the cow replying it is ready
- role shift to show the fox placing the pail and stool under the cow in order to milk, and holding the pail while thanking the cow with instrument classifiers

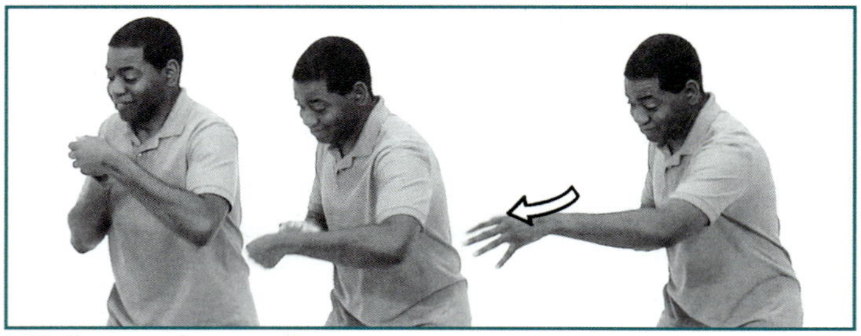

ICL*"spread grass"*

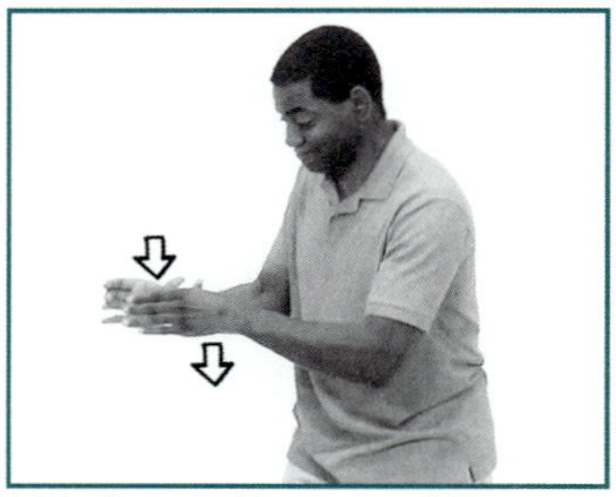

ICL*"put down pail"*

ICL*"put down stool before sitting"*

ICL*"milk cow"*

ICL*"hold pail"*

ICL*"hold pail"* (while thanking the cow)

- show the fox running to the left side (toward the woman)

The Fox and the Woman

When describing the exchange between the fox and the woman be sure to:

- use instrument classifier (ICL*"hold pail handle"*) with role shift to show the fox holding the pail while knocking on the woman's door

ICL*"hold pail handle"* (while knocking)

- role shift to show the woman opening the door, and commenting that the fox has her milk
- role shift to show the fox handing the pail to the woman, and the woman taking the pail and setting it on the counter with instrument classifiers (ICL*"hand over/take pail"*)

ICL*"hand over pail"*

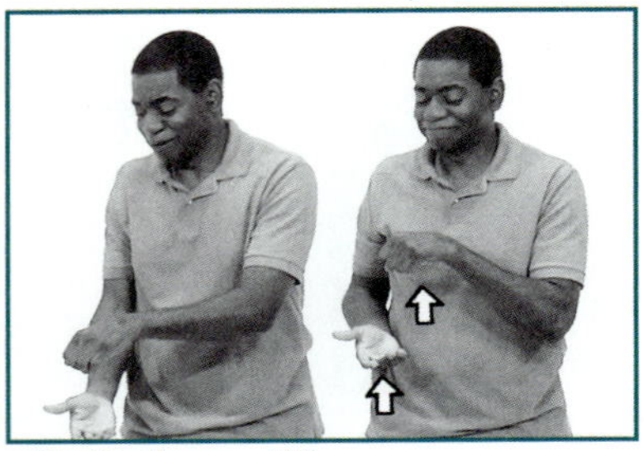

ICL*"take pail"*

Reminder! Signs with role shift must match the height and location of the characters.

Homework 12:7

GUIDELINES: YOUR PRESENTATION

You are to sign the story **One Fine Day**. To view the story refer to **Lesson 12:3**. Practice the story until you can tell the story in the same amount of time it took Melvin to tell the story (approximately six minutes).

KEY LANGUAGE ELEMENTS

Use the following to help you learn the story.

Title

Sign the way Melvin presents the title.

Opening

Melvin signs the **Opening**. He conveys the different emotions of the fox (and the woman) throughout the scene; and times the action and reaction in the "tail cutting" scene to add to the dramatic effect. In this segment, he mostly maintains eye contact with the audience.

Be sure to:

- use facial expressions to convey attitude and feelings
- achieve effective timing in the "tail cutting" segment
- use direct eye contact with audience (except during role shift).

Body

Review and apply the language elements covered in these lessons:

12:4 Character Placement
12:5 Conditional Sentences and Agreement Verbs with Role Shift
12:6 Instrument Classifiers with Role Shift

Closing

Melvin signs the **Closing**. Pay close attention to where Melvin places the cupboard, the thread and needle; how he shows the fox struggling to re-attach his tail and the woman attaching the fox's tail; and how he transitions into final remarks.

> **TIP:** Memorize the opening and closing to **One Fine Day** to give you the confidence and help you get over being nervous. The better you know the story, the easier it will be for you to focus on your character development and delivery.

Be sure to:

- maintain agreement among objects in the woman's space
- use ICLs to show how the woman handle objects
- make direct eye contact with the audience when giving final remarks.

Day of the Exam:

On the day of the exam, please do the following:

- wear solid colored clothes
- if your hair tends to fall into your eyes, pin it back or wear a ponytail
- don't wear hats (unless it has no brim) because the shadows will hide your face
- have nothing in your mouth—no candy or gum while filming. If you have something in your mouth, you run the risk of not executing the "facial grammar" correctly—possibly resulting in a lower grade.

Homework 12:8

THE LION AND THE MOUSE

Read the fable.

One day, a little mouse was busily searching for food. It was running up and down and around a sleeping lion looking for scraps. Suddenly, the lion woke up. The king of beasts grabbed the tiny mouse in its huge paw. The lion was about to swallow the poor mouse when the mouse said, "Please, let me go and I will do something for you some day."

The lion was amused. "I don't know how you can help me," it said, "but I am not so hungry, you are only a tiny mouthful, and you have amused me." And the lion let the little mouse escape.

Some time after that, the lion became caught in a trap. It roared and struggled, but it could not escape. The little mouse heard the lion's frightened roar and came to help. It saw the lion trapped in the ropes, and it busily went to work. It chewed on the ropes until the lion broke free from the trap and escaped. Forever after, the lion and the mouse remained best friends.

Moral: Even the weak and small may be of help to those much mightier than themselves.

TELLING THE FABLE

Fables are short stories that teach a moral lesson, often with animals as characters. These stories lend themselves nicely to practicing language elements specific to storytelling. Since they are simple, fables are also good for examining meaning to develop translations. Since **The Lion and the Mouse** is action-based, showing characters' movement and interaction with objects is central to telling the story well.

Use this narrative structure to help you present the story.

NARRATIVE STRUCTURE

I. Title

II. Background
- setting
- character(s) description
- other relevant information (that gives reason for what is about to happen)

III. Tell what happened
- transition
- character's movement
- character's interaction with object
- contact between characters

IV. Conclusion

V. Moral
- transition
- moral

LANGUAGE ELEMENTS

Review the following elements and incorporate them when rehearsing the story.

Title

When giving the title, sign or spell it word for word starting from your non-dominant side to your dominant side.

"and" (used in literal translation of titles or quotes)

Background

Expand on the written version by adding background.

- **setting**

  Establish a location far away, then name or describe the place

far away in the forest

- **character description**

  Describe each character when they first appear in the story. To describe the character:

  - name the kind of animal
  - describe two or three distinctive features of the animal.

distinctive features of the mouse

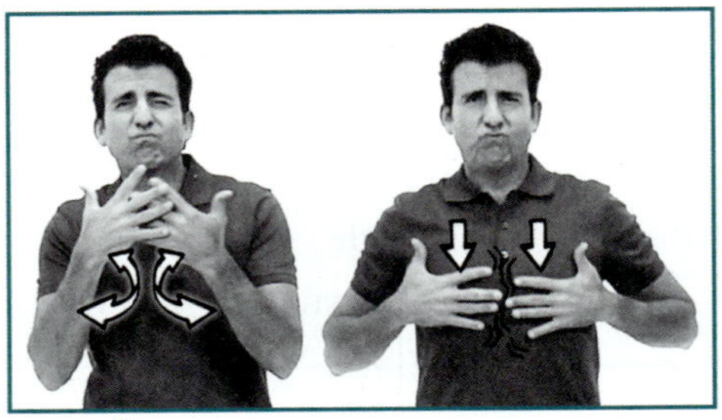

grey fur

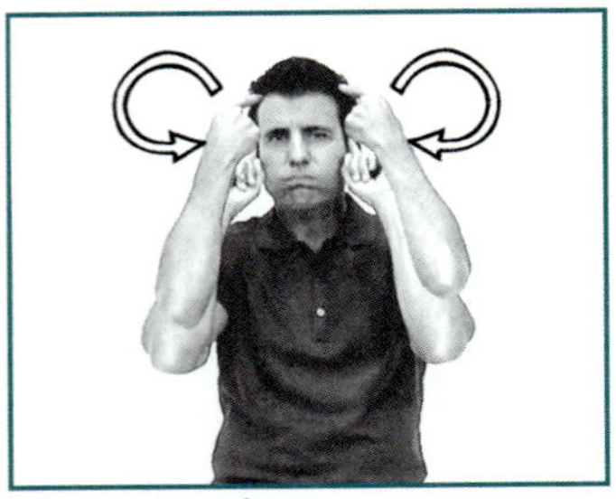

big round ears

snout

whiskers

distinctive features of the lion

broad shoulders

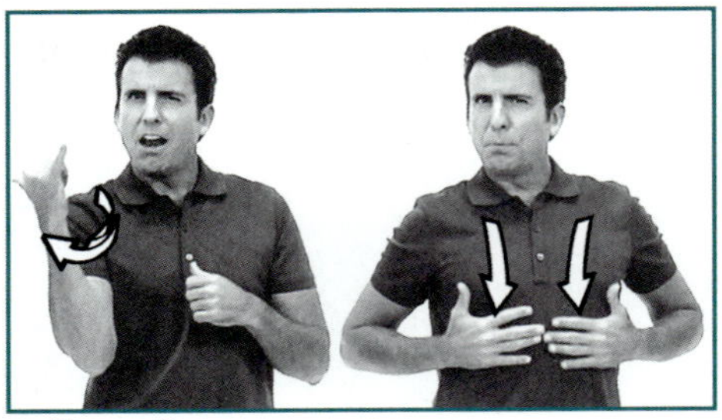

yellow fur

brown mane

Tell what Happened

- **transition**

  Use this transition to begin this part of the story.

"One day…"

- **character's movement**

  Three ways to describe a character's movement:

  1. ***Use signs that indicate movement***, such as signs for walking, running, going to, escaping, fleeing, zooming away, and so on.

sign: escape or flee from

sign: go off into the distance

2. ***Use role shift and body part classifiers (BPCL)*** to show the character in motion. Body part classifiers (BPCL) are classifiers used to represent the character's legs or feet in motion.

NOTE: all of the BPCLs shown here were done while role shifting the lion or the mouse.

BPCL lion's front paws walking

BPCL lion's legs lowering its body to ground, then crossing front paws for the head to rest on

BPCL mouse's four legs running

BPCL the mouse's back legs running

3. ***Use semantic classifiers (SCL)*** to show the direction of character's movement.

Semantic classifiers are classifiers that represent the whole character as opposed to a specific part of the body, and the direction the character is moving in.

SCL character moving forward in upright position

SCL character moving forward on all fours or belly

Combine the three ways to make a more interesting description of the character's movement.

Combine the sign (to run) with a BPCL (back legs running)

NOTE: use role shift when using a BPCL in the combination

Combine the sign (to run) with an SCL (moving forward on all fours)

Combine a BPCL (back legs running) with an SCL (moving forward on all fours)

Combine a BPCL (four legs running) with the sign (to go off into the distance)

- ### character's interaction with object

  Here are two ways to describe a character interacting with an object:

  1. ***use role shift with instrument classifiers (ICL)***

  role shift mouse + ICL (holding rope while chewing it)

  role shift lion + ICL (front paw being caught in the trap)

  2. ***use a semantic classifier (SCL)***

  This particular semantic classifier (SCL) shows the character's interaction with an object. It is used in conjunction with another classifier that represents the object (usually shown on the non-dominant hand).

  the lion (represented by the SCL) struggling in a trap (represented on the non-dominant hand)

the mouse (represented by the SCL) going up the tree (represented on the non-dominant hand)

the lion jumping out of the trap: the lion (represented by the SCL) jumping out of the trap (represented by the non-dominant hand)

THE TRAP

The written version of the story does not explicitly describe the trap so it is up to the storyteller to determine what the trap looks like and how it works. Here are two possible traps to use for the story:

- **Trap 1**, net dropping down on lion

rope (trap) out in front

lion walking along

paw trips on the rope

net falls down on lion

lion struggling in net on ground

pushes against the net

and roaring

- **Trap 2**, net pulling lion up into the tree

net (trap) on ground

lion walking along

paw caught the net

net folding up around lion

lion struggling inside net

pushing against the net

and roaring

- **contact between characters**

  Three ways to describe contact between characters:

  1. ***use non-dominant hand to represent part of the receiver's body, then show the initiator making contact with it.*** Parts of the receiver's body located below the waist (an animal's back legs), foot (or an animal's back paw), buttocks or tail, are represented on the non-dominant hand.

> **TIP:** Remember to name the object (tail) with raised brows, before describing the interaction.

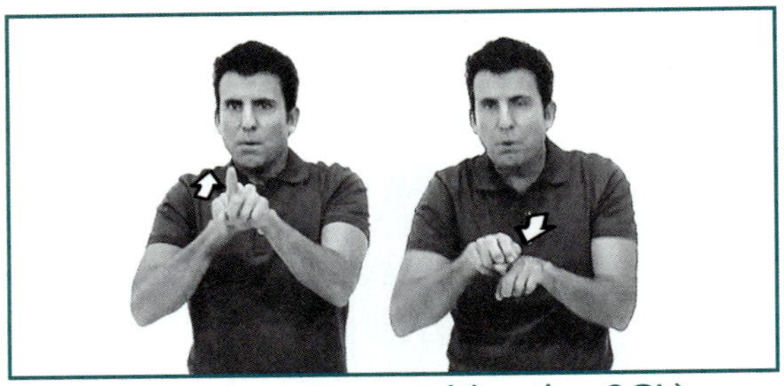

the mouse (represented by the SCL) walks on the lion's tail (represented by the non-dominant hand)

  2. ***role shift the receiver and show how the initiator makes contact.*** When you role shift the receiver, you can only show the initiator making contact with the receiver's head, face, chest, and arms (or an animal's front legs).

> **TIP:** Remember to maintain the role shift as the lion while showing the mouse running over the lion's head, arms and paw.

the mouse (as the initiator) running over the lion's (as the receiver) front leg and head.

3. ***role shift the initiator making contact, then role shift the receiver to show their reaction.***

TIP: Remember as the lion, grab the mouse with your non-dominant hand so your dominant hand is free to sign the lion's dialogue with the mouse.

role shift the lion (initiator) grabbing the mouse

role shift the mouse (receiver) reacting

Conclusion

"Forever after, the lion and the mouse remained best friends."

Use these signs to help you translate the conclusion to the story:

"from that point on"

"being best friends"

Moral

"Even the weak and small may be of help to those much mightier than themselves."

Transition into the moral with this phrase:

"the point of the story is..."

View. Watch John's translation of the moral.

Notice how he:

- reverses the order of "the weak and small" and "mightier" to enhance the flow of information that is to follow
- uses contrastive structure and establishes "the weak" on his right and the "mightier" on his left
- to maintain symmetry, he uses the same number of adjectives to describe each character
- uses the conjunction below to signal, contrary to popular opinion, "the weak and small" can help the "mightier"

TIP: When translating from one language to another, the obligation is to convey the meaning, not the exact words or the order the information is given in the original language.

"in spite of, regardless of ..."

Assignment

Telling the Story: "The Lion and the Mouse"

Follow the narrative structure and incorporate the language elements and translations discussed to present **The Lion and the Mouse**. Sign your story to two students and get written feedback from each. The feedback papers must have the students' signatures. Submit the papers when asked.

USEFUL VOCABULARY

The following vocabulary may be useful for telling the fable.

1.

2.

3. to search; to look for

4. to sleep

5. to wake up

6. to be hungry

7. go off into the distance

8. later on; some time after

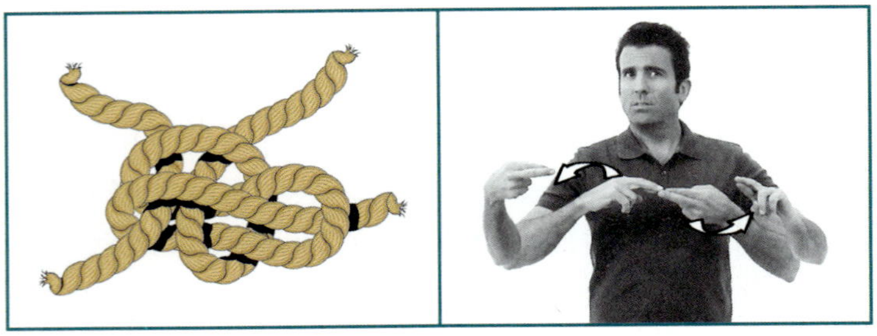

9.

10. to be prevented from (getting out); to be trapped

11. howling; shouting; roaring

12. to hear something

13. to escape or to flee

14. from that point on

15. to be best friends or pals

Homework 12:9

THE FOX AND THE CROW

Read the fable

One day, while he was out walking, a fox saw a crow swoop down and pick up a piece of cheese in its beak. The crow then flapped its wings and flew up onto a high branch in a nearby tree.

"Man, that's a tasty looking piece of cheese," said the fox to himself.

"Hey, I should have that cheese. I'm the fox and I deserve it," he said. "I'm a sly, smooth talking fox too. I'll have it soon enough.

The fox walked over to the foot of the tree. "Hi ya, Miss Crow" cried the fox.

"How are you today?" asked the fox. You're looking mighty fine. Is there something different about you? Have you changed shampoo?"

"Your feathers look so glossy and black and your eyes are sparkling like diamonds," said the fox, flattering the crow. "Hey, have you lost weight? Your figure looks great."

"Wow, if you can sing as good as you look then I'll have to call you Queen of all Birds" said the fox.

Flattered by all the compliments from the fox, and wanting to be called Queen of all Birds, the crow lifted her head and began to sing.

But the moment she opened her mouth the cheese fell out, and the quick fox jumped and caught it before it hit the ground.

"Yes!!!" yelled the fox, holding the cheese up over his head as he did his victory dance. "I got what I wanted."

Moral: Never trust a flatterer.

TELLING THE FABLE

In **The Fox and the Crow**, the plot is driven by dialogue. Subsequently, an effective presentation of this story depends upon the storyteller's ability to show the characters' personalities through their lines and responses. Use this narrative structure to help you present the story in ASL.

NARRATIVE STRUCTURE

I. Title

II. Background
- setting
- character(s) description
- other relevant information (that gives reason for what is about to happen)

III. Tell what happened
- transition
- character movement
- character talking to itself
- role shift sequence
- object passing between characters

IV. Conclusion

V. Moral
- transition
- moral

LANGUAGE ELEMENTS

Review the following elements and incorporate them when rehearsing the story.

Title

When giving the title, sign or spell it word for word starting from your non-dominant side to your dominant side. For "crow," you can either spell out "crow," or use the sign for "bird," then fingerspell CROW.

Background

Expand on the written version by adding the background.

- **setting**

  Establish a location far away then name or describe the place, for example, the forest.

- **character description**

  Describe each character when they first appear in the story. To describe the character:

  - name the kind of animal
  - describe two or three distinctive features of the animal

distinctive features of the Fox

pointed ears

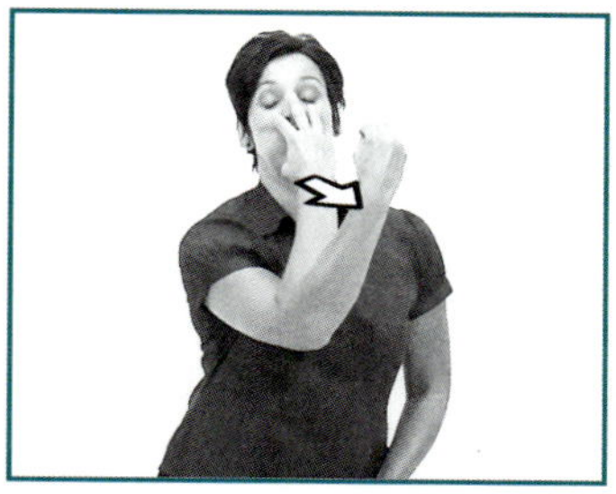

snout

bushy tail

distinctive features of the crow

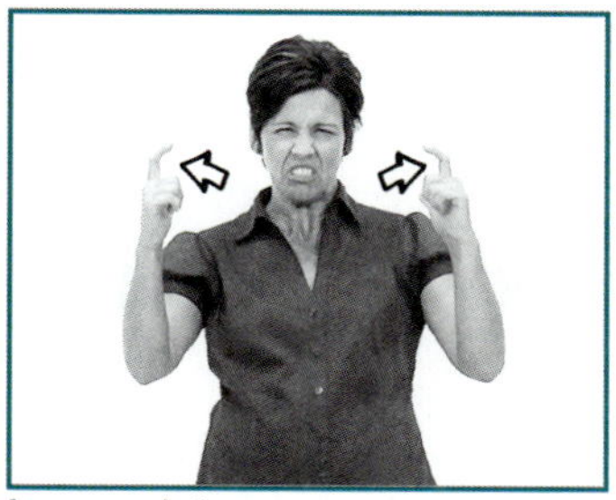

large, big

size of crow

NOTE: Throughout the story, use this sign when referring to the crow.

"bird"

- **other relevant information:**

  In Terrylene's version she gives the fox's personal qualities.

to be arrogant; to think oneself is better than others

to be smart or clever

Tell what Happened

- **transition**

  Use this transition to begin this part of the story.

"One day..."

- **character's movement**

  Remember when describing a character's movement in the story use a combination of at least two ways to show movement. For example:

TIP: Use role shift when using a BPCL in the combination.

Combine a BPCL (wings flapping) with an SCL (bird swooping down)

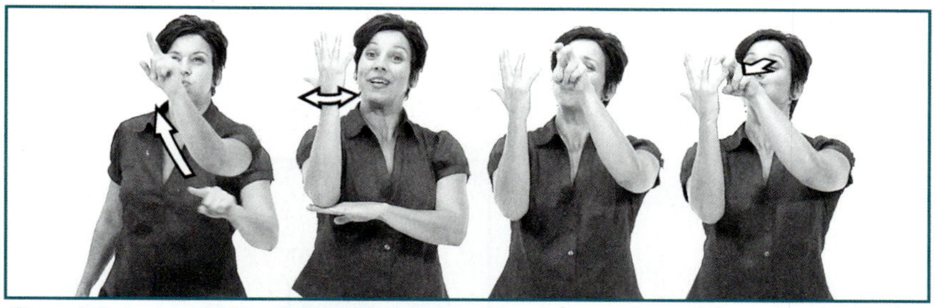

Combine an SCL (bird flying up) with a sign (the tree) and another SCL (alighting on the tree)

Combine an SCL (fox hopping on ground) and another SCL (moving forward) with a sign (to go off into the distance)

- ### character talking to itself

  To describe a ***character's thoughts***, role shift that character looking at the subject of its thoughts, and externalize what it is thinking by signing low and close to your body

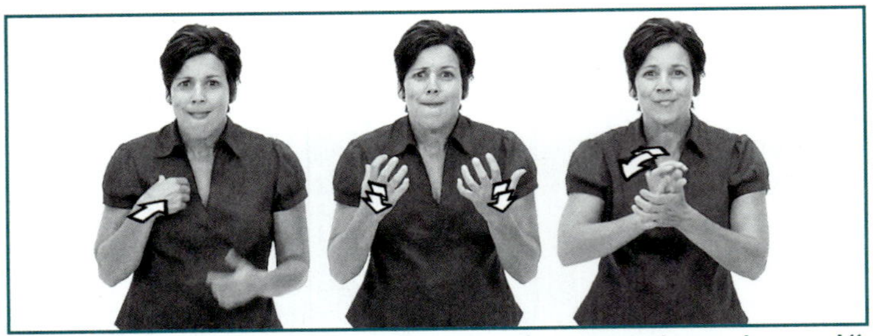

fox looks at cheese and thinks "I want that cheese!"

To describe a ***character's intentions***, role shift that character and look at the audience with a scheming facial expression and describe the character's intention or plan.

fox looks at audience and describes his plan for getting cheese from the crow

Notice Terrylene briefly breaks eye contact with the audience when she refers to the crow.

- **role shift sequence**
  Each time the fox addresses the crow, add the crow's reaction to complete the role shift sequence. Notice Terrylene maintains the cheese in the crow's beak with one hand while showing reactions by gesturing and signing with the other hand.

crow reacting coyly to fox's question about new shampoo

crow reacting to fox's comment about its feathers and eyes by fluttering its wing and batting its eyes

crow reacting to fox's comment about it's weight loss by fluttering both wings

crow reacting to fox's question about being the Queen of Birds by signing "yes"

- ### object passing between characters

  Use the sequence below to describe an object passing between characters. In the story, Terrylene follows this sequence to describe the cheese passing from the crow to the fox.

  1. name character, tell what it was doing (the crow began singing)

  2. use conjunction

  3. name object, tell what happened (the cheese fell out of crow's beak)

  4. name second character, tell what it did (the fox jumped up and caught the cheese)

  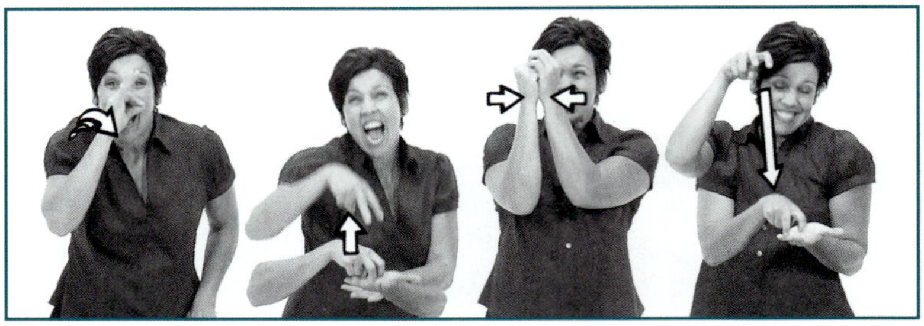

Conclusion

To conclude, add the crow's reaction to the fox's victory dance to complete the role shift sequence.

crow's reaction as the fox dances away with the cheese

Moral

"Never trust a flatterer."

Transition into the moral with this phrase:

"what can we learn from this?"

View. Watch Terrylene's translation of the moral itself.

REMEMBER: When translating from one language to another, the obligation is to convey the meaning, not the exact words nor the order the information is given in the original language.

Notice how she:

- Terrylene uses a conditional phrase "if someone is flattering you..."
- then, uses role shift to assume the roles of the flatterer and the flattered to illustrate the point of the moral
- and concludes with "don't do it" (believe or trust the flatterer).

Assignment

Telling the Story: "The Fox and the Crow"

Follow the narrative structure and incorporate the language elements and translations discussed to present **The Fox and the Crow**. Sign your story to two students and get written feedback from each. The feedback papers must have the students' signatures. Submit the papers when asked.

USEFUL VOCABULARY

The following vocabulary may be useful for telling the fable.

1. having a talent or unusual ability to perform tasks well

2. cajole; flatter; sweet-talk

3. soap for washing the hair; shampoo

4. sparkling or shiny (referring to the crow's feathers)

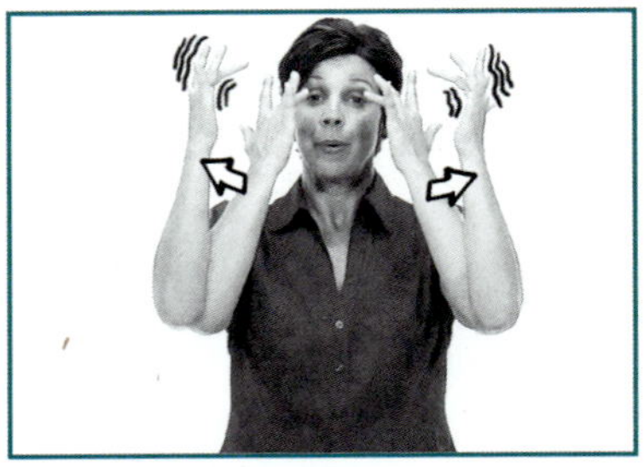

5. sparkling or shiny (referring to the crow's eyes)

6. large sparkling diamond ring

7. to lose weight; to decrease in amount

8. a sign that begins a hypothetical situation, for example, "If you can..."

9. to give a name or title to someone

10. female sovereign or monarch; queen

11. a disheartened reaction; to feel let down

12. unspecified person; someone

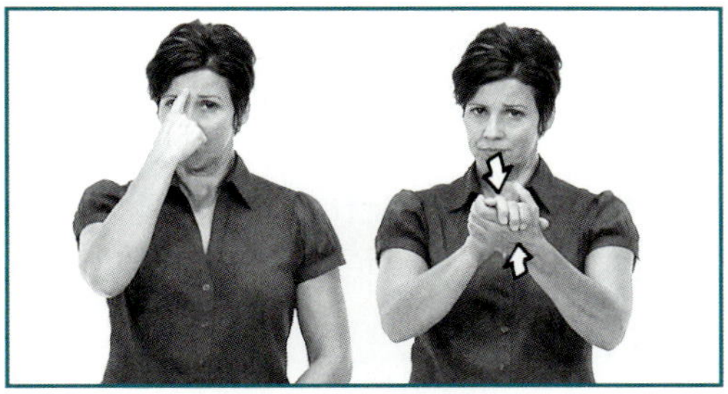

13. to accept something as true; to believe

14. to rely upon or place confidence in someone; to trust

Homework 12:10

GUIDELINES: YOUR ASSIGNED FABLE

Your assigned fable is: ______________________________

You will present it on (date): ______________________________

DEVELOPING THE FABLE

Use this narrative structure to help you develop your assigned fable.

NARRATIVE STRUCTURE

I. Title

II. Background
- setting
- character(s) description
- other relevant information

III. Tell what Happened
- transition
- character's movement
- interaction with objects and characters
- character talking to itself

IV. Conclusion

V. Moral
- transition
- moral

Worksheets. Refer to the worksheet for your assigned fable:

The Ant and the Grasshopper, pages 449–451
The Wolf and the Kid, pages 452–454
The Fox and the Stork, pages 455–457
The Dog and the Wolf, pages 458–460
The Scorpion and the Frog, pages 461–463
The Fox and the Goat, pages 464–466

View. Review the signs and classifiers pictured on your worksheet. Be sure to include them in your presentation.

The Ant and the Grasshopper, pages 449–451
The Wolf and the Kid, pages 452–454
The Fox and the Stork, pages 455–457
The Dog and the Wolf, pages 458–460
The Scorpion and the Frog, pages 461–463
The Fox and the Goat, pages 464–466

LANGUAGE ELEMENTS

Title

When giving the title of your fable, sign or spell it word for word starting from your non-dominant side to your dominant side. Be sure to include this sign when giving the title.

"and" (used in literal translation of titles or quotes)

Background

Refer to **Exercise 5** in your worksheet to review the background your group developed for your fable. Be sure to include these parts:

- **setting**
  Use this sign to establish a location "far away" before naming or describing the place.

"far away"

- **character description**
  Remember to describe each character when they first appear in the story. Refer to **Exercise 1** in your worksheet for character descriptions specific to your fable.

- **other relevant information**
  You can elaborate on the background as long as the information is relevant to the context of story. For example, in **The Lion and the Mouse**, John added the mouse being hungry as the reason mouse was looking for food. In **The Fox and the Crow**, Terrylene added a few of the fox's personal qualities to help set up the audience for how these qualities affected the outcome of story.

Tell what happened

- **transition**
  Use this to transition to begin this section of your story:

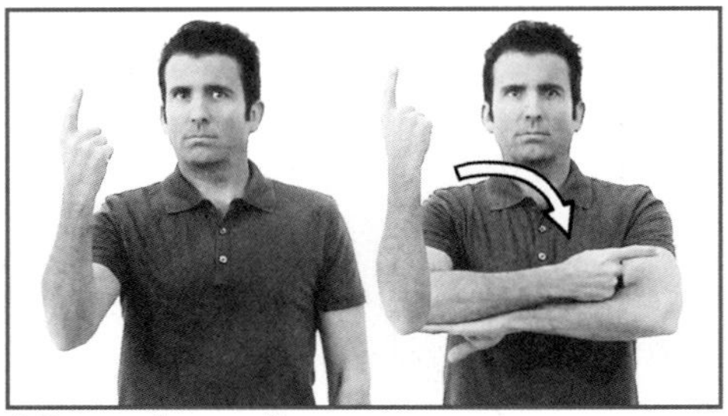

"One day..."

- **character's movement**
  Remember when describing a character's movement in the fable, use a combination of at least two ways. Refer to **Exercise 2** in your worksheet for suggestions specific to your fable.

- **interaction with objects and characters**
  There are principles for describing a character's interaction with an object, or for contact made with another character. Refer to **Exercise 3** in your worksheet for suggestions specific to your assigned fable.

- **character talking to itself**
  Refer to **Exercise 4** in your worksheet for suggestion(s) where and how the character(s) should talk to itself in your assigned fable.

Conclusion

Conclude your story before presenting the moral. In **The Lion and the Mouse**, John concludes the story by saying that the mouse and the lion were best friends afterward. In **The Fox and the Crow**, Terrylene describes the crow crestfallen while the fox dances away with the cheese.

Moral

Use one of these phrases to transition into the moral:

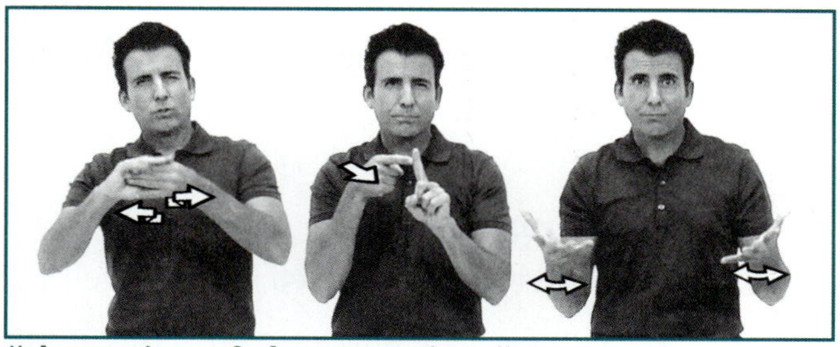

"the point of the story is..."

or

"what can we learn form this?"

Assignment

REHEARSE YOUR ASSIGNED FABLE

Develop your assigned fable by following the narrative structure and incorporating the language elements and translations discussed. Rehearse and be ready to present your first draft in class.

TIP: A large part of successful storytelling is directly tied to how well you engaged your audience. How does one do this? By bringing the story to life; by showing the characters' feelings, manner and attitude; by making eye contact with your audience; by telling the story in a very deliberate manner; and by pacing the story for emphasis and effect. This will require you to rehearse it well! So start working on your story now.

Day of the Final Presentation:

On the day of the final presentation, please do the following:

- wear solid colored clothes
- if your hair tends to fall into your eyes, pin it back or wear a ponytail
- don't wear hats (unless it has no brim) because the shadows will hide your face
- have nothing in your mouth—no candy or gum while signing. If you have something in your mouth, you run the risk of not executing the "facial grammar" correctly—possibly resulting in a lower grade.

Grading Criteria

You will be graded based on how well you:

- followed the narrative structure to develop the fable
- incorporated the appropriate level of detail
- incorporated the language elements covered in class
- demonstrated command of vocabulary and articulation
- engaged the audience and paced the story with emphasis and effect
- presented the moral's meaning effectively.

WORKSHEET: THE ANT AND THE GRASSHOPPER

One summer day a grasshopper was singing and chirping and hopping about. He was having a wonderful time. He saw an ant who was busy gathering and storing grain for the winter.

"Stop and talk to me," said the grasshopper. "We can sing some songs and dance a while."

"Oh no," said the ant. "Winter is coming. I am storing up food for the winter. I think you should do the same.

"Oh, I can't be bothered," said the grasshopper. "Winter is a long time off. There is plenty of food." So the grasshopper continued to dance and sing and chirp and the ant continued to work.

When winter came the grasshopper had no food and was starving. He went to the ant's house and asked, "Can I have some wheat or maybe a few kernels of corn. Without it I will starve," whined the grasshopper.

"You danced last summer," said the ant in disgust. "You can continue to dance." And they gave him no food.

Moral: There is a time to work and a time to play.

EXERCISE 1: CHARACTER DESCRIPTION

- name the kind of animal
- describe two or three distinctive features of the animal. Include the signs below:

ant

tiny size (1)*

pinchers (2)

grasshopper

bug eyes (3) *antennae (4)*

* These numbers correspond with the 12:10 video on your DVD.

EXERCISE 2: CHARACTER'S MOVEMENT

There are three ways to show a character's movement.

- use signs that indicate movement
- use role shift and body part classifier (BPCL) to show characters in motion
- use semantic classifiers (SCL) that show direction of character's movement

Excerpts. Translate the following excerpts incorporating the signs pictured below:

a. *"a grasshopper was …hopping about."*
b. *"he saw an ant who was busy gathering and storing grain"*
c. *"the grasshopper continued to dance"*
d. *"the ant continued to work…"*
e. *"he (grasshopper) went to the ant's house"*

a. ***SCL"grasshopper hopping (on the ground)" (5)***

c. ***SCL"grasshopper dancing (on the ground)" (6)***

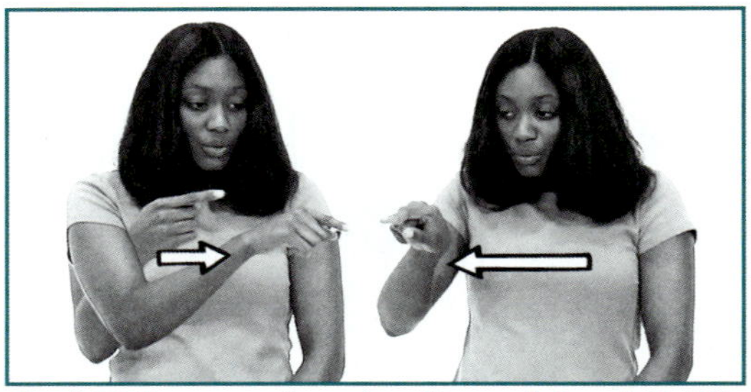

d. ***SCL"ant going back and forth" (7)***

EXERCISE 3: INTERACTION WITH OBJECTS AND CHARACTERS

Excerpt. Translate this excerpt showing how the ant handled the grain. Be sure to use role shift with instrument classifiers. Remember to name the grain (food) before describing what the ant did with it.

"(ant)...gathering and storing grain for the winter"

ICL *"ant carrying grain" (8)*

EXERCISE 4: CHARACTER TALKING TO ITSELF

- To describe a character's thoughts, role shift that character looking at the subject of its thoughts, and externalize what it is thinking by signing low and close to your body.
- To describe a character's intentions, role shift that character and look at the audience while it describes its scheme.

Excerpt. When translating the excerpt below, add the grasshopper talking to itself about its intention to ask the ant for food.

"When winter came the grasshopper had no food and was starving." ***(intentions)***

EXERCISE 5: BACKGROUND

Answer the following questions to help you further develop the background to your story.

- **setting**
  - *what kind of setting would you most likely find the ant and the grasshopper?*
  - *farm, country, garden, desert, beach, city, mountains, forest?*
- **character description: the grasshopper** (see **Exercise 1**)
- **other relevant information** and possible things to add to the fable's background
  - *what is the grasshopper's personality?*
  - *why is the grasshopper singing and dancing?*
  - *do the grasshopper and the ant know each other?*

EXERCISE 6: MORAL

Remember to use one of the transitional phrases before signing the moral.

*"**Moral:** There is a time to work and a time to play."*

WORKSHEET: THE WOLF AND THE KID

A wolf was chasing a young kid. The poor kid realized it could not escape, so it turned to the wolf and said, "Please, wolf, I know I am about to die, but before you eat me, would you do me a great favor. I have heard you are a wonderful flute player. Please play for me, and I can have one last dance."

The wolf quickly agreed because it also thought it was a great flute player. It played and the kid danced, but the shepherd's dogs heard the sound of the flute and came after the wolf. As the wolf escaped, it said to itself, "My purpose was to be a butcher, not a musician."

Moral: Those who stray from their true business often lose the prize in hand.

EXERCISE 1: CHARACTER DESCRIPTION

- name the kind of animal
- describe two or three distinctive features of the animal. Include the signs below:

wolf

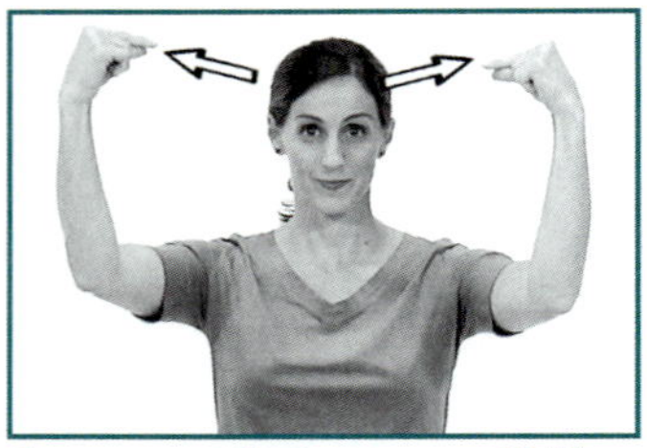

large pointy ears (1)*

teeth (2)

kid (goat)

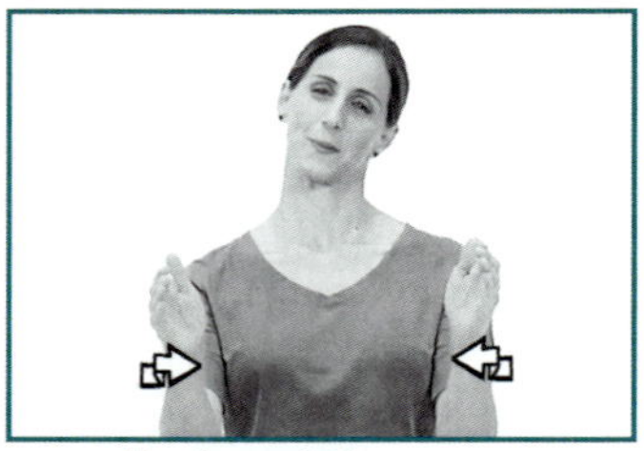

small size (3)

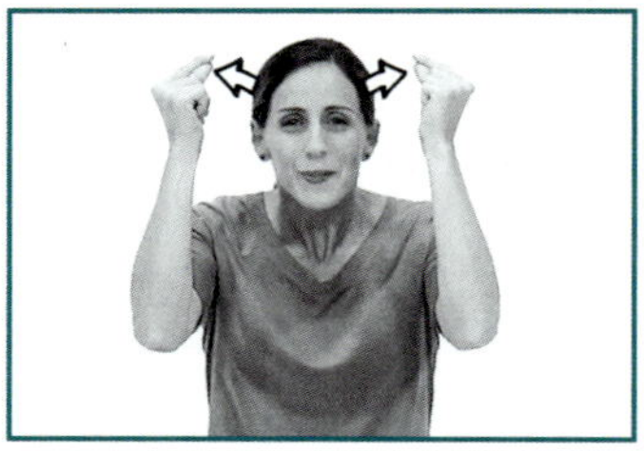

small pointy horns (4)

* These numbers correspond with the 12:10 video on your DVD.

EXERCISE 2: CHARACTER'S MOVEMENT

There are three ways to show a character's movement.

- use signs that indicate movement
- use role shift and body part classifier (BPCL) to show characters in motion
- use semantic classifiers (SCL) that show direction of character's movement

Excerpts. Translate the following excerpts incorporating the signs pictured below:

a. *"A wolf was chasing a young kid."*

b. *"...so it (kid) turned to the wolf.."*

c. *"...and the kid danced."*

d. *"...(dogs) came after the wolf."*

e. *"...the wolf escaped,..."*

a. to chase (5)

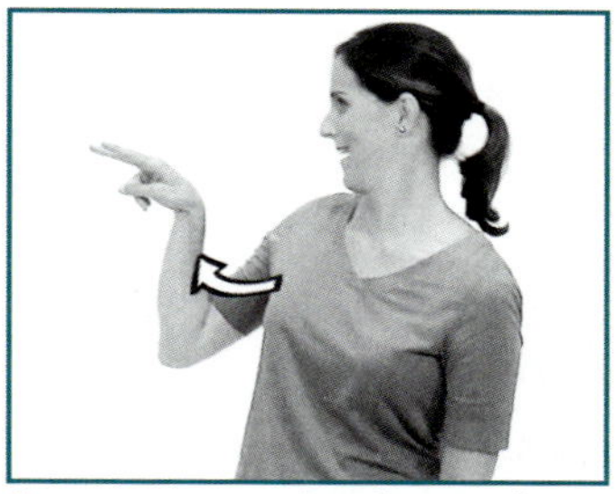

b. turn to look at the wolf (6)

c. SCL"danced" (on ground) (7)

d. plural classifier: "many came" (8)

e. BPCL"legs running" (9)

e. sign: to zoom off (10)

EXERCISE 3: INTERACTION WITH OBJECTS AND CHARACTERS

Excerpt. Translate this excerpt showing the wolf pulling his flute out and playing it. Be sure to use role shift with instrument classifiers. Remember to name the flute before describing the wolf getting it.

"(wolf) thought it was a great flute player. It played..."

EXERCISE 4: CHARACTER TALKING TO ITSELF

- To describe a character's thoughts, role shift that character looking at the subject of its thoughts, and externalize what it is thinking by signing low and close to your body.
- To describe a character's intentions, role shift that character and look at the audience while it describes its scheme.

Excerpt. When translating the first excerpt below, add the kid coming up with a strategy to save its life. For the second excerpt, add the wolf criticizing itself for being taken by the kid.

"...(wolf) said to itself, 'My purpose was to be a butcher, not a musician.'" ***(thoughts)***

"The poor kid realized it could not escape..." ***(intentions)***

EXERCISE 5: BACKGROUND

Answer the following questions to help you further develop the background to your story.

- **describe setting**
  - *where do you think the kid lived?*
  - *farm, country, garden, desert, beach, city, mountains, forest?*
- **character description** the kid (see **Exercise 1**)
- **other relevant information** (that gives reason for what is about to happen)
  - *what caused the kid to be separated from it's mother?*
  - *what was the kid doing before the chase?*

EXERCISE 6: MORAL

Translate this moral beginning with a transitional phrase:

*"**Moral:** Those who stray from their true business often lose the prize in hand."*

WORKSHEET: THE FOX AND THE STORK

One day a fox invited its friend, a stork, to come to its house for dinner. The fox cooked a delicious soup, but it decided to play a trick on its friend. It served the soup in a flat dish so the stork could only sip a little at a time with its long pointed beak. Meanwhile, the fox quickly lapped up the soup with its tongue. The polite, but angry, stork thanked the fox and went home.

A little while later, the fox received an invitation from the stork. The stork prepared a nice dish of chopped meat. The smell filled the room, and the fox could not wait to begin. The stork served the dinner in a tall pot with a narrow mouth. The stork easily stuck its long beak into the pot and pulled out piece after piece of the meat. The fox with its shorter nose could not reach the food in the pot, but the fox understood the stork's trick, smiled and went home hungry.

Moral: One bad turn deserves another.

EXERCISE 1: CHARACTER DESCRIPTION

- name the kind of animal
- describe two or three distinctive features of the animal. Include the signs below:

fox

snout (1)*

pointy ears (2)

stork

long neck (3) *long bill (4)*

* These numbers correspond with the 12:10 video on your DVD.

EXERCISE 2: CHARACTER'S MOVEMENT

There are three ways to show a character's movement.

- use signs that indicate movement
- use role shift and body part classifier (BPCL) to show characters in motion
- use semantic classifiers (SCL) that show direction of character's movement

Excerpts. Translate the following excerpts:

a. *"...(stork) come to its (fox's) house..."*

b. *"...stork...went home"*

c. *"...the fox received an invitation from the stork."*
(the fox went to the stork's house)

EXERCISE 3: INTERACTION WITH OBJECTS AND CHARACTERS

Excerpts. Translate these excerpts by role shifting the stork and the fox and using BPCLs to show them licking from the plates or the tall pots. Remember to name the plate or pot before describing what the character is doing with it. When describing mouth actions, be sure your mouth movements match the actions.

"(fox) served the soup in a flat dish..." (ladled soup into dish)

"...so the stork could only sip a little at a time with its long pointed beak."

"...the fox quickly lapped up the soup with its tongue."

"The stork served the dinner in a tall pot with a narrow mouth" (ladled soup into pot)

"The stork easily stuck its long beak into the (tall) pot and pulled out piece after piece of the meat."

"The fox with its shorter nose could not reach the food in the pot."

EXERCISE 4: CHARACTER TALKING TO ITSELF

"The fox with its shorter nose could not reach the food in the pot."

- To describe a character's thoughts, role shift that character looking at the subject of its thoughts, and externalize what it is thinking by signing low and close to your body.
- To describe a character's intentions, role shift that character and look at the audience while it describes its scheme.

Excerpt. When translating the excerpt below, add that while cooking, the fox came up with his idea to tease the stork.

"... it (fox) decided to play a trick on its friend (stork)." ***(intentions)***

EXERCISE 5: BACKGROUND

Answer the following questions to help you further develop the background to your story.

- **setting**
  - *where do you think the fox lived?*
  - *farm, country, garden, desert, beach, city, mountains, forest?*
- **character description: the fox** (see **Exercise 1**)
- **other relevant information** (that gives reason for what is about to happen)
  - *what is the fox's house like?*
  - *what kind of personality or tendency (likes to cook, likes to host parties) does the fox have?*
  - *and so on.*

EXERCISE 6: MORAL

Remember to use one of the transitional phrases before signing the moral.

*"**Moral:** One bad turn deserves another."*

WORKSHEET: THE DOG AND THE WOLF

A gaunt wolf was almost dead with hunger when he happened to meet a house-dog who was passing by. "Ah, Cousin," said the dog. "I knew how it would be; your irregular life will soon be the ruin of you. Why do you not work steadily as I do, and get your food regularly given to you?"

"I would have no objection," said the wolf, "if I could only get a place."

"I will easily arrange that for you," said the dog; "come with me to my master and you shall share my work."

So the wolf and the dog went toward the town together. On the way there the wolf noticed that the hair on a certain part of the dog's neck was very much worn away, so he asked him how that had come about.

"Oh, it is nothing," said the dog. "That is only the place where the collar is put on at night to keep me chained up; it chafes a bit, but one soon gets used to it."

"Is that all?" said the wolf. "Then good-bye to you, Master Dog." And with that, the wolf quickly turned around and ran back to the forest.

Moral: **Better free than be a fat slave.**

EXERCISE 1: CHARACTER DESCRIPTION

- name the kind of animal
- describe two or three distinctive features of the animal. Include the signs below:

wolf

"skin and bones" (1)*

gaunt (2)

dog

husky (3)

* These numbers correspond with the 12:10 video on your DVD.

EXERCISE 2: CHARACTER'S MOVEMENT

There are three ways to show a character's movement.

- use signs that indicate movement
- use role shift and body part classifier (BPCL) to show characters in motion
- use semantic classifiers (SCL) that show direction of character's movement

Excerpts. Translate the following excerpts incorporating the signs pictured below:

a. *"...house-dog who was passing by (the wolf)."*

b. *"...the wolf and the dog went toward the town together."*

c. *"...the wolf quickly turned around and ran back to the forest."*

a. SCL"someone coming by" (4)

b. SCL"two animals walking side by side" (5)

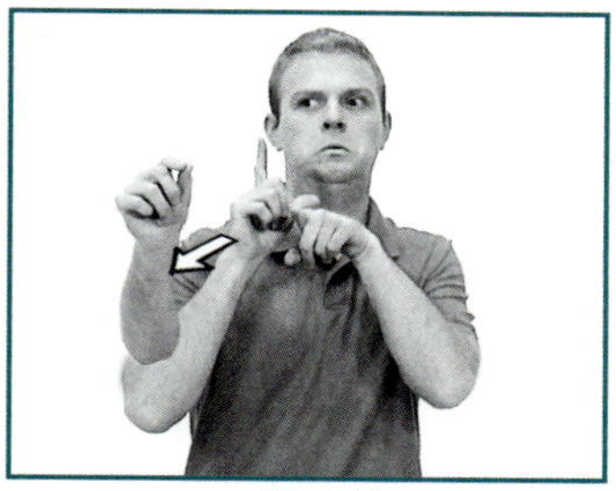

c. zoom off (6)

EXERCISE 3: INTERACTION WITH OBJECTS AND CHARACTERS

Excerpt. Translate this excerpt by role shifting the dog and showing the placement of the collar on its neck. Use instrument classifier to show the collar being put on and chaffing the neck, and then being removed to reveal the baldness.

"the hair on a certain part of the dog's neck was very much worn away ...where the collar is put on at night to keep me chained up; it chafes a bit"

EXERCISE 4: CHARACTER TALKING TO ITSELF

- To describe a character's thoughts, role shift that character looking at the subject of its thoughts, and externalize what it is thinking by signing low and close to your body.
- To describe a character's intentions, role shift that character and look at the audience while it describes its scheme.

Excerpt. When translating the excerpt below, add the wolf thinking that he doesn't want to be chained up.

> *"Is that all?" said the wolf. "Then good-bye to you, Master Dog."* ***(thoughts)***

EXERCISE 5: BACKGROUND

Answer the following questions to help you further develop the background to your story.

- **setting**
  - *where do you think the wolf lived? farm, country, garden, desert, beach, city, mountains, forest?*
- **character description:** the wolf (see **Exercise 1**)
- **other relevant information** (that gives reason for what is about to happen)
  - *why is the wolf hungry?*
  - *when do you think was the last time the wolf ate?*
  - *why did the wolf go to town?*

Useful Sign

"... gets used to it." (7)

EXERCISE 6: MORAL

Remember to use one of the transitional phrases before signing the moral.

> *"**Moral:** Better free than be a fat slave."*

WORKSHEET: THE SCORPION AND THE FROG

A scorpion, desiring to cross the stream, meets a frog on the bank of the stream and asks the frog to carry him across on its back. The frog asks, "How do I know you won't sting me?" The scorpion says, "Because if I do, I will die too."

The frog is satisfied, and they set out, but in midstream, the scorpion stings the frog. The frog feels the onset of paralysis and starts to sink, knowing they both will drown, but has just enough time to gasp "why?" Replies the scorpion: "It's my nature..."

Moral: It's hard to change one's character.

EXERCISE 1: CHARACTER DESCRIPTION

- name the kind of animal
- describe two or three distinctive features of the animal. Include the signs below:

scorpion

pinchers (1)*

stinger (2)

frog

bulging eyes (3)

croaking neck (4)

* These numbers correspond with the 12:10 video on your DVD.

EXERCISE 2: CHARACTER'S MOVEMENT

There are three ways to show a character's movement.

- use signs that indicate movement
- use role shift and body part classifier (BPCL) to show characters in motion
- use semantic classifiers (SCL) that show direction of character's movement

Excerpts. Translate the following excerpts incorporating the signs pictured below:

a. *"...meet on the bank of a stream"*

b. *"...and they set out." (carry him across on its back)*

c. *"...and starts to sink,..."*

a. SCL"jumping off the bank" (5)

b. BPCL"frog doing breast strokes" (6)

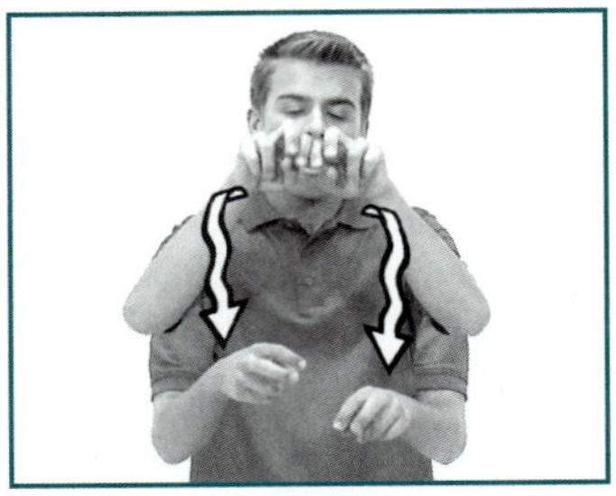

c. SCL"two of them sinking to bottom" (7)

EXERCISE 3: INTERACTION WITH OBJECTS AND CHARACTERS

Excerpt. Begin the translation of the first excerpt by role shifting the frog and then use SCL classifier to show the scorpion getting on its back before they set out into the water. For the second excerpt, use role shifting to show that while the scorpion was holding on to the frog, he stung the frog (using BPCL).

"... and they set out..." (carry him across on its back)
(for a more effective translation, be sure to show the frog swimming for a while)

"....the scorpion stings the frog..."

EXERCISE 4: CHARACTER TALKING TO ITSELF

- To describe a character's thoughts, role shift that character looking at the subject of its thoughts, and externalize what it is thinking by signing low and close to your body.
- To describe a character's intentions, role shift that character and look at the audience while it describes its scheme.

Excerpt. When translating the excerpt below, add the scorpion realizing that the frog could swim, and coming up with the idea to ask the frog for a ride to the other side.

"A scorpion, desiring to cross the stream, meets a frog..." ***(intentions)***

EXERCISE 5: BACKGROUND

Answer the following questions to help you further develop the background to your story.

- **setting**
  - *where do you think the scorpion lived? farm, country, garden, desert, beach, city, mountains, forest?*
- **character description:** the scorpion (see **Exercise 1**)
- **other relevant information** (that gives reason for what is about to happen)
  - *what brings the scorpion to the stream and why does it want to cross the stream?*

EXERCISE 6: MORAL

Remember to use one of the transitional phrases before signing the moral.

*"**Moral:** It's hard to change one's character."*

WORKSHEET: THE FOX AND THE GOAT

A fox one day fell into a well and could find no means of escape. A goat, overcome with thirst, came to the same well, and seeing the fox, inquired if the water was good. Concealing his sad plight under a merry guise, the fox indulged in a lavish praise of the water, saying it was excellent beyond measure, and encouraging him to descend. The goat, mindful only of his thirst, thoughtlessly jumped down, but just as he drank, the fox informed him of the difficulty they were both in and suggested a scheme for their common escape. "If," said he, "you will place your forefeet upon the wall and bend your head, I will run up your back to get out, and will help you out afterwards." The goat readily assented and the fox leaped upon his back and made off as fast as he could. When the goat upbraided him for breaking his promise, he turned around and cried out, "You foolish old fellow! If you had half a brain, you would never have gone down before you had inspected the way up, nor have exposed yourself to dangers from which you had no means of escape."

Moral: Look before you leap.

EXERCISE 1: CHARACTER DESCRIPTION

- name the kind of animal
- describe two or three distinctive features of the animal. Include the signs below:

fox

snout (1)

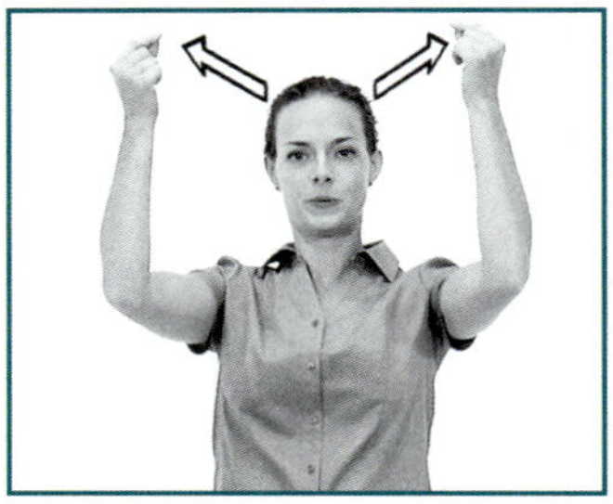

pointy ears (2)

goat

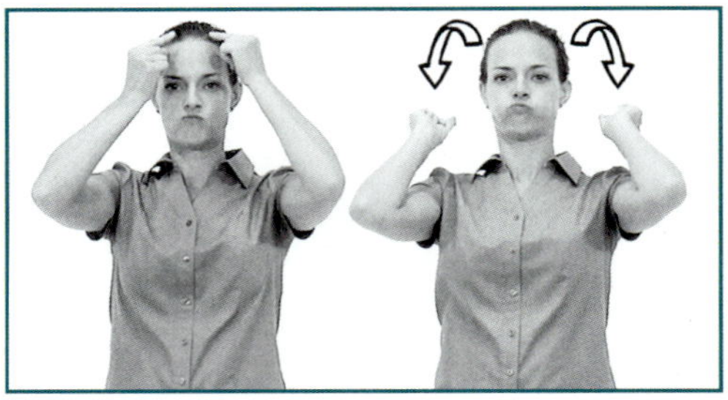

horns (3)

beard (4)

EXERCISE 2: CHARACTER'S MOVEMENT

There are three ways to show a character's movement.

- use signs that indicate movement
- use role shift and body part classifier (BPCL) to show characters in motion
- use semantic classifiers (SCL) that show direction of character's movement

Excerpts. Translate the following excerpts incorporating the signs pictured below:

a. *"A fox one day fell into a well..."*
b. *"A goat...came to the same well,"*
c. *"The goat... thoughtlessly jumped down"*
d. *"fox ...made off as fast as he could."*

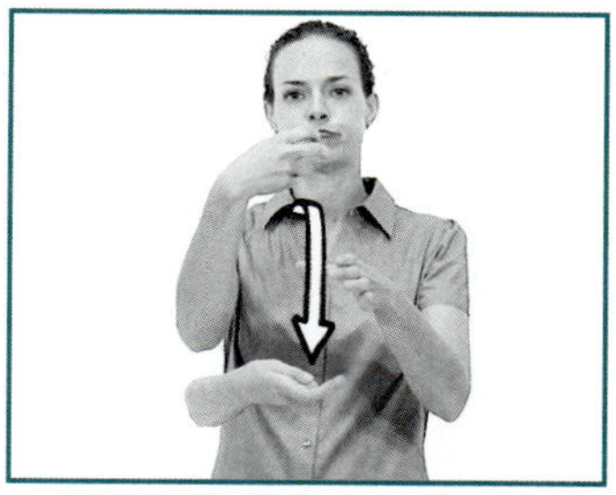

a. SCL"fell into the well" (5)

c. SCL"jumped down into well" (6)

d. to flee or run off (7)

EXERCISE 3: INTERACTION WITH OBJECTS AND CHARACTERS

Excerpt. Translate this excerpt by role shifting the goat leaning on to the wall, then using SCL to show the fox leaping onto the goat and out of the well.

"you place your forefeet upon the wall and bend your head, I will run up your back. The goat readily assented and the fox leaped upon his back and made off..."

place forefeet upon the wall (8)

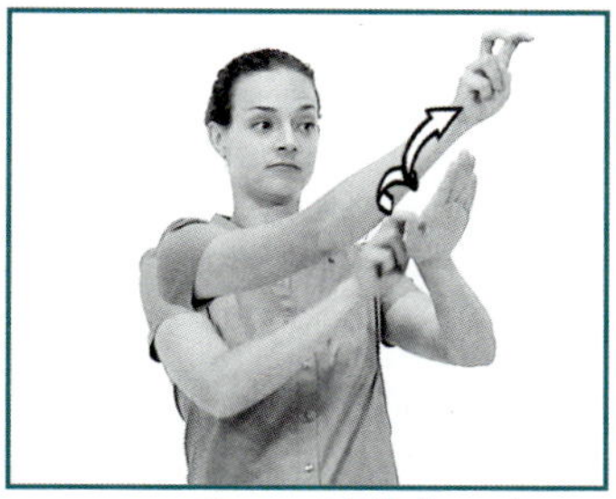

run up (goat's) back (9)

To show the fox or the goat drinking water, use this sign:

drinking water from inside well (10)

EXERCISE 4: CHARACTER TALKING TO ITSELF

- To describe a character's thoughts, role shift that character looking at the subject of its thoughts, and externalize what it is thinking by signing low and close to your body.
- To describe a character's intentions, role shift that character and look at the audience while it describes its scheme.

Excerpt. When translating the excerpt below, add the fox thinking of a way to get the goat to help him out without the goat realizing the fox's stupid mistake.

> *"Concealing his sad plight under a merry guise,*
> *the fox indulged in a lavish praise of the water..."* ***(intentions)***

EXERCISE 5: BACKGROUND

Answer the following questions to help you further develop the background to your story.

- **setting**
  - *where do you think the well is?*
  - *on the farm, in the country, garden, desert, city, mountains?*
- **character description:** the fox (see **Exercise 1**)
- **other relevant information** (that gives reason for what is about to happen)
  - *what led the fox to the well? what caused the fox to fall into the well?*

EXERCISE 6: MORAL

Remember to use one of the transitional phrases before signing the moral.

> *"**Moral:** Look before you leap."*

SIGNING NATURALLY

Exercises & Answer Keys

EXERCISE 1

Interview four students and fill in the blanks below:

NAME OF STUDENT	1	2	3	4
1. What year were you born?				
2. What year was the oldest member of your family born? Who?				
3. What year did you graduate from (pick one, high school, college)?				
4. What model year is your... (pick one, car, motorcycle, bicycle)?				
5. What was the best year of your life?				

EXERCISE 1A **UNIT 8**

Ask for Advice 1

This morning you were late for school so you rushed out of the house. On the way to class, you realized you forgot to give your dog his medicine. Ask for advice.

to rushed or hurry

medicine

Ask for Advice 2

This morning as your cell phone was recharging, you got ready for work. When you arrived at work, you realized you forgot your cell phone. Ask for advice.

to recharge

- Analyze the two situations above and construct your narratives following the sequence below.
- Rehearse your narratives.
- Pair off with a student that has **Exercise 1B** and follow the dialogue format.

Signer A: explain problem, ask for advice
- **tell when**
- **explain situation**
- **tell what you forgot to do (use conjunction)**
- **ask for advice**

Signer B: give advice

A: respond

EXERCISE 1: What Time?

Interview three students. Ask what time they do these things and write down the time.

NAME OF STUDENT	1	2	3
1. get up			
2. go to bed			
3. left home today			
4. arrived at school today			
5. start work (typically)			
6. finish work (typically)			
7. do ______________ (name activity)			

EXERCISE 1 UNIT 10

INSTRUCTIONS: Teacher will give prices of items in random order. Write the prices in the blanks below the correct items.

EXERCISE 1 UNIT 11

INSTRUCTION

Below, write the names of five people you know who have various personalities.

Hand your book to your partner (Signer A) who will select a name and ask about the person for a potential role. Go through the dialogue on the slide. When you are done, check off the role and the name you discussed and find another partner to repeat the activity.

You are done when all the names and roles below have been checked off.

Persons to discuss (check off when done):

- ☐ ______________________________
- ☐ ______________________________
- ☐ ______________________________
- ☐ ______________________________
- ☐ ______________________________

Potential role for that person (check off when done):

- ☐ travel companion
- ☐ roommate
- ☐ employee
- ☐ date
- ☐ babysitter

Ask for Advice 3

Last night you made a birthday cake for your classmate. This morning you were late and rushed out of the house. On the way to school you realized you forgot the cake. Ask for advice.

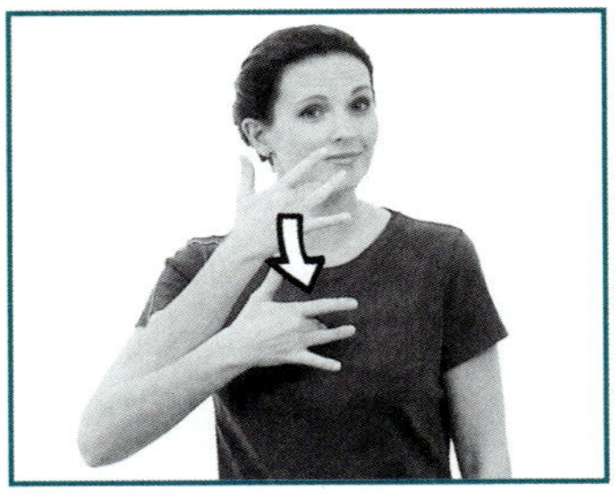

birthday (fingerspell CAKE)

to rush or hurry

Ask for Advice 4

This morning you let the dog out as you got ready for school. As soon as you got to school, it started to rain. You realized your dog is still outside. Ask for advice.

- Analyze the two situations above and construct your narratives following the sequence below.
- Rehearse your narratives.
- Pair off with a student that has **Exercise 1A** and follow dialogue format.

Signer A: explain problem, ask for advice
- **tell when**
- **explain situation**
- **tell what you forgot to do (use conjunction)**
- **ask for advice**

Signer B: give advice

A: respond

Sentences with "Have"

Pick the letter that represents the correct sign to use to translate "have" in each sentence below.

A

B

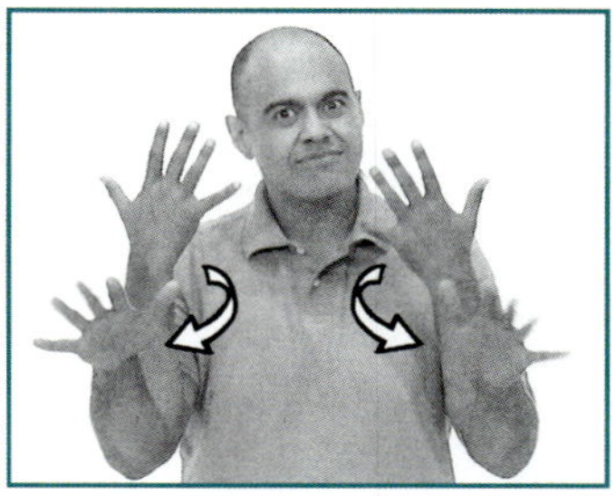

C

D

E

______ **1.** I don't have a plaid shirt.

______ **2.** My sister has 3 purses.

______ **3.** Rita already bought a dress.

______ **4.** He hasn't seen the movie.

______ **5.** I have sunglasses with red frames.

______ **6.** I have to call my doctor.

______ **7.** I have made cookies.

______ **8.** You have to tell me.

______ **9.** She has no leather jackets.

______ **10.** Grandfather hasn't taken his medicine.

to be adopted

Ask for Advice 1—Spills

You had borrowed your sister's (or brother's) pants last night to go out to eat. As you were biting into a hamburger, the mustard dripped onto the pants, leaving a yellow stain.

Ask for Advice 2—Awkward Conversations

During a walk in the park with your niece yesterday, out of nowhere, your niece asked if she was adopted. You told her you would talk about it with her later.

Ask for Advice 3—Something One Is Not Supposed to Do

Today at the restaurant where you work, while preparing food in the kitchen, you saw another employee who was preparing the salad accidentally flip the salad bowl onto the floor. Instead of throwing the ingredients away, he just put them back in the bowl.

- Use the **Grammar Notes** (pages 127–129) to help you construct your narratives.
- Rehearse your narratives until you can sign them without hesitation.
- Pair off with a student with **Exercise 2B** and follow dialogue format.

Signer A: explain problem, ask for advice
- **tell when**
- **explain situation**
- **tell what unexpectedly happened (use conjunction)**
- **ask for advice**

Signer B: give advice

EXERCISE 2: Describing a Neighborhood

Using the narrative outline, sign the following information. Pretend it is your neighborhood.

1. Tell where you live

- in a loft in Berkeley
- for the past 8 months, with two roommates

2. Tell what your neighborhood is like

- an industrial area with some buildings are converted into lofts
- freeway nearby which provides easy access to work and school
- mostly artists and blue collar workers live in the area

3. Tell what is next to your residence

- **across the street** – house; nice, friendly couple lives there
- **on your right** – liquor store; noisy outside the store
- **on your left** – house; nosy artist lives there
- **behind** – furniture factory

4. Tell what you like and don't like about the area

- **like** – cheap rent
- **don't like** – parking is difficult

5. Tell your future plans

- stay until you graduate from college, then move to a quieter place

EXERCISE 2A — UNIT 10

Ask your partners what the price is for the each of the items below and write the prices in the blanks. When asked, give the prices for items that are shown below.

$4.10

33¢

69¢

17¢ each

90¢

$1.15

$2.20

$4.88

$1.25

EXERCISE 2A UNIT 11

Translate these three hypothetical questions using the sequence below.

To ask a hypothetical question,
- **use hypothetical sign**
- **state sequence of events**
- **ask the question**

Question 1
How would you react if upon returning home from a three-month vacation, you received an $800 electric bill?

Question 2
How would you feel if you go out in the morning and find your car gone?

Question 3
How would you react if you got a card in the mail with $100 in it and no name?

Ask for Advice 1—Spills

Last Saturday, when you were house sitting for a friend and making your lunch, you had difficulty getting the ketchup out of the bottle when it suddenly gushed out and splashed on the white rug.

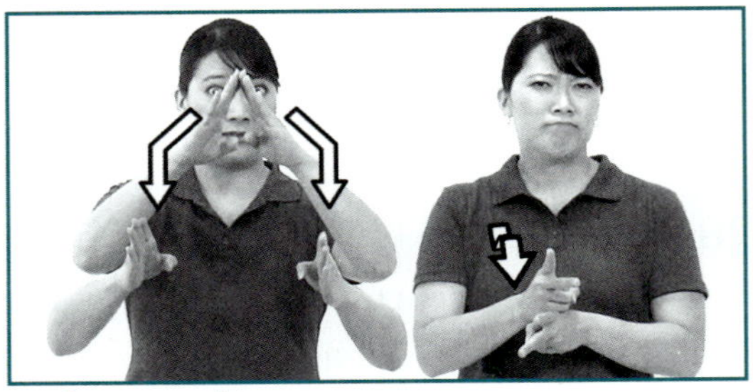

to house sit

Ask for Advice 2—Awkward Conversations

This morning during church service, your son, out of the blue, asked you if he had a brother. You told him to be quiet in church and that you would talk about it later. (His dad has another son the same age with another woman.)

Ask for Advice 3—Something One Is Not Supposed to Do

This afternoon you witnessed something improper at a wedding reception. You saw a guest at the next table putting silverware, salt and pepper shakers, and cloth napkins into her bag.

- Use the **Grammar Notes** (pages 127–129) to help you construct your narratives.
- Rehearse your narratives until you can sign them without hesitation.
- Pair off with a student with **Exercise 2A** and follow dialogue format.

Signer A: explain problem, ask for advice
- **tell when**
- **explain situation**
- **tell what unexpectedly happened (use conjunction)**
- **ask for advice**

Signer B: give advice

EXERCISE 2B

UNIT 10

Ask your partners what the price is for the each of the items below and write the prices in the blanks. When asked, give the prices for items that are shown below.

______

$8.69

______

______

______

______

15¢

______

25¢

______

______

$2.95

______

54¢

______

______

$6.25

______

______

$10.00

______

______

99¢

______

______

EXERCISE 2B

Translate these three hypothetical questions using the sequence below.

To ask a hypothetical question,
- **use hypothetical sign**
- **state sequence of events**
- **ask the question**

Question 1

How would you react if you were at a friend's birthday party and they ran out of birthday cake before you could get a piece?

Question 2

How would you feel if a meter maid was writing a ticket for your car and when you asked why, she pointed at the "No parking" sign overhead?

Question 3

How would you react if you were home alone and your friend snuck up on you and covered your eyes?

EXERCISE 2C UNIT 10

Ask your partners what the price is for each of the items below and write the prices in the blanks. When asked, give the prices for items that are shown below.

$1.05

$1.20

50¢

$3.45

$5.95

$7.50

75¢

$3.34

Translate these three hypothetical questions using the sequence below.

To ask a hypothetical question,
- **use hypothetical sign**
- **state sequence of events**
- **ask the question**

Question 1
How would you react if the adorable dog in the movie dies in the end?

Question 2
How would you feel if you find out the old lady living next door used to be a spy? (Tip: fingerspell "spy")

Question 3
How would you react if classes were canceled for a week?

EXERCISE 3 UNIT 7

Take turns describing one item in each row and giving information or a brief story about the item. Your partner is to circle the item and record the information below the picture. Remember to follow the sequences when describing the items.

Tops or Coats

- name item (color if only one)
- describe neckline, and sleeve length
- describe pattern
- describe other details

Bags

- name item (give color if only one)
- describe size and shape and its handle
- describe details
- tell how it is handled or carried

Hat, Scarf, or Eyeglasses

- name item (give color if only one)
- describe basic size and shape
- describe pattern and details

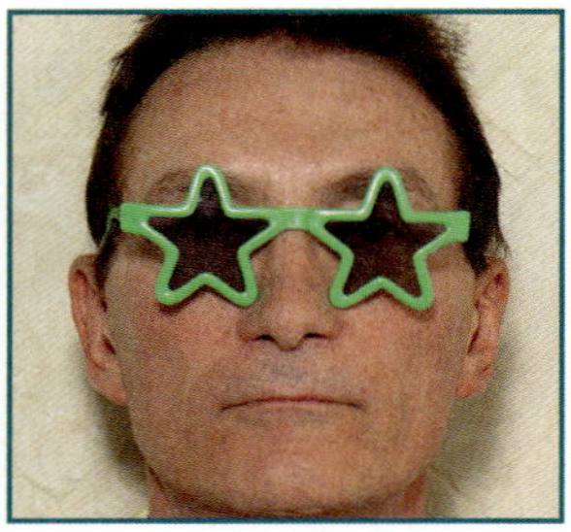

EXERCISE 2D

Translate these three hypothetical questions using the sequence below.

To ask a hypothetical question,
- **use hypothetical sign**
- **state sequence of events**
- **ask the question**

Question 1

How would you react if you pushed the wrong button and erased the pictures you were transferring to the computer?

Question 2

How would you feel if you accidentally fell down while walking into class?

Question 3

How would you react if it was the third time your friend failed to meet you at the coffee shop?

EXERCISE 3A: Phone Numbers — UNIT 8

Follow the dialogue on the slide and ask your partners what the phone number is for each name sign below. Fill in the blanks with the phone numbers.

235-1820

484-3337

779-1408

512-8506

You need the following:

1. coffee
2. auto insurance
3. hamburger
4. inexpensive toys
5. beer
6. paint

Follow the dialogue to get the location of the place, then write the name of the business in that location.

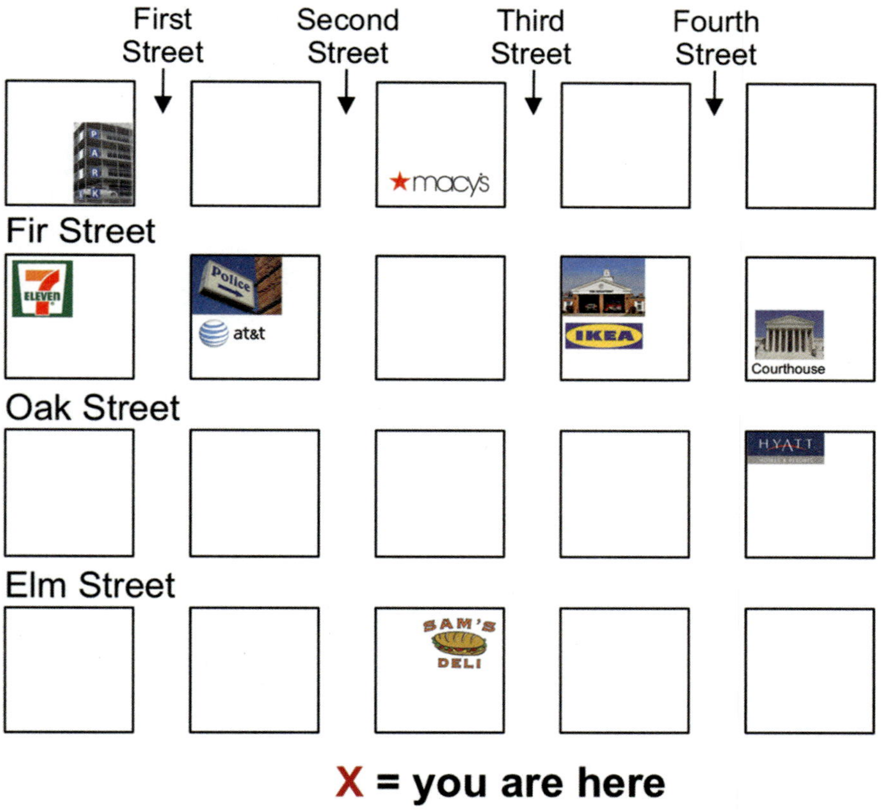

EXERCISE 3 UNIT 10

Decide with your partner which row of items belongs to you and which belongs to your partner. Now write the numbers corresponding to your items in various locations around the kitchen without showing your partner.

When ready, select one of your partner's items and ask where they put it. Write the number for the item in that location. Take turns asking and telling about all of the items.

Items 1–8:

1.

2.

3.

4.

5.

6.

7.

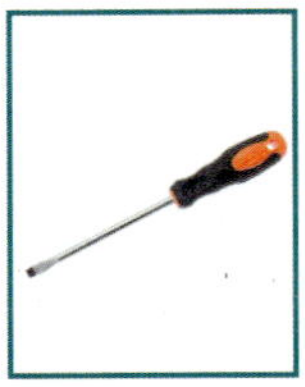

8.

Items 9–16:

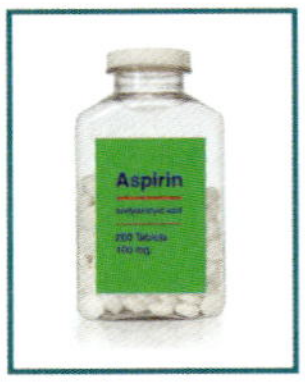

9.

10.

11.

12.

13.

14.

15.

16.

When done, check your partner's kitchen picture to see if the locations and numbers match.

EXERCISE 3: Two-Week Calendar

Mark your calendar with the dates shown on the slide. Then fill in activities you have already scheduled for the next two weeks. Include start and finish times for each activity.

Sun	Mon	Tues	Wed	Thurs	Fri	Sat

Now, think of four additional activities you would like to do during your free time. Write them here and find four students who are also free and available to join you. Fill in the information below.

	activity	*when*	*with whom*
1.	______	______	______
2.	______	______	______
3.	______	______	______
4.	______	______	______

EXERCISE 3B: Phone Numbers — UNIT 8

Follow the dialogue on the slide and ask your partners what the phone number is for each name sign below. Fill in the blanks with the phone numbers.

841-0732

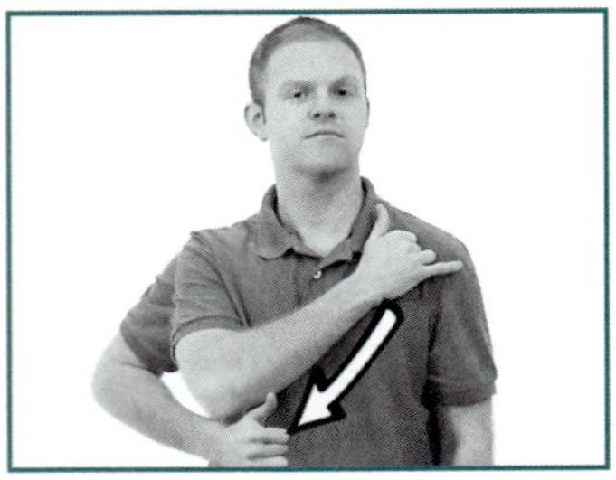

625-4764

970-2375

978-4100

You need the following:

1. furniture
2. sandwich
3. shirt
4. phone
5. milk
6. hotel room

Follow the dialogue to get the location of the place, then write the name of the business in that location.

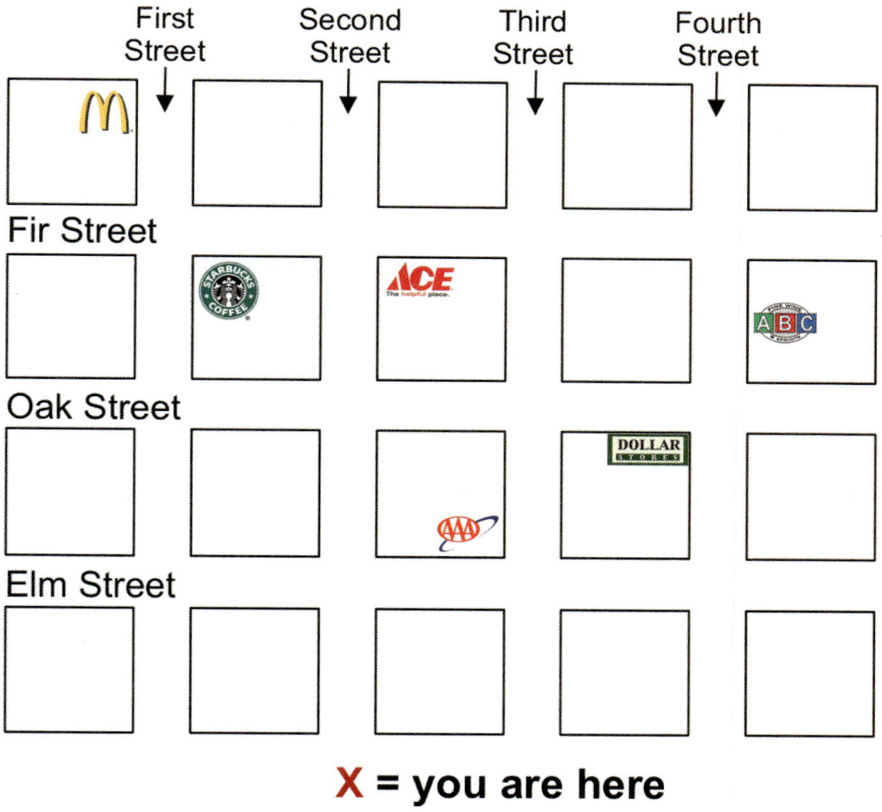

EXERCISE 3C: Phone Numbers

Follow the dialogue on the slide and ask your partners what the phone number is for each name sign below. Fill in the blanks with the phone numbers.

613-8441

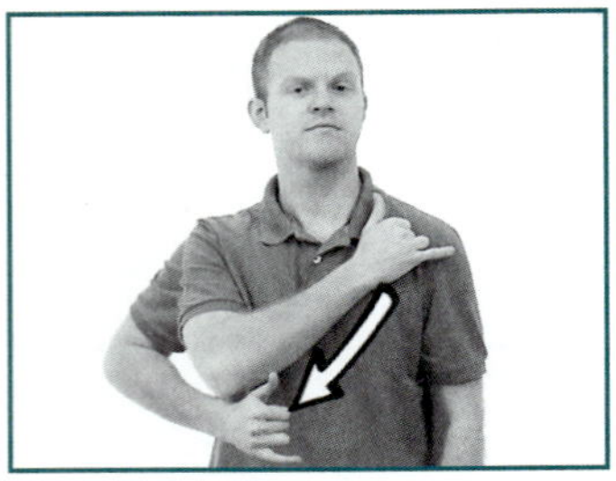

386-9408

209-6616

717-2336

Chris's Bucket List

Develop a narrative in ASL based on the information given below. Rehearse the narrative until you can give the information without looking at the page.

NARRATIVE SEQUENCE

1. Broach subject
2. State five goals
    - travel—go to Washington, D.C. to see the White House
    - personal—run a marathon
    - lifelong learning—live on a farm, learn how to make cheese
    - adventure—skydiving
    - community service—become a disaster volunteer with the Red Cross
3. Conclude

Challenge Yourself: Summarize your partner's five goals.

1. ______________________________

   ____

2. ______________________________

   ____

3. ______________________________

   ____

4. ______________________________

   ____

5. ______________________________

   ____

EXERCISE 4: Write the Names

Write down the topic of each conversation and the two places or brand names given.

topic	*names*	
1. ______________	______________	______________
2. ______________	______________	______________
3. ______________	______________	______________
4. ______________	______________	______________
5. ______________	______________	______________
6. ______________	______________	______________
7. ______________	______________	______________
8. ______________	______________	______________
9. ______________	______________	______________
10. ______________	______________	______________

EXERCISE 4B UNIT 11

Drew's Bucket List

Develop a narrative in ASL based on the information given below. Rehearse the narrative until you can give the information without looking at the page.

NARRATIVE SEQUENCE

1. Broach subject
2. State five goals
   - travel—travel to China
   - personal—have my picture taken with a celebrity (you name the person)
   - lifelong learning—take up a glass blowing class
   - adventure—ride in a hot-air balloon
   - community service—volunteer as a docent at a local museum
3. Conclude

Challenge Yourself: Summarize your partner's five goals.

1. ______________________________

____

2. ______________________________

____

3. ______________________________

____

4. ______________________________

____

5. ______________________________

____

EXERCISE 5A: Investigators

The Crime: Three days ago between 8 a.m. and 6 p.m. someone broke into a house in the neighborhood and stole a valuable painting.

You and your partner are investigating the crime. You and your partner will be assigned a pair of suspects. Your goal is to find discrepancies in their alibis. Work with your partner to create a list of questions to ask. After your interviews with the suspects, you and your partner will compare notes to see if the pair of suspects' alibis hold up.

Questions. Develop detailed questions to find discrepancies in the suspects' accounting of the day they spent together. Questions like if you went shopping, what stores did you go into, what time did you meet, what did you buy, what did it look like, how much did it cost, how did you pay, what time did you leave the store? You and your partner have 10–15 minutes to prepare the questions.

Interview. You will interview one of the suspects in the pair, separately. You have 10–15 minutes to get as much information as possible. Take notes during the interview.

Review. After the interviews, get together with your partner to compare notes on your suspects to see if there are any discrepancies in their story.

Good luck!

EXERCISE 5B: Suspects

The Crime: Three days ago between 8 a.m. and 6 p.m. someone broke into a house in the neighborhood and stole a valuable painting.

You and your friend are being investigated for the crime. Your goal is to work with your partner to create an airtight alibi for both of you. Each of you will be assigned an investigator who's aim is to find discrepancies in your alibi. After their interviews with you, they will compare notes to see if you and your partner's alibis hold up.

Your Alibi. You and your friend will have 10–15 minutes to create a detailed accounting of your activities together on the day of the crime to avoid being accused of the crime. The investigators will try to find discrepancies between you and your friend's answers. Your investigator will ask detailed questions about what you did together that day. If you say you went shopping the investigators may ask what time did the two of you meet; what stores did the two of you in go into; what did the two of you buy; what did it look like; how much did it cost; how did the two of you pay; what time did the two of you leave; what did the two of you eat; who paid; what did the two of you wear; who did you see; who drove; what you two did next.

Interview. You will be interviewed by one investigator and your friend by the other for 10–15 minutes.

Review. After the interview, go back to your friend and discuss how the interview went.

Good luck!

EXERCISE 5 UNIT 11

INSTRUCTIONS: Using the list assigned to your group, write the names of states or provinces in the correct locations on the maps (pages 501–502).

GROUP A	GROUP B	GROUP C	GROUP D	GROUP E
Colorado	Connecticut	Arizona	Delaware	Alabama
Hawaii	Illinois	Arkansas	Florida	Alaska
Indiana	Kentucky	California	Georgia	Iowa
Massachusetts	Missouri	Mississippi	Idaho	Kansas
Minnesota	Montana	Ohio	Michigan	Louisiana
North Dakota	Nevada	Rhode Island	Nebraska	Maine
Pennsylvania	New Hampshire	South Carolina	New York	Maryland
Tennessee	New Mexico	Vermont	Oklahoma	New Jersey
Texas	Washington	Wisconsin	Oregon	North Carolina
Virginia	West Virginia	Wyoming	Utah	South Dakota
Prince Edward Island	Nova Scotia	British Columbia	New Brunswick	Saskatchewan
Alberta	Manitoba	Newfoundland	Ontario	Quebec

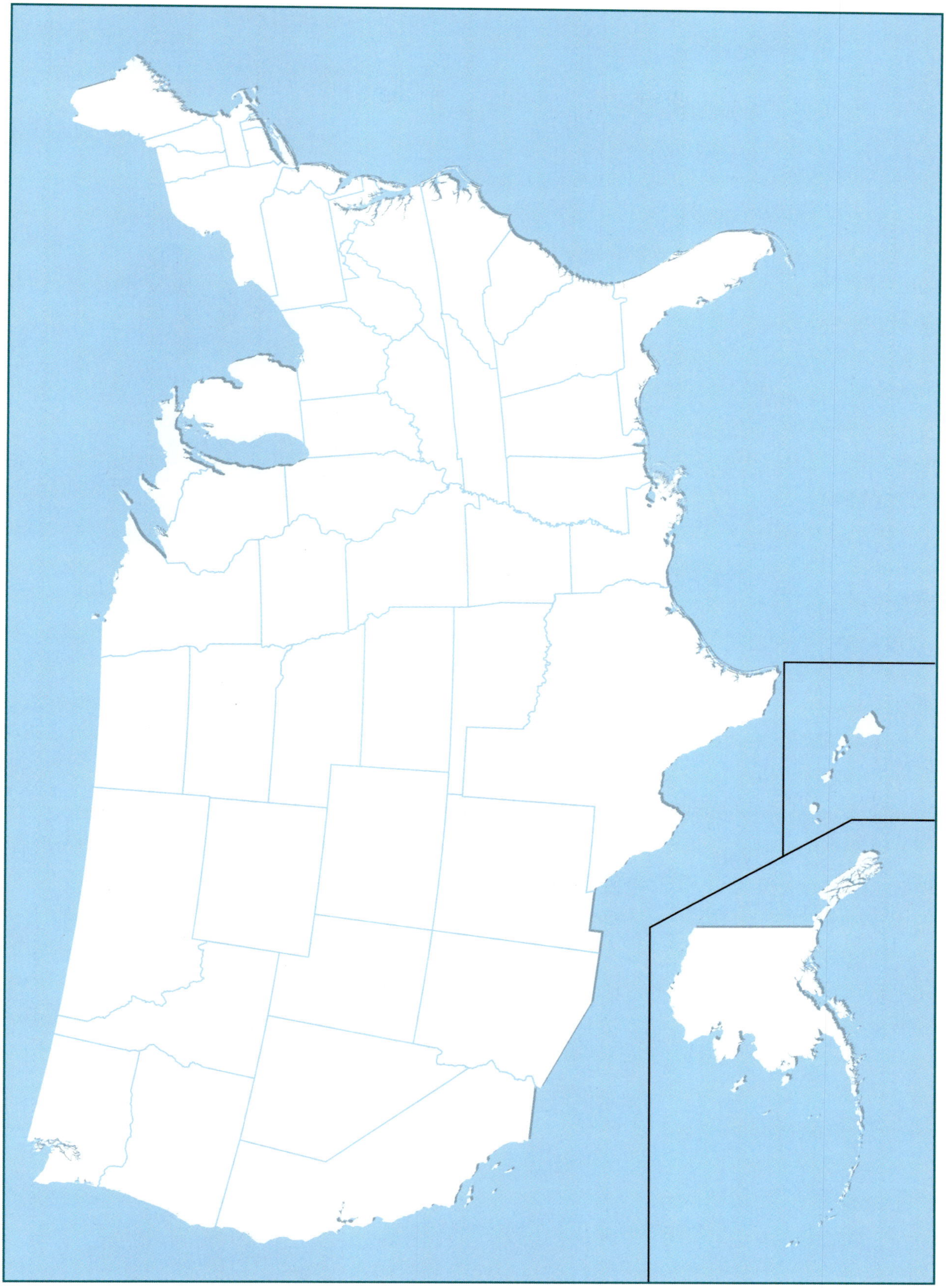

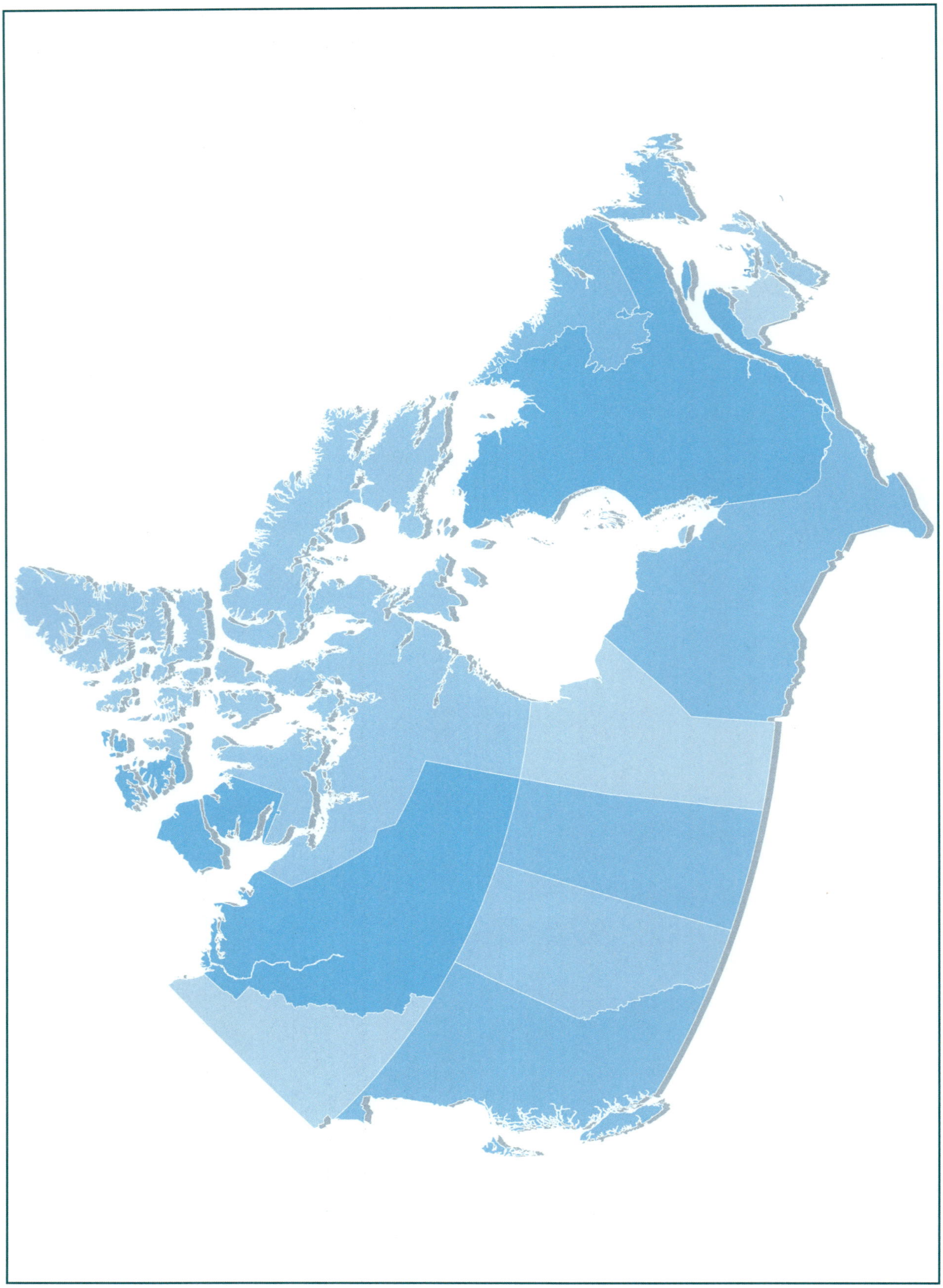

EXERCISE 6: STATE TRIVIA

INSTRUCTIONS: Discuss with your group the answers or best guesses to the questions below. Use this opportunity to practice your fingerspelling and reading others'! (Hint: no Googling.).

1. Which state boasts of being the birthplace of the greatest number of Presidents of the U.S.?
2. The Grand Canyon is in which state?
3. Yellowstone National Park is in which state?
4. Which state has the longest shoreline?
5. Which is the only state in the Union with a pennant-shape flag?
6. Which state does not have a natural lake?
7. The Alamo is in which state?
8. Which state is famous for its potatoes?
9. The Salem Witch trials of 1692 occurred in which state?
10. Mount Rushmore is in which state?
11. Which state do you have to travel to find the L.L. Bean Flagship store?
12. The Everglades are in which state?
13. The NFL Giants football team plays in which state?
14. The Gateway Arch is in which state?
15. In which state was the current President born?

UNIT 7 ANSWER KEY

HOMEWORK 7:2, page 14

Write the Word

1. suit
2. size
3. plastic
4. gold
5. silk
6. cotton
7. sun (glasses)
8. style
9. bag
10. suede
11. nylon
12. fleece
13. copper
14. silver
15. tux
16. wallet
17. wool
18. vest
19. boots
20. cell (phone)
21. polyester
22. fur

HOMEWORK 7:3, page 17

Guess My Number 1

1.	50	**(above)**	below	between
2.	10	**(above)**	below	between
3.	20-30	above	below	**(between)**
4.	25	above	below	between

Guess My Number 2

1.	50	**(above)**	below	between
2.	75	**(above)**	below	between
3.	60	above	**(below)**	between
4.	60-70	above	below	**(between)**
5.	61	above	below	between
6.	64	above	below	between
7.	62	above	below	between
8.	63	above	below	between

Guess My Number 3

1.	25	above	**(below)**	between
2.	75	**(above)**	below	between
3.	75-85	above	below	**(between)**
4.	95-100	above	below	**(between)**
5.	99	above	below	between

HOMEWORK 7:6, pages 43–44

Write the Translation 1–5

Translation: After the party, my friend took me to (or dropped me off at) the train station.

Translation: My roommate had a flat tire (on his way to work). I went and picked him up and took him to work.

Translation: My Dad dropped me off at school, then went over to my aunt's place to take her to the library.

Translation: I took my wife to the grocery store. After she was done shopping, I drove (or brought) her home.

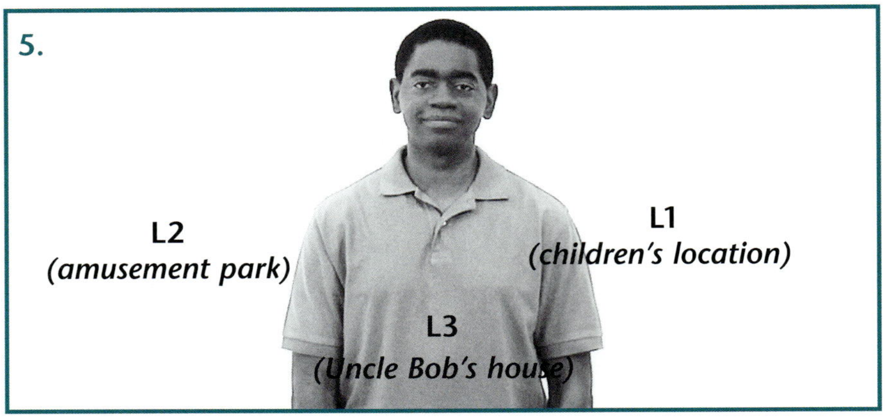

Translation: I took the children to the amusement park, then took them to Uncle Bob's house for a family meal.

HOMEWORK 7:7, page 45

How Many

Topic	Number Given	Reaction Used
1. hours worked	8	(1) 2 3 4
2. students in ASL class	3	1 (2) 3 4
3. books needed for ASL class	6	1 2 (3) 4
4. keys	2	1 (2) 3 4
5. children	34	1 2 3 (4)
6. people attending birthday party	70	1 2 (3) 4
7. small cans of soda pop	7	(1) 2 3 4
8. how many dogs he has	10	1 2 (3) 4
9. buses passing by Amber's house in one day	86	1 2 (3) 4
10. weddings Justin attended in the past month	16	1 2 3 (4)
11. number of cousins Terrylene has	73	1 2 3 (4)
12. hearing students in Suzanne's English class	52	1 2 3 (4)
13. fishes caught	19	1 2 (3) 4
14. pieces of candy left in the box	97	(1) 2 3 4
15. number of hot dogs winner ate at a contest	68	1 2 3 (4)

HOMEWORK 7:9, page 54

Write the Year

BONUS: In 2069 Iva will 100 years old, how old is she now?______

(subtract 1969 from current year to get the answer)

The sinking of the Titanic	1912
Start of World War I	1914
Wright brother's first flight (with engine)	1903
Young women's hair style of that period	1980s
First crossword puzzle	1913
First car Ford sold	1908
Barack Obama is elected President of the U.S.	2008
Hippie clothing style of that period	1968
San Francisco earthquake and fire	1906
London, England hosting the Summer Olympics	2012

HOMEWORK 7:10, page 57

Sentences with "Have"

Sentences 1–8

1. I have to wash my clothes.
2. My daughter hasn't bought a coat.
3. My friend has one plaid and one polka dot shirt.
4. I don't have a bicycle.
5. I have to brush my teeth after eating.
6. At the baseball game I have a very good view from my seat.
7. I had the men paint my house.
8. How did s/he know? Someone must have told her or him.

UNIT 8 ANSWER KEY

HOMEWORK 8:2, page 89

Write the Month

	month(s)	what the month(s) refer to
1.	*August, September*	*school year usually begins during those months*
2.	*June, July, and August*	*when people usually go on vacation*
3.	*April*	*when people pay their taxes*
4.	*June, December*	*June has the longest days of the year, December the shortest*
5.	*March, September, December*	*months with blue birthstones*
6.	*October, November*	*all five female cousins born in October all five male cousins born in November*
7.	*January*	*will go to South America on vacation (where it will be hot)*
8.	*February, May*	*Valentine's Day and Mother's Day (months associated with love)*

HOMEWORK 8:3, page 95

Sentences

Sentence 1: I told Renee to send you the flowers but instead she sent them to me.

A ☑ or B ☐

Write the English translation for the other signed sentence.

I told Renee to send you the flowers but instead I sent them to you.

Sentence 2: Lee called to tell me you have not paid him.

A ☐ or B ☑

Write the English translation for the other signed sentence.

Lee called to tell me he has not paid you.

Sentence 3: I was informed by Renee that Lee has already paid her, so I will now send Lee the package.

A ☐ or B ☑

Write the English translation for the other signed sentence.

Renee informed me that Lee has already paid me, so Renee can now send Lee the package.

Narrative 1

What did the dentist call JT about?

The dentist told JT to reschedule the appointment from Monday to Thursday.

What was JT's response?

JT told the dentist he will check with his wife first, then call back to confirm.

Narrative 2

What did Suzanne buy and when would it be delivered?

Suzanne bought a shiny red refrigerator, but it would be delivered to her house in two weeks.

What happened when she got ready to pay?

She forgot her checkbook so she mailed in a check when she got home.

HOMEWORK 8:4, page 101

Identify the Situation

2

6
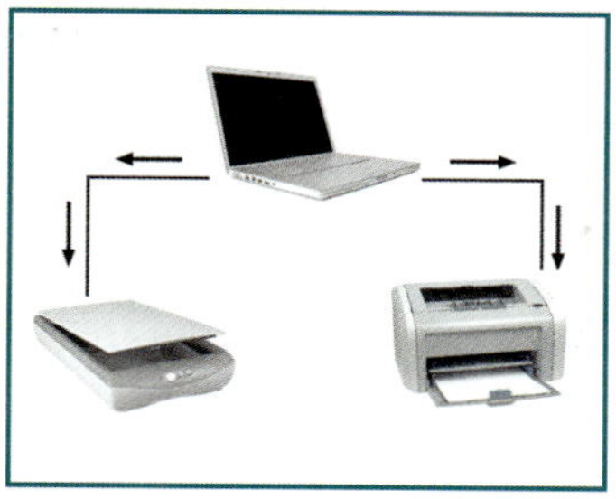

3

5

4

1

HOMEWORK 8:6, page 110

WRITE THE PHONE NUMBER

1. *202-456-1414* (For the White House switchboard)
2. *585-263-6250* (For the New York U.S. Senator's office)
3. *301-587-1788* (For the National Association of the Deaf office)
4. *858-625-0600* (For the DawnSignPress, Inc.'s office)

Useful Numbers

411 *to get the phone numbers of a restaurant, a company, or a friend who lives nearby*

511 *to get information about highway conditions, like accidents or highway repairs*

611 *to get phone company to identify and fix problems when you are unable to make a call from your landline phone or if there is a phone line breakdown*

911 *to call for assistance, like ambulance services if there is some kind of injury, death, an accident, a fall or difficulty breathing*

HOMEWORK 8:9, page 123

Narrative 1

Melvin and his friend went to see a movie. While watching the movie, the woman sitting next to him was using her smartphone. Melvin tried to ignore the light from the smartphone. After a while, he asked the woman to please turn off the smartphone. She got angry, and yelled at him. Melvin and his friend decided to change seats.

Narrative 2

One of Tonique's co-workers was really slow and tended to fall behind in her work. Tonique got angry and bawled her out. The co-worker phoned the boss to complain. The boss approached Tonique and asked her to be nice to the co-worker when giving instructions to her.

Narrative 3

At a party Suzanne attended, one of her friends told her to ask someone the size of his father's shoes. She asked that person and he got angry at her, explaining his father had no feet. She felt terrible and apologized to him. Then she noticed her friend and the guy laughing hard. They were playing a trick on her.

Narrative 4

When they were in high school, Iva and her friend borrowed her dad's brand new car to go see a movie. While driving, she drove through a red light. There were no police so she felt relieved. However, one month later, her dad received a citation from the police department. Her dad paid the citation and reprimanded her.

Narrative 5

John and his friend went to eat at a restaurant. At the end of the meal, he was told he could only pay in cash. John didn't have any cash on him, so he borrowed money from his friend and paid the bill. Some time later, John got a call from his friend saying he needed the money. John apologized and mailed him a check.

HOMEWORK 8:14, pages 145–146

Eugene's Name Signs

1. What name sign did Eugene's parents give him?
   letter "E" shaken in front of the body

2. In grade school his name sign changed. Why and how?
   letter "E" shaken in front of body plus "tall" (Because another student enrolled who happened to have similar name sign as Eugene. Since Eugene was taller than the new student, they added the sign for "tall" to his name sign, and the sign for "short" was added to the other student's name sign.)

3. At Gallaudet University, how did students refer to each other?
   by fingerspelling the person's last name, like La Cosse (Eugene's last name)

4. At Eugene's first job, what name sign did the children give him? Why?
   a descriptive name sign, which combined "beard" and "carpet flying in the air," a reference to the Mongol Prince who rode the magic carpet in the film "The Thief of Bagdad"

5. At Eugene's second job, what name sign did the children give him? Why?
   a descriptive name sign that described him fencing with a sword as in the movie "The Three Musketeers" because Eugene had a beard and mustache similar to those worn by the musketeers.

6. At Eugene's third job, what name sign did the children give him? Why?
   a descriptive name sign that indicated a short beard on the chin. Eugene again had changed his appearance letting his thin beard grow into a short beard confined to the chin area.

7. What name sign did Eugene end up with and why?
   "E" on the chin. Eugene was now clean shaven so the descriptive sign was substituted with the first letter of his name.

UNIT 9 ANSWER KEY

HOMEWORK 9:3, page 175

Write the Time

1. *7:45*
2. *6:00*
3. *9:03*
4. *4:15*
5. *2:55*
6. *11:11*
7. *8:50*
8. *1:20*
9. *9:05*
10. *5:35*
11. *12:10*
12. *3:00*
13. *7:30*
14. *10:01*
15. *5:18*
16. *6:40*
17. *2:25*
18. *12:05*
19. *1:00*
20. *11:59*

HOMEWORK 9:5, page 188

Fill in the Space

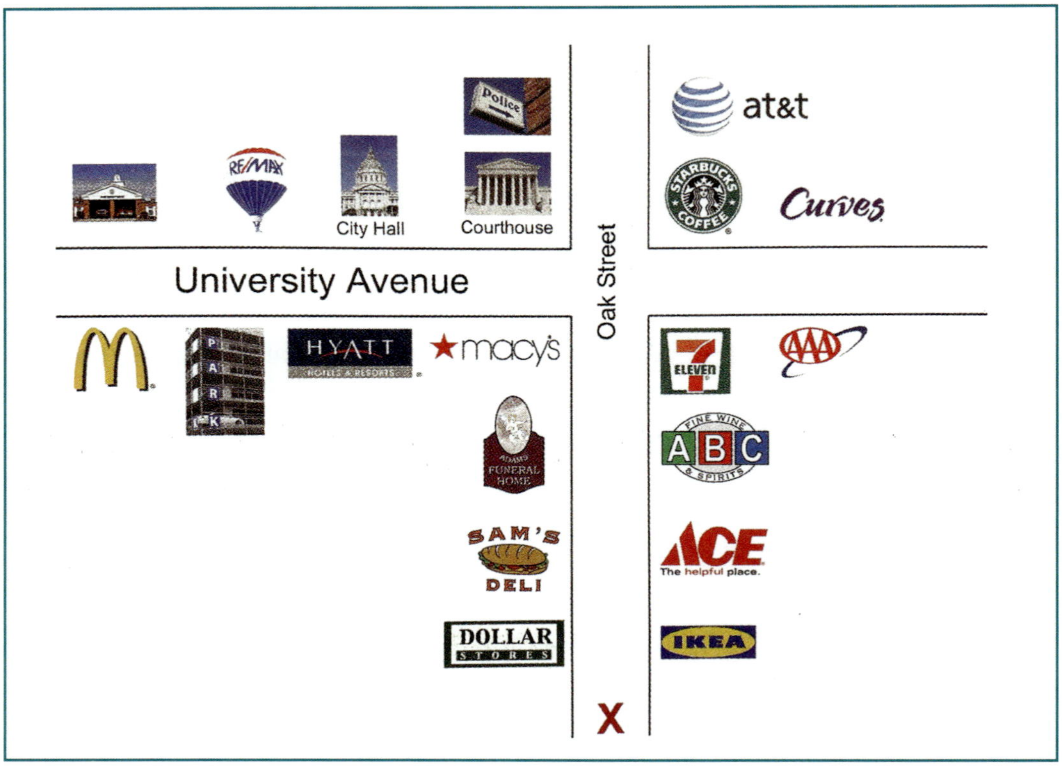

HOMEWORK 9:7, pages 197–198

Restaurant 1

1. name of restaurant ___*Hula Hut*___
2. dining area location ___*outdoors, near the water*___
3. draw the tables and their arrangement (or write the description)

4. draw the arrangement of the boats and the fish sculptures (or write the description)

5. draw the arrangement of the surfboards (or write the description)

6. type of food served at the restaurant ___*Mexican*___

Restaurant 2

1. name of restaurant *The Barn*
2. what is seen before reaching the restaurant *as you enter the farm, you drive down a tree-lined road. You will see a vegetable garden on the left, flowers on the right; as you climb up the hill, there is a cluster of 3 buildings*
3. what restaurant used to be *milking barn*
4. fill in the room with details

5. type of food served at the restaurant *fresh food from the farm*

HOMEWORK 9:8, pages 210–211
Turns 1–8

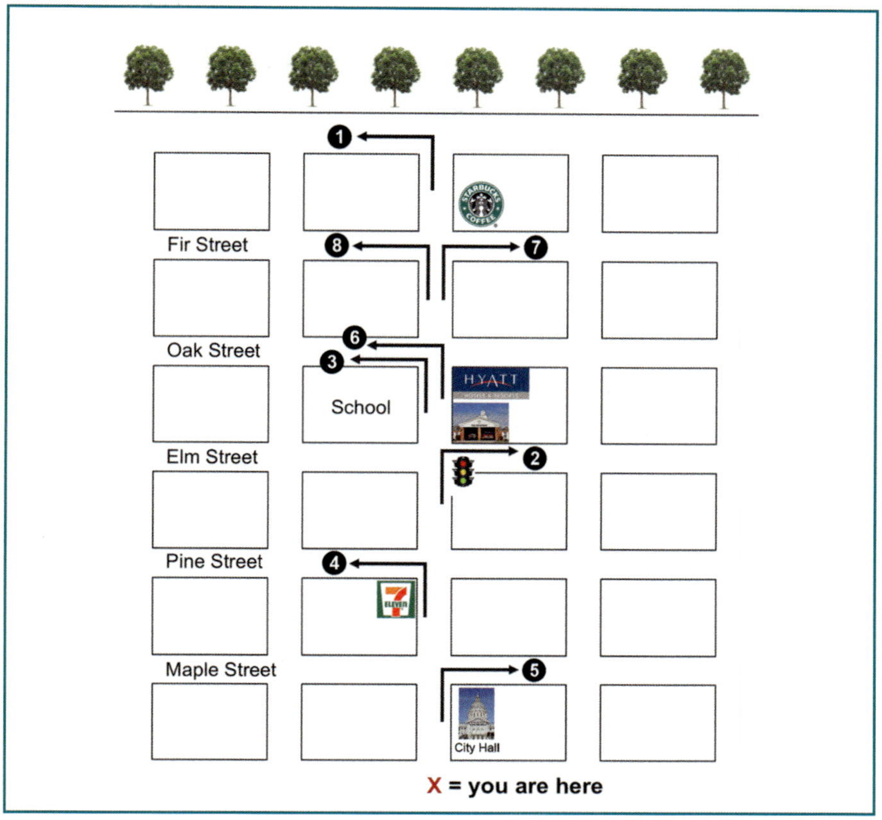

HOMEWORK 9:9, page 213
What Happens When

	Time	Who	What Happens
1.	*7:10 a.m.*	*Greg*	*took his dog out for a walk*
2.	*3:40*	*Sonya*	*exercised*
3.	*9:00*	*Emily*	*did the dishes*
4.	*6:25 p.m.*	*sister*	*went grocery shopping after work*
5.	*12:01*	*co-workers*	*went out to eat together*
6.	*1:15 p.m.*	*Holly*	*went to travel class*
7.	*2:05 p.m.*	*daughter*	*checked email on the computer*
8.	*8:40*	*roommate*	*showered, brushed her teeth and went to bed*
9.	*4:45 p.m.*	*Dad*	*stopped by a bar after work and chatted with friends there*
10.	*7:00 a.m.*	*Helen*	*woke her children*

HOMEWORK 9:11, page 224

Locations 1–10

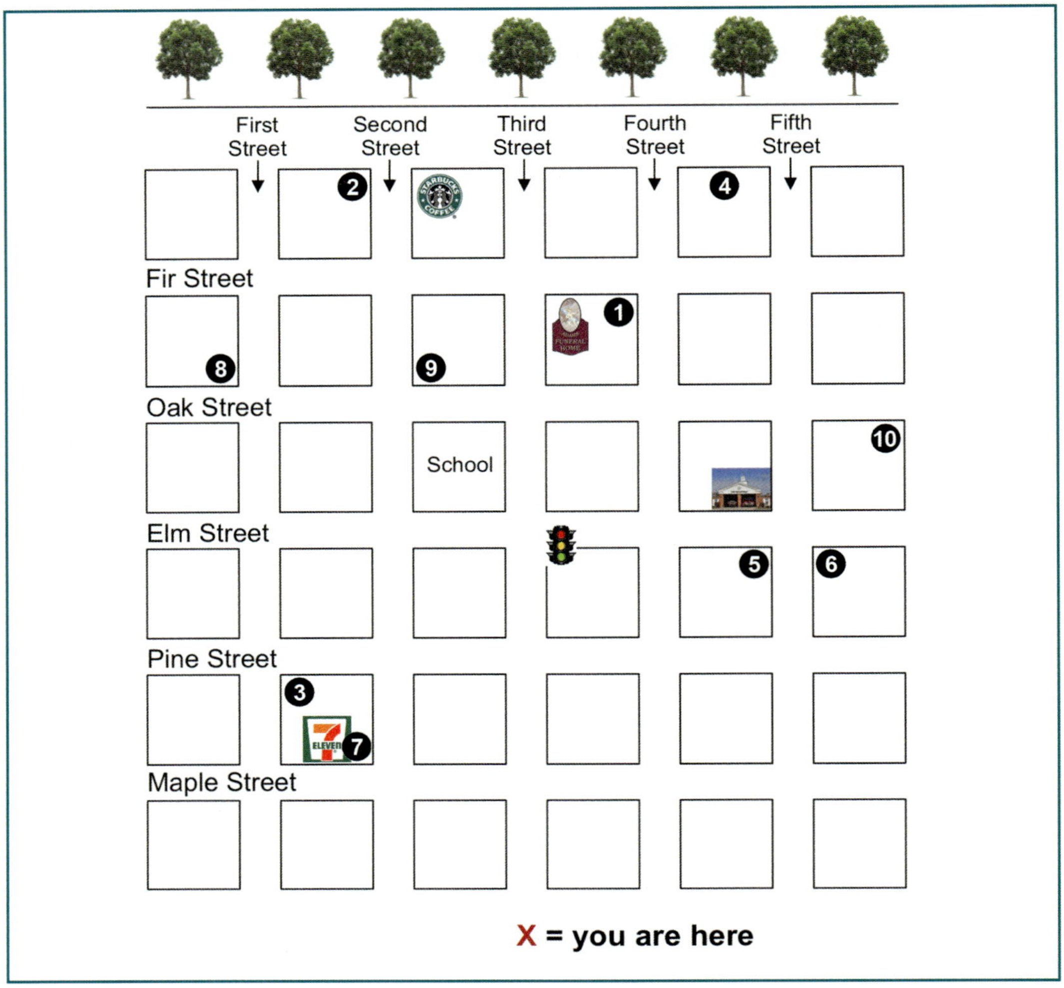

	name of business	*reason for going*
1.	*Macy's*	*need umbrella*
2.	*Sam's Deli*	*sandwich*
3.	*ReMax*	*looking for a house (to buy)*
4.	*Curves*	*exercise to stay slim*
5.	*City Hall*	*daughter needs birth certificate*
6.	*Ace Hardware*	*wall socket is broken*
7.	*AT&T*	*need a new cell phone*
8.	*Courthouse*	*got a ticket for speeding*
9.	*Hyatt*	*need hotel (the one you wanted is full)*
10.	*Parking*	*cheap parking*

UNIT 10 ANSWER KEY

HOMEWORK 10:2, page 255

Write the Amount

1.	*1¢*	9.	*29¢*	17.	*75¢*
2.	*89¢*	10.	*5¢*	18.	*25¢*
3.	*50¢*	11.	*70¢*	19.	*3¢*
4.	*18¢*	12.	*45¢*	20.	*55¢*
5.	*99¢*	13.	*30¢*	21.	*21¢*
6.	*26¢*	14.	*67¢*	22.	*10¢*
7.	*80¢*	15.	*20¢*	23.	*90¢*
8.	*15¢*	16.	*77¢*	24.	*40¢*

HOMEWORK 10:5, page 271

Write the Amount

1.	*$2.70*	9.	*$9.75*	17.	*$3.06*
2.	*$9.11*	10.	*$3.01*	18.	*$6.89*
3.	*$6.25*	11.	*$10.77*	19.	*$8.04*
4.	*$1.02*	12.	*$4.13*	20.	*$9.38*
5.	*$4.22*	13.	*$10.50*	21.	*$1.42*
6.	*$8.69*	14.	*$5.03*	22.	*$7.14*
7.	*$6.12*	15.	*$3.98*	23.	*$2.50*
8.	*$5.07*	16.	*$1.25*	24.	*$7.08*

HOMEWORK 10:6, page 278

Circle the Number

A.	(1)	2	3	E.	1	2	(3)
B.	(1)	2	3	F.	1	(2)	3
C.	(1)	2	3	G.	1	(2)	3
D.	1	2	(3)	H.	1	2	(3)

HOMEWORK 10:7, page 282

Ask Favor

Item	*Reason Given*
1. *knife*	*children are playing here, it's not safe having knife around*
2. *scotch tape*	*dollar bill is torn, needs to tape it together*
3. *stapler*	*did you leave it there? please return it to the kitchen*
4. *soap*	*no soap in the bathroom, people are coming here in 10 minutes*
5. *screwdriver*	*done assembling shelves, please take it back*
6. *camera*	*please hurry, want to take picture of dog and cat lying together*

UNIT 11 ANSWER KEY

HOMEWORK 11:1, pages 317–319

MINIDIALOGUES

Minidialogue 1

1. Summarize the information shared in the dialogue.
   While they were watching a football game on TV, Iva asked Ursula what a referee's hand signal meant. To which Ursula replied she was ignorant and she didn't know anything about football. Ursula suggested Iva ask the other person off screen (K on forehead) who is very knowledgeable about football rules and hand signals used by the referees. Iva asked why Ursula was watching the game. She replied it was fun watching the action.

2. Which sign(s) from above were used to describe each person's familiarity with the topic. Circle the letter(s):

   Ursula: A B C (D) E F G H

   The person off screen (K on forehead):

   (A) B C D E F G H

Minidialogue 2

1. Summarize the information shared in the dialogue.
   John needed to develop a chart for class but he had no idea how to use Excel spreadsheets. He asked David if he knew Excel. David said that at first he didn't know but after taking classes, he had become skilled and competent in using the software. John then asked David to show him how to use it.

2. Which sign(s) were used to describe each person's abilities? Circle the letter(s):

   John: A B C D (E) F G H

   David: (A) B C D E (F) G H

Minidialogue 3

1. Which sign(s) were used to describe each person's abilities? Circle the letter(s) and write what each person can do in how much time.

   JT: A B (C) D E F G H

   What could he do? In how much time?

   He could fingerspell the manual alphabet in less than 10 seconds.

   Justin: A B (C) D E F G H

   What could he do? In how much time?

   He could fingerspell the manual alphabet in reverse in less than 7 seconds.

   Melvin: A B (C) D E F G H

   What could he do? In how much time?

   Besides trumping the other two with the fastest time (in less than 5 seconds), Melvin did it using the British manual alphabet.

Minidialogue 4

1. Circle the letter(s) for the sign(s) that describe Terrylene's ability.

   Sign(s) Terrylene used to describe herself:

   A B C D (E) F G H

   Sign(s) Iva used to describe Terrylene:

   A B C D E F (G) H

2. List the steps Iva recommends Terrylene take to pursue her dream.

   a. take class to learn and master drawing skills

   b. move on to master watercolor painting

   c. then move on to oil painting

3. Circle the letters for the sign(s) Iva used at the end of each step.

   A (B) C D E F G H

HOMEWORK 11:2, page 324

Write the Number

	number	type		number	type
1.	*7*	*minute*	11.	*4*	*clock*
2.	*15*	*cardinal*	12.	*13*	*dollars*
3.	*2*	*age*	13.	*8*	*months*
4.	*11*	*days*	14.	*14*	*minutes*
5.	*9*	*cents*	15.	*3*	*weeks*
6.	*13*	*weeks*	16.	*15*	*cents*
7.	*5*	*days*	17.	*6*	*dollars*
8.	*12*	*clock*	18.	*10*	*age*
9.	*1*	*hour*	19.	*1*	*cardinal*
10.	*14*	*months*	20.	*12*	*hours*

Explain the Number, page 325

	number	type	what it refers to
1.	*7.15*	*dollars+cents*	*what it cost to buy popcorn at the movies*
2.	*10:05*	*clock*	*the time in the morning when the dog wants to go out*
3.	*1*	*cent*	*picking up a penny to bring you good luck*
4.	*4:10*	*clock*	*she has to stop at 4:10 for yoga*
5.	*2009*	*year*	*year he graduated college*
6.	*8*	*days*	*a road trip she took*
7.	*11:08*	*clock*	*solar eclipse that occurred this morning*
8.	*9*	*weeks*	*gestation period for dogs*
9.	*1.10*	*dollars+cents*	*amount of money he needs to borrow*
10.	*7*	*hours*	*doctors say it's best to sleep for a minimum of seven hours*
11.	*1912*	*year*	*it was a leap year*
12.	*2:15*	*clock*	*the time the dog sees the veterinarian tomorrow*
13.	*2*	*age*	*how old his rabbit is*
14.	*9.03*	*dollars+cents*	*what it cost for a sandwich with a drink plus tax*
15.	*6*	*minutes*	*how long it takes to walk to the train station from here*
16.	*5*	*dollars*	*the amount of the tip he left*
17.	*6.13*	*dollars+cents*	*the amount of loose change his mother had in her purse*
18.	*3*	*cardinal*	*the maximum number of turtles she can have*
19.	*12:14*	*clock*	*when the next bus will come*
20.	*3*	*months*	*how long school summer vacation usually is*

HOMEWORK 11:4, pages 339–341
MINIDIALOGUES
Minidialogue 1
Situation: *seeing a bird sleeping on a cat*

Whose reaction is more appropriate? ☐ John's ☑ David's

Why? *one is more likely to react with amazement rather than with discouragement*

Minidialogue 2
Situation: *finding your car keys locked inside the car*

Whose reaction is more appropriate? ☑ David's ☐ Ursula's

Why? *one is more likely to feel like annoyed with oneself than to feel scared*

Minidialogue 3
Situation: *your manuscript has been accepted for publication by a renowned publishing company*

Whose reaction is more appropriate? ☑ Ursula's ☐ Tonique's

Why? *one is more likely to be delighted rather than be filled with tenderness*

Minidialogue 4
Situation: *your son or daughter chooses to work rather than go to college*

Whose reaction is more appropriate? ☑ Tonique's ☐ John's

Why? *one is more likely to be disappointed than to be elated*

Minidialogue 5
Situation: *you got a "D" on the exam*

Whose reaction is more appropriate? ☑ Amber's ☐ Derrick's

Why? *one is more likely to react with shock than with relief*

Minidialogue 6

Situation: *you're wearing new clothes and shoes and someone pushes you into a swimming pool*

Whose reaction is more appropriate? ☐ Derrick's ☑ Terrylene's

Why? *one is more likely to feel upset than to be scared*

Minidialogue 7

Situation: *at a restaurant you accidentally spilled wine on your friend's mother*

Whose reaction is more appropriate? ☑ Terrylene's ☐ Amber's

Why? *one is be more likely to be embarrassed than be angry*

HOMEWORK 11:5, page 348

Circle the State

1.	Minnesota	**(Tennessee)**	Connecticut
2.	North Dakota	South Dakota	**(Maryland)**
3.	**(Utah)**	New Hampshire	Ohio
4.	**(Virginia)**	Pennsylvania	Vermont
5.	North Carolina	**(New Jersey)**	New Mexico
6.	**(South Carolina)**	South Dakota	North Carolina
7.	Georgia	New Mexico	**(Missouri)**
8.	Iowa	Idaho	**(Ohio)**
9.	New Brunswick	**(Nebraska)**	Nevada

Write the State, page 349

1.	*Indiana*	9.	*Louisiana*	17.	*Kentucky*
2.	*Wyoming*	10.	*Arizona*	18.	*Alabama*
3.	*California*	11.	*Nevada*	19.	*New Mexico*
4.	*Illinois*	12.	*Arkansas*	20.	*Alaska*
5.	*Mississippi*	13.	*Connecticut*	21.	*Michigan*
6.	*Oklahoma*	14.	*Texas*	22.	*Idaho*
7.	*Maine*	15.	*New Hampshire*	23.	*Kansas*
8.	*Rhode Island*	16.	*Iowa*	24.	*New York*

Write the Province, page 349

1.	*Quebec*	3.	*Alberta*	5.	*Ontario*
2.	*Saskawatchen*	4.	*British Columbia*	6.	*Manitoba*

HOMEWORK 11:8, page 365
Explain the Number

	number		*what it refers to*
1.	*1.29*	*money*	*what a loaf of bread cost a long time ago*
2.	*3:30*	*clock*	*her dental appointment had been postponed to 3:30*
3.	*2011*	*year*	*her brother's high school graduation*
4.	*4.42*	*money*	*price of scotch tape bought at the store*
5.	*10:18*	*clock*	*time in the morning second child (daughter) was born*
6.	*6.35*	*money*	*what it costs for a box of crackers*
7.	*11:58*	*clock*	*arrived at 11:58 PM, just in time to watch the fireworks*
8.	*2025*	*year*	*the year when robots will take the place of human pilots*
9.	*1969*	*year*	*year of the first moon landing*
10.	*9.59*	*money*	*what it costs for sleeping eye masks*
11.	*8:45*	*clock*	*the time tomorrow he will meet realtor to see a house he likes*
12.	*2:40*	*clock*	*the time tomorrow she will go to the Red Cross to donate blood*
13.	*1860*	*year*	*South Carolina became the first State to secede the Union*
14.	*7.50*	*money*	*how much he paid for parking*
15.	*1971*	*year*	*year Starbucks was founded*

HOMEWORK 11:9, pages 367–369

John's Bucket List

1. *volunteer—Peace Corps work with Deaf children*
2. *learn time management—stop procrastinating*
3. *go to France—see Clerc's birthplace and where he attended school*
4. *try parasailing*
5. *visit all ballparks in the U.S.*

Tonique's Bucket List

1. *try water rafting*
2. *collect films made by Deaf people for her library*
3. *learn to grow her own food*
4. *help people learn to communicate with deaf animals*
5. *ride a mule down the trail into the Grand Canyon*

Suzanne's Bucket List

1. *keep exercising regularly*
2. *live in Italy for one year, learn their culture, language and how to cook*
3. *learn names of flowers and how to arrange flowers*
4. *help adults learn to read*
5. *see grunion run in California*

HOMEWORK 11:10, page 377

State Trivia

	state or province	*information*
1.	*Connecticut*	*where the first American school for the Deaf is located*
2.	*Idaho*	*it's against the law to give a box of candy weighing more than 50 lbs*
3.	*Maine*	*blueberries mostly come from Maine*
4.	*Wyoming*	*the state with the smallest population*
5.	*Michigan*	*4 different flags flew over the state (French, British, Spanish, American)*
6.	*Illinois*	*where actress Marlee Matlin was born*
7.	*Ohio*	*only state with a pennant-shaped state flag*
8.	*Quebec*	*has its own Sign Language—Langue des Signes Québécoise (LSQ)*
9.	*North Carolina*	*the state closest to Bermuda*
10.	*Kentucky*	*has the largest underground cave in the United States*
11.	*Wisconsin*	*where the first typewriter was invented*
12.	*Vermont*	*the word "Vermont" means "green mountains"*
13.	*Hawaii*	*became a state in 1959*
14.	*Oklahoma*	*where the shopping cart was invented*
15.	*Ontario*	*where Canada's first Deaf, ASL-using politician came from*

STUDENT WORKBOOK INDEX